# HEGEL
# KIERKEGAARD
# MARX

# OTHER DELTA BOOKS OF INTEREST

Philosophy: *An Introduction to Its Problems and Vocabulary*
RONALD J. GLOSSOP

Existentialism Versus Marxism
GEORGE NOVACK, *Editor*

Philosophy and Revolution
RAYA DUNAYEVSKAYA

Camus and Sartre
GERMAINE BRÉE

The New Christianity
WILLIAM ROBERT MILLER, *Editor*

To Deny Our Nothingness
MAURICE FRIEDMAN

The Hidden Human Image
MAURICE FRIEDMAN

ROBERT HEISS

# HEGEL KIERKEGAARD MARX

## Three Great Philosophers Whose Ideas Changed the Course of Civilization

Translated from the German
by E. B. GARSIDE

A DELTA BOOK

A DELTA BOOK
Published by
Dell Publishing Co., Inc.
1 Dag Hammarskjold Plaza
New York, New York 10017
Originally published in German under the title *Die Grossen
Dialektiker des 19, Jahrhunderts: Hegel Kierkegaard Marx*
by Verlag Kiepenheuer & Witsch

Delta ® TM 755118, Dell Publishing Co., Inc.

Reprinted by arrangement with Delacorte Press/Seymour Lawrence

Printed in the United States of America

Second Printing

# Contents

FOREWORD                                                    ix

## Part I.
## HEGEL'S DIALECTICAL SYSTEM

1. Sources of Hegelian Thought                              3
2. Story of Hegel's Youth                                   18
3. The Conception of the System                             32
4. The Phenomenology: The Introduction                      45
5. The Phenomenology as a Whole                             58
6. From the Phenomenology to the Logic                      70
7. The Logic                                                83
8. The Dialectic                                            96
9. Heidelberg and the Encyclopaedia                         108
10. The System in Process of Change                         122

v

11. The Philosophy of History                               135
12. The Philosophy of Right and Its Fate                    148
13. The Dialectical Structure of the
    Philosophy of Right                                     159
14. Hegel's Theory of Social Forms in the
    Philosophy of Right                                     168
15. The Later Fate of the Dialectic                         180

## Part II.

# KIERKEGAARD'S EXISTENTIAL DIALECTIC

16. Hegel Kierkegaard Marx                                  187
17. Søren Aabye Kierkegaard: Dates and Events               203
18. Kierkegaard's Concept of Irony                          212
19. The "Indirect Method" and the Indirect Life            219
20. The Pseudonymous Works                                  231
21. The Religious and the "Pathos" of Dread                244
22. The Philosophical Writings                              259
23. The Final Stages                                        274
24. Kierkegaard's Dialectic                                 281

## Part III.

# THE MATERIALISTIC DIALECTIC OF KARL MARX AND HIS HISTORICAL MATERIALISM

25. A Sketch of the Life of Karl Marx                       295
26. A Sketch of the Personality                             304
27. The Development of Marxian Thought                      312
28. The Dialectic in the Youthful Writings                 319
29. The Theory of Revolution                                326
30. The Transition to the Economic                          336
31. The Critique of Hegel                                   346
32. The Conclusion of the Developmental Period
    and the Youthful Writings: The German Ideology          349

33. The Materialistic Thesis: Production as
the Motive Force of History                    354

34. Theory and Practice                         357

35. Recapitulation and Formulation of Historical
Materialism in the Critique of Political Economy   363

36. Capital                                     368

37. The Method of Capital                       376

38. The Utopian in Marx                         380

39. The Formal System of Dialectic in Marx      385

40. The Dialectical Approach in Marx            390

41. The Dialectic Process                       394

42. The Dialectical Goal                        397

SOURCES, QUOTATIONS AND SUPPLEMENTS             401

INDEX                                           425

# Foreword

The aim of all dialecticians has been to pit a "dialectical" logic against the so-called formal kinds, "classical" and Aristotelian, and the mathematical logic of modern times. Through this dialectical logic they expected to arrive at a deeper knowledge of actuality; indeed, they believed that only through this dialectic could actuality be grasped.

Is this a valid claim? And *which* actuality is to be contained? These questions can be answered only after making an examination of what dialectical thinkers have understood by dialectic and of how they went about filling the claims they made for it.

Three times in the nineteenth century the claim to know actuality through dialectic was realized. But in each case a different form of dialectic evolved. Hegel developed his dialectical system, Kierkegaard his "existential dialectic," and Marx his "historical materialistic" version. Each of these thinkers in his own way advanced an absolute claim to truth, each going about it differently.

Remarkably enough, this circumstance led to another development. Dialectical thought in the form given it by Marx came to have an influence on the history of mankind otherwise achieved only by the great religions. Thus was fulfilled, though quite differently from the way Hegel had anticipated, the claim that dialectical thought is an instrument of actuality.

This present inquiry traces the progress of dialectical thought from Hegel through Kierkegaard to Marx. In doing this it was indispensable to describe both the personal lives and the ideas of these thinkers. When compared with the many specialized works on Hegel, Kierkegaard, and Marx, this book cannot presume to do complete justice to these great minds; nonetheless the author hopes to depict, right down to details, a development in modern thought that first made its appearance in the nineteenth century, but which was not fully worked out until the twentieth.

For Hegel, Kierkegaard, and Marx are the fathers of modern thought. The twentieth century has brought to fruition the legacy handed down by the nineteenth.

In this work special pains have been taken to let the sources speak for themselves. Secondary literature is quoted only when used in the original text. Similarly, quotations from pertinent works by the author are made only when absolutely necessary.

ROBERT HEISS

*Freiburg, August 1962*

# I

## HEGEL'S DIALECTICAL SYSTEM

# 1

## Sources of Hegelian Thought

Hegel stands between the eighteenth and the nineteenth centuries. Reared completely in the eighteenth-century tradition, educated at the Protestant theological institute at the University of Tübingen and nourished in the spirit of Christian humanism, nonetheless he was far removed from the eighteenth century. His real influence came in the nineteenth, in which period he was a powerful and commanding figure.

Many thinkers can be characterized in terms of a single dominant theme, for example, Kant's idea of a "transcendental idealism." But although dialectic is methodologically basic in Hegel, he cannot be reduced to this theme alone.

Many attempts have been made to explain Hegel in terms of *one* line of thought. He has been understood as a dialectician, as the greatest systematizer of modern times, as the "philosopher of freedom," and yet again as a theologian or as an "ontological" thinker. But only partial aspects of the man are obtained this way, and not a conception of his real and great goal, which was to understand the "truth of the whole" and present a comprehensive synthesis of it.

In 1801 the young Hegel went to the University of Jena as a *Privatdocent*—an unsalaried university lecturer paid from his students' fees—with a clearly formulated goal in mind: to develop his own philosophical system. For six years he labored on this project, repeatedly announced its imminent publication, and meanwhile gained the reputation of being an obscure and unintelligible thinker that was to cling to him for a lifetime.

At the end of the Jena period, the first part of this system, in the form of the *Phenomenology of Mind*, welled forth out of him in an irresistible stream. Thereafter he never left the road that he had opened up. Piece by piece he developed his system, and piece by piece, through arduous and tenacious labor, he incorporated region after region of thought into it. Meanwhile the architecture and inner order of the system changed, and the parts became differently fashioned and shifted about relative to one another.

But the basic operative thought remained intact, the final goals fixed. All of Hegel's great works and lectures were built up and expanded according to the dialectical schema, all were conceived from the viewpoint of an "Absolute Spirit," which comes to knowledge of itself through its own workings. Always Hegel's effort was guided by a desire to reconcile "actuality with reason," to demonstrate the workings of the absolute and to show how absolute spirit (or mind) rules over all things with power and guile.

Yet behind Hegel's work as an uninterrupted continuum, which impresses by its tough conciseness, a closer look immediately detects a variety of single steps, a kaleidoscopic richness of insights and ideas and a multiplicity of spheres of thought. The more deeply you penetrate into Hegel's thought, the more you come to appreciate, beyond the final rigidity of the system, the continuously shifting and often scintillating versatility of the actual intellectual effort involved.

Herein lies the difficulty of any presentation that would do justice to the entire Hegel. Hegel can be explained from this or that standpoint, but the important thing is not any particular point of departure. Assign too much value to any one approach and the whole becomes distorted. Hegel's great disciples, Kierkegaard and Marx, made much of this vulnerability. Just one single decisive correction and at once the appearance of the whole is turned upside down into "historical materialism" or "existential dialectic."

Therefore, in undertaking to explain Hegelian thinking and thought structure, the only way is first to show the basic threads which he wanted to weave together into an unbreakable web. First of these is the idea of an "Absolute Spirit" or "Absolute Mind," which comes to self-awareness as it unfolds. The Christian idea of a personal and creative God is merged with this concept of Absolute Spirit.

The second basic Hegelian notion is the old idea that philosophy is the queen of the sciences, or intellectual disciplines, alone possessed of the ability to develop truth as a "whole." Again and again Hegel declared that his aim was to bring philosophy closer to being scientific in form, for "the true form in which truth exists can only be the scientific system of the same."[1]

Besides these two general sources of Western thought, the traditions of Christianity and of classical antiquity, there were others, too, which Hegel interwove with them in a unique fashion. Only then did the structure of Hegelian philosophy take shape, comprehensive, powerful, and in many respects monstrous as well.

It is above all important to view this Hegelian philosophy as a synthetic structuring of a historical epoch of long duration. It was born of the desire to unite the whole of Western thought into one unified, yet at the same time many-branched system. It is this whole—not the particulars of it—which is the truth for Hegel.

In his furious thrust to weld the universe and thought together, to reconcile "actuality with theory" and to understand absolutely everything, Hegel followed the example set by the thinkers of Christianity and antiquity before him. He shared the great medieval philosophers' ambition of arriving at a *summa* of knowledge, and at a time when knowledge was beginning to break asunder he worked out his all-inclusive system and wrote his *Encyclopaedia of the Philosophic Sciences*. On the other hand he did not renounce acuity and critical skepticism in his thinking. However much he may have concentrated on the relatedness binding single forms of thought together, this did not affect his determination to profile the individual forms and directions of knowledge in their specificity. Herein lies the monstrous quality of Hegelian thought.

Two additional sources of Hegelian philosophy also again and again stand out clearly: the basic philosophic tradition of the West as developed up to the time of Kant and the experience of history. Hegel knew the history of philosophy like no other thinker of his period. Even today his "Lectures on the History of Philosophy" are worth reading because in point of basic knowledge of the material his presentation is masterly and original. He is distinguished by his having found intelligible all philosophical lines of thought that ever appeared, whether in Christian, classical, or modern philosophy up to his day, and by having thought through both skeptical and mystical philosophies.

In many areas of his philosophy Hegel shows the breadth of grasp given only to the genuine historian, and this gift of a great historical tradition imparts a definitive quality to his work in another direction. It is no coincidence that Hegel should have fructified all later historic disciplines and that Marx's historical materialism should have arisen out of Hegelian thought.

For Hegel experienced history in a new and highly original way; he grasped it all in one encompassing vision, a vision from which his successors could not escape. In a certain sense we all think with Hegel and follow his train of thought when we view history. His conception of history colored nineteenth-century thought, and even the twentieth century remains under the same spell.

Here, then, begins the modern Hegel, whose system, to be sure, has fallen into ruins, but whose principles of historic interpretation have become dominant in many variations. This holds true to a point where not only the nineteenth century but even more so our own has brought the Hegelian legacy to a head.

If we turn to a characterization of the different single sources of Hegelian thought, we must give priority in time, if by no means primary importance, to the then prevailing philosophical tradition. At the time Hegel was beginning his work, facing him was the philosophy of Kant, a philosophy which, by the way, he did not know thoroughly until many years later.

It may be doubted, however, whether Hegel ever really learned much from Kant at all. As a thinker Kant did not attract Hegel. He was much more drawn to the great metaphysical thinkers like Plato and Aristotle, or again, Böhme, Descartes, or Rousseau.

But Hegel, no more than any other philosopher of the period, could not ignore Kant, and less so because Kant had broached a theme that was equally important to Hegel, the theme of dialectic. Kant had written the entire second part of his *Critique of Pure Reason* under the title of "Transcendental Dialectic," thus bringing up the very subject that was the basic principle of Hegel's thought. However, the Hegelian dialectic is as fundamentally different from Kant's, so far as there was a Kantian dialectic, as from Kierkegaard's or Marx's.

Kant's transcendental dialectic, and in general the whole critique of pure reason, as Kant himself expressly said in a letter to Garve, derives not from the metaphysical themes of "God's existence and immortality, etc.," but from the "antinomies of pure reason." It is the "scandal of the conflict of pure reason with itself" that Kant, as far as it went, wanted to do away with once and for all.[2]

The theme of antinomial reason is brought up at the very beginning of the *Critique of Pure Reason,* when Kant says that human reason, by virtue of its very nature, can raise questions that can neither be brushed aside nor answered, simply because they are beyond reason's scope. With this Kant was confronted by the old problem of "contradiction," the problem that is the starting point for the study of logic.

Yet Western thought thousands of years ago found a solution for this problem. The logical theory that when a contradiction appears cognition is thwarted, in consequence of which it is impossible for knowledge to be reconciled with contradictions, is an absolutely fundamental notion, operative in all kinds of scientific thinking.

This time-honored piece of wisdom, first precisely spelled out by Aristotle, was restated by Kant, but this time with certain qualifications. For as he saw it there are "unavoidable contradictions," which, as "natural illusions," cling "irremediably" to human thought.[3] They crop up again and again; they lie in the very nature of the human thinking process, waiting to be revealed over and over again.

In this fashion, one might say, Kant admitted the qualified existence of contradiction in order to avoid something worse. The cure for these phenomena is the limitation of pure reason, specifically the transcendental dialectic. This dialectic stands guard over thought like some sort of cognitional-theoretical policeman, keeping thought posted as to where the realm of "apparent" illusion begins. Transcendental dialectic is presented as the model of a kind of thought prone to betray itself.

The only real point of contact between Hegel and Kant lies in the theory that "apparent" contradiction may occur under certain circumstances. Yet the two men's points of view are still fundamentally different. The "illusion" of contradiction that Kant talks about is for Hegel the "appearance of the real."

Thus did Hegel quietly come to terms with Kant. He had kind words to say about him; among the greatest of Kant's merits, Hegel said, was the fact that he had "elevated dialectic to a higher plane" and conceptualized it as a "necessary activity of reason." But, he went on to note reprovingly, Kant's opinion that dialectic merely "plays games" and that "its whole strength resides solely in the fact that it glosses over contradiction," actually deserves "very little commendation."[4] When this argument over Kant occurred, Hegel's view had long since crystallized. Contradiction does exist, but dialectic is not a *negative* method at all, used only to expose illusion. Kant had failed to understand that dialectic is in fact a method for conceptualizing, for comprehending these contradictory phenomena.

In this manner Hegel ultimately rejected Kant's root idea, while at the same time learning much from Kantian dialectic and the antinomial theory. Hegel, as it were, turned the wheel of cognition backward. Once Kant had been comprehended, contained, and "sublated" (*aufgehoben*)—that is, once contradiction had been caught up and reconciled in a higher idea —once again philosophy's old and splendid goal, an all-inclusive metaphysic, came into view. So, full of conviction, Hegel turned back, carrying the banner of his belief before him: a people which "loses its metaphysic," he said, is a people in whom "Mind occupied with its own pure nature no longer really exists."[5]

In his determination to restore and render secure metaphysics as knowing's highest court of judgment, Hegel is entirely rooted in the Western philosophic tradition, for him imperishable. With this commitment his philosophic effort became as magnificent as it was all but despairing. Hegel the metaphysician lifted himself up to the level of almost hybrid formulations which one reads with a kind of skeptical amazement.

Hegel claims to know the realm of truth "as it is, stripped of all integument, in and for itself, implicit and explicit." He says he has grasped the *Darstellung Gottes*, that is, God as primordial representation or presence, "as he was in his eternal essence before the creation of nature and finite spirit*."[6]

Hegel the metaphysician found some recognition, but the great thinkers of the nineteenth century had nothing but scorn for his metaphysical objective. Here the Christian thinker Kierkegaard is completely in accord with the atheist Marx, who summarily rejected the Hegelian metaphysic as "mystification." Kierkegaard's reaction was very much sharper: "This Hegel fellow—oh, let me think Greek—how the gods would have laughed! Such a loathsome professor, pretending to have seen through the necessity of all things and then arrang-

---

* As used by Hegel, the term *Geist* means both "spirit" and "mind." There is no exact English equivalent of *Geist.*—*Tr.*

ing it all so he can reel off a lot of jabber about it. Ye gods!"[7]

Hegel is a two-faced Janus, embracing the form and content of the past with a tremendous power of synthesis and carrying it forward into the present. Meanwhile he cannot resist looking into an as yet unformed future. He thinks in terms of the past and the future opens up to him. Meanwhile his believing nature also contemplates, with perfect trust, eternal and absolute spirit. Yet the clearsighted and skeptical aspect of his intelligence sees other signs, too.

Hegel's pupil, Hotho, described his mentor as follows: "It was precisely in the depths of the seemingly undecipherable where this powerful mind pried and poked about with splendidly self-confident ease and calm." The older and by that time successful Hegel made the same impression on many of his contemporaries: sovereign, both sure of and at ease with himself, the master of philosophy. And according to the testimony of schoolmaster Leutewein the younger Hegel, too, had been a "pleasant companion," notable for a "certain joviality and barroom conviviality."[8]

But Hegel, as we have just said, was a man with two faces. The strain of cheerfulness in him, the self-assurance and perhaps even cockiness, poorly concealed the other side. Of himself Hegel said: "You know, for one thing I'm a timid person, for another I love peace . . ."[9] And it was certainly not by chance that his wife attested to his being one of those "hopeless people," the kind "who want nothing and ask for nothing."[10]

Beyond this, Hegel, as he once wrote, for "some years" suffered from "hypochondria to the point of exhaustion." An even deeper insight is provided by another comment he wrote in the same connection: "I know from personal experience this mood of the emotions, or rather of the reason, when, with engrossing interest and all the retributions thereby exacted, it has got itself entangled in a chaos of appearances . . ."[11]

Anyone seeking a practical explanation for this unsure and anxious Hegel might find an adequate one in the hard and deprived circumstances in which he lived for so long. He traveled the usual road of the scholar of his day. He graduated from the Tübingen religious institute as a foundation scholar, then went through the misery of working as a private tutor. After this he became an unsalaried university instructor, a *Privatdocent*, dependent for a living on his students' fees, and finally a professor, but one so poorly paid he could not possibly live on his academic earnings. For a while he was also a newspaper editor, then a teacher in a *gymnasium*. It was not until he was forty-seven that he finally became a full professor with a proper income.

In many ways his life was not an easy one. When he taught in the *gymnasium* his pay was often months in arrears. Besides this he was buffeted by the vagaries of history. By birth a Swabian, during his employment in Bavaria he was listed as a "foreigner." Eventually, as noted, he did become a professor in Berlin. But there, too, trouble dogged his steps: "I am just fifty years old and have spent thirty of them in these endlessly unsettled times of fear and hope, always hoping that sometime fear and hoping will be ended. Now I'm forced to see that it will always continue, indeed, in gloomy moments one is inclined to think that things will be getting worse."[12]

But this sort of surface explanation is not enough to understand Hegel the *thinker*, nor, specifically, a strain of thought in his work that justifies our speaking of him as a dark and somber man. This somber Hegel had a stronger and more pervasive influence than Hegel the systematist. It was to this dark side of Hegel that Marx attached himself, absorbing its every facet. Kierkegaard, too, was held by Hegel's dark side— or, more precisely, used the Hegelian mode of thought to develop new somber possibilities of his own. In his apocalyptic guise, if we may call it such, Hegel exerted an influence deep into our own times: it is as if the full potential of his kind of thinking was not realized until the twentieth century.

In his *Philosophy of Right*, Hegel said that every philosophy is a child of its own times. This comment applies with particular force to his own system. History itself was his vast source of cognitive material, and his general concept of history was conditioned by his specific experience of the history of his own period. This experience began with the French Revolution, and with the way that he and two partisan friends at the Tübingen Theological Institute, Schelling and Hölderlin, re-

acted to this great upheaval. They admired the French Revolution because they hoped that through it the world would be
reborn in a spirit of freedom and reason. When these hopes
were dashed by the Terror, the world fell apart for Hegel.
Then came Napoleon, who also excited Hegel's admiration.
He described Napoleon on the day of his triumphal entry into
Jena—a day that for Hegel also marked the end of his life in
that city—in these words: ". . . the Emperor—that world-
soul—I saw riding through the city on reconnaissance; it is
indeed a wonderful feeling to see such an individual . . ."[13]

Then Napoleon in his turn fell, and for Hegel it was the
most tragic thing imaginable; he mourned the "monstrous
spectacle, the sight of a tremendous genius committing self-
destruction."[14] Yet history went on; the Congress of Vienna
ensued and a new order for the continent took shape. For his
part Hegel became a professor in Prussian Berlin, and the
thinker who had once clung to the idea of revolutionary freedom in his last work became for many the philosopher of
reaction and the Restoration.

Hegel lived through all these things as one who hoped and
feared. However, it was not his own personal fate that engaged his hopes and his anxieties. For his personal fortunes he
had a cheerfully stoic formula. One had to keep an eye on the
"advancing world spirit," keep track of the path along which it
was rushing "with seven-league boots." This, he believed, was
"the safest way," safest, that is, in both the inner and outer
sense.[15]

He had early divined that the world was in a state of flux
and was heading toward an unknown goal. Already in Jena he
had concluded a lecture with the following sentiments: "We
live in an important period, a period in which the world-spirit
is experiencing a shock, emerging from its old form and finding a new one. The whole mass of hitherto existing ideas, the
ties that bound the world, have disintegrated, crumbled like
an apparition in a dream." Did he say this fearfully or hope-
fully? There is no way of knowing. But it was characteristic of
him to add: "A new emergence of spirit is in process of preparation. And it is philosophy especially that must bear witness
to and welcome its coming, even while others, feebly resisting,

cling to the past and reject its mass appearance. But philosophy, recognizing eternality at work, has to do it honor."[16]

In these words from the Jena period, Hegel's great metaphysical instinct is again evident—the instinct to recognize the eternal and enduring, the Spirit (*Geist*) at work. Yet intermingled here, too, we detect another tone. Hegel speaks about the disintegration of all ties: he describes the world as having melted away like an image in a dream. And if this thought is construed as having sprung from a mere random mood, a very important side of Hegel will have been overlooked.

Actually the dark and somber Hegel who "immersed himself with engrossing interest, and with all the toll that this exacts, in a chaos of appearances" goes back even further than the Jena period. It is a most remarkable fact how persistently unrecognized this dark side of Hegel has remained. It throws a curious light, indeed, on the very ability to read. You ask yourself what the reader actually does and does not read, or, more precisely, what the interpreter, as he reads, grasps and does not grasp.

To be sure, again and again Hegel clothed the dark elements of his teachings in the brighter raiment of his theory of Absolute Spirit, and thus there is some excuse for failing to catch the message. Nonetheless the dark underground is in his works, at every step, from first to last.

Hegel experienced history as conflict. He never forgot the French Revolution; he described it many times and for him it always stood as the supreme example of the deep-seated disunity of history. On the one hand he described this conflict in terms of a "splendid dawn,"[17] on the other as a "rage and fury of destruction."[18] In the *Phenomenology*, the Revolution is depicted in a chapter titled "Absolute Freedom and Terror."

In this model Hegel found reason and unreason firmly side by side. Again and again Hegel fashioned the image of an event that begins meaningfully only to change suddenly into senselessness. In the *Philosophy of Right* he cites Rousseau as having correctly recognized that the state is founded on will. But what Rousseau had not seen was that it was not individual wills uniting in contract that can found the state, but only objective Will, a general will that is rational *an und für sich,* "in and for itself," that is, implicitly and explicitly, essentially and operatively.

He goes on to say: "For this reason, when these abstractions [of Rousseau's] came into power, for the first time in human history they afforded the spectacle of the overthrow of the constitution of a great actual state and its complete reconstruction from a fresh start on the basis of pure thought alone after all that was existing and given had been destroyed. The will of the founders of the new state was to give it what they alleged to be a purely rational basis, but it was in fact only abstractions that were being used; the Idea was lacking; and so the experiment ended in the maximum of frightfulness and terror."[19]

As so often is the case, here Hegel presses his "on the one hand" and "on the other hand" into a single statement, sublates the two together by transcendence. "On the one hand" he sees the apparently rational and mighty power of the French Revolution, and "on the other" its degeneration into a most horrible and crude event. He rejects, while giving recognition to, this piece of history.

It was not only history that taught Hegel how to think in terms of double meanings. During the Jena period he wrote a fragment that no interpreter has ever given its due. This fragment depicts a curiously brutal God, torn within and ambiguous in his nature. It is a God who "becomes angered with himself" because "he has spread himself thin in a splendor of forms and lost his 'punctuality.'" Destroying his creations, he retreats back into the focus of his being, "rage devouring his creations into itself." Here Hegel is developing, as he himself says, "a barbaric point of view." But the whole fragment spells out the dialectic principle in one mystical vision. Having ventured forth out of himself, God returns again into himself. Such is the cycle of his eternal and ever new constructions.

Here for the first time, then, appears the Hegelian image of essential being as torn and divided within itself. In this, his very first description of it, we see how strongly Hegel was moved by this image. Even at this early stage he was rationalizing his mystical notion of a self-expanding, self-consuming God who reverted back into himself. For now he goes on to

tell us that the "root of philosophical need" is this very "disunity." Philosophy springs from "the living originality of the
Spirit . . . which, through itself, has restored and spontaneously reformed the disrupted harmony within itself."[20]

With each later step forward, Hegel's description of these
phenomena becomes more realistic and concrete. One of these
portrayals is found in the *Phenomenology* and stretches out
over almost a hundred pages. The chapter title is "The Self-
Estranged Spirit." Here the vision of spirit grown outside of
and beyond itself is no longer treated in mystical, but in abstract terms. Even if this chapter were not subdivided into
sections on "Culture," "The Age of Enlightenment," and "Absolute Freedom and Terror," one would recognize that what
Hegel is doing here is simply describing the period in which
he lived. For Hegel culture itself was self-estranged spirit, and
the Enlightenment equally represented the workings of the
process of self-estrangement. As the final act of the whole
drama there is again a description of the French Revolution.

The somberness of this portrayal exceeds by far anything
produced by later cultural criticism, even Rousseau's denuncia-
tions of his times. It is culture especially that Hegel indicts for
"venting scornful laughter on existence, on the confusion per-
vading the whole and on itself as well."[21]

Little though Hegel's contemporaries grasped his devastating condemnation of a world that was, in fact, their own, later
generations read the sequel to this portrayal with an open
mind. We find it in the *Philosophy of Right*, where Hegel
describes civil society. For him civil society is not a revolutionary achievement. And again the theme of a world torn
within itself comes up. Hegel's gaze is now directed at the
social and economic structure of the society surrounding him.
He depicts it in terms of "that which, in its extremes, has lost
its morality."[22] In this torn society, a creation of the modern
world, "each person is his own goal, all else is nothing to
him."[23] In the extravagance of its manifestations civil society
is "driven above and beyond itself," because with all its wealth
it is still not rich enough "to get around the overabundance of
poverty and the production of a mob."[24]

One can only marvel that neither the clarity nor the dev-

astating criticism of this description had any effect. But one
man, at any rate, read it with a receptive mind: Karl Marx. In
his youthful writings Marx already was thinking in terms of
the "self-estranged spirit" and cited Hegel to this effect. To be
sure, in Marx's *Capital*, where the economic downfall of civil
society is actually presented, Hegel is no longer quoted. By
this time he is accorded recognition only peripherally, as the
one who first used dialectic "in its general forms of movement
in a comprehensive and knowledgeable way."[25]

But Hegel's real discovery was not the dialectical phenomenon as such, even though he did apply it more broadly than
anyone before him. Much more important is Hegel's idea of the
"negative" as the *vis motrix* of history. Neither Kierkegaard
nor Marx escaped the spell of this notion, however strongly
they may have believed that Hegel's use of dialectic had
yielded false conclusions.

In the *Phenomenology* there is a description of the principle
of the negative as exemplified by death. Following this, Hegel
develops his notion of the life of the spirit. The spirit, he says,
does not exist by looking away from the negative while "keeping it free from devastation," but by "looking the negative
squarely in the face" and by "abiding with" the negative when
"it [the spirit] finds itself in a state of absolute inner strife."[26]

In his *Logic*, Hegel developed this maxim into a methodical
principle. Only when one recognizes that "the negative is
equally positive" can progress be understood, that is, the essential nature of the Spirit and its evolution.[27] It is at this
point that the Hegelian dialectic assumes its characteristic
form. The negative essences that Hegel describes under many
names are the initiators of all movement.

With this began the theory of creative contradiction, which
from the nineteenth century on gave rise to an enormous variety of schools of thought. While this theory was expanding,
developing, and gaining firmness, its original author was almost forgotten. The negative essences which Hegel depicted
again and again, though to be sure he did not invent them,
continued to live on. Indeed, they have become more and
more powerful and have taken on an ever more threatening
aspect.

The Hegel who saw these negatives so clearly, but who in the end merged them into the essential nature of a self-unfolding Absolute Spirit, has been almost snappishly rejected and rebuked as naive for his ultimate belief in God.

Seen this way, Hegel's attempt to tie the "negative" and his own world into the positive course of the Absolute Spirit is no longer relevant for our times.

Modernity no longer wants to see what Hegel saw in his day. It no longer believes in the notion which Hegel described at the conclusion of his *Philosophy of Right*: "Spirit has actuality only through being divided within itself in giving bounds and finitude to natural needs and the relationship to external necessity, and along with this by incorporating itself into these needs and relationship, thus overcoming them and therein achieving spirit's objective existence."[28]

While the defenders of absolute reason were falling into discredit and belief in reason at all seemed slowly to be vanishing, Hegel's visions of nothingness and menacing decline were looming all the more apocalyptically.

The synthetic strength which Hegel had ascribed to dialectic changed into a destructive force. And thus in the hands of Hegel's successors dialectic became an instrument which tore reality apart in all directions, which sharpened and extended opposites and ultimately split the world into two camps.

# 2

## Story of Hegel's Youth

Georg Friedrich Wilhelm Hegel was born August 27, 1770, the son of a *Rentkammersekretär*, or secretary in the internal revenue department in the dukedom of Württemberg. The Hegels had migrated from the Austrian province of Carinthia in the sixteenth century and since that time had lived in Swabia. Hegel himself was a completely typical Swabian. From time immemorial the Swabians have had their special place among the Germanic people. If we are to believe the Prussians—for example, Haym[29]—the South Germans are a harmless, homey, naive, comfortable people, whereas the Prussians have culture and circumspection and "keep themselves under control in wants and thought." But if we are to believe the South Germans, they brag about having an older culture, lay claim to having more heart, and run down the Prussians for being boastful and loudmouthed.

Beyond such superficial judgments, found in any case in all

countries from south to north, the Swabian has his own special place in South Germany. The great Protestant tradition separates the Swabians from the South German Catholics. Beyond this, Swabian Protestantism often goes into the mystical and pietistic. As difficult as it is ultimately to find true general characteristics for any race of people, a basic Swabian trait is perhaps a peculiar mixture of thoughtfulness and sobriety. In this respect, in all events, Hegel is representative of the Swabian type.

Source material on Hegel's childhood is none too abundant. According to his sister, Christine, he began to go to a German school at the age of three and was sent to a Latin school at the age of five. He won prizes in all his classes and from his tenth to his eighteenth year was first in his class. The zeal that he put into everything he did is shown by his diary entries, by the excerpts he made from the books he was reading, and other evidence. We most clearly see what he was like from his diary notes of the Stuttgart *gymnasium* period. Everywhere they reveal the precocious child. As a fifteen-year-old he wrote: "Ah, ha! Bad news from Hohenheim. Matter of the peasants, a bad lot, smashed all the Duke's windows at the castle in Scharnhausen." And after this: "Today was a holiday; but I didn't go to church, instead went walking in the Bopser woods with Duttenhofer and Autenrieth."[30]

The wisdom of the fifteen-year-old shows in another entry: "When I ate a whole lot of cherries, refreshed myself wonderfully and thought myself lucky, someone (actually older than I) watched me unconcernedly and said: when you're young you think you just couldn't go by a cherry-seller without (as we Swabians say) your mouth watering for some; but when you get older you can let almost the whole spring roll by without longing for them. This proposition, for me rather disagreeable (but as wise as can be), led me to think: in youth, when unbridled appetite could certainly get your health in a bad way, you are not allowed to eat so much, in old age you do not want to."[31]

And then, a year later: "All men intend to make themselves happy, and in order to make others happy some sacrifice 'temporal' advantages . . . [but] they have not sacrificed true bliss . . . But first I must get the concept of bliss clear in my mind."[32]

It is a favorite trick with many biographers to read signs of adult genius into the child. And to be sure it is possible, if one wants to be unqualified about it, to read the great philosopher of later years into such statements as the foregoing. But at bottom everything we know about the young Hegel tells us that whereas he was a diligent boy, eager to learn and precocious, there was no more to it than that. Indeed, it looks as if the young Hegel was just a bright young fellow like many another.

As the head of his class, Hegel gave the valedictory address when he was graduated in 1788. It was extraordinarily straightforward, unlike any valedictory you would hear at a modern commencement. In it Hegel described the stultification of the arts and sciences under the Turks and then praised, by way of contrast, the Stuttgart Gymnasium and its educational program. Listen to the beginning of one passage: "But you, dear friends and fellow students . . . be assured that we [Hegel] . . . have learned to realize what ill-effects will result from any failure to heed the warnings of our teachers and superiors . . . Give thanks with us to a gracious Providence for granting our youth just these teachers and educators . . ."[33]

Even allowing for another style and another age, we still believe that the picture here is of a typical model boy. Hegel, in any case, then went on to the university, that is, he became a ducal foundation scholar at the Tübingen Theological Institute, where he studied philosophy and theology for five years.

Now the impression changes somewhat. Information available on the Hegel of this period is no longer so clear-cut. Beyond any doubt, however, Hegel, as we would say today, was a late-bloomer, and as such at Tübingen made up for a lot of headway lost at the *gymnasium*.

Hegel's Tübingen period has been thoroughly researched and described many times, by Dilthey, Haering, and others. All agree that two events stood out in this phase of his life. One was Hegel's friendship with Schelling, five years his junior, and with Hölderlin, who was his own age. The other was Hegel's experience of the French Revolution.

These two experiences really go together. The Tübingen triumvirate of Hegel, Schelling, and Hölderlin were bound together by a rapturous youthful friendship. They took turns assuring each other of their solidarity, and they felt commonly united by a belief in a coming Kingdom of God, for which they waited in tense anticipation. This kingdom was not particularly, or at any rate exclusively, religious in coloration in the sense of being an ecclesiastical kingdom. But all three, with the prerogative of youth, looked forward to a complete transformation of social, political, and spiritual life.

Again and again the word "freedom" cropped up in their exchanges. They aspired to freedom of mind, repeated the French revolutionary slogan of liberty, equality, and fraternity. And so they became, they believed, possessed by the spirit of the French Revolution. A political club was organized at the Tübingen Institute. In this connection one might wonder what the institute was like at the time. It was indeed a theological foundation, a boarding school, and it had its strict rules and regulations. Yet all evidence indicates that the institute was in no way narrow and limited in outlook. Important scholars taught there. A free kind of Protestantism was taught, and we have it on the statement of a contemporary student that no restriction was placed on what kind of books could be read.

But the institute was financed during this period by the reigning Duke Karl Eugen, whose court was a faithful copy of the Versailles court before the Revolution. From anecdotes we know that the Duke heard about the political activity at his Tübingen theological school and discovered that the "Marseillaise" was being sung there, and so he made a sudden appearance at the institute and gave the students a dressing-down in a speech in the refectory. At the end he is said to have asked Schelling whether he was not sorry about the whole business. Schelling is supposed to have replied: "Your Grace, all of us have our failings."[34] Regrettably the anecdote does not tell how the Duke reacted to this.

But not even yet did Hegel in any way show any signs of his

future greatness. Rather it is more often reported that many of Hegel's fellow students who lived to see him grow famous said that at the time they never thought he had it in him.

Some of the commentary from student days is nonetheless worth mentioning, not so much because it throws light on the later Hegel but because it shows how he was evaluated at the time. At the institute Hegel was tagged as "the old man." We know of a drawing in which he is so portrayed, with this caption beneath: "May God stand by the Old Man." Another anecdote tells how Hegel liked to drink and how he often came to class not quite sober. On one occasion his dormitory proctor is said to have shouted at him when he came home: "Oh Hegel, you'll surely end up sousing all your brains away."[35]

All this sort of thing accords with the picture that school-master Leutewein, a fellow student and friend of Hegel's, gives of him in a letter, and to the testimony provided by the ephor Schnurrer. Leutewein has it that Hegel was well-liked by everybody, that a certain joviality and tavern good-fellow-ship made him a pleasant companion, but that he behaved in a rather *genialisch* way—that is, showed off how smart he was—and that his conduct was not always in line with cloister regulations.[36] And Schnurrer wrote: "Herr Hegel will be examined late this year . . . A little caution would do no harm. I doubt very much whether meanwhile he will have learned to accept with patience the self sacrifices that always go with a private tutoring position, at least at the beginning."[37]

All in all, reading these accounts, you simply get the impression that Hegel was of the stuff from which good, ordinary citizens are molded. As a result the question has often been raised and quite justifiably explored as to whether the young Hegel was actually revolutionary at all. His biographer Haym believed that Hegel's revolutionary convictions did not run very deep, and wrote that "it was a student fad by which even the sober and later so antirevolutionary Hegel was seized."[38] With deeper instinct Dilthey apprehended how decisive the experience of the French Revolution was for Hegel, yet Haering, quite to the contrary, asserts that Dilthey very much overestimated Hegel's oppositional character.[39]

Now, despite all the tavern joviality that Leutewein ascribes to him, Hegel was not one to let everybody know how he really felt about things. And so it must be taken into account all the more seriously that the same young Hegel whose pulpit delivery is said to have been "bad, inaudible and hesitant"[40] is on the other hand described as an inspired speaker for freedom and equality. But perhaps this, too, could really be discounted as mere student enthusiasm if we did not have ample evidence that his experience of the French Revolution still clung to him even in his declining years.

At a time when Hegel was already teaching at Berlin and when he considered himself to be a faithful servant of Prussia, he said in his "Lectures on the Philosophy of History":

> It was in consequence a splendid time of dawning. All thinking beings joined in celebrating this period. An exalted emotion dominated the times, an enthusiasm of the spirit thrilled the world as if the divine and the mundane at last had been reconciled.[41]

What is remarkable in this formulation is that Hegel obviously views the French Revolution almost mystically when he speaks in terms of a reconciliation of God with the world. Did Hegel misunderstand the Revolution to the point of failing to see its actuality?

This is not the case. For in the *Phenomenology*, Hegel's first work, a description of the Revolution is again of central importance. We shall speak later about this part of the *Phenomenology*, which bears the title of "Absolute Freedom and Terror." In any case, in this description it is made perfectly clear that he did in fact see the Revolution in its entire dimension.

One thing is certain: Hegel was not one of those who forgot the impact of the French Revolution. It remained within him; he meditated on it again and again and for it found ever new definitions. Yet it is also certain that an intellect of Hegel's type was really alien to the revolutionary, indeed opposed to it. Nonetheless, in dealing with the revolutionary for the first time, we encounter the powerful capability which lifted this thinker above the centuries and gave him his high rank.

For Hegel made out of the French Revolution a paradigmatic experience. A man who sought peace and preferred a bourgeois way of life, he saw in the French Revolution the signature of the whole human process. The stage setting of history could change swiftly, and the face of events undergo precipitate dialectic reversal. He learned, and the French Revolution was his model, that this world's events do not follow any rectilinear course and that there is no direct progress as was visualized by the thinkers of the Enlightenment. Rather, the scene is ruled by an eternal ebb and flow, and he who has not apprehended this fact has grasped nothing.

From this point of view it is irrelevant whether Hegel personally was revolutionary or antirevolutionary. Something else is more important. The dynamic element, the dialectic which Hegel built into his system, he experienced for the first time in the fact and fate of the French Revolution.

And at the same time we first see here that strain in this thinker's nature which permits us to speak of his genius. Like him, countless thousands of others witnessed the French Revolution and either found more or less reasonable explanations for it or did not comprehend it at all; Hegel himself came from an entirely different world of rigidly structured Protestantism to which, in fact, he clung his whole life. But however alien the French Revolution may have been to him, he must have understood what was going on and incorporated the event into his thinking.

Hegel's powerfully synthesizing mind declared itself for the first time in dealing with this subject, if functioning quite differently from the mind of a Kierkegaard or Marx. This becomes more evident when we learn that although during his Tübingen period Hegel was reading Kant and other philosophers and theologians as well, it was to Rousseau that he repeatedly returned with a true passion. Thus Leutewein reports on the Hegel of the Tübingen period: "His hero was Rousseau, in whose *Emile, Social Contract,* and *Confessions* he read constantly. He believed that through his reading he would rid himself of certain general prejudices and tacit assumptions, or, as Hegel himself put it, 'unfettered.' "[42]

This reasoning sounds rather naive, but it is completely correct. Hegel, the model boy, as we have described him, wanted to reach out beyond his limited world. He wanted to be rid of all prejudices and intellectual fetters so that he might grasp the whole of things.

And while he was following this course of action another and different nature emerged in him. As shown by his *gymnasium* valedictory address, he had grown up with a touching and almost blind trust in authority, and in this spirit of trust had accepted everything the prevailing system of education had offered him. Now this confidence began to waver, simply because he suddenly began to see the world in another light.

He had been at home in the Enlightenment, which looked into the future full of assurance and faced up optimistically to what it had in store. In the French Revolution he experienced the other side of the world, a grim and demonic side, simultaneously revealing the faces of freedom and of absolute terror. Some time was to pass before Hegel found his synthesis for these opposites, one able to bring both sides of the world together. The result was his philosophical system, which confronts us like some strange two-headed monster.

At this point we do not want to anticipate more than is necessary. But again and again we will encounter the same powerful intellectual capacity evidenced here in his reaction to the French Revolution, a capacity that makes the thinker Hegel what he is. Quite the opposite of Kierkegaard and Marx, he saw the dual aspect of this world and tried to comprehend it in his way. In doing this he arrived at the idea of a dialectic and of a dialectical way of thinking, but in the Tübingen period his dialectic had not yet been formulated and in the fragment "Popular Religion and Christianity," written by Hegel in this period, we find not a trace of it.

In contrast to other interpreters we shall abandon forthwith any exegesis of this and other youthful writings, which in any case have been exhaustively discussed by Dilthey and Haering, and immediately move further along the biographical line.

Hegel left Tübingen, meanwhile still seriously debating whether he should add the law to his theological and philosophical studies. Instead of doing this, however, he plunged

into the misery that so many younger scholars of his day had
to endure. He went to Switzerland and became a tutor in the
home of an old Bern family, called Steiger von Tschugg.
There he got to know the aristocratic oligarchy of Bern, and
about these people wrote peevishly to Schelling that "the intrigues at the princely courts by cousins male and female are
nothing compared with the combinations made here . . . To
get to know an aristocratic system of government, you have to
spend a winter here before Easter, when the supplementation
[of the Conseil souverain, or Supreme Council] occurs."[43]

We do not have much source material on these tutoring
years of Hegel, but enough to know that he was unhappy in
Bern and also to realize that he was continuing to pursue what
he had already started in Tübingen. He collected and stored
material and formulated part of it in writings which, in my
opinion, show precious little of the later Hegel, however often
this may be claimed in detailed analyses. These youthful
fragments, published by Nohl, deal with conventional themes:
the spirit of Christianity and the life and destiny of Jesus. In
our context we shall not go into this literature.

In 1797 Hegel left Bern and went to Frankfurt, again as a
private tutor. Hölderlin got him the post. Hegel wrote about
this move that he followed his friend's call "without thinking."
He also mentioned other prospects that he let go, apparently
meaning a private tutoring position in Tübingen.[44]

By this time Hegel was almost twenty-eight years old; when
he left Frankfurt three and a half years later and moved to
Jena he was thirty-one. His younger friend, Schelling, having
advanced meteorically, was already famous. Through Goethe's
intervention Schelling had already been given a professorship
at Jena, while Hegel was in Frankfurt. And before Hegel went
there Schelling's first system of "natural philosophy," *Ideas
Regarding a Philosophy of Nature*, had already appeared.

How was Hegel developing in this period; how were things
going with the philosopher Hegel? I have already mentioned
that Hegel's development has been minutely researched by a
number of authors and that the fragments from the period
found in Hegel's literary estate have been repeatedly interpreted, but the conclusions have varied. Naturally they have

been influenced by whether the scholar in question had his mind set on finding the old Hegel in the young one, or whether he approached the question without bias.

We are concerned here only with the latter approach. It is always rather annoying to watch biographers at work who, at any price, are determined to see their subject as a single, uniform personality, who reduce his life and works to a sort of mathematical equation. A man is no mere matter of arithmetic, for himself or for others.

To be sure, even in these early years Hegel showed many signs of what was to come, providing, of course, that one knows beforehand what the future Hegel is going to be like. For the unprejudiced observer, however, who does not look back from what is yet to be, the Hegel of this period was a highly uncertain quantity. A whole range of possibilities lay ahead.

Born the son of a ducal official, brought up in the atmosphere of Swabian Protestantism, he had so far studied theology and philosophy. His whole background would have led one to suppose that he would remain in a prescribed course and become a quietly working scholar of solid worth.

But there was another element in Hegel that only gradually came to the fore. In many respects this element was at odds with what we know of Hegel hitherto. It was first indicated, as we have already described, by his turning to the French Revolution. Then other signs of it began to appear here and there. For example, he took a notion to study the law. Then, remarkably enough, the philosopher and theologian suddenly wrote a piece which seems to be really extraordinary—it was called "On the Most Recent Internal Conditions of Württemberg, Especially the Infirmity of the Municipal Constitution." Thus once again, right in Frankfurt, his interest in politics and political action declared itself. It was in this period that Hegel collected his information on political economy. In 1798–99 he wrote a detailed critical commentary on the then well-known work by Stewart on political science.

This development is almost amazing. One might get the impression that the philosopher and theologian now wanted to become a politician. This politician, moreover, was on the side of the opposition. Hegel felt himself to be a reformer. The piece on the state of Württemberg as it was in those days is filled with criticism. Its abuses are described, and we are told that the bureaucracy and the members of the government by their very nature are opposed to all progress and reforms. The whole system—we are told—is inherently defective and a total overhaul is needed. The tone is polemical, as only a small sample will suffice to show:

> The commission must find it very convenient to have on hand men who speak and write for it and in an emergency even think for it. A majority of the membership meanwhile have been consuming their income in comfortable repose, at the same time also looking out for their own soul's salvation while letting the affairs of the country go as Providence and the leaders wish. Any flock would really be in a bad way if it had one shepherd to lead it in the morning and another at night.[45]

The piece continues in this vein. When Hegel, as the story goes, let it be known he had it in mind to write this critique to qualify himself for a post in the Württemberg government, his friends told him that publishing it would do him more harm than good. The young reformer in thought—for none of this ever actually reached the public eye—also criticized in these sharp words the then existing situation in Germany: "Outside of the despotisms, that is, states without any constitution at all," he said, "no state has a more miserable constitution."[46]

These are harsh words. Had they come out in print, had they taken effect, had they had consequences for Hegel himself, today we might have had another Hegel than the one we know. One might even indulge the wild notion that Hegel could have become a politician. Would German philosophy then have been deprived of one of its most influential exponents? Would philosophy's loss have been politics' gain?

However idle this question may seem, it must be considered if we are to know the man behind the works of Hegel. It has often been stressed that this political preoccupation also led to his acquiring a fund of information that enabled him to write certain parts of his *Philosophy of Right*. But none of his biographers can escape the fact that Hegel did in the end become a philosopher and a very effective one. In consequence they take his political activity as part of his theoretical accomplishment. The question still remains whether Hegel originally did not want to follow another path. Yes, it might even be asked whether Hegel was a politician *manqué*.

To be sure, Hegel's actual development followed a quite different course. Nonetheless for his later career it was extraordinarily important that for at least an interval Hegel should have wanted to get away from theory. This tendency was to show up repeatedly and was an active component of Hegel's philosophy.

Most biographers have, of course, noted this political tendency in Hegel, but for them it has been a peripheral thing. However that may be, it should not be overlooked that a strong inclination to political activism was at work in the youthful Hegel. And this theoretician of tremendous dimension, for us a veritable symbol of speculative thought in general, had in him still another tendency opposed to theoretical reflection.

In this connection the letters which Hegel wrote to Schelling that have been preserved deserve particular consideration. Often cited is a letter Hegel wrote to Schelling in 1795, that is, during the Bern period. It was written, as Haym says, in a mood of "revolutionary enthusiasm"; at times it has been taken seriously and at times not. In it Hegel said:

> The philosophers prove this dignity [of the human race], they teach the people how to feel and how not merely to demand rights ground down into the dust, but to take them themselves—seize them by force. Religion and politics have worked hand in glove, and the former has taught what despotism wanted, contempt for the human race, its incapacity for anything good, to be anything on its own. With the spread of ideas about how things ought to be, the indolence of established people in taking everything as it is will vanish . . . [Now the tone grows more urgent and at

the end we are told:] My summons is: strive toward the
sun, friends, so that the salvation of the human race will
soon mature . . .[47]

Reading these words, one understands how commentators
have talked about them in terms of youthful flights and revolutionary fads. But it must not be forgotten that after this
letter, both in Bern and Frankfurt, Hegel continued to pursue
this line of thought. Wherever he went he sought to get involved in the local political situation, and the flights of enthusiasm which the letter bespeaks were replaced by sharp
and expert political criticism. This criticism was directed at
the then prevailing political system in Bern, at the government
of Württemberg and the German government, and everywhere it became evident how greatly Hegel was attached to
the cause of radical opposition.

At the same time the last sentence that I cited is specifically
significant for Hegel the theoretician. For he is saying that it is
the existing leadership which has a monopoly on ideas about
how things ought to be, and that these ideas govern practice.
It was the spirit of this sentence which Marx evoked again and
again and which he interpreted as follows: as the idea of
revolution spreads the existing order will be overthrown by
it.

And this same passage was also to have its history within
Hegel himself, a development which I shall present later in
detail. For Hegel was to return again and again to this idea—
briefly put, the relationship between theory and practice. The
older Hegel, as already noted, was to say quite literally the
opposite of what he wrote at twenty-five. It is truly remarkable to see how the youthful Hegel was caught in irons between politics and theory. Later he was to change continuously with the passage of the years. What would have become
of him if, in his youth, other possibilities had presented themselves? Was he guided by personal circumstance or his given
disposition? But we can only stick to the facts. Hegel's father
died in 1800, leaving him a small legacy which made it possible for him to give up private tutoring. He decided to move
to Jena and the then famous university where his friend

Schelling was teaching. After a long silence he again wrote to Schelling, in a carefully thought-out letter in which he announced he had made up his mind "to spend some time in independent circumstances" and devote himself to work and studies already started. "Before I commit myself," he wrote, "to the Jena literary whirl I want to fortify myself by a stay at a third place. Bamberg occurred to me all the more because I have been hoping to meet you there . . ." He inquired for Bamberg addresses, etc.

At the end the letter turns to a description of his own state of mind. It would appear that his decision on the future had been made, and there was no more talk of politics. He said of himself:

> In my scientific education, which began from subordinate human needs, I had to be driven on to science, and at the same time to change the ideals of youth into forms of reflection, into a system; I ask myself now, while I am still busy doing this, where a way can be found back to involvement in the everyday life of men . . .[48]

This last passage could still be interpreted as meaning that Hegel was looking for some practical activity. But the die had in fact been cast. He would continue to work at scholarly pursuits. He had—and now for the first time that great magic word suddenly appeared in definitive context—developed a system. Obviously he had found what for him was to be a lifelong theoretical labor: a system and a theory of systematization.

# 3

## The Conception of the System

At the beginning of the year 1801 Hegel moved to Jena, which meant that he became connected with a university that at the time, as Haym says, was uniquely the center of German literature and philosophy. And indeed many great men had worked, or were working, at Jena during this period. Schiller had taught there, and Wilhelm von Humboldt had worked there. Fichte had reached the peak of his fame in Jena, Schlegel had worked there with Novalis and Tieck, and Schelling was teaching there. Goethe had close ties with Jena, though he actually lived in Weimar.

For six years Hegel stayed in Jena as docent and professor, although paid so little he could not live on his earnings. He left the city after the Battle of Jena and Auerstedt, in which Napoleon was the victor, and with that his Jena connection was ended.

Hegel came to Jena, as he wrote to Schelling, with the insight that the time had come for him to transform the "forms of reflection" of his youth into a "system." From this it could be inferred that he came to Jena with a completed philosophic system. Such was not the case. On the contrary, it would be nearer the truth to say that it was in Jena that the Hegelian system was created. Hegel's first great work, his *Phenomenology of Mind*, appeared in 1807, at the end of the Jena period. Marx called Jena the birthplace of the Hegelian philosophy.

All interpreters of Hegel agree that Hegel's real development did not begin until he went to Jena—or, as some have said, reached maturity there. Hegel wrote to Schelling that his "forms of reflection" had changed into a system, and in line with this some have felt they could detect the first outlines of the Hegelian system in the many fragments from the end of the Frankfurt period. For example, there is the so-called "Frankfurt Fragment of the System," which according to Nohl originally consisted of some forty-seven pages of manuscript, although only two pages have come down to us.[49] However, to the extent that the whole can be extrapolated from these two pages, Haering appears to be right when he says there is no justification here of speaking in terms of a system, either in a formal or a practical sense.

There is no doubt that Hegel went to Jena with the intention of creating a philosophic system. The process of actually doing this, however, was to last for six years. We even have the first preliminary draft of the project, published under the title of "Jena Logic, Metaphysics and Natural Philosophy."[50] However, if we compare these lectures with the system as it eventually appeared in the *Phenomenology*, it is as if we were looking at something entirely different.

The University of Jena lecture listings show how Hegel was in process of developing his system. In the winter semester of 1804–05 he was already offering a course of lectures called "The Whole System of Philosophy According to Its Own Dictates."[51] Even in 1802 and thereafter, he repeatedly called attention to the imminent publication of his book, and for his lecture series used the title "System of Philosophy" again and again. The component parts of the system were already becoming clear, as when Hegel delivered such lectures as "Logic and Metaphysics," "Philosophy of Nature and Mind," and beyond these gave others on the history of philosophy, indeed, even on geometry and arithmetic.

Thus the six years in Jena appear to have been filled with an unconditional and absolute striving to create a system. Many students of Hegel have assumed that he built up his system piece by piece during these years, working like an architect according to a plan that he had brought with him to Jena, elaborating the single parts and finally fitting them together. Indeed all the component parts such as "Logic" and "Philosophy of Nature" do appear in the Jena lectures and so it might be thought that they were ultimately united into a system.

But why did this composition take six years to complete? At the end of these six years, why was it that what had originally been intended as a short introduction within the larger framework of the *Phenomenology* came out as an independent work, and one actually not conceived at all in the earlier outline of the system? Still other questions can be broached.

When Hegel came to Jena he had no more than a bare notion of a system. His ambition was to create a philosophic schema different from any known before. Floating before his mind's eye in lively motion were its as yet unarticulated component parts. At this stage he might have had the individual building blocks, but he lacked nevertheless the constructive element out of which his system was to grow. And this constructive element or motivating force had to have special characteristics: it had to generate the system by means of a sort of inner movement, piece by piece. Without this dialectic the Hegelian system would have been unthinkable. For Hegel, system and dialectic were inseparable. This was not always to hold true, however. Kierkegaard and Marx were to accept the dialectic but reject the Hegelian system. So far as Hegel's historic significance goes, it must be said that his system has become extinct, but his dialectic lives on.

If we are concentrating in this chapter mainly on the basic elements of the Hegelian philosophy it is because access to it is impossible without understanding these two root factors.

For Hegel himself the idea of a system, rather than the dialectic device, was of primary importance. For many philosophers, one of whom was Hegel, systematization has a kind of magical attraction. The impulse to systematize appears again and again in philosophy; it is evident in ancient and in medieval systems, as well as in modern. The magic spell of systematization seems simple enough. A system is a means of understanding the whole in all its detail. It provides, so to speak, the greatest range of vision; it allows anything and everything to be put in its place and the whole to be comprehended.

Something of this idea of a system animated Hegel; he sought and found what he believed to be the universal order of things. But since time immemorial, and Hegel's system was no exception, the idea of systematization has always contained a drop of wormwood. Systems are transitory. Like all living things they are clearly born but to die. Hegel was constantly aware of this. He even says as much at the end of his *Phenomenology* when he speaks of Golgotha as the throne of the Absolute Spirit.

For us today the idea of a philosophical system has faded, not least the one developed by Hegel. The great philosophers who came after Hegel had nothing but mockery and contempt for his schema. Thus Kierkegaard, obviously with Hegel in mind, commented: "Every step that philosophy takes it sheds its skin, and into it creep the more stupid hangers-on."[52] And Nietzsche: "I am not stupid enough for a system."[53]—"System-building—is childishness."[54] And then, with undisguised malice: "The desire to make systems springs from a lack of honesty."[55] And these are not the only thinkers opposed to systematization. A much more recent and also much more academic thinker, Nicolai Hartmann, more than once declared in this connection: "The day of systems is past."

Whether they are completely over and done with, however, is open to doubt. Man's bent to see the whole from one visual angle is ineradicable. There is food for thought in the fact that although modernity may not give much credit to philosophical systems, nonetheless in political thinking, judging by those who engage in it, systematization still has the greatest significance. Such a system, for example, is Marxism, which explains everything, comprehends everything, and stretches everything out to fit on its Procrustean bed. Marx was a true disciple of

Hegel, so far as the universalism of his system is concerned.

When Hegel himself ridiculed systems that practice a "barren formalism," which are like a "grocery store" in which "tins bestuck with labels are lined up in rows,"[56] he was not far from sharing the point of view of modern critics of philosophical systems. If in spite of this he still believed in systematization, it was because he believed he had found "the one true method" of going about it. This method was his dialectic.

With this, as it were, we again come to the central concept of Hegelian thinking, which would be of interest to us if for no other reason than that it gave rise to a whole school of thought, in the fullest sense. However, our initial concern with the Hegelian dialectic will not be concentrated on the finished product of the method, as ingeniously developed by Hegel in the *Phenomenology* and all his other works. Rather we are much more interested, at this point, in how his dialectical method came into being.

Apparently there is a perfectly simple explanation for its origin. Hegel certainly did not invent the concept of dialectic. It can be traced back as far as the philosophies of classical times. Plato and Aristotle used dialectic. We must not forget, too, that Kant devoted an entire half of his *Critique of Pure Reason* to "Transcendental Dialectic." And immediately preceding Hegel, Fichte and Schelling were talking about dialectic and incorporating it into their philosophies.

The obvious and almost necessary conclusion is that Hegel took over the dialectic from many predecessors. The only argument against this conclusion, really, is the fact that in the history of philosophy the opinion on dialectic changes like a chameleon. At one point it is praised as philosophy's true method, only later to be exposed by Kant as absolute reason's jugglery, still later to take on the appearance of a mere rhetorical art, by means of which an opponent is cheated in an apparently logical way.

Hegel crossed swords with all these versions of the dialectic, often summarily and in short sentences. He was rather critical of the Platonic dialectic, and while praising Kant taxed him at the same time with having failed really to understand the dialectical method. Yet neither from Hegel's polemics, nor from his later dogmatic applications of the dialectic can we arrive at an idea of what he personally saw in it.

It is in fact my conviction that one must have had a concrete, firsthand experience of the actuality which Hegel called dialectical before the conceptual system of the dialectic can be grasped. This also provides an answer to the earlier question of why Hegel worked for six years on his system. He had always been thinking dialectically, as witnessed by many of his early fragments. He always saw, so to speak, with two different eyes, one seeing the *sic*, the other the *non*, the Yes and the No. The apprehension of actuality as structured in opposites, one might say, was born in him.

But he could not at first find full expression for this faculty, or, more precisely, could not bring dialectic to the heights of his intuition of its workings as he experienced them. When he finally found the way and the material to demonstrate the dialectic in all its fullness and immediacy, he wrote it all down in a great rush. The result was the *Phenomenology*. And it was not by chance that the *Phenomenology*, as we shall see upon closer inspection, implies a sort of historical view of consciousness.

On the whole one might think that Hegel came to be aware of the dialectic directly and concretely through history itself. For he lived through just such times as we are experiencing today: times witnessing a rapid change in the so-called historical truths. His day was characterized by the ups and downs of history; he lived through the French Revolution and its results, the rise of Napoleon and his downfall. Historical actuality and the stage on which it was played changed repeatedly in Hegel's period. He himself was not only an observer of events, but beyond this personally experienced the effects of historical change in his own lifetime.

Thus it could look as if it were the flux of history, the reciprocity of revolution and reaction, the rise and fall of power on which his recognition of the dialectical principle was based. It must also be noted in this regard that for this same reason the one work by Hegel which became relatively popular was his *History of Philosophy*, since the material of history lends itself better than any other to dialectical interpretation.

However, I do not believe that it was historical empiricism through which Hegel gained dialectical experience and a dialectical point of view. He saw things dialectically, the dialectical experience was more deeply rooted in his nature and the dialectical method as he later ingeniously elaborated it was far more essential to him than at first meets the eye.

There is a document from the period of Hegel's early development, first recognized and printed by Rosenkranz, the great philosopher's pupil and biographer, and later reprinted in 1936 in Hoffmeister's *Documents Contributing to Hegel's Development*. It is remarkable that this piece of work should never have found an interpreter although it has now been there for all to see in print for over a hundred years. But it has never caught anyone's attention and none of the many gifted Hegelian interpreters has taken notice of it.

From the Jena period there are a series of fragments which depart drastically from the usual Hegelian style. They show no trace of the didactic, abstract, and often extraordinarily laborious style with which we are familiar in Hegel. In place of the abstruse abstractions that, so to speak, were Hegel's daily bread, appears a limpid quality, a plasticity rich in imagery and metaphor.

Anyone who has really read and learned to know Hegel will have discovered this side of him, indeed, in all his works. Suddenly he will throw abstractions aside and out will come an image, most often a somber one, fraught with graphic power; for example: The Absolute Spirit sitting on a throne of skulls. And remarkably enough Hegel, in the same passage, continues with a modified quote from Schiller—"Out of the chalice of this spirit realm / about him foams his infinitude."[57]

The so-called aphorisms from the Jena period are similar in nature. One of them goes: "Fools become wise through hurt, the clever people on the other hand remain unwise through all hurt." Another time he defines a political party in this manner: "A party becomes a party when it disintegrates into itself." And a third example: "A mended stocking is better than a torn one; not so the self-consciousness." These aphorisms are saturnine indeed. He begins a longer passage with: *"Ora et labora! Pray and curse!"*[58] To add to the Latin phrase "pray and work" his own "pray and curse," sounds rather sinister and impious coming from a theologian.

This is the first but not the last time in Hegel's thought that we shall come across his dark side. This gloominess was rooted deep in his nature and, more importantly, was constantly ready for action in the underground of his thought. It often seems as if he were able only with great difficulty to conceal and curb this demonic streak in his being.

The fragment earlier mentioned in connection with Rosen-kranz and Hoffmeister and which has gone unnoticed springs out of this same dark side:

> God, become Nature, has spread himself out in the splendor and the mute periodicity of his formations, be-comes aware of the expansion, of lost punctuality and is enraged by it. This fury is the forming, the gathering to-gether into the empty point. Finding himself as such, his essence pours out into the restlessness and inquietude of infinity, where there is no present, but a wild sallying forth beyond a boundary always reinstated as fast as it is tran-scended. This rage, in that it is a going forth, is the de-struction of Nature. The going beyond the formations of Nature is in effect likewise an absolute falling back into the self, a focal return. In doing this God, in his rage, consumes his formations. Your whole extended kingdom must pass through this middle-point, this focality; and by this your limbs are crushed and your flesh mashed into liquidity.

When we pause over this passage from Hegel's early years, an image of "God" takes shape before our mind's eye. But he is an extraordinary God, the like of which is unknown in the Christian religion. This God of Hegel's bears a distant resem-blance to the Titan Cronus of Greek mythology. Cronus, as we know, swallowed up all his children at birth except Zeus, who was saved, and who later forced Cronus to disgorge the others.

This God, like Cronus, is also grim. But instead of becoming enraged by his children, he is angered by his creations, by his own "riotous venturing forth" out of himself. And in this rage

he consumes all that he has formed, crushing limbs and flesh
into liquidity.

Thus he is a God who is dissatisfied with himself and because of this, tears down what he has built up. But while
Hegel is describing this in the most drastic terms, he is repeatedly sounding other themes as well. This God, to be sure,
overrides his own manifestations, but at the same time
this constitutes a going-into-himself (*In-sich-selbst-gehen*),
indeed, an act of "becoming a focal point."

Contemplating this image, one has the impression of watching a mystic painter painting the picture of a mysterious divinity. And whereas in this passage the image of self-consuming
annihilation is triumphant, the fact becomes evident that the
process is a necessary one.

Now Hegel continues, and I shall quote from him only in
extracts: "God's anger with himself over his otherness, over
being fixated here as the fallen Lucifer, turns against God and
his [Lucifer's] beauty makes him vainglorious." And in succeeding sentences Hegel repeats that it is God's anger, the
inflammation of his being which "grates in him and consumes
his vainglorious splendor." Then it goes: "Nature consumed
rises up in a new ideal form as a shadow kingdom that has lost
all vestige of its first existence, [and which has become] the
manifestation of its [Nature's] spirit after the death of its life.
This new form, however, is the overcoming of evil, the having
endured in the fiery pain of the focal point, where in the
process of refining all dross has been left behind in the crucible, leaving a residuum that is pure nothingness. It [the new
form] rises up as free Spirit, which sees Nature only as a
means of its transfiguration." The image, accordingly, has
undergone a change. Lucifer, and in him the Christian
mythos, has become visible. At the same time a new process
appears. Out of this God who destroys his manifestations a
shadow kingdom arises in a new, ideal form, in which free
Spirit is transcendent.

Now follows a third passage, which begins with Hegel's
saying: "Such myths, such intuitions are the intuitions of
*barbarism*." With this everything suddenly seems to be solved.
What Hegel had in mind, then, was to describe the bar-

barian's view of life. Could this be so? This is by no means the case. For again the previous image suddenly appears, hardly changed. Hegel goes on to say: "The form of these intuitions annihilates individuality, or rather here it is a case of raged against, this evolved and again self-subsisting Absolute." And he goes on to describe how the former intuition undergoes a second process. Slowly it becomes clearer what he means. The second process is the science (*Wissenschaft*) or knowledge of "that divine course of life [*Lebenslauf Gottes*] out of which knowing itself proceeds." It becomes evident that a second cycle (*Kreislauf*) is appended to the self-destructive divine cycle first described. Hegel calls it the second cycle of the Absolute which, now "having become Spirit," creates the process of becoming in itself.[59]

It is unlikely that this fragment can be entirely penetrated, in its almost monstrous mixture of figurativeness and abstraction, by interpreting it, as it were, sentence by sentence and word by word. But all the more impressive is how Hegel, out of a somber image of a self-destructive God, out of a process whereby God contemplates his own destruction of himself, evolves nature, the world, and the spirit. Of course all this remains imagelike, in the nature of metaphor—later it will be conceptually fixed.

Also impressive is the nucleus of this process, visualized partly in images, partly in concepts. We refer here to the notion of "cycle," which later on in Hegel crops up again and again. It appears for the first time quite uncontrolled and raw in the image of a self-consuming God, then returns as the cycle of the Absolute, and the third time around is called "the cycle which contemplates itself."

If I now make the claim that the Hegelian dialectic appears in this allegory, it is also plain that this image concealed in a myth relates to the later, rationally elaborated idea of the dialectic more or less as the metaphor of the cave relates to the rationally presented Platonic theory of ideas. It is incontrovertible that here Hegel is graphically experiencing and painting in words what he was later to perfect in a world of concepts and more concrete intuitions. Nonetheless this allegory in one way or another was to have a lingering effect.

Thus we read in the introduction to Hegel's *Logic*, which contains an abstract and conceptual presentation of the dialectic, this passage: "On this account it can be said that this content [of the *Logic*] is the representation of God, of how he is in his eternal essence before the creation of nature and of a finite spirit."[60] This sentence has a hybrid sound, and one wonders how Hegel could suddenly lower himself to such a statement, but perhaps still very much lurking in the immediate background is the fragment that Hegel wrote in Jena.

This allegory, moreover, contains all the elements found in the later rational dialectic. Here, first of all, we have the immediate Absolute, characterized as God. Secondly the "monstrous power of the negative," as Hegel later called it, appears in the image of a God enraged by himself into tearing his creations into pieces. And we are repeatedly told in the same fragment that this rage is likewise "an absolute going into himself" of God, an act of becoming the "middle point," or what might be called the central, focal point of godhead.

By God's giving birth to himself, the cycle of Spirit begins, to rise up to ever new levels. This notion also comes up in later works, in the *Phenomenology*, the *Philosophy of Right*, and other writings as well.

But let us pause a moment over this dark and mythic allegory without anticipating the later dialectic; in so doing, we recognize the great components of the Hegelian world. This world, for one thing, contains the whole realm of classical notions curiously intermingled with those of Christianity; it is, indeed, the world of Christian humanism in which Hegel was brought up. Combined with it, in odd admixture, is the abstract conceptualism evolved by European philosophy after Descartes up to the time of Kant. As a third component is added something one might not at first be inclined to expect. This is the world of mysticism, that Western strain of thought found both in Nikolaus von Kues and Böhme. In an otherwise very critical presentation of Böhme's philosophy in his *History of Philosophy*, Hegel himself remarked that "this robust mind indeed has an enormous barbaric capacity to make use of actuality as concept."[61] And Marx was not so far off the track when he accused Hegel of mystification.

To turn Hegel's own words on himself, it is simply something to marvel at, the barbaric power of synthesis with which Hegel forces together the diverse elements of the European and Occidental worlds. Seen from this standpoint, the early fragment we have been examining is again unique.

Indeed, the whole fragment, contained in a mere two pages, relates to the later Hegelian system as a dream to reality. This reminds us of the fact, a fact the modern world is apt too easily to forget, that all conceptualization ultimately originates in an intuition, a sort of vision of the way things are. The road that Hegel henceforth was to travel consisted mainly in the translation of this dark vision into actuality, using the medium of rational and philosophical conceptualization, that is, the language of modern philosophy.

Meanwhile the question remains to be answered why we are bringing up this fragment at this point and what relation it has to dialectical thinking, or indeed to the dialectical method. The answer is simple as soon as one has a notion of the rhythm, or, rather, the lawfulness of the movement which fulfilled this image. Hegel's God split himself asunder by becoming enraged with himself. His rage, the negation of himself, did not, however, lead to his destruction, but to a new unity. Therefore Hegel can say that this process of annihilation was both a retreating into himself and a genesis of the "middle point," a focality of godhead. Out of the antithesis, in the image understood as the kindling of rage, "consumed Nature rises up in a new, ideal form." But this cycle does not happen only once. It recurs. Thus systematic knowledge (*Wissenschaft*) is also understood as a self-devouring process which at the same time leads to new formations.

Hence, at the end of the fragment, we find this sentence: "Knowing makes each moment of intuition, by itself an impenetrable, fixed form unrevealing of what is inherent in it, which arises, does its work and vanishes into another action, into a process in itself, or into something of a spiritual nature."

The process which Hegel sets forth here in a formative vision is nothing more or less than the dialectical one. He shows us the characteristic component parts: unity, division, and a new unity arising from division. This triad, forever renewing and perpetuating itself, has been expressed schematically in the old formula: thesis, antithesis, synthesis.

At the same time it is evident that Hegel gave the old formula a new twist. The triad, forever renewing and perpetuating itself, an endless cycle, is not only the secret of the world but the secret, too, of the philosophy that comprehends it.

Although the fragment contains the nucleus of dialectical thinking in a mythical image (actually, in fact, in a mythical intuition), Hegel is as yet unable to present his insight in a comprehensive way at once palpable and conceptualized. The labors of the Jena years were devoted to doing this. He made repeated attempts to make a systematic philosophy out of this cyclical process and may not have been satisfied with any of them. When he finally succeeded and for the first time condensed dark intuition into a complete picture, the *Phenomenology of Mind* took shape all in a rush.

# 4

# The Phenomenology:
# The Introduction

Before we turn to the *Phenomenology*, there are some
dates in Hegel's inner and outer life to add to
those already considered.

On his thirty-first birthday, August 27, 1801, Hegel qualified
for lecturing at Jena. Jena was the university, as we have
noted, where Fichte had taught in 1799. His departure had
not diminished the university's power of attraction, though the
onset of political insecurity and other factors were having
their effect. By and large Jena kept its high reputation until
1806. Schelling worked there until 1803.

Hegel qualified himself as a university lecturer by writing a
Latin dissertation—*Dissertatio philosophica de orbitis plane-
tarum*—a philosophical-scientific piece of work in which he
developed the philosophical implications of the Keplerian
laws. That same year he wrote another piece called "On the
Difference between the Systems of Fichte and Schelling."

Both were the work of a beginner, but the second clearly

shows certain signs of intellectual qualities peculiar to Hegel. Thus, as in all of Hegel's later works, we find that the introduction is a sort of summary *in extenso* of the main body of the argument, reminding us that some have felt most of the introductions subsequently written by Hegel are the most readable part of his writings.

Some thoughts emerge in the piece on Fichte and Schelling which we are to find later on again in Hegel. An example is the idea that in philosophy there are neither "predecessors" nor "successors," and that each philosophical system or form is a "true one" in its way. And the basis for this? The Absolute and its manifestation or appearance—reason—are "eternally one and the same." In every temporal manifestation of reason a philosophy proper to it is realized, which dissolves once the period in question is ended. Here the great operative principle of Hegelian thought is proclaimed in general terms: absolute reason is the truth of the world.

Bound up with this notion is a second noteworthy idea, one that in a certain sense seems to contradict the first. Philosophy grows, Hegel says, out of *Entzweiung*, which means "bifurcation" or "discord." As he puts it in so many words: "Discord is the source of the philosophical need." In other words, each system of philosophy is only a part of the total thought generated in any one period of time. Because this is so, and because each system takes on a fixed, definitive form, it tends to repress thought's vital movement. "The firmer and more splendid the edifice of understanding," says Hegel, "the more restive becomes the striving of that part of life trapped in it to escape from it into freedom."[62]

In this antithesis we see the theme of tension which runs through all of Hegel's works. On the one hand there is a desire to have a completely rounded-out system, man's desire to know the whole in its enduring relationships. Opposed to this is another and opposed desire, grounded in the knowledge that the same whole is in a state of eternal flux, driven by a dynamic impetus.

Besides this and a series of critiques, Hegel published no important work in the Jena period until the *Phenomenology of Mind*. Hegel read all his university lectures, which were obviously difficult to understand. He stuck to his written texts and, as far as we know these manuscripts, they were long and unrelievedly abstract trains of thought. Some of his lecture courses were never given at all for lack of listeners.

During these years Hegel did not succeed in establishing himself on an adequate financial footing. He was simply an unpaid *Privatdocent*, whose income was limited to his lecture fees. For the most part he lived on a small bequest left him by his father.

In 1805, however, he was at last made a professor, but not until after many pleas on his part and with the aid of Goethe's intercession did he manage to get a salary in 1806. He wrote gloomily about it all to his friend Niethammer: "I have finally got a salary (?) of—one hundred, imagine—one hundred thalers."[63] Even in those days a hundred thalers a year was a tiny sum and certainly not enough to live on. In consequence Hegel wrote many begging letters in the hope of gaining a full professorship. But this was not to be granted him until ten years after his departure from Jena.

Just how straitened Hegel's circumstances were is made evident by the fact that he was repeatedly forced to borrow money. In 1806 Goethe empowered his friend Knebel to lend Hegel a sum "up to ten thalers." Karoline Schelling about this time wrote to her husband that she had heard no one knew how Hegel was able to manage.

We do not know exactly when the *Phenomenology* came out, but obviously a major part of it must have gone to press at the beginning of 1806. Thereafter the work expanded in the process of its writing, and the publisher had to wait for the rest of the manuscript. But finally, as Hegel himself attests, on the night of October 12 or 13, 1806, it was done. We know this to be so because Hegel later wrote in a letter that he had completed editing the manuscript the night the Battle of Jena ended.

It is plain to see that the *Phenomenology* is a work whose content the author had been turning over in his mind for a long time, but at the same time it is also evident that the book itself was written with extraordinary speed. Hegel himself was conscious of the haste of its composition. He wrote to Schlegel that to make the whole "clearer and more finished would still take a lot of time."[64]

The *Phenomenology* seems to be formed out of a single flow of thought. But this flow proceeds irregularly. Sometimes the stream slows to a standstill and the reader has the feeling he is drowning in a flood of abstractions. In these sections it seems as if the argument were moving in circles. However, for the first time the Hegelian dialectical structure is strictly and schematically maintained for all to see. From now on Hegel was to fashion all his philosophical works and lectures in this schematic manner. For this reason it is perhaps worthwhile to take a closer look at the structure of the *Phenomenology* as revealed in its table of contents.

The book is divided into three parts: (A) Consciousness, (B) Self-Consciousness and (C) Reason (by some translated into English as "Free Concrete Mind" to give some idea of the special Hegelian usage of *Vernunft*, which otherwise almost invariably means "reason"). But remarkably enough the third part, which for the sake of differentiation we will call Free Concrete Mind, has three subdivisions: (AA) Reason, (BB) Spirit and (CC) Religion. In addition there is a short concluding chapter: (DD) Absolute Knowledge.

Each of the above parts, with the exception of the second, which is divided into two, is again subdivided into three subparts, and often these subdivisions are themselves again divided into three segments. The whole, therefore, is a progressive trichotomy, which schematically looks something like that shown in the chart.

The architectonics of this ground plan is intended to show the dialectical technique not merely of the whole, but of divisions and subdivisions as well. How are we to understand this dialectical interplay? Concrete consciousness (A) confronts itself in self-consciousness, and reason as synthesis unites consciousness and self-consciousness. But the process of dialectical fission continues. Reason (AA) stands opposed to Spirit (BB). Religion (CC) is the synthesis of reason and spirit. The final section, Absolute Knowledge (DD), crowns the whole.

The dialectical splitting process also continues in the subdivisions. In the first stage consciousness divides into "sense-

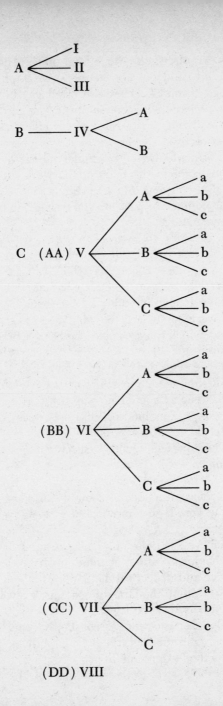

certainty," "perception" and "force and understanding." Curious subdivisions suddenly appear, as for example under the second subpart in part C. Here are listed (a) Self-contained individuals associated as a community of animals and the deception thence arising, (b) Reason as lawgiver, and (c) Reason as the test of laws.

This table of contents, unlike similar tables, does not provide a real insight into the body of the work. Rather it is a curious round of concepts, in part abstract and reminiscent of psychological notions, in part arbitrary conceptual constructs of a descriptive nature.

Basically it is useless to try to get a grip of the *Phenomenology* through its table of contents. For the table provides only the dialectical outline of the whole, which in itself seems to be schematic, yet which is nonetheless very odd. For ordinarily when we acknowledge something as a scientific or philosophical method, we assume it to be identified with the subject matter at hand, which is not completely the case here.

Hegel himself may have felt this defect. When he got through with the book he may very well have realized how heterodox and strange his procedure must have looked to others. In a letter to Schelling announcing the work he wrote that the whole book is "an interlocked criss-crossing" (*ein verschränktes Herüber und Hinübergehen*).[65] In any case, he sent the printer a long preface of almost seventy pages to be added to the *Phenomenology*. Titled "On Scientific Knowledge in General," it is a treatise in itself. This piece of work is manifestly a masterpiece, intended to show the author's method, in a brightly checkered give-and-take of attack, defense, and pronouncement.

At this point we shall cite only one passage from this preface, thereby hoping to arrive at some understanding of what the constructive and dialectical method is all about. For if we looked no further than the table of contents, we would be led to ask ourselves: is this framework a sort of canon in which the basic melody of the work is constantly repeated? Is the constructive organization of the whole perhaps largely no more than a method of presentation?

Hegel gives the answer to these questions in the passage we

shall now quote. Its lines are very strange indeed, in part telling about appearance, in part giving a definition of truth. There have been many translations of this passage into English, none the same. An excellent one by Walter Kaufmann reads:

> The appearance is the coming to be and passing away that itself does not come to be or pass away; it is in itself and constitutes the actuality and the movement of the life of the truth. The true is thus the bacchanalian whirl in which no member is not drunken; and because each, as soon as it detaches itself, dissolves immediately—the whirl is just as much transparent and simple repose.[66]

For comparison here is the same passage translated by the nineteenth-century English student of Hegel, J. B. Baillie:

> Appearance is the process of arising into being and passing away again, a process that itself does not arise or pass away, but is *per se*, and constitutes reality and the life-movement of truth. The truth is thus a bacchanalian revel, where there is not a member, a part of it, that is not drunk; and because every member no sooner becomes detached than it *eo ipso* collapses straightway, the revel is just as much a state of unruffled and simple calm.

Whichever version you may prefer, the first sentence addresses itself to appearance, but obviously not to what we usually understand by the term, as when we speak of the "evanescence of appearances." For Hegel defines appearance not as something that arises only to fade away, but as that which constitutes the "reality and movement" of truth.

Here, be it noted, we have now gained a clue as to why the title of the book is *Phenomenology*, that is, quite literally, the theory of phenomena. What Hegel clearly has in mind is to provide a phenomenological theory of appearance. This title, incidentally, was by no means original with Hegel; others before him have used the same term. Even Kant had used it to label a section of his *Critique of Pure Reason*. But all previous usage had of course no bearing on the Hegelian adaptation of the concept, any more than the "phenomenology" and the "phenomenological method" found in Husserl's philosophy are derivative from Hegel.

In all events, the second proposition is an altogether remarkable one, offering a definition of truth quite opposed to what we usually understand by the term. In the usual scientific way of knowing things we understand truth to be a judgment, a cognitive statement that is fixed and secure. To be sure, we are also well aware that even science only seldom knows eternal, absolutely assured truths, and it is clear to everyone that scientific advance can make, as they say, today's truth tomorrow's error.

But Hegel's proposition goes a long way beyond this conception. Here we are told directly that truth is a moving, shifting thing. In a wild and splendid image Hegel calls truth a "bacchanalian revel, no member of which is not drunk." He then goes on to say that each single member of this revel of truth collapses, dissolves. as it detaches itself from the whirl, and that on this account the bacchantic revel is likewise a state of simple and transparent calm.

We have now arrived at a central point in the Hegelian philosophy, namely, a concept of truth divorced from the customary scientific notion. In the Hegelian concept, clearly, there is no single truth. Each individual truth is a part of the whole that takes shape and then vanishes. What is true is not a matter of single truths, but a continuous movement, in which these single truths come and go. The following sentence also expresses this notion very clearly: "Judged by that movement, the particular shapes which mind assumes do not indeed subsist any more than do determinate thoughts and ideas, but they are, all the same, as much positive and necessary movements as they are negative and transitory."[67]

This much is now clear: the Hegelian apprehension of truth is completely different from the conventional one. Putting it in a more conservative way, we might say that Hegel's emphasis is not on single truths, on the individual results of knowledge, but on truths as part of a process and on advancing knowledge as a movement. To put it another way, Hegel was not so much fascinated by individual truths as such, as by the movement of thought in its dynamic continuum. Yet curiously enough our more matter-of-fact language still does not suffice for an understanding of Hegel—for why, again, is this dynamic also a simple and transparent calm?

The question is less complicated than first appears. What looks to us like the constant movement of knowledge is in fact only a form moving within itself. This form Hegel called the "Absolute Spirit." The content of the *Phenomenology* is nothing more than an interpretation of the "system" of this movement, and the concept of truth just discussed above is, so to speak, only the quintessence of the movement.

The whole preface can be summarized in the passage cited above, which appears about midway in the piece. With this the content has been capsulized. I have already noted how polemic and positive affirmations alternate in motley succession. Shortly before and after the passage just quoted Hegel polemicizes against the customary notion of truth and in the process makes violent critical attacks as bewildering to us as they were in his own day.

He assails mathematical truth and knowledge in a way that at first seems absurd, impossible. To cite one passage in this long exposition, he declares that mathematical demonstration is "an activity that remains external to the matter," that mathematical knowledge is "defective," that it "proceeds on the surface, does not touch the thing itself, the essence or the concept of it, and on this account is not comprehension."[68] Historical knowledge fares no better with Hegel, as for example when it is concerned with such factual matters as "when was Caesar born?"[69] The kind of factual determinations found in history, and in another form in mathematics, are a species of knowledge unworthy of philosophy, Hegel contends.

It becomes obvious, therefore, that what Hegel is attacking is the conception of truth almost unanimously accepted up to his day. As Hegel says, he is placing emphasis on the fact that truth does not consist of "dead, fixed" propositions, since such propositions only give rise to a sort of tabular knowledge. In this way science becomes a "lifeless schema" and "scientific organization" degraded into "tables." Hegel endlessly scolds, and in so doing comes out with some pretty strong epithets, as when he speaks of the "barren formalism" of this kind of knowing, of the "monotonous whistling" of such wisdom, of science as something in which every living thing is "stuck away in jars," as a "monotonous formalism" in which "everything in heaven, on earth and under the earth is plastered by a mud of paint" as by a painter whose palette holds only two colors.[70]

But the final and stubbornly repeated reproach is that the scientific form of knowledge changes what is really alive into something dead and produces propositions that are lifeless and fixed, immovable and rigid. In a general way it is already clear that Hegel, to a degree exhibited by few other thinkers before him, looked away from the stores of knowledge accumulated during millennia and turned his gaze elsewhere: on the dynamic, the process, the movement of knowing, or however else you may describe this aspect of the scientific event of cognition. Very well, this is not the first time we have heard the reproof that knowing and reasoning are removed from life. "Gray is all theory," Goethe said, "and green the golden tree of life." This theme has been sounded in all sorts of variations in all periods, but in fact we expect to hear it least of all from the mouth of a philosopher and instead from those who are in the thick of things and not concerned about contemplation and theory.

For this reason one is all the more curious to find out how Hegel develops his argument. Let us ask in all naiveté, what better approach does Hegel have to offer? What kind of conceiving and knowing is valid for him and his philosophy?

With this we come to the affirmative, as distinguished from the polemic, content of the *Phenomenology*, to the positive theory of dialectical knowledge. Neither in the body of the *Phenomenology* proper, nor even less in the preface is Hegel the least systematic about developing the positive side of his thought. Quite the contrary, odds and ends—we are now referring to the preface—crop up at random and the whole picture, certainly, cannot be pulled together after only a first reading. To unite the pieces one must look now to the beginning, now to the end of this introduction.

Yet, tenaciously and with great effectiveness, ideas repeatedly come up which we are already acquainted with in metaphor, if we recall the Jena fragment about God enraged with himself. This fragment constitutes a single movement in which the themes of destruction, dismemberment and anger stand out again and again. And at the conclusion it is shown how the process just described is a kind of cycle.

There are, then, three basic notions involved, and these three appear again in the preface: 1) A movement is being described. 2) This movement, splitting within itself, breaks up into opposites. 3) The movement is viewed as a complete cycle. Now, however, a fourth is added, the notion of a "system."

Hegel starts with this last idea in his preface. In something like twenty pages he argues that philosophy is possible only as science and system: "The true form in which truth exists can only be the scientific system of the same."[71] Yet even as Hegel is describing this idea, into it creep other more important notions. One is struck by the fact that the aim of the preface is not to present the kind of systematic concepts customary hitherto in philosophy, but something quite new. In this new approach the notions of "movement" splitting itself into "opposites" and as occurring in a "cycle" dominate.

In order to reproduce these ideas as they appear in the preface it is necessary to turn to the decisive concept which Hegel developed. This notion is not easy to grasp, but it contains the conceptual secret of the dialectic.

Let us now make use of some direct quotations to explain the Hegelian notion of the self-movement of concepts. "The truth is the whole," says Hegel. Then he immediately adds: "But the whole is only the essence perfecting itself through its development."[72] In ensuing paragraphs Hegel, in ever new variations, expounds the notion that the whole can be grasped only as becoming, which from the beginning anticipates whatever result may occur. Such anticipation, he asserts, must proceed from the fact that the result is contained seedlike in the beginning, but Hegel does not speak in such naturalistic locutions. He expresses his interpretation in such characteristic concepts as *an sich* (in or by itself, implicit) and *für sich* (for itself, explicit). "While the embryo is to be sure implicitly a human being, it is still not human for itself; being human for itself is only educated reason making it that which it is in itself. Only this is its actuality."[73]

All this can be comprehended without difficulty, even if one is critical of this or that part of the argument. The real difficulty, however, begins as soon as one turns to the notion of "self-movement of concepts." For Hegel the aim of his philosophy is to "sublimate fixed, determinate thoughts and by this means actualize and inspirit the universal." His intention is to make "fixed thoughts fluid" and to strive to attain a movement of thought, that is, of philosophical thinking, by means of which "pure thoughts become concepts," and only then come to be "that which they are in truth: self-movements, circles [or cycles], that which they are in substance, spiritual entities."[74]

The average reader may not read such propositions casually, but even so he may perhaps attach no great importance to them, which may mean that he has passed over the sentences immediately preceding in the preface without having it dawn on him how they relate to the ones just cited. This passage reads:

> Death, if so we may call this unactuality, is the most terrible of things, and to hold fast to what is dead requires the greatest strength of all. Beauty, which has no strength, shrinks from understanding because it asks this of her and this she cannot do. But the life of the spirit is not a life that recoils from death and stays clear of its devastation, but one that endures death and in it is maintained. Spirit gains its truth only by finding itself in absolute dismemberment. This power of spirit is not in the nature of the positive looking away from the negative, as when we say of something that it is nothing or that it is false, and so being done with it move on to something else: rather the spirit is this power only when it looks the negative in the face and abides with it. This abiding is the magic force which transforms the negative into being.[75]

Thus, while Hegel is in process of describing the movement of philosophical thought, in the same train of ideas he suddenly leaps into another dimension. An almost triumphal image takes shape before our eyes. Death is evoked. It is plainly referred to in terms of the negative. To this extent the idea continues to spell out the enormous power of the negative. But simultaneously we are told that the force and life of the spirit consists in "holding fast to that which is dead," in "looking the negative in the face," and by thus abiding with the negative "convert it into being."

This is the historic passage which heralds the first appearance of the *angeschaute Nichts*—nothing (or nothingness) contemplated or intuited—and the *negative Wesenheit*—the negative essence—ideas later to show up again and again in Kierkegaard, Nietzsche, and the existentialist philosophers. But Hegel, as it were, cloaks this nothingness in the force of the sovereign spirit, which, by abiding with the negative, has its life.

It may now be asked what this has to do with the self-movement of concepts. In a literal sense, nothing at all. In Hegel's image all that is actually claimed is that spirit converts, "sublimates" the negative and transmutes it into being. It is not until some paragraphs later that the thought is taken up again and we are told that the negative is not a "defect" but "the soul, the moving spirit."

Thus the notion of the self-movement of concepts which Hegel affirms in the *Phenomenology* actually remains indeterminate in its methodological aspect, and not until his *Logic* will it be described more precisely.

We, too, for the time being, shall leave open this most difficult and most disputed component of Hegelian thought. Instead we shall now turn to the text of the *Phenomenology* itself. We have already said that it was originally intended to be an introduction to the whole Hegelian system, but grew into a book in its self. This is linked with the problem of self-movement, for the *Phenomenology* is nothing more than a portrayal of the "self-movement" of the spirit and to this extent an illustration, as it were, of the "self-movement of concepts."

# 5

---

# The Phenomenology as a Whole

When we turn to the *Phenomenology* as a whole and ask what it is all about, we might begin to answer this question by quoting a short extract from the preface. Aside from occasional comments, it is the only passage which provides a kind of brief summary of the contents of the book. Otherwise Hegel rambles on in terms of general reflections and methodological and polemical exposition. The passage goes like this:

"The task of leading the individual from his uneducated standpoint to that of knowledge had to be taken in its general sense: we had to contemplate the general individual, the self-conscious spirit, in its formative development." This sentence clearly tells us what the *Phenomenology* aims to do. It is intended to provide a systematic history of the development of consciousness, and therein show the history of consciousness in general. And where does this history lead to? The answer, hidden in the same sentence, is to the general individual, to the self-conscious spirit. Hegel then goes on to say:

> As to the relation between these two [the particular and the general individual]: in the general individual every moment is made evident as it acquires concrete form and its own shape. The particular individual is incomplete spirit, a concrete form in whose whole existence one determination dominates, while others are present only in blurred outline. In the spirit standing on a higher level than another, the lower concrete form of existence has been reduced to an insignificant moment; what formerly was the matter itself is now only a trace; its form is veiled and become simply a shade. The individual whose substance is spirit at a higher level skims through this past much in the same way the student of a higher science skims through preparatory knowledge long since mastered in order to recall their content to mind; he recalls the memory of the same without being interested or abiding in it. The particular individual must also pass through the educational stages of the general spirit according to content, but as forms already put aside by the spirit, as stages of a way already worked out and made even; thus we see that, in respect of information, what in former ages occupied men of mature spirit has sunken to the level of mere information, exercises and even children's games and in pedagogical advance we can detect the history of the world's culture delineated in faint outline.[76]

Here the content and procedure of the *Phenomenology* is described in relatively simple language. It contains, as it were, the shadowy outline of past stages of spirit, memories of which—so we are told in our summary of the *Phenomenology* —are retained. The gradations of the shadow outline, as we would expect, proceed from the lower and incomplete spirit to the higher. At whatever stage the higher spirit may be, it keeps its precedent form as a "trace."[*]

Still another proposition in this summary is worthy of no-

---

[*] *Geist* in this context appears to mean both "mind" and "spirit."—*Tr.*

tice. Each particular individual, seen from the standpoint of the whole, is an incomplete spirit, but the general spirit is unfolded when all gradations of incomplete spirits are propagated. For this reason the *Phenomenology* is, so to speak, a display case for the single, qualitatively revealed and concrete forms of mind-spirit's existence, a sequence of vanished forms which fuse together into the whole of spirit in general.

Is the *Phenomenology*, then, something in the nature of a historical interpretation? Yes and no. This Hegelian presentation is historical only insofar as the historical substrate shimmers through. Thus, as the *Phenomenology* runs its course, figures and episodes suddenly appear, like forms out of the dusk, from classical history, from the days of the Romans, from the Middle Ages and from modern times. Often they are hardly recognizable; the whole is portrayed from afar. The *Phenomenology* becomes more historical the closer it gets to Hegel's own times. Now the figures become clearer and contemporary existence is described almost unconcealed.

But then, too, the whole is not history at all. For within this half-veiled historical information lurk the abstract binding segments which actually clamp the whole thing together systematically. For instance, there is a chapter on perception, another on "contemplative reason," indeed, a third on physiognomics and phrenology and many others. Viewed from this angle the whole looks like a strange mixture.

The book's mysterious charm, and it still continues to be read after 150 years, is due in part to this interweaving of abstraction and intuition. Beyond the chapters just named there are still others such as "The Unhappy Consciousness," "The Law of the Heart and the Frenzy of Self-Conceit," "Self-Contained Individuals Associated as a Community of Animals and the Deception Thence Arising: The Real Fact," and finally "Consciousness in Self-Estrangement," of which last more later in detail.

All of this is ingeniously woven together, in such fashion as not to lose track of transitions and contrasts. But it can happen that in the middle of an abstract passage Hegel will launch into this kind of description: "On one fine morning, whose noontide is not bloody, when the infection has penetrated all

organs of the spiritual life, then only in remembrance is preserved the former way of the spirit, as a story that has faded,
one knows not how, and the new serpent of wisdom lifted up
for adoration in this manner has painlessly sloughed off only a
shriveled skin*."[77]

Again and again Hegel resorts to such metaphors as if abstraction is suddenly no longer enough for him. Thus in the
section on "The Unhappy Consciousness" he says how "Its
thinking as such is no more than the discordant clang of ringing bells, or a cloud of warm incense, a kind of thinking in
terms of music that does not get to the length of conceptual
thought . . ."[78]

Then in their turn come segments in which great intellectual
periods of Western history are described in their fullness of
form, as when stoicism and skepticism are interpreted.

Haym once said, with justification, that the *Phenomenology*
became a "palimpsest," and that "over and between the first
text we discover a second one."[79] Yet another image comes
forcibly to mind. As in a modern abstract painting a second
image is developed on the basis of the initial sensuous impression, one in which all contours of what is actually seen are
effaced; similarly the *Phenomenology* is an abstraction painted
on the silver foil of a historical intuition.

Finally, the *Phenomenology* has been compared to Dante's
*Divine Comedy.* "Holding to the author's hand," says Haym
when this simile occurs to him, "we are led through the regions of the departed spirits, see the sufferings of some and
rejoice in the bravery, the happiness and the beauty of others,
and finally, in the heaven of the Absolute, enjoy the blessed-
ness of knowledge based on the Spirit itself."[80] Haym is alluding to the final chapter of the *Phenomenology*, in which "Absolute Knowledge" appears as the crown of the whole.

And indeed the *Phenomenology* can be read as if it were a
moral tract ending in the triumph of the good. This dialectical
sequence of conceptualized history can be understood as if, in
the last analysis, it does no more than proclaim the ineluctable
progress of the spirit. According to this interpretation, Hegel

* Hegel is borrowing his imagery here from Diderot's *Rameau's Nephew.*
—*Tr.*

can also be looked upon as an optimist who, starry-eyed, accords recognition to the ultimate harmonious synthesis.

But there is something else which contradicts such an interpretation. The closer Hegel approaches a description of his
own times and the clearer the picture becomes, the more negative the portrayal. It is as if Hegel felt no value endured any
longer in his own day. Even the title of his description of then
modern times proclaims this. Hegel called this section "The
Self-Estranged Spirit."

The section which Hegel simply called "The Spirit" begins
about halfway through the *Phenomenology*. It is the penulti-
mate section, excepting the concluding chapter on "Absolute
Knowledge."

"The Spirit" section is divided into three parts. The first is
called "Objective Spirit: The Ethical Order"; the second,
"Spirit in Self-Estrangement"; the third, "Spirit Certain of Itself: Morality."

The formal dialectical relationship here is as follows: The
true spirit, as ethical order,* divests itself of its negation, the
"self-estranged spirit." It then turns back into itself in positive
form and becomes a "spirit certain of itself," that is, one identified with morality. According to dialectical law this third
stage is the synthesis of the first two. But even the page-count
shows that Hegel gave most attention to the description of the
"self-estranged spirit." It also becomes apparent as one reads
that in this part Hegel is depicting the contemporary world.
To be sure, this middle section of the dialectical movement
contains only a portrayal of the negative, yet even taking this
into account it is still remarkable how pessimistic and critical
Hegel becomes.

Also striking is the title of the subsection in its entirety,
"Spirit in Self-Estrangement: The Discipline of Culture and
Civilization," the latter being summed up in the German word
*Bildung*, literally, "education," whether in a broad or narrow
sense. One wonders if Hegel can be identifying education
with "self-estrangement," and it turns out that he is. The passage reads: "The means whereby the individual here has valid-

---

* *Sittlichkeit*, a German word with no English equivalent, but suggesting
morality associated with or rooted in custom.—*Tr.*

ity and actuality is education. Its [education's] true original nature and substance is the spirit of estrangement of natural being."[81]

Hegel might be correct in equating education with gain and property. He still belonged to a closed educational world, one that would hardly be possible today. Deeply anchored in the spirit of Christianity, saturated with a detailed knowledge of antiquity, well read in contemporary European literature and even linked with the arts, he was still really living in the spirit of Christian humanism. And at that time an educational universality was perhaps still possible—a cultural breadth no longer attainable today.

The allegation that science and culture spoiled natural man had already been made by Rousseau. Are we then seeing Hegel's favorite author of the Tübingen period suddenly make an appearance here? Is he simply appropriating Rousseau's thesis? Should this be the case, then it would have to be said that Hegel was incomparably more radical than Rousseau.

Near the beginning of the subsection there is an overall description of the "self-estranged spirit." Hegel puts it this way: "Nothing [in self-estrangement] has a spirit grounded and indwelling in itself, but [all] is outside itself in a strange one; the balance of the whole is not unity sustained of itself and assurance of having turned back into itself, but rests upon the estrangement of its antithesis. The whole, therefore, like each single moment of it, is a self-estranged reality."[82]

In his *Divine Comedy*, Dante described Hell, but for him Hell is a region in the afterworld. Hegel, on the other hand, portrays a hell that is right here with and in us. To summarize the text of this subsection in key phrases, using Hegel's own terms, self-estrangement is seen as a world of "absolute disruptedness" and "total lack of substance," where a "destructive rooting about in the natureless earth" holds sway. In this realm "all objectivity is wiped out," and at the same time "the self-consciousness is confused." The "pure ego" is "beside itself and contemplates itself distractedly." All that "has continuity and universality, all which is called lawfulness, good and right" is "dispersed and gone to the dogs."

The world of self-estrangement is completely at odds with

itself. This world arises out of education and cultivation, for Hegel expressly says of this spirit: "It is the absolute and universal perversion of actuality and of thought, their entire estrangement from one another; it is pure education."[83] The description ends as ominously as it began: "The dismemberment of consciousness, in its self-awareness and self-expression, is laughing existence, as well as the confusion of the whole and oneself, to scorn; at the same time it is the fading away, still self-aware, of this whole confusion."[84]

What is Hegel really describing? A mood, a vision, a reality? Pondering this question, we recall that Hegel had already used the same tone once before in the Jena fragment. The God who, angry with his own wild rushings about and the loss of his "middle point," his centrality, destroys everything—this mythical or mystical vision could have been the very godfather of the present description.

We posed the question whether this portrayal reflects a mood, a vision or a reality, and actually one must say that it reflects all of them. But the substrate of the image is unmistakably that process of development whose last act Hegel believed he had detected in the French Revolution. A third section, which bears the title of "Absolute Freedom and the Terror," has always been recognized as modeled on the French Revolution. Leading to this third stage, however, are the two preceding ones: education and enlightenment, both of which as forms of the self-estranged spirit end up in terror.

If we should try to describe what Hegel had in mind in simpler and perhaps more concrete terms, we might put it something like this: Everywhere in the modern world, as he saw it, an unbridled and unlimited wish to know and understand was at work. It was a free-spirited world, knowing no other law than the advancement of knowledge. The spirit of progress, it was believed, would lead to a free world. But Hegel saw things differently. The spirit of the times was self-alienated and inwardly distraught. He did not view the spirit of enlightenment like Kant, who had described it as "the emergence of mankind from its self-imposed infancy." To be sure, he recognized the rightfulness of the Enlightenment, yet at the same time saw another side to it. He described the Enlightenment as a period of "vulgar skepticism," which in its self-complacency had lost the power to believe and no longer knew anything about Absolute Being. He accused the Age of Enlightenment of not being enlightened about itself. And there is a certain ambiguity when, at the end of the subsection on "The Truth of the Enlightenment," he says: "May heaven be transplanted here on earth below."

Finally, as Hegel saw it, the third stage appears: "Absolute Freedom and the Terror." The description begins with absolute freedom, which starts out as a positive thing and which is depicted as the universal will, transcending and including all particularity. We are told that this undivided substance of the absolute freedom takes its seat upon the throne of the world with no power able to offer it resistance. But now the description becomes more negative and one of Hegel's strangest images appears, when he says: "The beyond of this, its actuality, hovers over the corpse of the lost dependence of the real or believed being only as the exhalation of a stale gas, of the empty *Être Suprême*."[85]

Already it is becoming clear that absolute freedom is inherently an empty concept. Hegel tells us about it this way: "The only work and deed, therefore, of universal freedom is death, and indeed a death that has no inner scope and fulfillment, for what it negates is the unfulfilled point of the absolutely free self; in consequence it is the most cold-blooded and meaningless death of all, with no more significance than cleaving the head of a cabbage, or swallowing a drink of water."[86] Hegel obviously has his eye on the last stage of the French Revolution, the Terror and rule by guillotine.

Now the question of what Hegel is really getting at can be answered. The substrate of history that he has in mind is human development up to the French Revolution. This he sees as a great continuity stretching back through the centuries, which began with the self-estranged spirit and through the Enlightenment led to an idea standing radiantly emblazoned at the start of the French Revolution: the idea of liberty, equality, and fraternity. But what others doubtless saw as the debasement of this idea into the subsequent development of the Revolution into rule by terror, Hegel saw as the inherent consequence of a spirit that had lost its reality.

In this sense Hegel necessarily had to arrive at terror out of the idea of absolute freedom. But he did not go about it like the usual historian, who assembles details and finally shows how in the course of any development other forces can come into play. For Hegel a development such as the Terror can be deduced out of the law of dialectical change into an opposite. According to this law, upon the concretization of any particular form of the spirit, the negation of this concretization and its sublimation and transcendence must follow. The spirit lives by always keeping in motion, by changing one form of its existence into another and thus always arriving at higher stages.

It is basic to this Hegelian notion that any way of looking at humanity as progressing in slow and logical steps must be abandoned. Rather, as Hegel believed, humanity advances, so to speak, by logical leaps and bounds, by a constant changing of position, a springing from one extreme to the other, and by taking, from time to time, two steps which in the Hegelian sense cancel each other out, thus achieving a higher form.

It was at this point in the *Phenomenology* that Hegel was first able to demonstrate concretely this law of dialectic, a law on which it was his intention to base his whole philosophical system. Here he was able to show how the dialectic worked with a material offering the most favorable conditions imaginable. For quite obviously if the notion of progressing in antitheses and by leaps and bounds applied anywhere, it applied to the realm of history.

If he was now successful in imposing a certain order, namely a dialectical one, on the historical substrate, it is worthy of note how much this ordering of historical things depended on an experience and mood already announced by Hegel in the preface. We now see why the idea of the negative and of abiding in dismemberment of spirit was so often emphasized in the preface and why Hegel could say that the life of the spirit is gained only by looking the negative in the face and abiding with it.

For Hegel this is both a human and a historical experience. History, he instructs us, does not remain suspended in the negative. It overcomes the negative by living through it, by abiding with it, sweating it out. This, he said, is the magic power which "converts being."

At every turn, in consequence, the *Phenomenology* is shot through with this peculiar and, one might say, fundamentally stoical tone, the message of which is look death and the negative squarely in the eye. Thus Hegel is able to paint, so to speak, the picture of a self-estranged world as having an unmoved countenance, though within torn to shreds, and to know at the same time that out of devastation the next stage of history must arise, new and pure, like a Phoenix from the ashes.

This is the basic vision guiding Hegelian thought, and, however freighted down with fact it may be, it remains a visionary view of history throughout. Is it also a prophetic vision; does it provide a view of the future? One is hesitant about answering this question, and again it may be said that Hegel can indeed be taken this way. He has been criticized for his "optimism and quietism" (Haym). In any case, whoever reads Hegel this way is bound to find this philosophy of confidence in the power of spirit a comforting outlook on the world.

Meanwhile it cannot be denied that a deep strain of skepticism accompanies this trust in the power of the spirit. As already shown in the *Phenomenology*, and as will be shown in later works, Hegel, however optimistic he may have appeared, was in fact filled with a profound mistrust of the world of his period. In the *Phenomenology*, in any event, he certainly describes a thoroughly critical situation, although of course it can be assumed he also believed this situation had already been overcome.

The chapter that Hegel wrote on the self-estranged spirit was to have a sequel of historical importance—among the readers of the *Phenomenology* was the young Karl Marx. He did not care for, he wrote as a twenty-year-old to his father, "the grotesque craggy melody of Hegelian philosophy," but time proved he was unable to escape from it. It was to be a

long time before Marx was to be finished, in his way, with
Hegelian thinking. How much Marx was impressed by it we
know from his youthful writings. It was Marx who made the
comment that the *Phenomenology* was the "birthplace and
secret of the Hegelian philosophy."

Just as the student Hegel read Rousseau over and over
again and was certainly influenced by his cultural criticism, so
was Marx fascinated by the Hegelian description of the "self-
estranged spirit." Marx took over from Hegel and extended
this notion of a world alienated from itself. It must be frankly
said that it became for Marx the basis of his outlook on the
world of his own time.

The Marxist theory that the capitalist age is unavoidably
destined for destruction derived from the Hegelian vision of a
world self-estranged. This can be demonstrated sentence for
sentence. When Marx first proclaimed the misery of the capitalist system and the proletariat, his pronouncement grew entirely out of the notion of self-estrangement and the picture of
it that Hegel had drawn in the *Phenomenology* forty years
before. Marx said it this way:

> The owning class and the class of proletarians represent
> the same human self-estrangement. But the first class feels
> comfortable and assured in this self-estrangement, and in
> it possesses the appearance of a human existence; the sec-
> ond feels destroyed in estrangement, in it perceives the
> impotence and the actuality of an inhuman existence. To
> use an expression of Hegel's, it (self-estrangement) is in-
> dignation in depravity over this depravity . . .[87]

This very expression stems from the section in the *Phenomenology* on the self-estranged spirit. Hegel coined it for
Marx when he said: "The language of spiritual dismemberment is also the perfect language and the true existing spirit of
this whole world of education." And immediately went on to
say: "This self-consciousness, whose depravity reaches rejec-
tive indignation . . ."[88]

In Marx's hands Hegel's ambiguous abstract conceptual
forms become filled with a realistic content. What Hegel in
the last analysis presented as metaphysical powers are per-

sonified and actualized by Marx. Later Marx was to say proudly that he had recognized "the mystifying side of the Hegelian dialectic" at an early date and had given the "German mode" a "rational form." This is not the place to discuss the manifold relationships between Hegel and Marx, especially the development of particular Marxist theories as already prefigured by Hegel. But let the result, at least, be anticipated. From this moment on the thought of revolution and world revolution marched in step with dialectical thinking and the dialectical theory. Both meshed together from now on like cogwheels. Henceforth Stahl's words—"Revolution is the work of our times, struggles for and against it fill our history" —were to have worldwide application.[89]

The structure of the historical process, which reaches into our own day, deserves to be spelled out in its special Hegelian form. Out of an immediate intuition of his period, Hegel created what he called the dialectical method. In the *Phenomenology* he set out for the first time in the direction of developing this dialectical method of thinking in the light of historical events and relationships. Here for the first time the history of the spirit was conceived in terms of conflict between ever newly evolving antitheses and as a gradual upward progression of configurations of the spirit arising out of this clash. Hegel himself, however, did not stick to history alone. For him history was a means to an end, the way to a metaphysics.

Insofar as Marx took this same road, he turned the conceptual world developed by Hegel toward actuality as he saw it. He backtracked on the path that Hegel had traveled. The methodology that Hegel had created out of his intuition of actuality was for Marx the key to a new way of looking at things. Thus arose the dialectical theory of revolution and historical materialism.

At the same time Marx turned Hegel's approach dialectically in the other direction, Hegel's metaphysical idealism became a messianically prophetic belief. Out of the Hegelian attitude, according to which the world was ultimately viewed as the unfolding of Absolute Spirit, came a political religion, which no longer understood itself as theoretical contemplation but as political practice.

# 6

---

# From the Phenomenology
# to the Logic

N ow the *Phenomenology* was finished and with this
Hegel's stay in Jena had also run its course.
As shown by the history of its genesis and by
all of the comments made by Hegel in the course of working
it out, the whole book was written down like a rhapsody.
Hegel had now turned into words, sentences, and printed
sheets the weight that had been weighing him down.

The entire work was written under almost barbaric pressure. Piece by piece it had grown under his hands. The first
part of the system itself had developed out of the original
introduction. But even half a year before this, about the middle of 1806, Hegel still did not know how long the book would
be, and it is to be assumed that the second half of the book
especially, and with it the chapter on the self-estranged spirit,
grew even longer while being written.

With the finished work before him, Hegel was only partially
satisfied. He wrote to Niethammer that while reading proofs

he planned to lighten the book of a good deal of its ballast. He also wrote to Schelling that by working the argument out in detail he might have done injury to the whole. But he was right about the special procedure and unique thinking of this book when in the same letter he said to Schelling that "by its nature" it involved such "an interlaced crisscrossing" that even if it had been better rendered it would still have cost him considerable time to perfect.[90] But in the second edition, he wrote on another occasion to Niethammer, "everything will be better."[91]

The first thing he had to do, however, was get out of Jena. Obviously he had used up his paternal inheritance, but hoped to be able to live during the coming winter on his honorarium from the *Phenomenology*. The appeals for money that he sent to Niethammer are proof of how hard up he was. For a moment he found himself in a horrible position. A couple of days before the Battle of Jena he had mailed the finished manuscript and now did not know whether it might be lost in the wartime confusion. At this juncture everything was up in the air, and the only certain thing was the need of a job to keep him alive.

Hegel seems to have got his next position through Niethammer. But fate dealt very ironically with Hegel. Grinning at him, it sent his way an entirely different kind of work from what he was used to. Hegel now took over the editorship of the *Bamberger Zeitung*, a small provincial daily. He was tolerably happy in his post simply because he finally had a paying job which could at least support him after a fashion. To be sure, here, too, his income was so small that he could not count on being able to stay for too long. Anyway, it was a secure position of sorts that he looked on as transitional, for he had not given up his hopes of becoming a full professor.

So he took the job and supposed the "business" would interest him, since he did indeed "follow world events with curiosity." At first his Bamberg letters sound content enough. In early October 1807 he wrote that he was leading a pleasant and "untroubled" life.[92] But by the end of March 1808 the tone changes and he wrote about the "vegetative pace of a newspaper existence" that dragged on "without further chal-

lenge,"[93] and finally, a half-year later, he said he was longing
to escape from his "newspaper galley."[94]

For about two years Hegel was employed as a managing
editor, as we would call it today. The newspaper, besides
being a local daily, was operated under special conditions.
Since Europe was then basically under Napoleonic rule, directives emanated in a roundabout way from Paris. Hegel could
not do much more than assemble the news without benefit of
interpretation. It is a credit to his organizational talent that he
succeeded in doing this much well. Haym was certainly right
when he surmised that an inherently poor newspaper was
about as well edited by Hegel as it could be.

Anyone who skims through back copies of the *Bamberger
Zeitung* today can really find nothing of Hegel, and anyone
anticipating the discovery of some trace of the Hegelian intellect or even of his style is in for a complete disappointment.
And Hegel was clearly bored with his paper. He once wrote
that composing newspaper articles meant about as much as
"eating straw." On another occasion he asked Niethammer for
a coffee machine made in Munich because the time had come
to put more spirit into his job. He complained about the
peaceful times. The journalist, so Hegel said, had a hard time
"providing the fodder for public curiosity," since these "melancholy times of peace," from the newsman's point of view,
were like "lovely moonshine and a fine police force for
thieves."[95]

Besides this, newspaper life also had its seamy side. Hegel
got into difficulties with the government by denouncing, in
one of his articles, a plan to post three garrisons in the town.
He was asked on pain of having the paper shut down to name
the military person who had told him three garrisons were to
be posted. It was no military person who had told him the
secret—which in any case was not really a secret at all—but a
printer. The man had got his information from a torn piece of
the proof of a royal decree. Thus in the end it was a relief for
Hegel to be offered, again through the intervention of his
friend Niethammer, the post of rector and professor at the
Nuremberg Gymnasium. He took over his new duties in

Nuremberg in December 1809. During this period he was to write the second part of his system, *Science of Logic*.

Yet before we begin describing the Nuremberg period more closely, and beyond that go on to an exposition of the *Logic*, the most curious study of logic ever written, let us make a couple of observations on Hegel's inner development. He stayed in Bamberg two years, and eight in Nuremberg, in all, ten years spent away from a university. In 1813 the wars of liberation began and at their conclusion the new Prussia came into being. In the capital of this new Prussia, Hegel, the Swabian, was to take over the chair of philosophy at the university and to remain there to the end of his life. Prussia's ascendancy was also to be Hegel's.

The question intrudes as to what was Hegel's stand in the ups and downs of political history. This question is all the more urgent because Hegel the thinker was close to history. The *Phenomenology* is a history of the spirit into which external political happenings are interwoven. Beyond this the *Phenomenology* develops the viewpoint that the history of actuality unfolds along dialectical lines, and that the dialectical law of the spirit is at the same time the law of actuality.

So it has to be expected that Hegel reacted to contemporary events according to his philosophical position. Or was he one of those thinkers who, as it were, keep two sets of books, one for everyday reality, another for theoretical work?

The question is as difficult to answer as it is simple to pose. There is really no simple answer to it. In his interpretation of Hegel, Haym made a cardinal point of going into this matter. He says—actually in blunter language—that Hegel was an opportunist. The young Hegel who had been so enthusiastic about the Revolution and who had proclaimed the millennium of freedom ended up as a Prussian government employee and glorified the Prussian police state. For Marx, too, the question of Hegel's politics was quickly answered: Hegel was a bourgeois thinker through and through. To be sure, he had grasped the essence of the dialectic, but it had served him only to mystify and to exalt the status quo. Both answers are basically quite similar. But the facts are the following: It is quite correct that Hegel was an admirer of the French mind. It may be thought strange that this thinker, of all people, a veritable prototype of the German intellect, had such a propensity for the French and Latin spirit. Yet such is the fact, and one can only look for reasons.

Indeed, it was not only Napoleon whom he admired; his admiration was just as great for the French people. Although from personal experience he knew that the French had pillaged and plundered, he still wrote from Jena:

> Through the [blood] bath of their revolution the French nation has not only been freed from many institutions that the human spirit had outgrown like children's shoes, and which in consequence had weighed both on them and others as mindless fetters, but the individual has rid himself of the fear of death and of his everyday way of living, which, the change of scene, has no more hold on him; this gives the French the great strength they show toward others. They bear down on the reservedness and torpor of others, who, finally forced to give up their sluggishness toward actuality, get involved in it, and perhaps, while preserving their inner nature in the [new] environment, excel their teachers.[96]

Napoleon, therefore, is a kind of champion of the world-spirit, and through the Revolution the French nation has achieved a higher dignity and thereby—so it sounds—become the teacher of mankind. Why? Because mankind has been jolted loose from the apathy and torpor of its usual existence and made free in the face of death.

Again the motif is sounded that we have heard so many times: The only true life of the spirit is that which maintains itself in devastation and death, which looks death squarely in the eye. In connection with the first theme, a second makes its appearance: We are living, Hegel says, in a time of transition, a period in which the stage setting of the spirit is undergoing a change, and as a result those who were snugly secure in the old setting are losing their bearings.

But now the flow of events would change course. Napoleon was to fall in the ensuing years and the French people had to carry all the burdens that the Revolution and Napoleon piled on them. What was Hegel to say to this? Again it is his letters that provide the answer. When Napoleon's fate was sealed, Hegel wrote:

> Great things have happened all around us. It is a tremendous spectacle, to see an enormous genius destroy himself.—That is the most tragic thing of all. The whole mass of mediocrity with its leaden force of gravity keeps on pressing leadenly without let or appeasement until that which is higher is reduced to its level, or below. The critical point in all this, the basic reason why this mass has power and remains up there on top as the chorus, is that great individuality must concur in it, and therewith destroy itself.

> Moreover, if I may sing my own praises, I predicted the whole revolution. In my work (completed the night before the Battle of Jena), on page 574 I say: Absolute Freedom —(it is described before this; it issued from the purely abstract, formal freedom of the French Republic, from the Enlightenment, as I showed)—proceeds out of its self-destructive actuality to become *another* land (I had here a *land* in mind) of self-conscious spirit, wherein it (Absolute Freedom) counts as the true in this unactuality, in which thought the spirit refreshes itself insofar as it *is and remains thought*, and knows this being, comprised in the self-consciousness, as the perfect and entire Essence. It is the new form of Moral Spirit.[97]

Curious sentences, but referring directly to political actuality, however fantastic they may sound. To the extent that they are intelligible, they reveal that for Hegel Napoleon was an enormous genius who had destroyed himself, and actually had to yield to the leaden weight of mediocrity. Hegel boasts of being a political prophet. One feels how literally he meant this. In the *Phenomenology*, that is, at a time when Napoleon was at the height of his power, Hegel had anticipated his downfall. The necessity of this event was grounded in the very spirit of the *Phenomenology*. Napoleon represented the last stage of that Absolute Freedom which must destroy itself.

It is not made quite clear whether Napoleon is seen as still being the propagator of this freedom, as can be assumed, or whether he is regarded as the dialectical synthesis after the annulment of freedom by the Terror, a synthesis in which the accomplishments of the Revolution are preserved even while at the same time absolute freedom is limited.

Finally, Hegel's notion that this process is now continuing in another land is plain enough; it continues as a new stage of the historical spirit and draws forth the form of the "Moral Spirit." But Hegel does not say where it is that this spirit is gaining form and actuality.

The last sentences of the passage are extremely difficult to interpret. According to Hegel absolute freedom lives on in the new form of the spirit. It persists as thought. As absolute freedom it has lost actuality because it has destroyed itself, but it is and remains thought in which the spirit refreshes itself.

In detail the sense of the argument is obscure, but taken as a whole the basic thought of the *Phenomenology* stands out powerfully: history is governed by the dialectic of the spirit. The individual, however much of a genius he may be, must accommodate to the thrust of the world. In the dealings of the world-spirit he plays the part of puppet, although "world-historical individuals" are almost the world-spirit's managing directors.

Out of curiosity we might ask: Where is the whole trending; is the world-spirit actually striving toward a goal? We must return to this question later on. Hegel has often been criticized on the grounds that his philosophical system really anticipates the whole continuum of history. Burckhardt, among others, felt this about Hegel's approach and said, with undisguised annoyance, "This bold anticipation of a world-plan leads to error, because it proceeds from false premises."[98]

For the present, however, all we ask is: How far can the master who knows the world-plan see into the future? We are able to infer from the letter just cited, we believe, that Hegel felt the future was at least not completely closed to him, since he—like others as well, actually—predicted the downfall of Napoleon. The answer to this question is found in a letter to

Niethammer, written toward the end of the Nuremberg period when Hegel had a positive prospect of being called to Heidelberg. In this letter he said:

> The more general conditions and expectations of the world as well as those of more local circles more than anything lead me to general points of view, which remove the particular and the local further from my thoughts, however much they may engage my feeling. It is my firm belief that the world-spirit of our times has given the command to advance. Such a command is obeyed: this essence strides on irresistibly through thick and thin like an armored, close-ranked phalanx, its movement as imperceptible as the sun's. Countless light troops for and against it flank it round about, most of them without the least idea of what it is all about, and get nothing out of it but cracks on the head as from an invisible hand. All humbug stalling tactics and phony windbaggery cannot help an iota. You can, so to speak, reach the shoestrings of this colossus and on them smear a bit of shoe-polish or dirt, but you can never untie them, much less take off the divine shoes—as Voss has it, q.v. mythological letters et al.—with the elastic spring-soles, or even his seven-mile boots, if he should put them on. The best thing to do (namely, internally and externally) is definitely to keep a close eye on the advancing giant; this way one can even make a stand, and for the edification of the whole busy and eager company oneself help out with smearing on the cobbler's wax meant to hold the giant fast and find heart's delight in lending a hand to the earnest hustle-bustle.

It is a splendid military image. The motorized world-spirit, as we would say today, is ineluctable in its advance, but—the next stage and its goal are known to it alone. What stage is coming next Hegel does not know. All that he knows is that the advance must be watched closely. The letter ends as follows:

> I have been expecting the reaction we are currently hearing so much about. It is determined to be right. *La*

*vérité en la repoussant, on l'embrasse* [by rejecting the truth one embraces it] is a profound Jacobin motto . . . The most violent reaction against Bonaparte, has it changed much in the nature of things, in good and evil, leaving aside the farcicalities and crumby successes of the personal ants, fleas and bedbugs? And these antlike, flea- and bedbuglike personalities, what else can we do but take them as the good Lord intended, that is, use them as ma- terial for jokes, sarcasms and pleasure in the discomfiture of others? What we can do to this good end is help them, should need arise, to achieve their perfection.[99]

From what this letter tells us, all that Hegel basically knows about the future is that history and the world-spirit guiding it are conceived to be swiftly advancing. And, as if it were ir- revocable, once again Hegel's old thesis that we are in a time of transition comes to the fore. Concomitantly some new themes appear: belief in genius, contempt for the masses and the average.

However, if one insists on asking whether the almost revolu- tionary enthusiasm that the young Hegel expressed in 1795 in the letter to Schelling cited earlier was still in force, then it must be said that the picture had indeed changed. To be sure there was a kind of echo of it in a letter in the year 1808 which went like this: "Theoretical work, I become more convinced each day, gets more done in the world than practical; once the realm of ideas is revolutionized, actuality cannot resist."[100]

It is striking, nonetheless, how Hegel's thinking has changed. No more talk now about ideas as to how things should be. Of course we are told that actuality cannot hold fast against a revolutionizing of ideas, but this is to come about through the work of theory, not brute force. And this passage has to be read differently again in the context of the whole letter. Hegel was writing this letter on the occasion of having been given the hope by Niethammer of getting a position at the Nurem- berg Gymnasium.

The thirty-eight-year-old Hegel had become a cautious man. Getting the position in Nuremberg was now his goal. He wanted to have a steady job, and after two years in the Nuremberg post he was still writing: "Here at the Gymnasium I am a professor of preparatory philosophical sciences and the Rector, and, leaving aside my hope of sometime getting into a university, to me personally the most preferable thing, I have a settled career and beyond this a professional occupation for the most part compatible with my studies."[101]

But the Nuremberg interlude was not altogether an easy one. The monthly stipend always arrived too late, even though a certain financial stability had been achieved. Toward the end of 1811 Hegel even got married.

For years he ran this *gymnasium*. It became evident, as when he had been employed as an editor, that there were plenty of things to which he could turn his organizational talent. It was a very poor *gymnasium* by modern standards. Hegel had to do all the administrative work himself, even to the writing of lists and reports, and he had no *Pedell*, or proctor, to help keep order. The building was inadequate and at one point was threatened with closure. When Hegel would plead for advances for some piece of equipment or other, he was told there was no money. Hegel's letters teemed with laments of this sort.

On the whole Hegel seemed well on the way to becoming one of those civil servants who, notwithstanding a certain justifiable feeling of grievance toward the powers that be, does his best to do his duty. We have a description of his workaday manner. "As teacher and rector," one of his pupils later wrote about him, "in respect of his students Hegel combined seriousness and dignity with a sympathetic friendliness, an appreciation of individual circumstances and a readiness to give counsel. Laxity in student deportment, the root of all evil in all *gymnasia*, naturally was not permitted; still, provided that it did not deteriorate into excess, much was overlooked that today would not be allowed . . . Otherwise Hegel saw to the maintenance of order with the greatest possible strictness." The same student, himself, by the way, later on teacher and headmaster at Hegel's school, goes on to tell how once he called on Hegel to ask to be relieved of some obligation. "But," he wrote, "how quickly we were rousted out of there! To this day I hardly know how we made it down the stairs."[102] From this description we gather that whereas Hegel was not lacking in open-mindedness and friendliness toward the students, on the other hand he could exercise authority.

Hegel had been called to this *gymnasium* as professor of "philosophical propaedeutics," that is, elementary or preparatory philosophy. In other words, he was to work in his own field. In the *gymnasia* of the period a three-year course of instruction in philosophy was obligatory. The curriculum, or *Normativ*, laid down by the office of education was as follows: The first year of introductory instruction had to begin either with logic as the "formal" part of philosophy, or with the theory of religion, right (law), or morality. In the second year cosmology and theology, as well as psychology, had to be taught. Compulsory in the third year was a course offering examples of speculative thinking, or an encyclopedia—a comprehensive summary—of philosophy.

From the first Hegel did not like this compulsory curriculum. Furthermore, with the passage of the years he became increasingly skeptical about the value of teaching philosophy in a secondary school. To be sure, he had earlier said that philosophy was as *docibel*—teachable—as geometry, and had also ventured the opinion that philosophy had to be taught and learned, but actual practice seemed to make him doubt this notion. In 1801 he wrote: "At the same time, more and more every year it seems as if there is too much teaching philosophy in the *gymnasium* . . ."[103] A year later he was saying that "perhaps all philosophical instruction in the *gymnasium* may after all be superfluous, that for the youth of *gymnasium* age the most suitable and, *by virtue of its substance*, the true introduction to philosophy may be the study of the ancients." Official expert opinion submitted by Hegel on this question, however, was something else again. Here he kept the last opinion just quoted under his hat. Actually, in the end he never completely made up his mind about the matter. He wrote: "How am I, the professor of introductory sciences, to be the only one to quarrel with my profession and my position, to strip myself of my own bread and butter."[104]

After all, he did teach philosophy, although unfortunately we do not know what his *gymnasium* courses were like or what effect they had on his pupils. But the manuscript on which his course was based had been preserved and published by Rosenkranz in the collected works under the title of *Philosophical Propaedeutics*. Out of Hegel's original copybooks and, in part, from student transcripts of what he dictated to them, a book over 200 pages long has come into being.

There is no doubt that this treatise reads more easily than many other Hegelian writings, and it is not the worst way to get acquainted with the Hegelian philosophy, here presented in an abbreviated, comprehensive outline. In part the book is structured according to the education minister's directive on the course. A first section contains legal, moral, and religious theory, a second one the phenomenology of the mind and logic, and a third the theory of concepts and a philosophical encyclopedia.

Actually the whole is the Hegelian philosophy in a nutshell. The systematization is somewhat different: the phenomenology, for instance, is no longer in first place, but second. The first section, which has the superscription "Legal, Moral and Religious Theory," according to the official norm, is a sort of anthropology, a theory of human nature, with its rights and obligations. The last part, on the theory of religion, is treated very briefly and covers no more than two pages.

The second book, the one on phenomenology, is written in paragraph form, the same form that Hegel used in his *Encyclopaedia of Philosophic Sciences* and *Philosophy of Right*. He chose a method of presentation such as a jurist would use in a lawbook or a decree. Nonetheless the dialectical partition or grouping is retained. A few passages from this *Propaedeutics* cannot give an idea of the whole, nor can they be expected to. However, I will choose passages which show Hegelian thought in much simpler form than found elsewhere. To be sure, these passages were written for *gymnasium* students and so, as Hegel saw it, very much simplified. Nonetheless they contain the nuclei of Hegelian thinking.

"Man," he says, "on the one hand is a natural being." He then goes on to define the nature of man as follows: "As such [as a natural man] he behaves according to impulse and chance, as an inconstant, subjective creature. He makes no distinction between the essential and the unessential. Secondly, he is a spiritual, rational creature. Viewed from this aspect he is not by nature what he is intended to be."[105] This is the basic Hegelian idea of development, here expressed in its simplest fashion. Man simply by nature is not what he is meant to be; he is a creature in the process of becoming. Later Hegel defines reason in these words: "Reason is the highest union of consciousness and self-consciousness, or knowledge of an object and knowledge of oneself."[106] Here the dialectic of consciousness to self-consciousness and reason which Hegel developed at length in the *Phenomenology* is suddenly clarified in a perfectly simple fashion. The three stages now seem almost obvious: 1. Consciousness is consciousness of something. 2. As self-consciousness the ego contemplates itself and the expression for this in its purity is I = I, or I am I. This second definition is found word for word in the *Propaedeutics* and is rounded out by a third statement already cited: Reason as the union of consciousness and self-consciousness.

The propaedeutic definition of an idea is equally characteristic: "The idea is the unity of the concept and the reality; the concept insofar as it determines itself and its reality, or the actuality which is as it is intended to be and contains the concept of itself."[107]

Let these examples suffice. All in all, this abbreviated systematization of the Hegelian philosophy is certainly not only one of the most instructive, but one of the clearest pieces of philosophical writing that Hegel ever composed. And one thing at least he got out of the work: he learned to take his audience into account and to a certain extent, in contrast to the Jena period, learned to accommodate his listeners.

# 7

## The Logic

**H**egel's *Logic* came into being in the Nuremberg period. In February 1812 he announced to Niethammer:

Nine sheets of my "Logic" have been printed. Before Easter, perhaps, another 20 will have been. All I can say about it right now is that the 25–30 sheets are only the first part, that they contain nothing of logic usually so called, that they are metaphysical or ontological logic: first book on Being, second book on Essence, provided that the second book can be fitted into the first part. I am up to my ears in it. It is no small undertaking to write a book of the most abstruse content 30 sheets in length during the first semester on the job.—But *injuria temporum!* I'm no academic: to do the thing right I would need another year, but I have to have money to live.[108]

Hegel speaks of a book "of the most abstruse content." The self-deprecation suggested by the word "abstruse" should not be taken too seriously; here, actually, it has more the sense of "abstract." However, it is notable, as in the case of the *Phenomenology*, that Hegel is concerned about not "doing the thing right," of giving his book the proper form.

The first part of the *Logic* actually did come out in 1812, but four more years were to pass before the second was published. On one occasion, when Niethammer proposed he write a logic in the conventional sense, Hegel replied: ". . . that anyone like myself who for many years has nested with eagles on wild crags and who is used to breathing pure mountain air should now learn to eat off the carcases of dead or (modern) stillborn thoughts and vegetate in the leaden air of empty palaver . . . Sir, let me pass up this bitter cup!"[109]

From the foregoing one might expect that in his *Logic* Hegel will appear in his most arbitrary guise, evolving his metaphysic in the pure air of abstract thought. And that, indeed, is exactly how Hegel's *Science of Logic* strikes us today.

This book was intended to be the second part of the Hegelian system, the first part being the *Phenomenology*. Hegel repeatedly explained how the second part related to the first. In the *Phenomenology* he had already said that the second part of the system, the *Logic*, would present the dialectical movement in process of organizing itself into a whole. In the introduction to the *Logic* we are told that in the *Phenomenology* the consciousness is presented in its progression from the first concrete antithesis of this progression and from the object to absolute knowledge. In the first part of his system Hegel described the dialectical evolution of consciousness with a background of historical events shimmering throughout. In the *Logic* this sort of thing is left out. All discussion of the empiric, sentient consciousness is abandoned. The intention here is to show the Idea as pure knowing bereft of any other consideration.

The logical development is also meant to unfold dialectically, or, as Hegel puts it, to present "the conceptual system in general," how it forms and perfects itself in an "ineluctable, pure course taking in nothing from without."[110] When one opens the *Logic*, it comes to light that again Hegel has written a long foreword, which this time combines a preface and introduction, with a second preface added in the second edition. Here again almost seventy pages precede the text proper. As in the *Phenomenology* this foreword is polemical, accusatory, and defensive. It is hard to tell whether the preface and introduction were written before or after the text. It is noteworthy, however, that the basic methodological principle appears in the introduction compressed into a few sentences. Being concerned above all with this principle, we shall look more closely at this part of the introduction. As for the rest of the prefatory material, we shall turn first to the text itself, as we did with the *Phenomenology*.

The text of the *Logic* is an imposing structure of almost 1,200 pages, and is much more difficult to read than the 500 pages of the *Phenomenology*. Before the reader's eyes abstract concepts are developed in ever new series of columns. A countless number of concepts from the most diverse regions of thought make their appearance. There are concepts familiar to us from ordinary logic, such as judgment, syllogism, quantity, and quality. Then concepts of a most general kind appear, such as Being, Nothing, and Becoming, and then again concepts borrowed from the natural sciences, such as mechanism, chemism, teleology.

The development of the whole is strictly trichotomous. The *Science of Logic* consists of three books, each book again has three sections, each section is divided into three chapters, and so it goes. Only seldom does Hegel depart from this triadic scheme, yet occasionally it is in fact abandoned and then perhaps four smaller subsections will appear in one of the subchapters.

But before considering the text itself, we shall have to digress long enough to ask why it was that Hegel called this work *Logic* at all. For it is perfectly clear, as he himself said in the letter earlier cited, that his logic has nothing to do with the conventional kind of logic written up to that time. Why, then, did Hegel insist on using the name "Logic," why did he not give the book another title, for example, "The Theory of Categories."

The answer seems simple enough. Hegel was convinced that he was writing a true logic, one which corresponded to the development of the knowing process. He expounded this claim for his logic with unmistakable clarity when he said something like this: "In order that the dead bones of logic be animated by the Spirit into having vigor and content [*Gehalt und Inhalt*], its method must be one whereby it alone is capable of being pure science."[111]

All previous logic, then, is so much dead bones. Of it Hegel says:

> Indeed, the need for a reform of logic has long been felt. In form and content, as it appears in the textbooks, it has fallen, one might say, into disrepute. It is still dragged along, more out of a feeling that a logic cannot be entirely dispensed with and because of a continuing habituation to the tradition of its importance, than out of a conviction that its usual content and preoccupation with empty forms has any worth and usefulness.[112]

Let it be said at once that traditional logic, which Hegel dismissed as dead bones, very much came back to life when Hegel's *Logic* came out. The best and most penetrating critique came from a logician, the philosopher Trendelenburg. And even today for logicians the Hegelian *Logic* is beyond the pale of discussion so far as having any pretense to being real logic.

Hegel claimed that formal logic was obsolete, and thereby, again, hangs a tale. Even Kant had praised logic as the only scientific discipline in philosophy. He said: "That logic has traveled this sure course (namely that of science) since the most ancient times is evidenced by the fact that since Aristotle it has not been permitted to take one backward step . . ." He then goes on to say: "It is also remarkable that up to the present it has also been unable to take one step forward, and thus to all appearances seems to be closed and perfected."

He then states this fact: "That logic has succeeded so well is an advantage for which it merely has its limitedness to thank, in that it is empowered, indeed bound, to abstract all objects of knowledge and their differences, and therefore in it the understanding has nothing more to deal with than itself and its form."[113]

This was, in fact, the concept of logic that had been current for a long time. By common knowledge Aristotle had laid down the foundations of the science. He had been the first to marshal the laws holding good among concepts, judgments, and syllogisms and to demonstrate the special relationships according to which certain judgments are mutually exclusive or capable of accommodation. From him came the theory of syllogisms. He had already provided all constituent parts. The Middle Ages then dovetailed these constituent parts and constructed that system of formal logic which earlier, so to speak, had been regarded as the elementary school for thinkers.

Actually again and again voices were raised to express displeasure with formal logic. Descartes, Bacon, Leibniz, and others found fault with it. One time the complaint would be that formal logic did little good because it did not teach you how to think, but only how to correctly express what had been thought. Another criticism that often cropped up was that logic was nothing but a summation of the obvious. Thus in actual fact formal logic was no longer held in much esteem, even though Hegel's claim that it was held in contempt was not true.

The hostility that Hegel showed toward formal logic was ultimately grounded in the fact that he was fighting against a whole trend of thought, namely, to think "logically." He visited the same sort of almost incensed obloquy on other forms of scientific thought, for example on mathematics and history. And this criticism was always directed against the fact that this kind of thinking was taken for granted in modern science and in the science, or disciplined thinking, of all periods, and that moreover this mode of thinking found its most basic expression in formal logic.

For formal logic teaches that science, or disciplined thinking, must work with fixed, unambiguous concepts. As soon as we use ambiguous concepts scientific thinking becomes impossible. All fallacies rest on such ambiguities, and actually can arise only when judgments are inherently equivocal. Scientific knowledge is found only where the related concepts, judgments, and inferences meet logical requirements.

Now let us recall Hegel's assertions relative to the concept as already expounded in the *Phenomenology*. Fixed concepts are dead. They must be made "fluid," they are nothing more than self-movements and "circles" (*Kreise*), or perhaps "cycles." This is already enough to make it clear that Hegel wanted no part of a methodological principle oriented in terms of unequivocal, fixed concepts. Even at this point he stood opposed to previous tradition and was of a mind to revolutionize it.

This tendency in Hegel, then, already shows in the *Phenomenology*. There, to be sure, it was only underpainted in the picture and, as it were, carried along by the flow of history. Now, in the *Logic*, the underlying approach was to be dropped and concepts developed out of one another in pure self-movement.

Let us take the first example of concept as self-movement which Hegel offers us in the text. In the first chapter Hegel deals with three concepts: Being, Nothing, and Becoming. In this example we can see what Hegel understood by the fluidity of concepts, and objectively examine his claims of how the self-movement of concepts is fulfilled.

He begins this chapter with a definition that is inconspicuous and obvious: "Being is undetermined immediacy." This implies, therefore, that Being is the most universal concept of all and, by definition, indeterminate. It is a concept which comprehends everything about which we simply say: It is— and predicates nothing more than this. This definition corresponds to the function of "is" as a copula in a sentence. We can say of every phenomenon, even the most ambiguous, that it "is."

In the course of describing the concept Being in this fashion and in other terms, Hegel again arrives at the conclusion that Being is "pure indeterminateness and emptiness." Now a dash comes in the text, announcing the dialectical transition, and this sentence follows: "There is nothing in it (in Being) to be intuited . . . as little as there is anything in it to be thought . . . Being, the undetermined and immediate, is indeed Nothing, nor more, nor less than Nothing."

With this the dialectical transition has been completed.

Being has become Nothing. It makes little difference how we go about construing or understanding this transition. Whether we arrive at the concept of Nothing after pondering over this peculiarly empty concept of Being, whether we say that the concept of Being necessarily requires the antithesis Nothing, or whether we simply affirm, as Hegel does, that Being *is* nothing—we have in any case slipped out of one concept into its opposite.

Hegel then continues along this line, in effect actually moving backward. He now discusses the concept of Nothing. Of Nothing he says it is "complete emptiness, lack of all determination and content, implicit indeterminateness." He comes to the conclusion that this general indeterminateness and lack of definition are really the same as "pure Being." In other words, if before the concept of Being led to Nothing, now Nothing leads to Being. And so we are no longer surprised at Hegel's third step: "Pure Being and pure Nothing are thus the same." The two concepts merge together and the truth common to both of them, according to Hegel, is: "This movement of immediate disappearance of one into the other—Becoming."[114]

The reader cannot be blamed for viewing this line of thought with the greatest mistrust. Is all this nothing more than sleight-of-hand? Have not the concepts here been pulled and twisted out of shape until there is no difference between them? Being is Nothing, Nothing is Being, and finally, out of this word game, Becoming suddenly springs at us, as it were, in a single sentence.

What actually is going on here? Formal logic would say it is all nothing but a tawdry play on words using abstract concepts, and can be seen through immediately once we test it with concrete concepts. A table is a table, and not a chair, and a chair is not a table. To claim that a table is also a chair and vice versa, and finally to make a third thing out of them, is so much nonsense.

It is further conceivable, turning away from this logical argument, that it might be justifiable to ask: Where will we end if we fluidify concepts in this matter? We could make white into black and something else out of a mixture of the two, and with this we lose every hold on thinking and all scientific thinking is at an end.

Therefore, if I now take up the cudgel for Hegel, I must do it in full awareness that I am shifting into another dimension of thought. Bearing this in mind I ask: Is the world of actuality in truth as unequivocal as formal logic would have it? Does not formal logic arbitrarily weave a net of fixed concepts over actuality, so as to permit distinctions to be made in terms of fixed forms?

Yet is not actuality far more mobile than this? Yesterday we had war, today we have peace, but there is also a third, intermediate state moving between war and peace, which today we call the "cold war."

Is it not the same with all actuality? I can cite an example which Hegel himself used in the *Phenomenology*:

> The bud disappears as the blossom bursts forth and one could say that the former is refuted by the latter. In the same way the fruit declares the bloom to be a false existence of the plant, and the fruit supplants the blossom as its (the plant's) truth. These forms are not only different, they also displace each other because they are incompatible. Their fluid nature makes them at the same time elements (or moments) of an organic unity, wherein they not only do not conflict, but are each one as necessary as the other, and it is only this equal necessity that is constituent of the life of the whole.[115]

This example is often used to illustrate the Hegelian dialectic. At first it is tempting, for it does indeed demonstrate by an everyday example the gliding transition that is of the essence in the dialectic. It shows how in the process of a plant's maturation various forms of the phenomena change and contrast with each other, and it becomes clear how nonetheless these stages are bound to each other, with the fruit coming forth from the blossom, the blossom from the bud.

But upon closer inspection many objections do in fact arise. The beautiful third step, which leads from bud to bloom to fruit, in actuality is a process subject to division into more than three parts. Besides, one particular in the whole growth process of the plant has been arbitrarily chosen. The whole process in fact does not begin with the bud, but very much earlier, for example with the seed.

However, let us leave such objections aside, since our primary concern is to understand Hegel. It then cannot be denied that the notion of movement has here been expressed in a living event, in which the change of phenomena of necessity leads from an initial stage to subsequent ones. The same process is carried out in all evolutionary events. In this same fashion we can understand the evolution of human life, we can conceive historical events in these terms and fit all forms of development into the same picture.

Into which picture? One in which a whole—in our case the plant—is broken up into partial phenomena and partial states which can be clearly distinguished one from the other, while at the same time the notion of a whole is assumed which, as Hegel puts it, conceals within itself these partial phenomena as *elements* (literally, as *moments*).

Returning now to the example found in the *Logic*, we find the facts of the case are the same. Being, Nothing, and Becoming are partial aspects of a whole. Hegel juxtaposes these concepts like bud, blossom, and fruit. Out of itself Being releases Nothing, and out of Being and Nothing, Becoming arises—like fruit from bud and bloom.

But where is the whole, corresponding to the plant, that holds Being, Nothing, and Becoming together? Hegel develops this dialectic in a section called "Being." Therefore we must assume that the concept of Being is to be broken down into the three stages of "pure" Being, "pure" Nothing, and "Becoming." And such is Hegel's notion. And to this dialectic is connected a higher stage, which Hegel calls the level of "Existence." In contrast to the pure and empty concept of Being, Existence is defined as "determinate" Being.

This gives us an idea how the *Logic* as a whole will develop from here on. Step by step the concepts will become more specific and narrower. They will be "concretized." Again and

again new forms of the logos—concepts in the Hegelian sense
—make their appearance. This Hegelian logic marches on in a
dialectically continuous process to the final concept of the
Absolute Idea, which overlaps and contains all others within
itself.

Thus the *system* of concepts is meant to unfold and structure itself before our eyes in a splendid conception of one
continuous movement; from a very first, primordial beginning,
guided by the dialectic as by an Ariadne's thread, we wander
on, as we did in the *Phenomenology*, through the maze of
concepts involved in human cognition. Wandering on in this
manner, the manifold, endlessly extended and divided world
of the *Logic* begins to take shape in our mind's eye. And so at
last we envision a kind of harmonious order, one ruled, kept in
motion, and formed by the one law of dialectical evolution.

We now have a better understanding of why Hegel in his
preface defined the goal of his *Logic* as follows: "The system
of concepts has to be built altogether in this way—and be
perfected in an irresistible, pure progression, taking in nothing
from without."[116]

Now at last we see, too, how fascinating is this idea of
"system" which hovers before Hegel's eyes. We can share his
feeling for it. Before Hegel's eyes, as no less before our own,
arises the mighty complex, endless and incalculable, of knowledge. Even more than Hegel we are in an age of specialization, in which every form of knowledge takes a separate
course and a final unity is no more to be found. But Hegel
sought this unity; in his dialectical way he wanted to bind all
separateness together. He was governed by a powerful will to
synthesize. In the dialectic he thought he had found an instrument to do this that was at once simple and omnipotent. It
could do something no other scientific instrument could: arrive at a final and comprehensive synthesis.

We understand the boundless enthusiasm that always over-
came Hegel when he talked about his dialectical method.
Sometimes this enthusiasm was almost moving, sometimes it
seemed like hubris and arrogance. At one point in the introduction to the *Logic* Hegel says: "How would I be able not to
suppose that the method I follow in this system of logic—or

rather which the system follows of itself—might not be subject to greater perfection, greater improvement, but at the same time I know that it is the only true one."

And it is the same in this introduction: "This realm is truth, as it is without integument, in and for itself. On this account it can be said that this content is the representation of God, as he is in his eternal essence, before the creation of nature and of any finite spirit."[117]

All this we can understand if we look at the method as a sort of splendid poetical idea and acquiescence in Hegel's tacit assumption, which goes something like this: Everything is interconnected with everything else and all parts, in the last analysis, are a whole.

But it was not Hegel's intention at all to poetize. The notion of conceptual romanticism, of the poetry of concepts and conceptual poetizing, comes from F. A. Lange, who in 1866 wrote a much read *History of Materialism*. Into this romantic category he put German idealism, the philosophies of Fichte, Schelling, and Hegel. But meanwhile Hegel himself was firmly convinced that his was no "conceptual poetizing," but a "scientific" philosophy.

In his *Logic* Hegel claimed that the dialectic method was the only true one, and similarly, in his *Phenomenology*, he called the dialectic a "scientific method." On another occasion in the *Logic* he says, full of hauteur: "It is clear that no interpretations can be counted as scientific which do not follow the procedure of this method and which do not conform to its simple rhythm, for it is the procedure of the thing itself."[118]

Here we have reached the critical point in the Hegelian philosophy. What does "science" mean in this context? Is the dialectical method in fact a scientific one? This point is important not only for a discussion of Hegelian philosophy, but for that of Marx as well. For Marxism also maintains to this day that by virtue of its dialectical thinking it is able to evolve a scientific view of the world and a scientific politics.

We shall return many times to this question of the scientific character of the dialectical method, particularly during the discussion of the Marxian dialectic. Meanwhile the matter is not susceptible to being dealt with conclusively within the context of a discussion of the Hegelian *Logic*. We can do no more, indeed, than excerpt an admittedly important subsection, and answer the question of the extent to which Hegel understood his dialectical method as scientific in the *Science of Logic*.

It has already been indicated where the basic difficulty lies. The real mystery of the dialectical method lies in the "fluidity" of concepts, and in that event which Hegel apprehends as the "self-movement of concepts." For formal logic there is no such thing as self-movement of concepts. To put it plainly, in formal logic this kind of thing would be viewed as so much nonsense. The essential nature of concepts, in formal logic, resides in the fact that they differentiate, separate, and lift up unequivocal relationships out of actuality. A concept is more scientific the more sharply and exactly it carries out this function.

Once we can no longer differentiate between concepts, black counting as much as white, Being indistinguishable from Nothing, round meaning the same as quadrangular, then there are also no more true or false concepts. From the dialectical point of view, false and true concepts are all lumped together and with that, says formal logic, good-by to scientific comprehension.

In consequence Hegel has often been criticized from this standpoint. It has been said that from the outset, and certainly when he turned to dialectical thinking, he ventured onto ground that made scientific thinking impossible. But it would be grossly underestimating Hegel to imagine that his claim to thinking scientifically can be done away with, so to speak, with a stroke of the pen. This procedure is altogether too simple.

However, it is certainly necessary to investigate Hegel's claim to being scientific, and an inquiry made into what it consists of and what it is based on. When we do this it will be shown that the idea of science which floated in Hegel's mind can in no way be made to conform with the idea of scientific knowledge as developed by the exact sciences. Moreover, Hegel knew this himself, and spoke with undisguised contempt of such "subordinate" knowledge.

Doubtless the "science" which Hegel was striving after cannot be granted the same recognition due mathematics and the natural sciences. But to simply dismiss Hegel's understanding of things as having nothing to do with science, in any acceptable sense of the word, is another matter. This can be decided only when the thrust and reach of its method, that is, of the dialectical method, has been tested.

# 8

## The Dialectic

Twice during this period Hegel presented the dialectic: once in the *Phenomenology*, once in the *Logic*. A space of nearly ten years separated these two statements. After the *Phenomenology* Hegel left Jena and wrote the *Logic* during the Nuremberg years, work which grew more slowly and more steadily in form and content. This second performance obviously required the greater effort.

Both works, using quite different material, had the same goal, which was to give a concrete demonstration of the dialectical method and dialectical thinking. Thus they took different routes toward the same destination. The chapter on Absolute Knowledge is found at the end of the *Phenomenology*, and on the Absolute Idea at the end of the *Logic*.

Although method and goal are almost identical in the two works, nonetheless, because of their disparate content, they are only conditionally comparable. However, they do complement each other since the *Phenomenology*, according to the notion of system then prevailing with Hegel, was the first part, and the *Logic* the second, of the whole. The entire conception of the system became clear when Hegel announced that a third part of it, *Philosophy of Nature*, was to follow.

The two works are comparable in that each demonstrates the unfolding of dialectical thinking as a methodological progression, albeit in different contexts, now as demonstrated in the stuff of history, now in the stuff of the logos. In this sense these books can be defined as Hegel's basic works. To be sure, again and again he was to deploy his dialectical thinking in new material; but by and large the dialectic was developed in these two works.

Thus we can now pose this question: What, actually, is this dialectic?

Herewith it immediately becomes apparent that the Hegelian dialectic had different roots. This fact also became evident in later years. Marx learned about the dialectic through the *Phenomenology*, but many of Hegel's pupils learned of it through the *Logic*. The subsequent breakup of the Hegelian system, its separation into different schools, was foreordained by the difference between the two roots.

For Hegel himself, beyond any doubt, dialectical thinking was at the bottom unified. Having found his method, for him it was a universal and comprehensive instrument, applicable to and demonstrable in any kind of material.

Dialectical thinking, Hegel maintained, had already been developed in principle in the *Phenomenology*, and there he is especially critical of other "subordinate" methods of thinking and philosophizing. But not until the *Logic* is the dialectical method really spelled out in a methodological sense.

Now it was perfected, now Hegel could make the presumptuous claim that his method was "the only true one," that it was the realm of truth unshrouded, indeed, that it was nothing less than a demonstration of God as he was "in his eternal essence before the creation of nature and of any finite spirit." At the same time Hegel made the claim that dialectic was the only scientific way of knowing things.

The introduction to the *Logic* from which we have taken these quotations, therefore, spells out the nature of dialectical thinking in a new way. To be sure, many statements are repeated that have already appeared in the introduction to the *Phenomenology*, yet at the same time the supplements and additions to the first description are extraordinarily important.

At first, then, we see the basic ideas already expressed in the *Phenomenology*. For instance, Hegel repeats his proposition that the task of his dialectic is to change "fixed and fast concepts" into "fluid" ones. In the preface to the *Logic* it is also stated that the dialectic shows the "self-movement" of concepts, and that on the strength of this a science is developed. Hence, as Hegel puts it, the presentation of the *Logic* presupposes the "concept of pure science and its deduction" to the extent that the *Phenomenology* is the deduction of the same. In other words, whoever had read the *Phenomenology* as prerequisite had been introduced to the concept of pure science and its method.

If a critical consideration may be interpolated here, one might ask whether it is admissible to carry over the dialectical method as evolved in the *Phenomenology* into the *Logic* without further ado. Does not each body of material require its own method? Do we not understand by "method" a definite procedure suited to the material at hand, showing how to elucidate a specific material according to specific rules?

This is precisely the proposition that Hegel contradicts. Only that method can be right and true which includes *all* regions of thought and elucidates the *whole* of thought. Hegel strove toward a final unity of cognitive thinking. If he has often been praised as a comprehensive systematizer, this falls in line with his wish to restore that unity in scientific thought threatened with loss by specialization.

We have already brought up the question of why Hegel gave his work the title *Logic* when in fact it departed completely from any kind of logic previously known. The reason is now evident: formal logic was a last vestige of what had once been the inner unity of science. However, for Hegel it had ceased to be even this. His sharp critique of formal logic, as already shown, was aimed at the fact that whereas in actuality it might perhaps provide a kind of formal and sterile unity, it was no longer able to arrive at the actual living unity of knowledge. Therefore its "dead bones" had to be brought to life through the spirit to gain "content and vigor."

In addition to these reflections, notions, and wishes, the introduction to the *Logic* once again developed the dialectical method. Although Hegel took pains to point out that in both the *Phenomenology* and the *Logic* the same kind of thinking is at work, every so often he had to justify a different application of the dialectic. Thus for the more closely observant reader the differences in usage also become apparent.

The material that Hegel first chose for dialectical treatment was historical. It is immediately apparent how any historical material is a priori suited for dialectical thinking. The reason is simple. The principle of the dialectical method, which is to evolve a whole in its divers ramifications, to show methodologically how this whole breaks down into single steps, is best suited to historical events.

For these events a priori exhibit the process of movement which the dialectic apprehends. All historical events admit of being regarded from a viewpoint according to which they represent opposed opinions, contradictory attitudes and contrasting elements. It is a truism that history proceeds in movement and countermovement. It likewise seems to be unequivocally clear that the movement of history repeatedly leads to a kind of equalization in which antinomies are sublimated.

The movements of the historical process, great and small, can be grasped from this standpoint. Whole epochs covering centuries can be traced back to this schema just as well as the small, everyday movements of history.

Thus the development of Christianity was completed in a slow ascendancy lasting for centuries. While this movement was reaching its peak in medieval thought, a countermovement emerged and came to full expression in Protestantism and the Reformation. At this stage of development the historical process was reversed. Christianity in its previous form suffered negation and had to be re-formed root and branch and led back to its original form.

If "contradiction" or antithesis appeared here in the Hegelian sense, then an equalization, an accommodation was carried out in a third stage. Brothers originally hostile to each other moved together again. The common, basic principle of Christian thinking finally reunited them once and for all. The overriding idea of Christianity again won the day. The antinomies were not erased and continued to exist, but behind the differences a final community again emerged.

Even the smaller movements of history can be understood in this manner. Every movement so important for our own lifetime, say changes in style and taste, or in clothing, can be understood without difficulty in terms of the dialectic. Here, too, the principle of movement and countermovement rules; here, too, the fact holds true that what was valid at one stage will be dismissed at the next. The statement that something is "old-fashioned" imports nothing beyond the fact that what before was the ultimate in acceptability is now no longer recognized.

Finally the same principle can be projected into science. If here there are no "modes" in the narrower sense of the word, opposed and contradictory opinions do appear just the same. But they, too, in their development lead to agreement. Here, too, sudden and often radical changes of opinion occur in which a whole field of phenomena will be placed in a new light and prior opinions eclipsed.

Everything generated by the historical spirit and everything subject to history is destined to be born and to pass away. This proposition holds true however far we extend the continuum of historical thought. Sometimes this passing away can occur abruptly. There are times when the following thesis holds true: *Incende, quod erasti, ora quod incendisti.* The next epoch burns up what the one before had acclaimed, and worships that which the previous one had denied.

But occasionally, too, such movements are completed in a slow and plodding way, and centuries, millennia may pass before what had been a valid principle yields and is negated. But that all history is a shifting spectacle of events, that every historical process, sooner or later when its time has come, suffers change—this seems to be one of the simplest laws of history.

In his *Phenomenology of the Mind* Hegel elevated this

process to an abstract schema and a basic idea. In this work he laid open the history of the human spirit and at the same time sublimated this process to the level of "absolute" validity. This schema (in its most general form the methodological key permitting the process of historical movement to have order impressed upon it) started out as a methodological instrument and evolved into an absolute mechanism. The sense of this was rooted in the conviction on Hegel's part that we do not merely use the dialectical schema as a means of apprehending history but that the schema as such actually dictates history.

Thus the phases of the history of the spirit singled out by Hegel become in the process of their fulfillment self-subsistent forms, following the absolute process, appearing and passing away according to the law of dialectic. History is the self-movement of mankind in which individual man fulfills his destiny. To this modern idea a second one has been added. While history is being consummated and the self-movement of mankind made manifest, in this process the Absolute Idea and the Absolute Spirit are revealed.

It was Hegel's intention to have the same dialectical schema attested in its absolute validity in the *Logic*. The difficulty here is clear from the start. The continuum of concepts is accommodated directly by the dialectic. The historical continuum is processlike and dynamic, but at first sight the logical continuum, insofar as it is not viewed in terms of its historical development, seems static.

The task of apprehending this static continuum dynamically again requires new assumptions. Above all, the notions underlying the static ordering of science have to be overcome. These are the principles of formal logic which decree that there is a difference between true and false and make a fundamental distinction between a thing and the concept of it. Hegel had already pointed out in the *Phenomenology* that: "True and false are among the determinate thoughts which are considered to be immobile separate essences, as if one stood here and the other there, with no community. Against this view one must insist that truth is not a minted coin which can be given and pocketed ready-made."

The sense of this proposition is clear: truth and falsehood

are mobile, shifting things. But Hegel now goes on to say: "Nor does something false exist, any more than something evil exists . . . Falseness (for only that is what we are talking about here) would be the other, the negative of the substance which, as the content of knowledge, is the true." This proposition is also clear: what is "false" at any given time is relative to what is true, insofar as it is the negation of truth.

Now at last comes the decisive thought and, as is so often the case with Hegel, it is very obscurely formulated: "But the substance is itself essentially the negative, partly as the differentiation and determination of the content, partly as simple discrimination, i.e., as self and knowledge in general. One can indeed know something falsely. But that something is known falsely means that knowledge is not identical with its substance."[119]

What is this passage trying to convey? To the extent that it can be interpreted at all, it can only mean that all falseness arises from differentiation and separation. A statement is false if it is separated from truth. Yet Hegel's statement contains much more than this. "Falseness," that is, *is* already in the substance. As Hegel puts it, the substance itself is "essentially the negative."

Before we move on to the introduction to the *Logic*, where statements are clarified step by step, let us get a firm grip on this hypothesis. In effect it goes like this: The true and false are both contained in the substance, but we can speak in terms of falseness only insofar as the "negative" of the substance is in evidence. This means that true and false are merely different ways in which the substance appears and reveals itself.

With this basic hypothesis we have really already reached Hegel's goal: true and false are linked together and almost identical. Hegel then proceeds to the consequences of this conclusion. If true and false belong together, if true and false are forms of conceiving and bound together in this manner, then under this aspect idea and thing are one.

This inference is emphatically elaborated in the introduction to the *Logic*. The real and true logic must abandon the distinction between "idea" and "thing." The true logic, in Hegel's words, presupposes "deliverance from the antithesis of consciousness." No longer is there a separation of subject and object. Hegel's *Logic* "contains the idea, insofar as it is just as much the thing in itself, or the thing of itself, insofar as it is as much pure idea."[120] In this manner, according to Hegel, we arrive at "objective thought," which is the "content of pure science."

What Hegel had in mind is clear. He abrogated the fundamentals evolved by formal logic. He denied both the determination of true and false as they are found in formal logic and the differentiation between "concept" as such and that in which the concept is grounded. New determinations were to replace the old. The new determinations would be a means to an end. To be achieved is that "fluidification" of concepts that is the basis of dialectical thought.

With this, the problem which Hegel had already solved once in the *Phenomenology* appeared for the second time. In the *Phenomenology* he had, as it were, made the idea of consciousness fluid in its history. He had shown the progressive development of this concept through the great stages of consciousness, self-consciousness, spirit, etc. At the same time he had demonstrated the "self-movement" of the concept in a specific object.

Now for a second time this self-movement was to be demonstrated, but minus the historical background that everywhere shines through the *Phenomenology*. It was precisely this historical background in the *Phenomenology*, however arbitrarily interpreted, that had made it possible to show self-movement. If the same task were to be performed for a second time in the *Logic*, with the historical background sweepingly abandoned, then a fresh start had also to be made in establishing the "self-movement" of concepts.

This was Hegel's main problem, which he finally solved in a memorable passage:

The only thing for securing scientific progress—and for which perfectly simple insight it is essential to strive—is

> the recognition of the logical proposition that the negative
> is equally positive, or that the contradictory is not dis-
> solved in nullity, in abstract nothing . . .

We interrupt this long sentence only to explain the statement so far. The scientific progress that Hegel had in mind is
the process in which the logic will be developed dialectically.
The prerequisite for this development, according to Hegel, is
the recognition that the negative is equally positive. Hegel is
repeating a claim already made several times before. At the
same time he is adding a new and extremely important note:
the contradictory is not dissolved into nullity.

With this thesis he disputed the fundamental logical proposition that two mutually contradictory statements cancel each
other out and that both cannot be valid at the same time.
Hegel's explanation why this proposition is not valid now follows: The contradiction is not dissolved in nullity, "but essentially only in the negation of a particular content . . ."

> . . . such a negation is not all negation, but it is the
> negation of the specific thing which is dissolved, and con-
> sequently is specific negation; that in the result is con-
> tained that out of which it resulted—which really is a
> tautology, for otherwise it would be an immediateness, not
> a result.[121]

Here the passage, developed nothing less than rhapsodically, comes to an end. In the last statement in it Hegel asserts
that contradiction represents only a "particular" and "specific"
negation. Negation does not dissolve everything, but lets a
partial content stand and in the final result takes along this
partial content.

One must turn to a perfectly simple example to bring home
what Hegel is driving at. He is developing the notion of a
negation which does not completely negate the hitherto existing content. This can be claimed of certain negative judgments. For instance, the statement that this cow is not black
can be understood as meaning that the original concept "cow"
remains and that in the negation the additional attribute of
"not black" has been added to it.

For Hegel all negative judgments are obviously of this nature. Every negative judgment contains a positive remainder that is extended. There are no blankly negative judgments. But Hegel goes a step further than this. Every contradiction is also an extension of knowledge, insofar as the negative judgment pertaining to the contradiction enlarges or extends the original facts of the case.

Formal logic before or after Hegel never recognized this claim. It can see no extension of knowledge at all in two propositions actually contradicting and mutually excluding each other. At most, formal logic can only say that a set of mutually exclusive propositions appear to be a cognitive cul-de-sac impossible to escape until one of the two propositions can be negated.

But for Hegel there was no such blind alley in the knowing process. For him, indeed, contradiction represents an advance, and each negation, in its way, is a positive act of cognition leading to higher and broader levels. This conviction comes to light in the concluding part of the section:

> Since what results, the negation, is a definite negation, it has a content. It is a new concept, but higher and richer than the one preceding it; for it has been enriched by the negation of the opposite of the precedent concept; therefore it (the new concept) contains it (the negation), but also more than it, and is the unity of it (the precedent concept) and its opposite.

These propositions complete the train of thought, once again expressing the idea that every contradiction is productive, that in its negativity it is a continuation of the knowing process, leading on to higher and richer concepts. Should there be any doubt that Hegel is describing the self-movement of the concept in this complex of ideas it is dispelled when, after interposing a dash, he goes on to say: "—The system of concepts has to be generally constructed in this way—and be perfected in an irresistible, pure motion, admitting nothing from the outside."

The theory of the self-movement of concepts, therefore, had been completed, the practical instructions for using it definitively laid down. The whole picture of the self-movement of concepts has been made plain for us to see. Every statement is just as positive as it is negative. When a negation appears, the first step toward a higher concept has already been taken. The new concept follows as a synthesis, as a unification of the negation, and that which has been negated.

It is obvious that according to the principles of formal logic such a theory does not hold up and there is no self-movement of concepts. But the fact remains that the complete negation of a proposition does sublimate the proposition negated. Hegel's theory can also be defended from the historical point of view. In this context it is valid to say that whenever something comes along that legitimately contradicts some form of theoretical or practical knowledge, for the most part this occasions new forms of knowledge. In this sense error frequently has been the basis for later advances.

But this historical movement of concepts as they fulfill themselves in time and their origin in the continuous striving to widen the horizons of knowledge can be conceived as self-movement only when cognition is conceived to be the servant of an absolute metaphysical process unfolded by man's mediation, rather than as an instrument of, or having its origin in, the human spirit.

This is certainly Hegel's view. The "Absolute Idea" and "Absolute Knowledge" are actualized in human beings. The stages of truth and error through which human knowing passes are stages of the metaphysical essence, that is, the Absolute, Divine Idea as manifested and actualized in human beings. Man himself carries out the Idea. One might almost say he is the functionary of the Absolute Essence, as Hegel called it. Hegel's *Logic*, therefore, at the same time is a metaphysics, that is, a demonstration and explication of the Absolute Essence. To repeat Hegel's own words, his logic is a representation of God.

As we follow the path which Hegel took methodologically and materially from the *Phenomenology* to the *Logic*, the inner consistency of the Hegelian system can be recognized from the history of the human knowing process. But the idea of the Absolute and of God was also to be demonstrated through the logic of the same cognitive process. So far the system had unfolded in two stages, first in the history of human self-consciousness, second in the idea of a new, abstract logic, always following the same way. Now the road was to be traveled for a third time in the "Philosophy of Nature."

Yet the system's claim to totality gives one pause. God and logic, spirit and nature, the history of man and metaphysics— all these have been fused into a unity that at first sight seems to be nothing but an arbitrary concord. Thus everything had been conceived, all understood.

But this was not the first time that a claim to totality had appeared. The same claim had been made in medieval thought, where the "logical" proof of God had been developed. In another way, but with a similar goal in mind, out of the logos Hegel had evolved a proof of the Absolute Spirit. This time the argument was dialectical and arrived at another kind of trinity, that of spirit, nature and logos, which together represented the Absolute. The logos, become dialectical and historical, developed this new trinity in a new way.

Later results of all this give even more cause for reflection. A few more steps along the road of dialectical thinking, Kierkegaard and Marx appeared. As different as these two thinkers were, and as much as each may have deviated from Hegelian thought, nonetheless they, too, raised the same claim to totality and defended it no less stubbornly. For them, too, the dialectical instrument was a means of arriving at the absolute.

Yet for each of them the nature of the absolute changed. With Marx it lost its otherworldly character. His dialectical materialism absolutized another kind of data—the class struggle, the movement of history and of economic forces, the economic progress of the spirit. Kierkegaard, on the other hand, described paradox, the paradox of existence, fear and nothing as absolute realities.

Both reviled and rejected Hegel, while on the whole still recognizing him as the master. In any event, they still carried on the dialectical method and dialectical thinking. Moreover, they brought to light the deep-seated ambiguity of the dialectical instrument and they showed how dialectical thinking as such can be used to reach any goal.

# 9

---

# Heidelberg and the Encyclopaedia

In the middle of the year 1816 the last and conclusive part
of the *Science of Logic* went to press. Hegel was now
forty-six years old and still headmaster or rector at
the Nuremberg *gymnasium*. The hope that shortly he would
be called to a university had, to be sure, loomed on the horizon
again and again, but so far nothing definite had materialized.
In 1812 Hegel had written to Niethammer:

> . . . the litany of getting to the bottom of things, of
> drawing conclusions, of separating, of making things flow,
> of piecing out basics, which on the subjective side repre-
> sents a similar litany of misery, vexation, delay, expecta-
> tion, disappointment of expectation, etc.—[is] a dismal
> tune I have been playing over and over for four years with
> no end yet in sight, and which if it should finally come to
> an end where I am, I might have to start all over again
> somewhere else. Things being what they are, I have, so to

speak, irrevocably lost any belief in better days to come . . .[122]

In other words, he was in one way fed up with his Nuremberg existence, yet in another way satisfied. Although it was not good, it could have been worse. But now, at last, his wish was actually to be fulfilled. When the call to Heidelberg came and was verified, he wrote to one of his future colleagues: "Well, then, we may have reached a point where I can soon look forward to my release from the crapulous school-and-studies way of life."[123]

Besides getting an offer from Heidelberg, which he accepted, he was also sounded out by the University of Erlangen. At Erlangen he would have taken over a professorship of philology. This appointment went through, but shortly before it became effective Hegel accepted the Heidelberg offer. At about the same time, still another inquiry arrived from Berlin asking whether he might want to take over the chair of philosophy there.

It is noteworthy that all the universities that dealt with Hegel about appointments were obviously concerned about his obscurity and unintelligibility. When he was under consideration at Heidelberg, one of the professors there had to make inquiries whether Hegel's "oral delivery was not especially good, and obscure." The answer turned out to be satisfactory. Word came that at the Nuremberg Gymnasium he was well-known for the excellence and clarity of his teaching methods.

This rumor about Hegel's obscurity also reached Berlin, and no doubt went back to the Jena years, when apparently he read his lectures, lectures that were not always understandable.

Hegel knew about this. He once wrote about his Jena activity:

> My first attempt at lecturing there, from what I hear, left a prejudice against me in that place. I was really a beginner, hadn't yet worked my way through to clarity, and in oral delivery was bound to the letters in my notebook. Nearly eight years of practice at Nuremberg, where one is in a constant give-and-take discussion with one's

listeners and where being clear and on top of the situation
of necessity comes about of itself, since that time has given
me complete freedom.[124]

Hegel now felt he had progressed to clarity and, so he believed, found freedom of expression. He wrote his letter of
resignation to the Munich government and began his teaching
career at Heidelberg full of expectation. The intermediary
official who forwarded his letter of resignation through chan-
nels to the ministry of education commented that Hegel had
proved satisfactory and was respected in Nuremberg, and that
nothing stood in the way of his release from service since he
was a "foreigner." For by birth he was a Württemberger and a
"foreigner" in Bavaria.[125]

Thus the portents under which he took the Heidelberg post
were highly auspicious. He began his lectures in the winter
semester of 1816–17. They were at first sparsely attended, but
he was able to announce he had a considerable number of
listeners for the summer semester of 1817. He had words of
praise for the "laughing, romantic and fruitful countryside"
around Heidelberg.[126] In half a year he wrote his *Encyclopaedia of the Philosophic Sciences*, which came out as a
manual for his lectures.

This was Hegel's third major work, following the *Phenomenology* and the *Logic*. Its title, *Encyclopaedia of the
Philosophic Sciences in Outline*, indicates that Hegel was now
presenting his whole system in an abbreviated form.

Again Hegel chose the method of presentation first used in
the *Propaedeutics*. The whole work is constructed according
to a strict trichotomy, that is, each part again split up into
three divisions, each division into A, B and C sections, and
almost all these sections again divided into a, b and c (and
sometimes even d) subsections.

At the same time there is a running numeration of paragraphs, of which there are 577 all told in the *Encyclopaedia*.
These paragraphs vary in length; often they run to many sentences, but others are quite brief.

The first edition of the *Encyclopaedia* was published in
1817, the so-called *Heidelberg Encyclopaedia*. Later, in 1827,

Hegel had another and larger edition brought out, in which the basic structure of the first *Encyclopaedia* was preserved. However, the individual paragraphs were now provided with "exemplifications," mostly designated as addenda.

Later the publishers of Hegel's works once again expanded the whole on the basis of lectures and transcripts and a third form of the *Encyclopaedia* was brought out after Hegel's death. By this time the work had grown into three volumes.

Moreover, in Hegel's lectures on the *Encyclopaedia of Philosophic Sciences,* which he repeated twice in Berlin, he incorporated additions at appropriate places into the oral material, some, for example, taken from his big *Logic.* These additions, too, were used in the third edition by the publisher Henning.

In its final published form the *Encyclopaedia* bore the title *System of Philosophy.* In other words, the outline of the Hegelian system represented by the *Heidelberg Encyclopaedia,* in which the whole was compressed into some 550 pages, in the course of years became the full-blown framework of the system, resulting in a three-volume work of over 1,500 pages.

Is the *Encylopaedia* then, the definitive version of the system, complete with all finishing touches? Is it what Hegel had been striving for since Jena? If we assume this to be the case, then it must be said at once that what Hegel submitted as the finished version of the system is not identical in structure with earlier versions. If we leave out of account the very brief formulation of the system as sketched out for classroom use in the *gymnasium,* and compare the *Encyclopaedia* with the outline of the system in which the *Phenomenology* is designated as the first part, the *Logic* as the second, a striking change is evident. In the *Encyclopaedia* outline of the system, the *Phenomenology* has lost first place. It is no longer the "beginning" of the system. Rather it is the *Logic* that has now taken first place.

The first volume of the large *Encyclopaedia* is given over to logic, with the philosophy of nature following in the second volume. The third volume contains the philosophy of the mind (spirit), and in it the *Phenomenology* appears compressed into a relatively short segment of about one hundred pages.

From this we must conclude that his whole philosophic system, as Hegel developed it, was mobile and changeable in structure as individual parts can be combined in different ways. The system as it was first organized had an introduction, the *Phenomenology*, which in a certain sense was historical; in the later structure it is the *Logic* that takes the lead.

The encyclopedic organization of the system shows a clear sequentiality. First comes logic, obviously the basic framework of all philosophy, since it represents "pure" thought. Next comes the philosophy of nature, in which "pure" thought is substantialized on the basis of natural events, and finally follows the philosophy of mind (spirit), in which pure thought and concept reach their third stage.

Thus we are now confronted by a closed and pellucid and formal version of the system: concept, nature, spirit (or mind). At the same time this form of the system completely actualized the whole basic notion of the Hegelian philosophy. The idea of it ascends in a single, repeated dialectical movement, beginning with the simple and immediate concept of Being, to all forms and configurations of the idea. Out of a first concept, Being, the whole concept is developed, as Hegel announced it would be, in one "irresistible progression."

Hegel's ultimate purpose again becomes evident, in that this great cycle of thought presumes nothing beyond the first empty concept of Being. All further stages in the dialectical movement flow out of this initial concept. The sum of knowledge is evolved on the basis of one dialectical guideline, presupposing nothing but the pure self-movement of thought.

Leaving all else aside, Hegel's artistic and compositional achievement is impressive. For the system as here organized is more than a mere formal construction. As the title *Encyclopaedia* suggests, Hegel is now concerned with presenting the *whole* of knowledge in general within the framework of a philosophical system.

It is an astonishing performance. Never again after Hegel—with the possible exception of Nicolai Hartmann—has any thinker undertaken such a vast project, literally attempted to present the *summa* of knowledge of his period from a philosophical point of view. Yet this was precisely what Hegel intended.

We are not surprised, therefore, to find that everything, as it were, had its place in the system. Just a glance at the table of contents shows the stupendous plethora of factual knowledge laid out for display.

In the second part, the philosophy of nature, we find sections on both physics and chemistry. There is a discussion of the Keplerian laws, and of galvanism as well. The section on organics deals with geology and biology. Zoology is explored in detail. The human body is discussed in terms of the function of the muscular apparatus, of the lung- and liver-systems, of the circulatory and digestive systems. There is a chapter on worms and mollusks, another on the art of medicine.

In the third part, the philosophy of spirit, in a chapter or section called "The Subjective Spirit," the subjects of anthropology, phenomenology, and psychology are treated. In an ensuing chapter on the "Objective Spirit" is a discussion of jurisprudence, comprising in abbreviated form the later Hegelian philosophy of right and the state. Everything is incorporated into the system: the philosophy of art has its place no less than the philosophy of religion. And, to emphasize the fact once again, the system meanwhile evolves in an irresistible progression through many stages to an ultimate stage, with which we are already acquainted as the Absolute Spirit.

The particulars of the system are as impressive as the structure as a whole. Hegel familiarized himself with every subject imaginable in his day. Naturally enough, now 150 years later, the scientific detail of the *Encyclopaedia* is completely obsolescent because of the uninterrupted advance of specialized science and because the continuity of this development has entirely changed the world of knowledge. Nonetheless it still must be borne in mind that Hegel did make an attempt to include all contemporary knowledge down to the smallest detail.

Thus the Hegelian system above all is a collective accomplishment, beyond being a triumph of construction. It is one of the last attempts to display knowledge encyclopedically on a unified basis. It is certainly one of the last philosophical attempts to rise above the individual sciences and, in a certain sense, proceed on the assumption of knowing more than the scientific specialists.

Yet also evident in the Hegelian *Encyclopaedia* is the hopeless struggle between the philosopher of universal scholarship and the scientific expert in a certain field. Even in Hegel's time the mass of specialized knowledge was constantly changing, if perhaps not as rapidly as it is today. In consequence even then the specialized scientist who really knew his own discipline regarded the Hegelian presentation of his field of knowledge with great skepticism. Today, when even a scientific or technical handbook is valid only for a decade and the state of research in some fields seems to be outrun with each morrow, the scientific material of the *Encyclopaedia* has inevitably become obsolete.

All that is left of the *Encyclopaedia* for us today is its basic methodological idea. This idea was first developed in the *Phenomenology*, then in the *Logic*, and again demonstrated in the *Encyclopaedia*. How, then, does the dialectic look in this last work?

The center of gravity and the idea behind the construction have suffered a shift. This is shown by the fact that the logic is the first part of the system. The logic displayed in the *Encyclopaedia*, whether in the short Heidelberg form or in the later expanded edition, is a more or less abridged version of the larger *Logic*. The whole is now provided with an introduction which more thoroughly than ever before describes what philosophy's task is.

However, Hegel's notion of what this task is has not changed. As on previous occasions, he reiterates the opinion in the brief introduction that his encyclopedic presentation offers "a new treatment of philosophy, which furthermore, as I hope, will come to be recognized as the only true one, one that is identical with its content."[127]

All other earlier claims are also repeated. In the preface to the second edition again Hegel expresses the view that philosophy must be "the scientific knowledge of the truth."[128] It can direct itself only toward the recognition of the "Absolute";

indeed, Hegel now describes the history of philosophy as "the history of thought's discovery of the Absolute."[129]

This process of discovery, as Hegel now expressly states, combines philosophy with religion, and we are told "That religion can indeed exist without philosophy, but not philosophy without religion, which rather includes religion within itself."[130]

Further along in the preface the business of philosophical thought is expounded. The essence or nature (*Wesen*) of spirit is defined: in the philosophical approach above all it "becomes *itself*, in the deepest sense of the word, for its principle, its unmixed selfhood, is thought." But the spirit is also dialectical. Therefore, spirit in the form of dialectical logic takes first place in the structure of the system:

> The insight that the nature of thought itself is the dialectic, that as understanding it must end up in the negative of itself, in contradiction, constitutes a main aspect of the logic. Also despairing of being able *out of itself* to resolve the contradiction into which it has got itself, thought turns back to solutions and consolations which have fallen to the spirit's lot in other of its ways and forms.[131]

We will recall that in his first essay on "On the Difference between the Systems of Fichte and Schelling" Hegel said that "bifurcation" (*Entzweiung*)—sometimes translated as "disunion"—was the source of the philosophical need. The present statement formulates the same idea even more pregnantly. Thought as thinking in order to understand must end up by contradicting itself. Here is the only point where Hegel joins forces with Kant.

For Hegel, as for Kant, philosophy's ultimate aim was an attempt to resolve the contradictions generated by the process of understanding. But if Hegel's point of departure was the same as Kant's, he went off on a different tack. He took the way of the dialectic. In the *Encyclopaedia* is found a definition of the dialectic which, though it offers nothing new, is couched more succinctly and precisely than any before:

"Thinking as understanding sticks to fixed determinations and the differences among them; for it a limited abstractness of

this sort is counted to be subsistent and essential." Then in the
next paragraph he goes on to say: "The dialectical moment is
the self-sublimation of such finite determinations and their
transition into their opposites." Thus Hegel holds to his idea
of the self-movement of concepts. He then adds this commentary:

> The dialectic is usually thought of as an external art,
> which arbitrarily brings forth a confusion in certain con-
> cepts and a mere *appearance of contradictions*, in such
> way that this appearance, not the determinations, is a null-
> ity and the intelligible, on the contrary, much more the
> true. Further, this dialectic often is nothing more than a
> subjective seesaw system, a *système de bascule* of argu-
> mentation that goes this way and that, where content is
> lacking and nakedness is concealed by the same ingenuity
> that has created such argumentation.—In its peculiar de-
> terminateness the dialectic, on the contrary, is the proper,
> true nature of the determinations of understanding, of
> things and of the finite in general.

Thinking about this rather heretically, one might almost go
even further and say that according to this the true dialectic,
as Hegel developed it, is a sort of objective seesaw system in
which the spirit moved upward stage by stage to the last
height. Looking at it this way, the other goal of the dialectic,
in any case of the dialectic which Hegel had in mind, becomes
clear.

Up to now we have always emphasized the view that the
dialectic has its final substratum in the actuality of the historical movement. But for Hegel it has, in fact, a second meaning, one which he also expresses briefly and pregnantly in this
same passage:

> Everything finite has to sublimate (or transcend) itself.
> The dialectical, therefore, is the moving spirit of scientific
> progress and is the principle whereby alone immanent re-
> lationship and necessity come into the content of science,
> just as in it (the dialectical) in general lies the true, not
> the external, transcendence above the finite.[132]

Each one of Hegel's systematic works ends on the same note: the Absolute Idea. The question of what the Absolute Idea actually is can be answered in several ways. For Hegel it is the "Idea that knows itself," "reason thinking itself," it is the "Absolute Universal (or General)."

In developing knowledge, philosophy marches forward to a final unity and necessity—the Absolute Idea—in which everything finite vanishes into the infinite. Obviously Hegel meant this to be taken quite concretely and literally. All of understanding's assessments and all individual forms of knowledge must somewhere be parts of a whole. In this whole, on the other hand, the relationships of the individual parts must become clear without having the differences among them disappear.

The dialectic succeeds in doing this, as Hegel saw it. The dialectic alone is capable of sublimating the limited postulates of understanding and of pressing forward to that notion which manifests itself as the transcendence of all that is finite. Thus one could almost say that the Absolute Idea is also the end product of the dialectic. The more these Hegelian trains of thought are recognized in depth—themes, moreover, which are not new and which earlier had already appeared in the *Phenomenology* and the *Logic*—the clearer becomes the Hegelian metaphysic. Revealed here is the double sense, the ambiguity of the Hegelian method.

On the one hand the dialectic is made to comprehend historical movement, and, indeed, in my conviction it is actually derived from Hegel's experience of history. Yet for Hegel the dialectic also had a second task. It was intended to go beyond the finite into the infinite and absolute, and it is this that gives the Hegelian dialectic a hybrid character. It is born of historical empiricism and—as later happened in the case of Marx —can be understood as a way of looking at history. Out of the dialectic in this sense grew Marx's historical materialism.

Hegel gave it another goal, however, the task of discovering and knowing the absolute and eternal. Then the Hegelian dialectic acquired its unique and specific significance. It was lifted up and beyond its claim to validity as a method of understanding history and made into a comprehensive method dealing with everything whatsoever. It took on philosophy's ancient task: metaphysics.

This becomes evident above all in the *Encyclopaedia*.[133] Here the Hegelian system is presented in its entire scope, though to be sure in an abbreviated form and on that account all the more precisely structured. Now the system meets the reader's gaze as a solidly armored phalanx, an ordering of the world complete in every particular.

The three-staged arrangement of the world, as Hegel saw it, stands out clearly. At the beginning of the world stands the undeveloped, immediate concept, which is developed dialectically in three great steps. Starting with the immediate concept, this evolution proceeds through and beyond nature to the absolute spirit. The structure of the system reflects this progression of logic, philosophy of nature, and philosophy of the spirit. Logic, of course, develops the basic spiritual material of the world, the concepts. In the philosophy of nature the actual, sensuously intuitable and operative world is evolved. The third level is reached in the philosophy of spirit: the self-contemplating and Absolute Idea, in which history, nature, and concept are all interwoven.

Hegel started with the experience of history and in it found the dialectical method. He then applied this method to logic, something he had actually had in mind from the start. By so doing, he believed, he tore down the old logic to its foundations and rebuilt it into a dialectical logic. Now he was still faced with the task of incorporating the world of facts into this system of historical and conceptual composition, the world that we designate as "nature."

This final evolution took place in the *Encyclopaedia*. We find it first mentioned in the abbreviated *Heidelberg Encyclopaedia*, in later editions in a volume of its own devoted entirely to a presentation of nature. And how did Hegel envisage "nature," how did he incorporate this region of understanding and knowledge into his system?

Hegel himself was living in a period in which scientific thought was more widespread than ever before. Hegel's day was no longer the period of Descartes and Leibniz, that is, the beginning of scientific thinking. Rather it was the period of

classical physics, chemistry, and other disciplines in the realm
of natural science, and above all the period, too, of a powerfully burgeoning technology.

That is, another notion of nature was in process of development. This can be seen more clearly if we look at our own
time and our idea of nature, in which what was then but
nascent is now obvious. We no longer understand nature as,
for instance, Rousseau understood it. For us nature no longer
is a "good and happy condition" opposed to civilization. Our
concept of nature is closer to Kant's, who saw it as a unified
and orderly complex of *phenomena*.

To be sure, a remnant of the romantic belief in nature clings
to our modern notion of it, and we still have a tendency to
view nature to some degree as the omnipotent and friendly
mother. But at the same time, in step with the growth of
physical science, for us nature has become a gigantic field of
actuality moving within a brazen ring of lawfulness, the
provenance of which in the last analysis we do not know.

For physical science tells us nothing about who organized
the world and nature as they are. It tells us about the laws
governing the movements of the cosmos. It teaches how we
can make these laws serve us, in proportion to the evolution of
technology. In this sense we not only believe in physical science and nature, but obey their laws.

Meanwhile another side of nature has become more and
more evident through the physical sciences—or should we say
another side of man? We have discovered that we can misuse
nature, or at any rate use it so that the forces of devastation
and annihilation are operative alongside those that maintain
and preserve. On the one hand nature is a useful and willing
slave, in the form of technology giving our lives new foundations and making less work for us. On the other hand, for the
first time in mankind's history the possibility has arisen that
man can destroy himself through the powers of nature made
subservient. Whether this possibility is realized or not,
whether it is a mere notion born of madness and fear—it is
still there.

In earlier times, too, there were visions of the downfall of
the temporal world, for example, Judgment Day. In our day

this image has changed, insofar as a kind of suicide of mankind must now be considered thinkable. This notion, naturally,
can also be united with that of Judgment Day, so far as it is
assumed that a creator of this world incorporated mankind's
self-destruction into his plan.

If we examine the Hegelian concept of nature from this
point of view we get a totally different picture and one that is
curiously pleasing to us. Hegel begins by developing his concept of nature as follows: "The first question here is, why did
God himself determine to create nature?"[134]

We will remember that Hegel had already answered this
question once before, in the "Jena Fragment." There he said
that God "had spread himself out in the splendor and mute
cycle of formations" and had become angry about it. "This
anger," he went on to say, "is the destruction of nature." Nature was an act of God, but a negative act of self-destruction
and a step in God's dialectical unfolding.

Something of this idea has been retained even now in the
*Encyclopaedia*. In the order of the Hegelian system, nature is
the second stage and thereby the negative of the pure logos
and before the third stage, that of spirit. And so Hegel tells us
in his definition of the concept of nature: "Nature has arisen as
the Idea in the form of otherness. Since the Idea in this form is
the negative of itself, or itself externalized, nature is not external and relative as opposed to this Idea (and as opposed to
the subjective existence of the same, the Spirit), rather ex-
ternality constitutes the determination under which it (the
Idea) is nature . . ."

An elucidation of this follows in a corollary. "If God is the all-
sufficient, the unneeding, why does he decide on something
plainly unequal to himself? The divine Idea is precisely this, to
resolve to put this Other out of himself and take it into himself
again, so as to make it subjectivity and spirit . . ."

This quotation may serve to show how Hegel evolved a
concept of nature that was basically theological in origin. It
must be added that the development of this concept was not
completed until later in Hegel's career. In the *Heidelberg Encyclopaedia* the word "God" does not appear in this context,
that is, in the transition from logic to the philosophy of nature.

It was not until the last draft of the *Encyclopaedia* that a theological concept of nature was added. When this was done everything became perfectly clear. Hegel puts it bluntly this way:

> God has two manifestations, as Nature and as Spirit; both forms of God are temples of the same (that is, of himself), which he fills and in which he is present. God as an abstraction is not the true God, but only as the living process of creating his otherness, the world, which, apprehended in divine form, is his Son; and not until he is unified in spirit with his otherness is God subject. This, then, is the definition and goal of the philosophy of nature, that Spirit should find in it its own essence, that is, the concept in nature, its antitype.[135]

At first sight this definition of nature and natural philosophy may seem surprising, but on closer inspection its inner consistency becomes evident. The Hegelian system, by this time perfected as a trinity of logos, nature, and spirit, in this form returns to the Christian faith. Hegel's system becomes a symbol of Christian humanism permeated with many rational elements. We now begin to appreciate the cogency of interpreting Hegel, as is so often done, as in the last analysis a theological philosopher. Just as the young Hegel developed his dialectic out of the idea of God, now the older Hegel again identified his dialectic, by this time fully elaborated, and his dialectical system with the Christian God. The only question is whether such an interpretation can cover the entire Hegel.

# 10

## The System in Process of Change

Hegel's Heidelberg years, like those in Bamberg, were only a brief interlude. When Hegel came to Heidelberg he felt, as he wrote to Niethammer, like a "neophyte university professor," who "really, for the most part, had to create the sciences" on which he was lecturing.[136] And the beginning was not encouraging. At first Hegel had scarcely any students to listen to him, although he was soon able to announce that he had a fair number.

At the outset of the Heidelberg period the *Encyclopaedia* stands out as the ground plan, by this time definitive, of the Hegelian system. We are reminded by it of how far the system has come. Back in the Jena days, in the announcements advertising Hegel's lectures, there had been several allusions to a manual of the system that was soon to appear. And the Jena lectures themselves had contained pieces of all parts of the system, that is, logic, metaphysics, and the philosophy of nature.

Then, at the end of the Jena period, the *Phenomenology*

had appeared as the first volume of the system, followed by the *Logic* as the second, this to be succeeded by a third on the philosophy of nature. The structuring of the system, therefore, began with the historical dialectic of the spirit, went from there to the *Logic*, with the philosophy of nature evolving as a third step.

But Hegel did not stick to this arrangement of the system. Another sequence appeared in the *Encyclopaedia*. Now logic had first place, followed by the philosophy of nature, with the philosophy of the spirit coming up last. Phenomenology took a back seat and was assigned a relatively limited role in the philosophy of the spirit.

In the new arrangement the logical, rather than the historical, was emphasized. It has to be assumed that this ordering of the material was what Hegel had been driving at from the start. However historical his thinking and however much the historical approach may have facilitated the development of the dialectical method, for him what had occurred in history and what was possible in history were still bound up in an ever greater dimension.

By this time, in any case, the ordering of the system had been decided, and henceforth Hegel would begin to work at the task of extending it. Hegel was a marvelously industrious and steady worker. At Heidelberg he gave lecture courses such as the *History of Philosophy* and "Aesthetics" that were later to appear in his collected works. Still later, in Berlin, his lectures on "Philosophy of World History" and "Philosophy of Religion" were also added.

Hegel was constantly mastering new masses of empirical material and incorporating them into his system. This activity is reflected in his collected lecture series, published after his death and running, all told, to ten volumes. It is also shown in the later editions of the *Encyclopaedia*, which in contrast to the first grew to three volumes.

Each of these works bears witness to the scope of Hegel's reading. The *History of Philosophy*, for example, is an astonishing mine of information. It is made attractive by the fact that Hegel went directly to the original material and presented it as such.

This also holds true for the other works and lectures as well. If, in the later "Philosophy of Nature," which came out as the second volume of the *Encyclopaedia*, he was able to discuss chemical and physical processes and theories, and zoology, botany, and medicine as well—all thanks to a groundwork of intensive study.

Even to this day the "Philosophy of World History" is a highly readable book, although outdated in its historical parts. For Hegel's own period, however, it was an authentic world history and philosophy in one, framed in terms of the historical knowledge of the day.

The "Philosophy of Religion" and the "Aesthetics" give still another picture, which shall be mentioned here only in passing. The "Aesthetics" and the "Philosophy of History" were among the most popular lecture courses of the Berlin period; in them Hegel developed the concept of the beautiful, historical art forms and a system of the arts. Using the dialectical method with sovereign self-assurance, Hegel wandered through the whole realm of the beautiful and the arts in their myriad ramifications.

Hegel's "Philosophy of Religion" is unique. Again the dialectical method seems to have been created to interpret and comprehend the manifold aspects of the religious theme. We find religion in all its forms, in all its modes of appearance, both determinate and indeterminate; before our eyes unfolds a panorama of the religious spirit, not unlike what we found in the *Phenomenology*.

One of Hegel's great talents was meditation, the power to immerse himself in a subject and to see through it from all sides. The "circling" kind of thinking that Hegel speaks about so often is adhered to both in the "Philosophy of Religion" and in the "Aesthetics." Inseparable from this dialectical approach, and working to the advantage of the method, are the ever-changing determinations or definitions. If, for instance, the different concepts of God appearing in the "Philosophy of Religion" were systematically collected, it would be found that they were endlessly changing. Yet it is not only the historical concept of God that changes in the Hegelian approach; Divinity and God himself shimmer in a thousand hues.

To be sure, shot through the entire "Philosophy of Religion" is the definition of God as "the absolute truth, the truth of everything" and of religion as "absolute knowledge." At the same time the dialectic leads us from an abstract and almost empty concept of God to the more substantive forms appearing in history. The god of magic and the god of the Brahmins as well, the gods of Greece and Rome, likewise the God of Christianity move on and off stage, in accordance with the dialectical method and in the light of philosophical contemplation.

As for Hegel's own private concept of God, it is hardly possible to formulate it. Hegel, to be sure, was of Protestant persuasion and sharply rejected Catholicism. This rejection went so far that one day while lecturing in Berlin he got into an argument with a Catholic priest, who felt he had been slandered by Hegel's exposition of the Catholic theory of transubstantiation, and filed a complaint with the university authorities.[137]

On the other hand, Hegel's Protestantism verged into the mystical. He could speak of an "implicitly existing unity of divine and human nature" and claim that "this subjectivity of human nature is God himself"[138] and teach that "the human is God immediately present."[139]

Starting with the *Encyclopaedia* as an outline, in the Heidelberg and Berlin years Hegel ranged through all realms of the spirit, describing and ordering, classifying and systematizing. The dialectic method served him as measuring rod and guideline. In a certain sense it enabled him to understand and conceive everything; it was able to show the necessity of the transient and the imperishable, likewise of the natural and the supernatural.

The effect of all this on Hegel's career was phenomenal. Honors were heaped on him, and students came to him in droves. Indeed, many non-students from the city attended his lectures. He once wrote in a letter that now he was even having "majors, colonels, privy councilors among his listeners."[140]

So however much Hegel may have liked Heidelberg, when he moved to Berlin a new and larger world opened up to him.

When Hegel left Heidelberg he wrote a remarkable passage in his letter of resignation to the Baden government. In it he says he is not accepting the call to Berlin merely because of the considerably larger salary, but also because of the prospect "in advancing years of having more opportunity to shift from the precarious business of teaching philosophy at a university to another activity and to be able to find employment in it."[141]

What is this supposed to mean? What activity was Hegel looking forward to in Berlin? This question must be left open. One thinks, to be sure, of Hegel's earlier desire to get into politics or government. We are struck by the fact, in any event, that now, all of a sudden, he sees teaching philosophy as a "precarious business," and just as he was about to get the professorship he had longed for for so many years. And since his letters from Heidelberg show that he was quite satisfied there, and since on one occasion he even went so far as to say that he found his change of location to Heidelberg "continuously pleasing in every respect," his stay in that city cannot have been the immediate occasion for this new wish.[142]

Meanwhile Berlin was obviously a splendid fulfillment, even if his other wish was not to come true. The once almost unintelligible docent, unable to manage without his notes, became an academic lion. We have an impressive and often quoted description of what Hegel was like while lecturing. His pupil, Hotho, later co-publisher of Hegel's collected works, described him as follows:

> When I saw him again after a few days at his professorial chair, I could not get used either to his style of delivery or to his train of thought. Exhausted, morose, he sat there in a huddle, head hanging, and while he was speaking kept leafing and searching high and low in his long folio notebooks; the steady coughing and clearing the throat interrupted any flow of speech, each sentence stood there all by itself and came out with an effort, all chopped up and jumbled; each word, each syllable broke loose reluctantly, whereupon it was given a strangely profound emphasis by the metallically hollow voice with a broad Swabian accent, as if each was the most important. Never-

theless his whole appearance compelled such deep respect, such a sense of dignity and attracted one so much by the naiveté of a most overpowering seriousness, that in spite of all my uncomfortableness, and although I may have understood little enough of what was being said, I found myself held for good. However, no sooner had I, in a short time, accustomed myself through zeal and perseverance to the external aspect of his lectures than their inner merits sprang more clearly into view and interwove themselves with the defects aforementioned into a whole, which in itself alone bore the measure of its perfection . . .

He had to bring up to the surface from the deepest depths of things the mightiest of thoughts, and if they were to have a vital effect had to be regenerated in him in an ever living present, even if they had been pondered and worked over again and again years before. A more vivid sculpturing of the difficulty and laboriousness of this process than the one afforded by his manner of delivery cannot be imagined. Like the most ancient prophets who, struggling all the more urgently to find words so as more forcibly to express what was contending in them, worked their way forward half-overcoming, half-overcome, he, too, strove and conquered in a heavy square-set way. Completely lost in nothing but the subject matter, he seemed to evolve it only out of and for the sake of itself, and hardly at all out of his own mind for the sake of the listeners . . . It was precisely in the depths of the seemingly undecipherable that this powerful mind burrowed and moved with magnificently self-confident ease and composure. Only then the voice rose, the eyes flashed sharply over the assembly and shone with the quietly lambent fire of a splendor born of deep conviction, while he, never lacking for words, reached out through all heights and depths of the soul . . .[143]

This report is from one of his most loyal followers, but the marvelous quality in Hegel's lecturing had been confirmed by other sources, likewise the sudden flaming up which—as Rosenkranz wrote—"progressed to a certain ceremonial sub-

limity which penetrated to the bone and marrow of an audience grown deathly still."[144]

Hegel, the Swabian, made a go of it in the Prussian capital,
"he conquered in a heavy square-set way." Actually he had his
enemies and critics, too, by whom on occasion he was emphatically taken to task. When Alexander von Humboldt was
giving a public lecture course on physical geography in the
winter semester of 1827–28, he protested against a "metaphysics without knowledge and experience," and spoke about
a "schematism narrower than anything ever coined in the
Middle Ages."[145] He did not cite Hegel by name, but obviously had him in mind.

Was Hegel changed by success and fame? In Hegel's letters
from this period we find old and familiar traits. How did he
write to Niethammer about his times? The world-spirit was
progressing, and the surest bet, intellectually and practically,
was to keep a sharp eye on it and track its movements.

But however sure he may have been about progress, Hegel
had never been filled with rosy optimism. To be sure he
taught development, and in this sense progress toward the
Absolute, but he did not teach an absolute progress. For the
spirit moved in contradictions, manifested itself in positive
and negative phases. Very much tied in with this limited belief
in progress, therefore, was Hegel's skepticism about his own
day. He was often overcome by deep skepticism. When still in
Nuremberg he wrote to Niethammer: "Everything is the same
old way with us here and *nobody*, moreover, is expecting a
turn for the better." His bride wrote the following note in the
margin beside this sentence: "Hegel belongs to the hopeless
ones who expect nothing and desire nothing . . ."[146]

But he adjusted bravely and tenaciously to circumstances.
The Jena, Bamberg, and Nuremberg years show how he tried
to make the best of the situation and continue to work in his
own world under everyday burdens. He never talked much
about the crises he experienced. Only occasional remarks reveal that he was well acquainted with the precarious side of
existence. A letter to Windischmann from Nuremberg contains
the following remarkable passage:

. . . this descent into dark regions where nothing turns out to be fixed, definite and sure, where brightnesses flash on all sides, but next to abysses made by them all the darker, where one is misled by the surroundings, casting false reflections rather than illuminating—where every path is no sooner begun than it breaks off again and runs out into the indefinite, loses itself and tears us away from our destination and direction. From personal experience I know this state of mind, or rather state of reason, once it has got itself involved, with interest and the intimations arising from it, in a chaos of phenomena, and when, though inwardly certain of its goal, has not yet come through to clarity and a detailed grasp of the whole. For a few years I suffered from this hypochondria to the point of exhaustion; every human being, after all, has indeed such a turning point in his life, the nocturnal point of contraction of his nature, through which narrow passage he is compelled and thereby strengthened and assured in his inner security, and of security as well in his usual daily round. And if he has already made himself incapable of being engrossed by that, assured of security in a noble inward existence.—Go on with confidence; only the science that has led you into the labyrinth of the mind is capable of leading you out and healing you . . .[147]

Nowhere in Hegel is found a more precise description of his own experience, which he speaks of here by implication. All that we know is the result of it: he had been through a nightly contraction of his being, suffered to the point of exhaustion, but had made his way through to security.

All the traits of the Hegelian personality that appeared in earlier years continued in force. Even in Berlin, as shown by the letter just cited, he went through periods marked by a certain discouragement. But now he had arrived at security, achieved authority, indeed, even power. In Berlin, Hegel not only held Germany's top chair in philosophy, but became, as Haym said, the philosophical dictator of Germany. He was now a much more important public figure; he was marveled at. But he was also subjected to attack.

One cannot speak in terms of any deep structural change in the Hegelian personality in Berlin, but his public image changed in keeping with his new situation. While he was filling out the basic outline of his system with *Inhalt und Gehalt* —content and intrinsic value—certainly feeling himself to be at the pinnacle of his philosophical grasp, the philosophy that made him what he was and which he propagated in his lectures now had to stand up to the test.

In line with the character of the system, involved here was not only its philosophical authenticity but its validity in actual fact. For Hegel's thought had always claimed to be universally relevant. He had created the dialectical method to comprehend the whole of things and the Absolute. The dialectic was not intended to be limited to the process of cognition and the world of the intellect. It was supposed to cover world history and the actuality of mankind as well. In this regard Hegel had never imposed any limitations on himself. His dialectical thinking, he believed, was omnipotent and yielded the truth regardless of application.

This was the claim made by Hegel, not to be measured or conditioned. He was as deeply suspected by some as he was marveled at by others. Hegel himself lived up to his presumptions by encyclopedically digesting and articulating the whole realm of knowledge. He had been in Berlin hardly two years before he wrote *Grundlinien der Philosophie des Rechts oder Naturrecht und Staatswissenschaft im Grundriss*, in English called "Outline of the Philosophy of Right or Natural Law and Political Science in Compendium." This was his last great work. After it he published hardly anything more in the Berlin years. Apart from smaller works, and new editions of works previously published, this course of lectures constituted his entire Berlin labors.

The *Philosophy of Right*, therefore, is the last work to show the whole Hegel. Before discussing it, let it be said that none of his other works was as sharply attacked as this one. Over and beyond this it brought Hegel significance in world history, for out of the debate surrounding the *Phenomenology* and, above all, the *Philosophy of Right* grew the thinking of Marx. In a certain sense the argument over the *Philosophy of Right* was one of the precursive factors of Marxism as expounded by Marx himself. This gave the book, in any case, a world historical status, the effect of which in all its scope and depth did not become visible until our times.

Before turning to this final Hegelian influence, one prefigured in the *Philosophy of Right* but not brought to fruition until after his death, let us describe the immediate consequences of his ten years in Berlin. The shining façade, the fame well-earned, have already been described, but the obverse side is all too easily lost sight of.

The complaint has often been raised that in Berlin Hegel became the faithful, the all *too* faithful, servant of the Prussian state, which by extension also means the ruthless defender of the spirit of the Restoration. Haym has leveled the accusation that the preface to the *Philosophy of Right* is nothing but "a scientifically formulated justification of the Karlsbad police system and the persecution of demagogues."[148] Hegel, in other words, became a philosopher who defended injustice and bondage.

Haym based this interpretation on the "conservatism, quietism, and optimism" of the Hegelian system, and here was merely repeating, apparently unaware, what Marx had already said in a much sharper way. Marx, to be sure, was an outsider with regard to the philosophy of the period. Haym, however, was not and plainly uttered an opinion shared by many others.

If we examine Hegel's attitude during the Berlin days, it will be seen, admittedly, that the inherent difficulty and ambiguity of Hegelian thought shows through the surface of glittering success. Yet it is not Hegel's own personal equivocation that comes to light, but the ambiguity of dialectical thinking as such. At some point Hegel himself may have realized this state of affairs, but he never openly admitted it. Rather he said often that the dialectic was the only true philosophical method.

If once again we subject Hegel's dialectical thinking to analysis, first of all the assumptions that go with it must be stated. The first of these postulates is that dialectical thinking is scientific. The second assumption does away with the hitherto existing concept of scientific truth as laid down in formal logic. The third assumption is the idea that truth is in the concept of the "whole," replacing the traditional belief in many isolated truths. It is not until the fourth assumption that the dialectic appears, to affirm, namely, that this truth of the whole is reached through concepts which glide and flow and are self-moved. Out of self-moving concepts arises the product of the dialectic. By means of the newly created instrumentality of the shifting concept, which goes from positive to negative and back in a steadily *ascending* line, the evolution of the Absolute is known and realized.

From this approach Hegel never swerved. The final criterion of his truth was always the whole. But what whole? For Hegel it was the historical whole, as evident to him in his time. It was the whole to which the spirit had arrived *up to the present*. He was already subscribing to this notion in Jena, when, at the close of the 1806 summer semester he said that the spirit had taken a leap forward beyond its hitherto existing form. Much later he repeated this same idea in another way when, at the end of the *Philosophy of World History*, he wrote: "Thus far has consciousness come." And went on to say: "Only *this* insight can reconcile Spirit with the history of the world and with actuality—viz., that what has happened and is happening every day would not have done so without God, but is in essence his very own work."[149]

Hegel's repeatedly acknowledged disposition to reconcile the "ideal with the real" produced his marvelous syntheses, so splendid to outward view. But this procedure can succeed only to the extent that the whole stands given, a priori, before one's eyes. For Hegel this whole is in fact present, as is the Absolute Spirit. Thus he succeeds in showing the whole despite, indeed on the basis of, the endless contradictions that he discovers.

It cannot be denied that Hegel made every effort to combine the spirit of synthesis and the compulsion to synthesize with the exigencies of scientific thought, with a readiness for criticism and critical thinking. But whether he really succeeded in doing this all the time remains questionable. There can be no doubt that one line of thinking was at odds with the other.

Nonetheless a basic assumption of dialectical thinking is that ultimately arriving at a synthesis is guaranteed. This kind of thinking to be sure acknowledges contradiction, regarding it as a vital and productive element, since contradiction introduces a next higher and richer stage.

Supportive of the mighty synthetic strength of dialectical thought is the method's deep ambiguity. This double meaning resides in the ambiguity of the dialectical concept of truth, which can view the particular at one time as positive, at another time as negative. However, this possibility of looking at anything two ways at any given time is of little help to the criterion of "the whole is the truth."

This was to come out most clearly in the Hegelian dialectical method as applied to historical events. Hegel himself adhered strictly to what was obviously a wise limitation of the use of the dialectic. He always applied the dialectic to history only last. He interpreted the present and the given on the basis of the past and of historical stages that had already run their course. He built up the whole out of its parts.

This is just the critical point. Is the whole as given at any point in time positive synthesis or negative contradiction? That which is given, is it a unity of everything and of all parts, or is it perhaps disunion and a falling apart? Strictly speaking, the dialectic provides no answer. Indeed it cannot, because the positive can just as well be reversed and become negative.

Hegel himself had to face up to this very question, in his own day and political situation. To be sure the dialectical method opened up an opportunity for him to use it in a sibylline way and thus avoid any real decision. But Hegel did not avail himself of this way out. That is, he did not shirk deciding whether things in his day were positive or negative, true or false, good or bad. Rather he took his stand on the belief that the period then reached was one of equilibrium, of a composition of conflicting forces.

Not even twenty years after Hegel's death, and with the same dialectic assurance that Hegel had made his earlier claim, Marx was to characterize the identical period as a time of disintegration and decline, and was to demonstrate that dialectical progression would lead to the destruction of the same state for which Hegel had provided a metaphysical justification.

When we come to deal later with the lectures on the *Philosophy of World History*, and especially with Hegel's *Philosophy of Right*, our concern will be to advance our exposition of Hegelian thought. Yet in dealing with these two Hegelian works from the Berlin period we are equally concerned with finding out how Hegel related his dialectical claim to universality to local political history.

For it is one thing to erect a theoretical system that is applicable in the realm of cognition, science, and the spirit, and another to build a theoretical system that, as Hegel intended, would also universally explain historical and political actualities. Even if Hegel himself, to be sure, did not raise any direct claim that the dialectic penetrated into politics, nonetheless the possibility of doing this, as Marx in fact later did, was based on the universality of Hegel's claim.

# 11

## The Philosophy of History

I n the winter of 1822–23 Hegel gave his lecture course on
the *Philosophy of History* for the first time, a series
he was to repeat four times. The form in which these
lectures were printed in Hegel's collected works seems in the
main to have been based on their final presentation during
the winter of 1830–31, one in which the whole lecture course
had certainly been compressed. A later and much more comprehensive edition arranged by Lasson and others, one which
required four volumes in contrast to one in the collected works,
contains a much broader spectrum of the powerful material
which Hegel gradually developed during the period of his
lecturing.

This lecture series at any rate certainly did not come into
being in one semester. To some degree we can trace its development. According to what we are told by the publisher of the
one-volume edition in the collected works, in the first winter
that Hegel gave the course he seems primarily to have worked

out his philosophical concept of history, which in the final, definitive work became an introductory section.

According to what Gans reports, in this first course Hegel spent a good two-thirds of the time on the presentation of China. Then, little by little, as he continued to work his way into world history and source material at his disposal, sections that at first had been executed in lengthy detail were shortened, while new ones were added.

Only gradually, then, did Hegel press on beyond the times where he made his start. Indeed, it was not until the last version of the lecture series that a more exact treatment of the Middle Ages and modern times made its appearance. And even in this last series it is still noteworthy that out of a volume of 560 pages only fifty are given over to modern times, that is, Hegel's modern times. Hegel did not adopt a perspective in which the present stood out in the foreground. Rather he pushed the present back in favor of the past.

Did Hegel, therefore, evolve the new out of the old, did he proceed in an unbroken historic train from the beginning to modernity? This view is only partly correct because he was not writing a world history totally devoid of prejudice or point of view. He brought along a systematic viewpoint and had his world history appear according to it. At the time of the first lecture course he wrote to Duboc: "It is also a very interesting and pleasurable business for me to have the peoples of the world pass in review. But I still don't really know how I'm going to make it through to our last Eastertide."[150]

This casually written sentence does not, however, express the fact that the real task is not "to have the peoples of the world pass in review," or that the serious background of an otherwise pleasant business is to impress order on world history and structure it dialectically. Yet this is what does happen, according to a principle developed in the introduction, and which, reduced to its simplest form, tells us: "World history is the advance of the consciousness of freedom."

The second publisher of these lectures, Hegel's own son, Karl, more than anyone noticed that during the five semesters that the course was given, Hegel tried various ways of mastering the material. This fact is mentioned in the preface Karl

Hegel wrote for this second edition. Apart from the amplifications and abbreviations already mentioned, Hegel adhered "so little to subdivisions once having made them" "that in every lecture he changed them, and, for example, once discussed Buddhism and Lamaism before India, another time after, now limited the Christian world more narrowly to the Germanic peoples, again brought in the Byzantine Empire, and more of the same."

He defended this procedure against "those who see rigorous thinking in a formal schematism," and he believed that "the security of the thought and the certainty of truth, like life itself, can be liberal in such things, and formal understanding, by taking offense at this, just shows that it has not grasped the philosophical idea and life in essence."[151]

We note that the strictness of the dialectical method indeed has a certain pliability. As already shown in the later editions of the *Encyclopaedia*, and now again in the *Philosophy of History*, it becomes evident that the dialectic permits a certain freedom of combination.

Trying to understand this, we have to keep in mind that the "whole" is the decisive factor in dialectical thinking and consequently the individual parts lend themselves to being combined. Dialectical thinking calls first for a correct understanding of the whole, out of which the ordering of particulars follows.

In all events this is the way Hegel operates in his *Philosophy of History*. The keynote to understanding the whole is formulated in the first big section: history is defined as the progress of the consciousness of freedom. One thinks of the young Hegel, who saw the French Revolution as an outbreak toward freedom, indeed, one also thinks of the Hegel of the *Phenomenology*, who recognized that absolute freedom lapses into terror. Now, however, the object of history is no longer progress toward freedom, but progress of freedom in the consciousness. But this is more precisely explained:

> The Orientals do not yet know that the spirit, or man as such, is implicitly free; they only know that One is free, but on this very account such freedom is only caprice, wild-

ness, dullness of passion, or a mildness and tameness of the
same, which is itself only an accident of nature, or a
caprice.—This One, therefore, is only a despot, not a free
man. The consciousness of freedom arose first among the
Greeks, and on that account they were free, but they, and
the Romans likewise, knew only that *some* are free, not
Man as such. Even Plato and Aristotle did not know this.
The Greeks, therefore, not only had slaves, and their life
and the basis of their fine freedom bound up with slavery,
but their freedom itself was in part only a fortuitous, transient and limited bloom, in part at the same time a rigorous enslavement of the human.—It was the German na-
tions which were first, under the influence of Christianity,
to attain the consciousness that man, as man, is free, that
freedom of the spirit constitutes his very nature: this consciousness arose first in religion, the inmost region of the
spirit; but to incorporate this principle into the worldly
nature, that was a broader task, which to solve and carry
out requires a long, difficult process of education. . . . The
thorough educating to, and permeating of the worldly condition by the same [principle] is the long process which
constitutes history itself.[152]

In no work of Hegel's can one see as well into the constructive action of dialectical thinking as in the *Philosophy of History*. The methodical structurization, the constructive lines,
the way the thing is worked out can be closely followed.
World history is viewed from the standpoint of being a way to
freedom. This way is a part of the Absolute Spirit's becoming
an Idea that knows itself, is conscious of itself. What was *an
sich*, or implicit, in consciousness, becomes *für sich*, or explicit, in history, though this actualization takes thousands of
years to accomplish.

In this initial statement the following three-step historical
progression is formed: Orientals, Greeks and Romans, and
Germans. Each epoch accomplished a part of the work of
history and advances consciousness by so much. This is the
basic division within which the dialectical process can be developed.

Yet this initial and entirely simple point of departure is intertwined with a series of other ideas. Hegel defines his philosophical historiography, based on the notion that reason rules the world, in contrast to other forms of history, as "original" and "reflective." Yet he knows and expressly says that nothing great can be accomplished in the world without passion. Thus he has to determine the relation between reason and passion. For this he finds a most peculiar solution. Absolute reason, he says, uses the passion of great individuals to accomplish its ends. He describes the great "world historical individuals" which the spirit of the age made use of "in the realization of its concept." They live by passion, nonetheless they serve the spirit:

> They never found calm enjoyment, their whole life was labor and trouble, their whole nature naught but their passion. The goal once reached, they degenerate, empty husks of the kernel. They die early like Alexander, they are murdered like Caesar, transported to St. Helena like Napoleon. This fearful consolation, that men of history have never been what one calls happy—this consolation can be drawn from history by those who stand in need of it.[153]

However, in this introduction and statement of fundamentals Hegel does more than examine the relationship between the individual and history. He looks closely into the material of history, the peoples of the world, the forms of their organization, their geographical conditions. Everywhere it becomes clear how profoundly Hegel understands things. Let us cite only one example. "The history of the world," he says, "is the interpretation of spirit in *time*,"[154] and thus, we might add, its interpretation in the various materials of history. As the individual spirit is ultimately the servant of the Absolute Spirit, likewise the spirit of whole peoples. Each of these partial spirits of the Absolute Spirit has its place, temporally and systematically, in world history. Each appears when it is necessary, and vanishes when the necessity for its appearance has been fulfilled.

Hegel examines the historical process all over the planet, and considers the geographic forms on which evolution is based: the arid highland, the valley plains, the shorelands. He divides up the world according to the advantage of this one or that—Africa, Asia, and Europe. He sets America apart as "the land of the future, where, in the ages that lie before us, the significance of world history will be revealed," and defines it as a land "of longing for all those who are bored with the historic arsenal that is Europe."[155]

The book's groundwork, first and foremost, is a presentation of the stage and the figures, together with the props, the scenic material, used in the theater of world history. Not until later do we come to the presentation of the drama of world history itself, as Hegel saw its unfolding. And, as one gets deeper into the main body of the work, at every hand one recognizes Hegel's clear and farsighted gaze, already evident from the introduction.

One stands lost in admiration before this grandiose and all-inclusive conception of world history, a scheme in which everything has its place. The advantages of dialectical thought become ever more impressive. It is able to grasp every unity and every disparateness as well, the endless multiplicity of events as well as the grand thrust of the whole. The dialectic of history itself is only a part of the great dialectic in which "the Idea progresses to infinite antithesis."

The more familiar one becomes with this or with other works of Hegel such as the *Philosophy of Fine Art*, the more one is inclined to acknowledge the methodological qualifications of dialectical thinking. The procedure seems virtually made, on principle, to comprehend any infinitely diverse multiplicity that fluctuates back and forth. One witnesses how the particular gets its meaning in terms of the whole; the triadic structure, apparently so schematic, loses its formalistic character. One becomes sensible of the fact that the dialectical method is an instrument which, in expert hands, can impress order on what at first sight seems to be chaos.

But alongside these advantages the dark side of this kind of thinking stands out quite clearly. No other method offers such great possibility of arbitrarily defining appearance. No other method is so greatly fraught with the danger of falsifying knowledge through prejudice. And no other method can be so deceptive about simulating the necessity of a relationship where none exists.

Once his *Philosophy of History* is subjected to critical examination, these shortcomings show up in Hegel, too. Once the basic claim has been made that world history is nothing more than the advance of the consciousness of freedom, everything has been predetermined. The goal of history is already anticipated, and whether correctly or incorrectly remains to be seen. Not only the goal, but the way leading to it is predetermined, and using this method it is only too easy to prove that everything had to turn out the way it did.

The great advantage of dialectical thought lies in its power to think synthetically on the one hand, analytically on the other.

Used this way, the dialectical method basically provides only methodological directions, for example, keeping a close eye on all contradictory phenomena, always having the whole in mind and with the most painstaking care watching for all changes, however insignificant.

The great heuristic value of the dialectical method, therefore, lies as much in the scope of its purview and ability to grasp complex circumstances as in the possibility it provides of bringing the most diversified phenomena under a unified point of view. This Hegel demonstrates again and again. Whether he undertakes to represent esthetics, world history or religious history, or simply an encyclopedia of the *summa* of knowledge, he always manages to view the material, however vast, as a whole, and to articulate it and bring out its relationships.

But with these undeniable advantages the dialectic has disadvantages as well. The synthetic application of this kind of thinking can all too easily suddenly shift into syncretism. The necessity of proceeding in terms of a "whole" can easily lead to arbitrary definitions of this whole. It follows in turn that the parts of the whole can be falsely assessed, whereupon the pattern of relationships becomes skewed.

When this happens the constructive and clarifying ability of dialectical thought goes sour, the whole as a whole and in all its parts is falsified, and what should be a discerning act of recognition becomes mere scenography, as arbitrary as it is badly drawn.

All these defects can be found in Hegel, too, and for them he was censured in no uncertain terms after his death. Posthumously Hegel was subjected to destructive critical pronouncements, some of which may be cited. Haym confirmed that Hegel had taken "empiricism and forced it together and knocked it into shape without hesitation or scruple in order to serve his idea." Kierkegaard maliciously compared the dialectical process with a cow's stomach that digests everything three times, and recommended that future masters of philosophy ruminate in four rather than three stages.

Arbitrariness as a weakness of dialectical thinking can also be found in Hegel's *Philosophy of History*. If history represents the advance of freedom in consciousness, it remains to be demonstrated how this omnipotent and absolutely progressive consciousness is translated into actuality. Hegel made this easy by speaking in terms of the "cunning of reason," which utilizes the workings of passion for its own ends with a slyness that is actually human rather than ideal in nature. By this means the extremely complicated process of the influence of thought on actuality, as well as the relationship between theory and practice, is greatly oversimplified. And since for Hegel the primacy of the Absolute Idea is taken for granted, it is easy for him to regard world history as the "true theodicy,* the vindication of God in history."

Thus out of the Hegelian definition of historical evolution, in itself debatable, arises a whole bouquet of metaphysical assumptions, and of consequences as well, which can be contested. Marx was to mount his critique of Hegel on this basis, and reproach him with having made the thinking process into a "demiurge of the real," and of having failed to recognize the effect of material conditions.

Hegel's *Philosophy of History* illustrated the uncertainty of dialectical thinking in another way, that is, in its handling of that phase of history in which Hegel himself lived. First of all,

---

* *Theodicee*, or "theodicy" in English, is a word coined by Leibniz, meaning the vindication of the justice of God in permitting or promulgating natural or moral evil.—*Tr.*

Hegel is inordinately brief in his discussion of his own times. The modernity of Hegel's lifetime—the period of the French Revolution and of Napoleon and the post-Napoleonic years— is dealt with in the last ten pages of the book, which is most surprising in view of the gigantic amount of material at hand.

Now a remarkable juxtaposition appears. As already noted, Hegel talks with undisguised enthusiasm about the French Revolution, as far as the idea behind it goes, describing it as a "splendid sunrise." He glorifies it as a resurrection of the spirit of freedom. In it he sees the revalidation of "the principle of the freedom of the will" and praises the rebirth of the "concept of justice."

But to this he links a discussion of the French Revolution as it actually happened. He examines the career of Robespierre, and describes the course of events already treated in the *Phenomenology*. Robespierre, "a man for whom virtue was a serious matter," established the rule of "virtue and terror."[156] The dialectical process of development continues to run its course. The regime identified with Robespierre had to fall because of the need for an absolute governing power, which Napoleon provided in the form of military force.

"With the vast might of his character," so Hegel describes Napoleon, "he then turned his attention to foreign relations, subjected all Europe and diffused his liberal institutions in every quarter." He had conquered, "but never was the powerlessness of victory exhibited in a clearer light than then." Now Napoleon had to go under: "The disposition of the peoples, i.e., their religious disposition and that of their nationality, brought about this colossus, and in France constitutional monarchy, with the *Charte* as its basis, was restored."[157] Now Hegel enters into a discussion of his own immediate present. He describes the situation on the Continent in France, Austria, Germany, and England, while Spain and Italy also come in for a brief mention. In this description Germany comes off best. The laws concerning human rights, though to be sure they arose through the French oppressors, come in for praise. Rights and religion have been reconciled through Protestantism, and the Prussian bureaucracy and state are lavishly lauded.

Other countries, however, get a scolding. French liberalism is very sharply criticized by Hegel. He predicts that agitation and unrest are going to continue there. Austria is viewed, on the whole, as a backward country. Government has less to do in England than anywhere else, Hegel claims, and says that this is what the Englishmen think freedom consists of. Nonetheless in point of "the freedom to possess property," England is marked by "an incredible backwardness," because the great estates there are majorats, that is, entailed and inherited according to the right of primogeniture.[158]

In the course of this exposition it becomes quite clear that Hegel actually believed that the conditions of German life were the most advanced. This is certainly a curious way of looking at things since many have felt that the Prussia of that period was in fact a police state that thoroughly suppressed personal freedom. And Hegel became nearly, or altogether, a defender of the Prussian state when he made the statement that in other countries only a "formal freedom" obtains, and turned against liberalism, saying it had "gone bankrupt on all sides, first the great firm in France, then its branches in Spain and Italy; twice, in fact, in the states where it had been introduced."[159]

Now with this unabashed accolade it cannot be denied that Hegel is a servant, a pawn of the Prussian state. He felt fine about the way things were; in Prussia he had found fame and peace. It was this reaction and none other that gave rise to the suspicion so often voiced about Hegel. Hegel, it was suspected, betrayed the basic principles of his thought. The philosopher of world history as the progress of freedom in consciousness ended up as the champion of bondage and reaction. The Hegelian system became, simply because Hegel had a full professorship at Berlin, the philosophical "dwelling place of the spirit of Prussian reaction."

This accusation was in fact most strongly supported by the *Philosophy of Right*, to be discussed in the next chapter. Yet it also hits home in the *History of Philosophy* as well. For it is certainly strange that the thinker who had made consciousness of freedom the measuring-stick of history, should, at the end of his *History of Philosophy* visit his strongest criticism on just those states that had striven most to extend freedom in all areas of life. The great program of liberalism, as it had taken shape in political science, economics, and sociology, was based on the belief that free unfolding of the inherent tendencies and strengths of the individual guaranteed continuous progress in civilization, culture, justice, and the economic and social order.

Yet remarkably enough it was precisely this liberalism which Hegel condemned, which he claimed was everywhere bankrupt in all directions. Hegel said this, moreover, in a period that was quite different from our own.

Perhaps he had a presentiment of our modern experience, that a boundless liberalism can in fact pose a danger? Or, what is probably closer to the truth, was his experience of the French Revolution and its quick deterioration into the Terror still haunting him?

We cannot really give a final answer to this question. But one thing remains strange and incontestable. For some reason Hegel suddenly began to mistrust the further advance of freedom of consciousness. As Haym put it, he even conceded there was a sort of "elective" between his system and the Prussian state. Like it or no, he fell into the ranks of the reactionary movement.

The young Hegel who had enthusiastically believed in the power of free and independent ideas became a man who publicly warned against too much freedom. More than that, it would appear that the old Hegel had done an about face, that the youthful revolutionary in his old age had grown into a fullblown reactionary.

What really happened? Did Hegel, as some suppose, actually change his beliefs for opportunistic reasons? Did he subscribe to the principle of *Wes Brot ich ess, des Lied ich sing*— whose bread I eat, his song I sing? Or did he see more deeply than most of his contemporaries into emergent reality? Or were there yet other reasons that led him to take this new stance?

Whatever the truth of it, Hegel in any event now appeared in an ambiguous light. This ambiguity is not confined to the fact that he became, or so his critics accused him, an apologist of a freedom-limiting state against all his own principles. It goes much deeper than this; he became equivocal in a quite different sense.

For no philosophy more than Hegel's ever expounded the principle that spirit, and with it everything human, is in constant movement. Repeatedly he had said that his times were a period of transition, repeatedly he had prophesied that the world as hitherto existing would collapse like an image in a dream.

But it now evolved that the aging Hegel in fact wanted to disavow this notion and that instead he inclined to the hope that history had entered into a more peaceful stage. That he at least wished this to be the case is expressed almost pathetically at the end of the *Philosophy of History* in these words: "At last, after forty years of war and indescribable confusion, a weary heart might fain rejoice in seeing an end to, and the pacification of, all these disturbances."[160]

What Hegel wanted, then, was peace and quiet. He had been a man who with great acuity apprehended and understood the fact that history is forever in a state of flux, and beyond that in his own personal lifetime had lived through a period of intense historic activity. He, personally, was weary of commotion and change, and believed it would be a fine thing if history and the spirit of the age could move into a more tranquil phase.

It was at this point that Hegel's self-deception began. History did not in fact subside into motionlessness at all, as our own twentieth century was to demonstrate with a vengeance. Hegel's proposition that the spirit of the age declared itself as an advancing process remains in force, for how long yet we do not know, and—to use Hegel's own terminology—carries along with it the Hegelian negativities and processes of "self-sublimation."

The special instrument Hegel had expressly contrived to grasp history's movement, and beyond that the movement of thought itself, was as much at Hegel's disposal as it ever had been. He had always taught the objectivity of this instrument, always defended it and undertaken to prove it in ever new areas. So it was only natural that just once he should, as it were, give it the supreme test in applying it to the present. He did this in part, as we have shown, in the *History of Philosophy*. But it had already occurred a first time in a work that had come out earlier in 1821, the much-cited *Philosophy of Right*.

This *Philosophy of Right* is both famous and infamous, and with a certain justification. If one had to characterize it before really getting to know its content, one would have to say it demonstrates both the splendor and the shortcomings of the dialectical method. The splendor of it again lies in the method's ability to give an all-encompassing presentation, the weakness in the fact that the defects of the procedure for which Hegel was censured here stand out in bold relief.

So much by way of anticipation. Only an analysis of the *Philosophy of Right* can clarify what has just been said.

# 12

## The Philosophy of Right and Its Fate

Hegel's *Philosophy of Right and of the State* ranks in importance with the *Phenomenology* and the *Logic*. It was his last great work, appearing two years after he had taken over his professorial post. In it, one can say, the nature of the finished, completed Hegel stands revealed.

In style and structure it was all of a piece with works previously published. In many places the way language is used brings to mind the *Phenomenology*. As in this earlier work, images of the highest intuitive power occasionally break through. But in the construction of the book, the second principle of Hegelian thought as developed over many years is completely dominant.

That is, the *Philosophy of Right* has the same strictly formal structure as the *Logic*. It was intended to be used as a compendium for the lectures, and hence is divided into numbered paragraphs, like the *Encyclopaedia*. The broad descriptive strokes which appear most strikingly in the *Phenomenology* are here less prominent, and the definitional and apodictic character of the individual propositions is underscored by the paragraph form.

In structure the whole has become smoother and more manageable, although here, too, from time to time Hegel writes mammoth sentences, interrupted by many dependent clauses, which are extremely difficult to follow. Here, too, Hegel consistently uses his triadic method of organization. The book as a whole is divided into three parts: "Abstract Right," "Morality," and "Ethical Life."

At the beginning of the preface Hegel explains that the work is "an enlarged, and especially a more systematic, exposition of the same fundamental concepts which in relation to this part of philosophy are already in a book of mine designed previously for my lectures, *The Encyclopaedia of Philosophic Sciences.*"

According to this statement the *Philosophy of Right* must be a sequential, linear extension, as well as a detailed elaboration, of a section of the *Encyclopaedia*. And this is actually the case, to the extent that it has the same tripartite division into right, morality, and ethical life which served as the ground plan of the *Heidelberg Encyclopaedia*. However, material which in the *Encyclopaedia* is compressed into twenty pages cannot actually be compared to the detailed presentation in the *Philosophy of Right and the State*. Under the guise of a formally similar schema, much has in fact been changed. Thus, while in the *Encyclopaedia* the whole chapter comparable to the book is titled "The Objective Spirit," now an apparently narrower designation has been chosen, *Philosophy of Right and of the State*.

But more than the title has been altered. One has only to leaf through the book to realize how greatly the subject has been enriched in point of content by its expansion from the *Philosophy of Right* into a book of some 300 pages. Many new sections and chapters have been introduced. Whereas in the *Encyclopaedia* the third basic section, "The Ethical Life," is divided into three subsections— 1) "The Individual Folk," 2) "International Law" and 3) "General World History"—in the

*Philosophy of Right* a new kind of partition is used. Now we have: 1) "The Family," 2) "Civil Society" and 3) "The State." In this example we already see how the theme of the book has been extended relative to the basic plan of the *Encyclopaedia*. The same goes for remaining sections. To be sure, the basic conceptual-dialectical approach has been retained and taken over apparently unaltered. But the addition of new subjects and themes, as well as the enrichment with concrete material, indicates that the *Philosophy of Right* is something more than a mere amplification of the original dialectical concept.

Indeed, closer study of the work does reveal another and different Hegel. The ingeniously speculative thinker who, during the years since Jena, had developed his system in an orderly, schematic progression using the dialectical instrument he, himself, had discovered, has to be sure lost none of his speculative vigor. But now he incorporates empirical fact and personal experience into the speculative process and because he does so, the more the ordering power of his thinking stands out in contrast to the empirical facts and the more Hegel begins to clash with actuality.

It was most clearly to be the fate of the *Philosophy of Right* to make public contact with the actuality, indeed the political actuality, of the period. This contact was especially emphasized by the preface, in which Hegel unmistakably and in clear language took a philosophical position on the political situation in his times.

The dialectical method is designed to be a constructive procedure showing the inherent unity of spirit in the course of its development. In a certain sense Hegel is always describing the dialectic of the spirit: in the *Phenomenology* he does it on the basis of the evolution of consciousness and self-consciousness, and in the *Logic* on the basis of the evolution of the world of concepts. Now, in the *Philosophy of Right*, he describes the dialectic of the human spirit in the light of social reality.

For Hegel this was a truly new theme indeed. In the *Phenomenology*, of course, there were many passages that had a close relationship to the social actualities of mankind, for example, the disquisitions on "Wealth" or on "Labor," and, in a broader sense, the dialectic of "Master and Servant." But now, in the section on "Civil Society," the theme of economic production is subjected to a detailed and fundamental analysis. Moreover, a basic train of thought devoted to human needs is found in the *Philosophy of Right*.

Much more innovation could be mentioned. All in all, as must be more precisely demonstrated, when this book is compared with Hegel's earlier writings it becomes perfectly clear how greatly the range of Hegelian thinking has been extended. There are indications in the *Philosophy of Right* that Hegel is simply developing a kind of philosophical anthropology, the first intimations of which once again are to be found in the *Phenomenology*.

By and large it can be said that the *Philosophy of Right*, as a final work, reveals the mature and inwardly realized Hegel, and it has to be emphasized that throughout the presentation he both hews to the line of the system and uses the dialectical method.

However, closer inspection reveals that the *Philosophy of Right* is not, in fact, a unified work covering the whole spectrum of Hegelian thought, while at the same time it introduces certain corrections of an earlier posture. These corrections are hardly perceptible. They are concealed insofar as Hegel, as ever, remains true to his system and dialectical method. Indeed, they come clearly to light only when the young and the old Hegel are analytically compared, whereupon the recognition dawns that in many ways the Berlin Hegel has surrendered.

There is still one more matter to discuss before turning to the work itself, a circumstance that clings to the whole book and which cannot be seen apart from it. This book had a highly diverse influence, illustrating the old saying that all books have their own fate. This influence attaches first to the preface, which has been taken as a political avowal of the Prussian state, and it cannot be denied that Hegel does make such a commitment. If the blame visited on him for making this commitment holds up, then the whole work will all the more forcibly tend to prove Haym's contention that in it "He-

gelian philosophy established itself as the philosophy of the
[Prussian] restoration."

But it may be doubted that Hegel deserved this rebuke to
the extent, and in the way, it was intended. There is also no
denying, however, that the preface in particular, with its
famous-infamous proposition to the effect that "What is real is
rational," did in fact redound to Hegel's advantage.

However, if one seizes on this proposition and proceeds to
measure Hegel's *Philosophy of Right* by it, one may overlook
how much the same proposition derives from other considerations besides the consistency of Hegelian thought. In such case
there is a failure to understand the new perspectives opened
up by the *Philosophy of Right* whose deeper import has not
been recognized. It has not, for instance, been realized or generally appreciated that Hegel developed the ground for his
theory of the state in the section on civil society. It is extremely odd that in the literature on Hegel no one has ever
remarked how, in this section, Hegel subjects civil society to
criticisms exceeded in sharpness only by those of Marx. Why
the Hegelian critique of civil society has gone unremarked,
either by the philosophers or the Marxists, remains an insolu-
ble mystery.

There is still more to this enigma. Anyone who reads Hegel's exposition of civil society today, and who knows even a
modest amount about these theses later advanced by Marx,
cannot get around the fact that all the basic elements of Marxian thought are contained in this section of the *Philosophy of
Right*. No assumption could be more natural than that Marx
based his initial points of attack, far more than he ever admitted, on the *Philosophy of Right* lectures.

Now, as we know, Marx was not only acquainted with the
*Philosophy of Right*, but had read it with minute care. Among
Marx's youthful writings there is a critique of the Hegelian
philosophy of the state, as expounded in the *Philosophy of
Right* beginning with paragraph 261 and ending with paragraph 313.[161] This manuscript unequivocally establishes the
fact that Marx had to have read the third section of the *Philosophy of Right*, the part essentially concerned with the philosophy of the state.

But meanwhile nowhere in Marx's work can be found any statement permitting one to conclude with certainty that Marx also knew the preceding paragraphs 142–256. It is precisely these paragraphs which deal with the family and civil society, and in this segment there are some sentences which again show how the Marxian ideology had been anticipated.

One would only be too glad to say that the Hegelian critique of civil society found at least one congenial reader, namely, Marx. That such was the case is apparently established by the fact that, strictly speaking, all Marx did was to amplify on theses developed in principle by Hegel, while giving them a historical materialistic inflection. Even more noteworthy is the fact, again, that Marx called on Hegel many times to bear him witness, but without uttering a single word about the Hegelian critique of civil society.

Thus in the manuscript on "Political Economy and Philosophy," for instance, he asserted that Hegel had taken the "standpoint of modern political economy" and had seen labor as "the essence, the self-authenticating essence of mankind." But when he did this he called on the *Phenomenology*, not on the *Philosophy of Right*, to bear him out.

Until new sources come to light it simply cannot be decided whether Marx had or had not read this part of the *Philosophy of Right*. Until then it will remain a mystery whether Marx, as proposed above, took his basic theorems from the *Philosophy of Right*, or developed them independently from the intrinsic consistency of his own thinking. It is also conceivable that Marx had indeed read this part of the *Philosophy of Right*, and then forgot it, and in working out his *Capital* assimilated it without actually being aware of what he was doing. But all such assumptions remain conjecture.

Thus we are confronted by a most remarkable and, in its way, unique state of affairs so far as the influence of the *Philosophy of Right* is concerned. The criticism visited on the work, however justified it may be, ultimately overlooks the real core of Hegelian thought. The projection by Marx of the basic tenets of the *Philosophy of Right* has never been acknowledged. And, finally, it must be clearly said that neither Hegel's contemporaries nor the later compilers and inter-

preters of the *Philosophy of Right* took cognizance of the basic
theory of the work, hidden to be sure, but still demonstrable,
to the extent that it is anthropological and sociological.

In other words, however great the influence of the *Philosophy of Right and the State*, it is greatly based on misunderstandings. In a certain sense all authors have let themselves be
deceived, because they proceeded on the fair assumption that
Hegel wrote the work for self-serving reasons and in defense
of the Prussian state. The only one who really grasped, or
could grasp, the magnitude of this work—Marx—was likewise
caught up in polemic, and used only those parts of Hegel on
which he could base his critique.

This claim is indeed so decisive that it must be proved in
detail, as we shall now attempt to do. It must also be agreed
in advance that this peculiar and unique misunderstanding of
a famous work was not *entirely* adventitious. It was ultimately
rooted in the fact that a work whose structure is so full and so
tightly integrated has *several* aspects, and for that reason
many meanings.

This survey of the whole of the *Philosophy of Right*, as we
have developed it, provides us with guidelines for the interpretation of particulars. We shall discuss in succession the
preface, the systematic structure, and finally the contents of
the book. This division is necessary if this many-leveled work
is to be understood with perfect clarity.

To prove our claim, let us begin with an analysis of the
preface. It is that part of the whole work which was justifiably
interpreted from a certain point of view and which above all
seems to show that Hegel's chief concern in his *Philosophy of
Right* was to legitimize the Prussian state.

As soon as Hegel took over his Berlin teaching post he
became generous in his praise of Prussia. He opened his lectures in Berlin with a short address to the students. In this
address, among other things, he expressed these sentiments:

> And it is this state especially, of which I, myself, have
> been made a part, that has raised itself up by virtue of
> intellectual superiority to its present importance in the

world of reality and politics, placed itself on equal footing in power and sovereignty with states superior to it in material resources. Here the cultivation and the efflorescence of the sciences is one of the most essential elements of the state itself.[162]

When the *Philosophy of Right* appeared, Hegel sent it to the lord chancellor, Prince von Hardenburg, with a note in which he said that the "scientific endeavor" of the book was to demonstrate the basic principles "which the nature of the state in general needs," and then goes on to say that a "concurrence" will be shown with "that which under his [His Majesty, the King's] enlightened regime and under the guidance of Your Serene Highness, the Prussian state, to which therefore it must give me special satisfaction to belong, has had the good fortune in part to obtain, in part still to obtain."[163]

Even if such phrases are taken simply as marks of respect, the preface of the book shows that in fact Hegel had more in mind than mere courtesy. Three themes stand out in this preface. The first is Hegel's critical rejection of those who stand opposed "in hostility to that which is publicly acknowledged." The second is Hegel's defense of his thesis of the actuality of the rational. The third has to do with the relationship between theory and practice.

If the argument of the preface is followed in detail, it will be found, first of all, to turn against philosophies which, in the "shallowness of their thinking," promulgate allegedly new theories about the state. Named as the "ringleader of these hosts of superficiality" is Jakob Fries, who is accused of producing a "broth of heart, friendship, and inspiration" instead of a scientific conception of the state.[164]

This line of argument gives Hegel an excuse to discuss the relationship between reason, science (in the sense of philosophical science) and actuality. He calls for a recognition of the "actual," just as the natural sciences have to be based on the actual. He claims—obviously referring to his own philosophy—that this recognition has been "placed in closer touch with actuality," and in pursuing this thought arrives almost abruptly at a proposition which he emphasizes in italics in the text: "What is rational is actual, and what is actual is rational."[165]

Now, it can of course be said that the first part of this proposition is not a new statement at all, but in fact an old and often iterated Hegelian idea. But the obverse side of the proposition, the second part saying the actual is rational, goes one step further than before. In this connection particularly the proposition can be taken as meaning that the existing (Prussian) state in its actuality corresponds with the rational.

If any doubt were still possible about this interpretation, further statements in the preface would dispel it. Hegel now talks about the relation between theoretical knowledge and practice. He inveighs fervently against people who would instruct the state how it should be. Again he says: "To understand what is, that is philosophy's task." He rejects it as absurd "to imagine that a philosophy can transcend its contemporary world." And then goes on to say: "If his (a philosopher's) theory does in fact go beyond it (the contemporary world), if a world is built *as it ought to be*, then to be sure it exists, but only in his imagining—in a soft element allowing anything to be incorporated into it at will."[166]

A change in Hegel becomes apparent in these passages, one going so far that the Berlin Hegel disavows things the younger Hegel once said. Had not the youthful Hegel written to Schelling that with the spread of theories as to how everything should be, established people who took everything for granted would be jolted out of their lethargy? And had not Hegel, much later, written to Niethammer that theoretical labor gets more done than practical, and that once the realm of ideas is revolutionized, actuality can no longer resist?

All this, the belief that theory is the battering ram with which actuality can be moved, seems to have been forgotten. Now Hegel has the opposite idea, that theory must justify existing actuality. And in the concluding words of the preface he once again endorses the same notion. He says that philosophy always arrives on the scene too late to "instruct the world how it should be." Philosophy expresses as idea that which is already actual. It is not until actuality has matured that the idea appears and builds its "intellectual realm." These reflections and the preface conclude with the following famous passage: "When philosophy paints its gray on gray, then has a form of life grown old, and with gray on gray cannot be rejuvenated, but only understood; the owl of Minerva spreads its wings only with the fall of dusk."[167]

These are resigned, almost melancholy words when one reflects that the young Hegel had started out believing that the theory of and the consciousness of how things ought to be would revolutionize actuality. Now this belief has gone. Hegel has capitulated to actuality. Theory does not light the way for actuality, but limps after it.

Hegel's renunciation of one of his earlier beliefs is here plain enough to see, now speaking as negatively about what "ought to be" as the young Hegel had affirmatively. The only question is, what were the real grounds for such renunciation and resignation? Was it merely Hegel's growing old, or the wisdom of the aging Hegel, that led to renunciation? Or was it that Hegel was defending the state that had called him to a university professorship?

All of these and similar answers seem to us all too simple and easy to come by. If Hegel now claimed that philosophy could only understand, but not teach, actuality, he was doing no more than acknowledging the consequences of his dialectical thinking. This dialectic had been created to show that something must necessarily arise and be, and also to demonstrate that something must also pass away and lose its actuality.

Hegel's dialectic can look at any actuality two ways. It can demonstrate why something must of necessity arise and be as it is, and can also recognize that this same actuality must yield to a new and different one and thus perish. This is the lawfulness of a method which proceeds on the basis that the "negative is just as positive."

While Hegel was undertaking to raise this principle of a double purview to the status of a primary law of thought and of "scientific" philosophy, he had always believed he was correctly understanding the truth of the whole. Now he was caught in the ambiguity of his own procedure. When he came to live in a state whose principles he affirmed, and when he

wrote a philosophy of the state that justified both this particular state and the state in general, he had to deny the second
consequence of his dialectic. Now he could no longer say that
this state, too, had to pass away, no longer use the words from
the Acts of the Apostles* he had so often used: "Behold, the
feet of them which have buried thy husband are at the door,
and shall carry thee out."

Naturally Hegel could have applied the dialectical principle
with full force to his state, too, and as a result on the one hand
have shown the necessity, on the other the transience, of this
state. He would then have given full rein to the equivocality
of the dialectical way of seeing things, but also would have
had to write an implicitly ambiguous work.

This he did not do, and it is conceivable that having found a
good living in a place where he was somebody, he espoused
the state where he felt at home. Trying to make the dialectical
method unambiguous and to evade the fact that the positive is
always negative, too, he had to suffer the consequences—
namely that his own attitude became equivocal.

His later critics, Kierkegaard and Marx, were to recognize
this clearly. Each in his own way pointed out and proved this
ambiguity. Kierkegaard was to make a laughingstock of "absolute knowledge" as inaccessible, and Marx to regard Hegel
himself as a "self-estranged spirit."

But the ambiguity in which Hegel became trapped, and
which he first brought to light as the disavowal of his earlier
belief, is shot through the whole work. For this work, which
proves in unbroken line the necessity of the state as the actualization of the ethical, is dialectically structured. It follows
the dialectical law. The state is defined as the positive form of
the ethical, in which the "negative" of civil society has become
positive.

In the apportionment of importance and in the ordering of
the dialectical sequence, civil society is made the negative
moment or factor. Hegel describes civil society as negatively
as he does the state positively. With this the ambiguity of
dialectical thinking has been elevated to a monumental grandeur.

* From the King James Version. The rendering in the German Bible used
by Hegel is somewhat different.—Tr.

# 13

## The Dialectical Structure of the Philosophy of Right

As already noted, Hegel's *Philosophy of Right and the State* is divided into three main parts: "Abstract Right," "Morality," and "Ethical Life." This basic construction follows the dialectical principle. In first place appears abstract right, which really means natural right as the lowest stage of the objective spirit. After this comes a second stage which Hegel calls morality. A third state arises out of the synthesis of the first two. It bears the name of *Sittlichkeit*, a term which can be only imperfectly translated, but which here will be called the ethical life or ethics.

At first glance this structure seems to be highly arbitrary. For the first part of the book deals with the principles of right, of natural right, or, as Hegel puts it, of abstract right. The second part has to do with the basic problems of ethics, relating to good and evil, guilt and conscience. The third part, finally, has to do with a quite different field. It deals with themes that today we would call "sociological." It looks into the nature of the family, of civil society, and of the state.

Thus the *Philosophy of Right and of the State* combines three jurisdictions which at times can be quite differently treated. However, for Hegel these three themes belong together.

In the *Heidelberg Encyclopaedia* these three parts had been brought together under the heading of "The Objective Spirit." For Hegel, therefore, the facts of right, ethics, and society are objectifications of spirit. This makes sense, since the problems of right, as well as ethical and social problems, can all be treated from this inclusive point of view.

The basic idea which led Hegel to combine these three domains in the *Encyclopaedia* derived from the consideration that the subjective spirit in right, morality, and ethics is dialectically sublimated into universal and objective spirit. This basic construction was to remain intact in the *Philosophy of Right and of the State*.

All this is explained in the introduction. "In keeping with the stages in the development of the idea of the absolutely free will, the will," says Hegel, "is first to be understood as 'immediate,' second as 'reflected in itself' and third as 'the unity and truth of both these abstract moments.' "[168] In the first step he embodies the idea of an immediate and "abstract right," in the second the dimension of moral events, set off from and overriding right, and in the third the unity of right and morality, that is, *Sittlichkeit*, or the ethical life.

However, when Hegel set about accommodating the concrete world of phenomena to this schema, each of the foregoing stages had to be concretized. This resulted in the expansions of the text earlier mentioned. Each domain was freshly thought through. This involved an amplification of the three basic parts, and with quite different results. Whereas the two sections covering abstract right and morality ran to barely a hundred pages, the third section grew to about 150.

The relative importance assigned the different parts of the subject matter shows in itself that Hegel's real interest lay not so much in abstract right and morality as in the part which he titled *Die Sittlichkeit*, or the "ethical life," as nearly as it can be translated into English. Here again Hegel was not concerned with an abstract and theoretical handling of the problems of *Sittlichkeit*. In this part the usually abstract and speculative Hegel became to an astonishing degree a thinker who described and analyzed actuality.

The first two parts, compared with the third, often seem downright skimpy. The third part not only shows greater descriptive power and intensity of thought, but beyond this the first two parts, by comparison, have the character of being merely preparatory for the third. They seem to have been run through quickly to get to the really important part.

The constructive line followed by Hegel in building up the whole had already been prefigured in the *Heidelberg Encyclopaedia*. Right and the state, morality and ethics, as stages of the objective spirit, are actualizations of the idea of freedom.

This is not an entirely simple idea to accept. Are not right and the state, morality and the ethical life, as a matter of fact, limitations of freedom defined as voluntary, optional behavior? What is freedom, anyway? Hegel ran into the old problem of the two conceptions of freedom. Freedom can be understood as subjective arbitrariness, in Hegel's language as arbitrariness spontaneously vented—*als sich selbst auslassende Willkür*—but also as free *self*-limitation curbing the arbitrariness of action.

Hegel's philosophy has occasionally been construed as a philosophy of freedom, but any attempt to stick a single label on Hegel's thought is false. Hegel's philosophy can no more be understood as exclusively concerned with freedom, than exclusively as a "panlogism," an "ontology" or a "metaphysical theology."

However, characterizing Hegelian thought as a philosophy of freedom is a correct insight to the extent that the nature of freedom did indeed have a central interest for Hegel. Otherwise he would not have been able to give central importance in the *History of Philosophy* to the idea of world history as a development of the consciousness of freedom.

The real groundwork for this notion is laid in the *Philosophy of Right*. This is shown by statements in the introduction, that is, at the very beginning of the *Philosophy of Right*. Here Hegel meditates on the nature, the essence, of right. He lays down these claims: "In general the basis of right is the *spiritual* . . ." He finds the will to be its "particular seat and origin," which will is "free, so that freedom is both its substance and its determination, while the system of right is the realm of freedom made actual, the world of spirit brought forth out of itself like a second nature."[169]

This definition is followed by a series of deliberations and reflections the importance of which, as one reads along, can be only too easily overlooked since they are so terse and abstract. However, they contain decisive leading ideas, ideas that determine the structure of the *Philosophy of Right*. That is, Hegel distinguishes between "will" and "arbitrariness," or, more accurately stated, defines two basic forms of will. For him will in its initial form as "immediate" will is arbitrariness. As such it is dependent on "impulses, desires and inclinations." These determine will in its natural state.

Will as arbitrary to be sure is free, but "still not in the form of rationality." It is "finite" will and is not yet rational because as yet "indeterminate," which in Hegel's language means it has no spiritual goal. This "indeterminacy of the will" in its natural state, according to Hegel, is "the primordial seed of all determinate existence." It "contains determinations and goals in itself and only brings them forth out of itself."

Hegel now ingeniously finds the dialectical transition to the second form of will. This second form of will *beschliesst*, makes a choice, and *sich entschliesst*, determines itself, in the sense of voluntary self-limitation and self-direction. Only intelligent will can do this. As such it becomes truly free. It becomes, as Hegel says, "self-determining generality, the will, freedom." Only now does it become "the Idea in its truth."[170]

Thus in this manner the will grows out of the realm of the finite and becomes "truly infinite," because it has "turned backward into itself." In contrast to this infinite will, finite will is only "possibility, tendency, capacity." Only infinite will is the "will by itself," without qualification. At the same time it is now "universal, because all restriction and all particular individuality have been absorbed into it."[171]

It was this definition of free will, at this point highly abstract, which Hegel took as his dialectical point of departure.

He was now able to speak of the "objective will," which sublimates or transcends (*auferhebt*) the contradiction between subjectivity and objectivity. This free will, then, in its first form is the right, and, indeed, abstract and formal right, which merely limits the arbitrariness of the natural will. In its second stage this same free will becomes morality, which in turn stands above formal right, limiting the natural will by means of ethical norms.

In its third stage, finally, will that is free in and for itself, implicitly and explicitly, is raised up to the level of the great realities that impose bounds on arbitrariness, and which are manifested as the actualities of history. These realities are instinctive in the nature of humankind. They are family, society, and the state. All these forms of human togetherness, according to Hegel, represent free self-limitations of the free will. At any given time they have their appointed general and historical location.

Central to the basic conception of the *Philosophy of Right*, as in the *History of Philosophy*, is the idea of human freedom. In the *History of Philosophy* Hegel traces the development of freedom and its idea on the basis of history, which in his view represents the progress of freedom in the consciousness.

Whereas this same general route is followed a second time in the *Philosophy of Right*, Hegel goes about it in a quite different way. This time what is shown is not the forms of freedom and unfreedom as actualized in history, but rather the systematic forms generated by the human spirit on its way as self-developing idea.

As stages of progression we have abstract right, morality, and the ethical life. At the very beginning, therefore, it is Hegel's idea that human freedom is a priori bound up with the idea of right. This idea is subject to the human personality, and in it are grounded the definitions of property, contract, wrong, coercion, and crime developed by Hegel. According to Hegel, again, this abstract right is immediate, but at the same time limited. It must lead to a contradiction, to a collision between rights and thus to "unconstrained wrong."

As always, the generative principle here is contradiction. Out of the "collisions of right," of right subjectively claimed by the individual, which as such is necessarily moot and contestable as among individuals, arises the second form—morality. This is the next stage after abstract right and appears as the concrete form of human action and intercourse.

Thus, under this second heading Hegel is able to deal with ethical questions revolving around the concrete actuality of actions good and bad, rather than abstract right, and so the following come up for discussion: purpose and responsibility, intention and well-being, good and conscience, as well as the moral forms of evil, that is, those forms of evil inverted into an appearance of the good.

The dialectical synthesis of the two basic stages—abstract right and morality—is a third stage to which Hegel gave the name of *Sittlichkeit*, or "ethical life." Basic to *Sittlichkeit* is the notion that freedom—or the *idea* of freedom, to be exact— must develop and be concretized in ethical life. At this point Hegel suddenly launches into a description of the forms of social life: family, society, and the state.

Now, it is certainly valid to say that Hegel had a great interest in justifying the state, the existence of which he had in mind to prove as absolutely necessary. But in the face of all efforts to prove the necessity of the state, as it were, from the fact that all human beings must live together, Hegel had the other end in mind, that is, to explore *Sittlichkeit*. Thus he had to develop the preliminary stages of abstract right and morality to be able to show how the unification of these two "abstract" ideas grows into the actuality of social relationships.

Once again a new aspect of dialectical thinking is shown in the *Philosophy of Right*. Actuality had already been conceived as Idea in the *History of Philosophy*, and, indeed, in the *Phenomenology* as well. But in both these earlier cases actual historical development served as the guideline.

However, Hegel was not satisfied with this. He had something more in mind beyond demonstrating the Idea on the basis of actuality. His claim throughout is the development of actuality out of the Idea. He had already proceeded in terms of this claim in the *Encyclopaedia* and in the *Logic*.

Now the same claim was developed a third time. It was to be shown how the idea of freedom, in its dialectical evolution, releases the forms of human existence. Right, property, good and evil, family, society, and the state are nothing more than objectifications of the idea of freedom actualized in human beings.

It is highly noteworthy how Hegel went about realizing his claim. Behind the formal schema just developed, as it appears in the table of contents, stands a much more vital intellectual framework. Anyone reading the *Philosophy of Right* will run across some astonishing ideas, running far ahead of Hegel's time. Two groups of ideas particularly seem almost modern in the Hegelian presentation. One of them revolves around Hegel's notion of the structure of the human personality; the other has to do with his view of society and his analysis of it.

In the *Encyclopaedia*, to which Hegel refers again and again in the *Philosophy of Right*, he had already introduced an idea about the nature of the human "person." At the end of the section called "Subjective Spirit," under the heading "The Practical Spirit," Hegel discusses the relationship between instinct, or drive, and intelligence—*Trieb und Intelligenz*. Spirit as "intelligence," according to his definition, is "self-determination," and the spirit finds itself in intelligence. This self-determination gives rise to the *Idee des Sollens*, the idea of what ought to be, of obligation or duty.

This obligatoriness as a new form of self-determination stands in dialectical contradiction to will (*Wollen*) based on impulses, inclinations, and passions. These are not "rational" and acquire rationality only through intelligence.

The same thought is propagated in the introduction to the *Philosophy of Right*, but in a more precise way. To be sure, Hegel argues against those "who regard thinking as one special faculty, distinct from the will as another special faculty." Anyone who thinks this, Hegel says, proves "his complete ignorance of the nature of the will." Anyone, that is, who supposes that this intellectual will can disregard "every determinate state of mind in which I may find myself," to be sure arrives at a conception of freedom. But this kind of freedom is "the freedom of the void which rises to a passion and takes actual shape in the world," ultimately leading to a negative conception of the will. "Only in destroying something does this negative will have the feeling of itself as existent."[172]

Hegel claims that this form of "negative freedom" often occurs historically, for example among Asian Indians. Later, as an additional instance, he cites "the period of the Terror during the French Revolution." "This period," he writes, "was a shuddering, an earthquake, of irreconcilability toward every particularity; for fanaticism wants an abstractness, no articulation: where differences come into prominence, fanaticism finds this repugnant, and annuls them."[173]

As if anticipating Freudian psychology, Hegel asserts that the proper content of "empirical psychology" is the theory of the different human impulses, or drives.[174] He talks about "the impulse toward right, also the impulse to property and morality, also the impulse to sexual love, the impulse to sociability, etc."[175]

But actually Hegel is far from trying to find a definition of man in any impulse theory. On the contrary, this second form of will as natural and immediate is not the final one at all. Only that will which rises above the impulses and determines them is the actual, free will, and "only in freedom of this kind is the will *bei sich*—by itself without condition—because then it is related to nothing but itself and every tide of dependence on anything else falls away."[176]

Thus Hegel sees the human personality in terms of three stages of the will. At the first stage there is the empty will devoid of content, at the second the substantial will determined by impulses and desires, and at the third the really free and independent will. Man grows out of the dialectic of these three stages. Thus we come to this definition: "Man is implicitly rational, but he must also become explicitly so, by struggling to create himself, not only by going forth out of himself, but also by building himself up within."

If, accordingly, the theory of impulses has a significant role for Hegel, in later parts of the book the theory of "needs" has an equally important place in the theory of human society.

In all this discussion Hegel looks again and again at the difference between man and animal. In his definition of free will he had pointed out that the animal must obey his instincts, whereas man, "as the completely undetermined," stands above them. In a similar assessment in the "System of Needs," the point of departure is again the difference between animal and man. There we are told:

> An animal's needs and its ways and means of satisfying them are both alike restricted in scope. Though man is subject to this restriction, too, nonetheless at the same time he evinces his transcendence of it and his universality, first by the multiplication of needs and means of satisfying them, and secondly by the differentiation and division of concrete need into single parts and aspects, which in turn become different needs, particularized and therefore more abstract.[177]

The sense of this statement is as follows: in his needs the animal is secure and limited; man, however, is insecure and unlimited. This thought is similar to the earlier one. There, too, the difference between man and animal was evidenced by the fact that the animal is bound and determined by his instincts, whereas man is unbound and undetermined.

Man as an insecure, unbound and free essence is dialectical. As man evolves through the dialectic of will into personality, so does human society develop through the dialectic of freedom. The anthropology which Hegel provides in the introduction is followed by the theory of social forms. One is as dialectically determined as the other.

We now have to show in the ensuing chapter how Hegel's theory of social forms—the family, civil society, and the state —grew out of this basic position. In process of doing this it will become clear that the whole *Philosophy of Right* is bathed in a peculiar ambiguity. That is to say, on the one hand Hegel is a sharp and unsparing critic of his times, and especially of civil society, yet on the other he defends the status quo and particularly the Prussian state.

# 14

# Hegel's Theory of Social Forms in the Philosophy of Right

Hegel developed his theory of social forms of institutions in the third part of the *Philosophy of Right*. His aim was to show the totality of social relationships. Lending themselves to the triadic dialectical principle were distinctions which seemed to offer themselves almost spontaneously. For Hegel there were three stages of the social life: the family, civil society, and the state.

Thus the mode of attack in this part of the *Philosophy of Right* seems very simple indeed, not to say primitive. It could be understood as follows: the family is the elementary unit of social relationship, and out of it arises the larger unity of society and finally the comprehensive whole, the state.

However, this tripartite division is really not quite that simple. The Hegelian viewpoint is not governed by an idea that any momentary, larger numerical or quantitative unity constitutes a higher stage. Rather it is based on the idea that each of these forms represents a stage of "ethical life."

For Hegel the natural and immediate unity is the family, which he says is "characterized by love, which is mind's feeling of its own unity." The state is the perfected form of the ethical idea, the ethical whole. Between the two stands civil society, representing the difference between family and state.

Thus from the start civil society has a peculiar intermediate position of a negative kind. Because of its dialectical position, civil society could be the intermediary between family and state. But in Hegel's description, civil society much more nearly intervenes detrimentally between family and state.

This fact is underscored, moreover, by Hegel's observation that civil society is a modern invention. Its development occurred later than the state's. But the difference between family and state nonetheless assigned civil society a place before the state, regardless of chronology, in the process of dialectical progression. Civil society must have the state "as sovereign before it, in order to exist."

Already we see that Hegel accorded civil society a special role in his scheme. It stands opposed to the family on the one hand and to the state on the other. It assumes the state, but evolves later than the state and therefore really has the character of a late, though to be sure dialectically necessary, intermediate product.

Hegel is relatively brief in his treatment of the family. The family arises, if we follow Hegel's train of thought, basically out of a contradiction. But for Hegel the family is still the "immediate substantiality of spirit, characterized by love, which is spirit's feeling of its own unity."

For Hegel at this time love is not only a contradiction, but the most monstrous of contradictions, one which the understanding cannot resolve. Hegel explains it this way: Love signifies the consciousness of my unity with another. "The first moment in love is that I do not wish to be a self-subsistent and independent person and that, if I were, then I would feel defective and incomplete." "The second moment is that I find myself in another person, that I count for something in the other, while the other in turn comes to count for something in me."[178]

A remarkable definition of love, one which obviously derives completely from the notion that the person first of all is self-consciousness. For the argument clearly moves in this fashion: If the person surrenders his self-consciousness and independence, actually he surrenders himself. Since he does this in love, yet nevertheless continues to exist, the phenomenon is a contradiction.

No matter, for Hegel love is the basis of marriage. Yet, and here Hegel may be right, it is a dialectical basis. As he says, it is "at once the revealing and the resolving of the contradiction, and as resolution it is ethical unity."[179]

Yet Hegel drew no further inferences from this dialectical definition of marriage. For instance, he might have asked what happens when love ceases to be while marriage goes on. This did not interest Hegel. He proceeded on an opposite course, as in his later description of civil society, where again he drew only feasible inferences from the dialectical presentation.

He moved directly to define the family further, which he characterized in three aspects: marriage, property, and education. The subjective starting point for marriage, so he believed, is a special propensity among parents, or a precautionary measure on their part; the objective source, on the other hand, is two persons freely consenting to make *one* of themselves. By doing this they give up their natural personality, limit themselves, but still make themselves free by gaining their "substantial self-consciousness." The description of the family also includes a series of judgments which today strike us as dated. For instance, Hegel believed that whereas women can be well-educated, they are not up to the higher sciences, philosophy, and art. They are lacking in the ideal. On the other hand Hegel is more friendly when he compares the difference between man and woman with that between animal and plant. Men have more of an animal character, women are more plantlike. But then he raises a warning finger: if women were at the head of the government, the state would be in danger.[180]

When the additional definitions which Hegel gives the family are tracked down, they turn out to be mainly two: property and raising children. The family as person has its external reality in property, but it is only through the children that the unity of marriage has "an existence for its own sake and object."

Whereas the subject of the family is basically treated very briefly and summarily, as if it did not much interest Hegel, civil society is dealt with in greater detail. The greatest importance in the presentation is actually given to the state. But it is worth noting that the moment Hegel moves on from the family to civil society, the tone of the exposition changes completely. The dark and ominous streak in Hegel which we first encountered in the Jena fragment and then in the *Phenomenology*, crops up again. It is the same Hegel who, in the Jena fragment, described God as rent within himself, and in the *Phenomenology* as the self-estranged spirit.

Not only the tone of the recital changes; the dialectic instrument is used differently. Certainly Hegel saw the contradiction of love in the family. But all the emphasis in the description of the family is placed on the fact that it is an immediate unity, and later Hegel was to view the state as the fulfillment of *Sittlichkeit*, that is, the ethical life or mores. In his portrayal of civil society, however, he cannot do enough to show it to be a contradictory and strife-torn institution.

Even the first idea which gets the treatment of civil society under way takes the form of a criticism. Civil society, Hegel explains, represents the "loss of the ethical life."[181] This must also mean, no doubt, that in civil society the immediate ethical unity represented by the family has been abolished. Civil society appears to be an intermediate stage of dismembered or disjointed ethical life, later redeemed by the state. The state is the new, final, and perfected form of the ethical.

This, actually, is also the main idea which hovers before Hegel's analysis of civil society. As the difference between family and state, civil society is no more than a necessary evil. In depicting civil society, Hegel uses the same colors as in his description of the self-estranged spirit, and, frankly, one gets the impression that basically he is painting the same picture but using two different subjects and themes.

One could have the impression that the dialectical position

which Hegel assigns civil society as the difference between family and state necessarily leads to this sort of negative portrayal, but this is not the case. On the contrary, Hegel, like Marx apparently following in Hegel's steps, views civil society with the deepest mistrust and subjects it to the sharpest criticism.

Turning now to the actual description of civil society, we must repeatedly compare it with the Marxian description. A similarity, indeed a concurrence, will be shown. Whether Marx did or did not know this part of the *Philosophy of Right*, it is in any case incontestable that Hegel developed the basic features which in Marx are fleshed out in often painstaking theoretical discussion.

For us, Hegel and Marx are as one in their judgment of civil society, and this will certainly be even more true for future generations. Both saw it as the phenomenon of a social form thoroughly marked by signs of dissolution and disintegration, in the process of dialectical movement and unfolding. For Hegel, as for Marx, civil society was a dynamic phenomenon, changeable in its very essence, in the grip of a stormy developmental process.

This is not to deny the theoretical differences separating the Hegelian from the Marxian position. But the differences are irrelevant in respect to the way both thinkers see and experience civil society: rather they are differences of dialectical inference. For Marx, civil society necessarily arises dialectically out of economic conditions and the development of the conditions of production, whereas Hegel derives civil society from the dialectical development of the Idea dwelling in mankind.

Marx himself repeatedly emphasized this difference. In the preface to his "Sketch of a Critique of Political Economy" he says that in reviewing the Hegelian *Philosophy of Right* he reached the convictions that the conditions of the state and of right cannot be understood by themselves alone in their own terms—*aus sich selbst*—or in terms of the "so-called universal development of the human spirit."

Clearly there is some basis for this criticism of Hegel. Marx goes on to say that the conditions of the state and of right "are rooted in the material conditions of life," the totality of which, following the precedent set by Englishmen and Frenchmen, Hegel lumps together under the name of "civil society." Marx then made the following often quoted statement, to the effect that "the anatomy of civil society is to be sought in the political economy."[182]

Here Marx is tacitly claiming, in effect, that he is the first to strike out on this path. But this is a curious claim, for he himself has already said that Hegel conceived civil society to be the sum total of material circumstance. Does not this suggest that Hegel, too, turned his attention to material conditions? Did not Hegel, perhaps, also use the material approach?

Just how justified we are in questioning Marx becomes clear immediately once we turn to the Hegelian interpretation itself. In the description of the family, the institution of property is discussed, though not, to be sure, its basis in instinct and sex. But the analysis of civil society moves at once into an investigation of its basis in drives and other forms of conational behavior. It is this which gives the Hegelian analysis its peculiar character and which, to put it plainly, causes it to stand out. Hegel begins by examining the system of human need in the first section of his presentation. A second section on the administration of justice in civil society follows. In the third and last section the threads appearing in the first are again taken up. The development of the system of needs in civil society is shown; curiously enough, the section is given the misleading title of "The Police and the Corporation."

Thus the analysis of "material conditions" runs like a red thread through the whole presentation, which is interrupted only by the section on the administration of justice. In our discussion we shall bypass this section, since Hegel's truly original theory appears in the other two parts.

One is rather taken aback at first that Hegel, quite contrary to his usual way of looking at things, should be engaged at all by such considerations. However, it must not be forgotten that the young Hegel had written a kind of commentary on Dugald Stewart's *Economic Theory*. And, as witnessed in his last article written in Berlin on the English Reform Bill for the *Allgemeine Preussische Zeitung*, he had clearly made steady progress in his economic studies.

At the beginning of his reflections Hegel takes a dim view of society as a whole. He tells us that civil society is "the actualization of selfish ends," that this system of "all-around dependence" leads to a sort of "foreign state," one "based on need and understanding."[183]

He gives the reason for this supposition. Civil society is ruled by "particularity . . . given free rein in every direction to satisfy its needs." The particularity of civil society expresses itself in "accidental caprice and subjective desires." On the one hand "it is endlessly agitated and in a state of thoroughgoing dependence on external happenstance and arbitrariness," while on the other "it is held in check by the power of universality."

His indictment of this society grows even more severe when he begins to draw conclusions from this initial description. He tells us that civil society "affords a spectacle of extravagance and want as well as of the physical and ethical degeneration common to them both."[184]

Marx depicted the nature of the modern society of his own day in much the same way in a fragment written in his youth. It is a self-estranged society in which each person strives only to fill his own needs and all activity is governed by self-seeking. It is worth noting that in this context Marx uses the idea of "self-estrangement" derived from Hegel. Hegel had expounded this idea in the *Phenomenology*, but did not use it in the *Philosophy of Right*.

Hegel, too, singled out the unlimited, unbridled world of needs and their satisfaction as the main distinguishing characteristic of civil society. In a supplement to Paragraph 182 we are told that "in civil society each member is his own end, everything else is nothing to him." But without relating to others he cannot attain the whole compass of his ends, wherefore "these others are means to the end of the particular member."[185]

Thus does Hegel heap negative criticisms on civil society. He tells us in a supplement to Paragraph 185: "Particularity by itself is measureless excess and the forces of this excess are themselves measureless." He then goes on to say: "On the other hand, however, want and destitution are measureless, too, and the discord of this situation can be brought into a harmony only by the state which has powers over it."[186]

A closer analysis of the grounds for this interpretation is provided by Hegel in a succeeding section on the "System of Needs." Here he makes a distinction between man and animal. The animal has inherently limited needs and likewise implicitly limited means of satisfying them.

Man, however, can expand and multiply his needs without limit by differentiating them, in this fashion creating new and particularized needs. The satisfaction of needs parallels this development, with satisfactions simultaneously experiencing "a multiplication ad infinitum."

This process never flags, it is "illimitable." "What you take to be comfort at any stage can be discovered by you to be discomfort, and of these discoveries there is no end."[187] It is as if for Hegel civil society is driven by the pressure of indeterminate needs, by means of satisfying them and by pleasures, and that in this pressure there is no distinction between natural and artificial needs. To be sure, man finds liberation in this process of creating new needs, since "the strict natural necessity of need is obscured," but at the same time he behaves toward these new needs as if they were necessities of their own, not his, making.[188]

How keenly Hegel sensed coming developments, a process already under way in his time, is shown by the following quotations. At one point he says: "Finally it is no longer need but opinion which must be satisfied." And again: "Hence the need for greater comfort does not arise within you directly, rather it is brought forth by those who seek to make a profit by its creation."[189]

The same sort of thing is described by Marx in his turn when he says that "within private property" everyone speculates "on creating a new need in order to force a new sacrifice to it, to impose a new dependence and to mislead to a new form of pleasure and so to economic ruin."[190]

Thus the young Marx traced the ever expanding need-structure of modern society back to private property and, as he was

to say later on, to capitalism. Anyone who supposes that the
real difference between Marx and Hegel lies in this Marxian
interpretation, as has often been claimed, is on the wrong
track.

For in fact Hegel, too, had already seen and described this
relationship, as well as all its consequences. This brings us to
the third part of his description of civil society, which has the
title, as already noted, of "The Police and the Corporation."
The fact that there is no general recognition of just how much
Hegel anticipated Marx may be because this particular section
of the *Philosophy of Right* remains almost unknown and quite
evidently unread. In this section Hegel spells out the dialectical consequences of his conception of civil society. Here our
claim that Marx only said what Hegel had already recognized
is completely borne out.

Again Hegel repeats his negative characterization of civil
society as if he could not say it often enough. He tells us that
civil society is "the tremendous power that wrenches men into
itself and demands of them that they work for it, owe everything to it, and do everything by its means." Hence it is destructive of the family. "Civil society tears the individual from
his family ties, estranges the members of the family from one
another and recognizes them as self-subsistent persons . . . it
subjects the existence of the entire family to dependence on
itself (that is, on civil society) and to contingency."[191]

It seems as if Hegel were now asking himself where this
development was tending and what was the goal of these
dialectical tensions. It is as if a prospect had opened up before
him no less dark than those revealed by earlier insights. In any
case, Hegel saw and outlined the perspectives of this development. And again it becomes evident that they are the same
perspectives which Marx would later bring to his theory of the
collapse of civil society and the coming world revolution.

Actually Hegel did not foresee these last consequences; he
stopped short of them. This is partly accounted for by the
overall thrust of his systematic presentation. For him the state
stood above civil society and subdued it.

Consequently, the state, or rather the idea of the state, for
him represents deliverance from the almost chaotic dialectic of

civil society. He either did not see, or did not believe in, the catastrophe that for Marx was the only way out of the dialectical dilemma. Nonetheless this did not prevent Hegel from recognizing in civil society the dynamic development from which Marx drew his inferences.

In Paragraph 243 Hegel sketches the basis for this dialectical development in a passage, as so often with him, that moves with almost breathless haste.

In a relatively brief introductory sentence he makes the following assertion: "When civil society is in a state of unimpeded activity, it is engaged in expanding internally in population and industry." Then he goes on to show the dialectic of this situation in a long sentence. He believes that in such a development the amassment of wealth is, on the one hand, increased as a result of increasing population and industrialization. But on the other there is a growing "subdivision and restriction of particular jobs. This results in the dependence and distress of the class tied to work of that sort."[192]

Marx later expressed this same idea within the framework of his *Verelendungstheorie*, or theory of pauperization or progressive deterioration. But the thought process is the same regardless of context. The more the wealth of the capitalist class increases, the greater the misery of the proletariat. Marx demonstrated this in a series of economic considerations, for example in the growth of the army reserve, the unemployment arising on this account, and the consequent reduction in the price of labor, etc.

No such detailed proof is to be found in Hegel. Nonetheless he is clearly aware of the "pauperization of the proletarian class," to use the Marxian phrase. He says that the class bound to a special kind of work ends up with an "inability to feel and enjoy the broader freedoms and especially the intellectual benefits of civil society." He describes this even more explicitly in the next paragraph, where we are told: "When the standard of living of a large mass of people falls below a certain subsistence level" this leads to "a consequent loss of the sense of right and wrong, of honesty and the self-respect which makes a man insist on maintaining himself by his own work and effort." Thus a *Pöbel*, a rabble or lumpenproletariat, is created, and at the same time conditions which greatly facilitate the concentration of disproportionate wealth in the hands of a few.[193]

Hegel, to be sure, did not draw the same conclusions as did Marx. For Marx, the development shown by Hegel proceeds mechanically and leads to inevitable decline if the proletariat does not rise up and wipe out the society and state in power by means of revolution.

Hegel saw no such result. It was not part of his train of thought nor did he strive after it as did Marx. Yet the peculiar, almost paradoxical structure of civil society is clear enough to him when he says: "Hence it becomes apparent that despite an excess of wealth, civil society is not rich enough, i.e., its own resources are insufficient to check excessive poverty and the creation of a penurious rabble."

But having gone this far he closed the section on civil society. He did not look into the distance and the future. His thinking remained fettered to the present. For him the dialectical method was not a prophetic instrument. Its task was to grasp what currently existed.

And when just for a moment he did cast a glance into the future, the prospect was not illuminating. Such a glance is indicated in the last paragraphs of the section, in which Hegel points out that civil society is "driven beyond its own limits" by its own dialectic to seek to expand its production in other lands among other people. As the following shows, Hegel thought this out quite concretely. He was aware of the colonization and the expansion of the world economy taking place before his eyes. Then comes an almost ominous prophecy. He says of civil society: "Since the passion for gain involves risks, industry, though bent on profit, yet lifts itself above it; instead of remaining rooted to the soil and the limitations of civil life with its pleasures and desires, it embraces the element of flux, danger, and destruction."[194]

With this, Hegel ends the analysis of civil society proper and goes on to the subsection called "The Corporation." This subject is dealt with in a few pages. Thereafter begins the third, and now comprehensive, section on the state with which the *Philosophy of Right* ends.

We shall not go into this section in detail. In it Hegel discusses the right of the state internally and internationally, and to these two parts adds a very abbreviated section on world history. Basic to this section is Hegel's conviction that the state is the "actualization of the ethical idea."

The state as Hegel sees it is by no means a very human or friendly institution, like the one, let us say, outlined by Sir Thomas More. In his discussion of the family Hegel had already said that "love" no longer exists in the state, since "There we are conscious of unity as law: there the content must be rational and known to us." In a certain sense the Hegelian notion of the state is reason actualized.

This actualized reason, finally, is harsh and rugged. Hegel did not believe in eternal peace like Kant; he was, rather, a champion of the power-state which, for instance, does not take too kindly to freedom of the press and maintains that war is inevitable. Hegel was unsparing in his description of civil society, and similarly there is nothing at all utopian about his state. Yet despite it all he ultimately believed in the "perfectibility" of man, insofar as the human race progressed in its knowledge of self, in accordance with the law of the spirit.

# 15

## The Later Fate of the Dialectic

The mark left by the Hegelian system by virtue of the strength of its systematic thinking and its universality was of short duration. This was during the brief period in which Hegel's pupils saw in their teacher a thinker who had brought everything together in a meaningful way and recognized the "whole" of truth.

The time soon came, however, when the system was proscribed and ridiculed, the period when, as Marx said, Hegel was treated "like a dead dog." By 1837 Kierkegaard was writing that Hegel "had given currency to a logical trinity in the silliest way."[195] And in Kierkegaard's *Concluding Unscientific Postscript* we are told: "But then, the System also has more to offer than God had in both hands; this very moment it has more, to say nothing of next Sunday, when it is quite certain to be finished."[196]

Hegel now seems to have become a purely historical figure. He has found his niche in the history of philosophy, but this goes only for the great systematist and synthesizer as a person. It has been strangely different with the seed so unexpectedly, and for that reason so effectively, sown by his analyses. Whereas the Hegelian system as a structure fell into ruins, small elements and themes within the mighty complex became enormously influential.

This holds by and large for the dialectical method as developed by Hegel. The dialectic, too, came in for its share of scorn, as when Kierkegaard described Hegel as a master who had provided philosophy with a stomach that chewed its cud three times, and then sarcastically suggested that the next magister to come along should try four-stage rumination. Indeed, Hegel's dialectical method was no less boycotted than his system.

Yet the dialectical idea persisted and developed penetrating strength. Kierkegaard transformed it and evolved his own existential dialectic. Marx followed out lines of attack already prefigured by Hegel and developed his historical materialism dialectic. With both thinkers the so-called dialectic suffered a complete change of appearance, just as it had in coming from Kant to Hegel. Indeed, it could be supposed that nothing was left of the Hegelian dialectic. Marx "stood it on its head," as he said, and Kierkegaard imposed equally radical changes.

Nonetheless the fact remains, even if Kierkegaard could not do enough to make Hegel's dialectical thinking contemptible, that neither he nor Marx were able to escape the dialectical spell. But wherein lay this spell, what moved these later thinkers to hold to what they called dialectic?

There is no way of connecting Kierkegaard and Marx. The phenomena which they deal with, their points of departure, and the style and goals of their thinking are as disparate as could possibly be imagined. Yet common to both of them is the perception expressed by Hegel in his own day in these words: "The bonds of this world are torn apart; they are collapsing like the fabric of a dream."

Marx and Kierkegaard both saw the world as falling to pieces, and they were as one in their consciousness of the necessity of destroying that which existed. They both sing the same tune in this respect.

But only in this general respect do they show any similarity. As soon as they start elaborating on the inevitability of the coming catastrophe, or the goal toward which the development is trending, their points of view become extremely divergent. For Kierkegaard the reason behind world decline is the betrayal of Christianity, and its salvation the return to true Christianity. But for Marx the necessity of the event does not lie in man's corruption. Rather catastrophe is the result of a necessary evolution. And this process of evolution is material and economic in nature.

Whereas Kierkegaard placed all his hopes on having mankind mend its ways, do penance and return to the Christian idea, Marx offered another cure: Mankind must press on, move irresistibly toward world revolution, at the end of which the age of freedom would dawn.

Remarkably enough the dialectical method here still shows its ambiguity, notwithstanding different points of departure, changes in outlook, and equally changed goals. For again and again Marx teaches that the dialectical method in his adaptation of it is a true instrumentality, whereas Kierkegaard thinks of it only as a human experience, rather than a scientific method in the true sense.

But in this diversity of usage, in which the concept of dialectic vacillates this way and that, always evident is the functional aspect of this kind of thinking, as a means of splitting actuality apart, of breaking it into pieces and of transposing it into a "negative" element. Hegel had been cognizant of this function but now his proposition that the life of the spirit consists of "looking the negative in the face and abiding with it" acquired a new kind of omnipotence.

Now the negative and destructive outlook took on a broader form, one in which at times all actuality threatened to vanish. Descriptions of the negative, of "Nothing" and of the truth of Nothing, arose in all directions; any positive outlook whatsoever disappeared. Nothing is valid any longer—barring Nothingness itself.

Yet this Nothing in a mysterious way comprehended everything and everybody. The thoughtful observer will often feel that only the lighting has been changed, altering everything previously bright and positive into the shadowy and dark. In all events, in these later thinkers one trait can be recognized which Hegel, on the whole, did not have. He wanted to reconcile actuality and theory. But now we see an undisguised effort to make a militant instrument out of theory, one that would reform actuality, and which in its day undoubtedly was unremittingly hostile to existing actuality.

The threat of destruction became, to say the least, one of the most effective measures used by the dialecticians who followed Hegel. For both Kierkegaard and Marx prove "dialectically" that the threat of destruction does in fact exist. Indeed, the scientific Marx sees destruction as unavoidable if his directives are not followed.

It was under this sign of doom that the second act of the dialectical drama began. The first act had ended with Hegel. The idea of a dialectical-synthetic reason as developed by Hegel ran out as soon as it had unfolded. Quite obviously the second act of dialectical thinking is lasting longer. Moreover, it is being played out not in the realm of spirit, but in the real dimensions of political thought.

Whether one believes, with its advocates, that dialectical thinking is uniquely adapted to human actuality, or whether one believes that dialectical thinking is historically conditioned and merely a product of our times, is really beside the point to the extent that dialectic has in fact become an effective force. The power of this kind of thinking is unmistakable.

Now that we have critically thought through the ideas of the dialectic's first great exponent, the character of the instrument stands out with perfect clarity. It is ambiguous and serves the thinkers of destruction just as willingly as the harbinger of the self-fulfilling spirit. It is a two-edged sword.

The claim, first advanced by Hegel, that the dialectical tool is the "only true scientific method" is not tenable. The dialectical method works according to the hand and eye of him whom it serves. On this account the future cannot be plumbed by the dialectical method, and it cannot be questioned that dialectical method does not show the truth *an und für sich*, in and for itself, implicitly and explicitly.

Rather it always shows probabilities and possibilities, and

its results remain as ambiguous as its mode of attack. Anyone trusting it gives himself over to the enormous power of fantasy, and in the end to feelings of hope or anxiety. In all ages has man been thus guided and misled.

Dialectic is certainly no critical instrument of cognition, insofar as criticism is not mistaken for disintegration. In its past and present forms it is a constructive tool which achieves results from *für wahr Halten*, from believing something to be true.

# II

## KIERKEGAARD'S EXISTENTIAL DIALECTIC

# 16

## Hegel Kierkegaard Marx

Hegel died on November 14, 1831. The last great work that he left behind was the monumental *Philosophy of Right*. After this he had concentrated on teaching, and apart from some longer articles no further work appeared.

He died at the height of his fame. He dominated German philosophy, and figures like the young Schopenhauer and the aging Schelling were lost in the brightness of his sun. But the school that he founded failed to consolidate and soon fell apart into a Hegelian "Right" and a Hegelian "Left."

It almost seems as if Hegelian philosophy was shattered by the death of the master. As dominant as had been the living, teaching, and writing Hegel, little remained once he had fallen silent. To be sure, at first the phalanx of the Hegelian school seemed to be securely closed; immediately after Hegel's death his collected works were published, 1832–87, by a large group of disciples. But even while the whole great work was being published for the first time—at least the primary documents of it—criticisms of it arose simultaneously, which were sharp beyond all measure.

The mighty figure of Hegel himself had vanished; his dictatorial thinking, that in polemic had destroyed his opponents, had a spokesman no longer. None of his followers could even dream of filling his shoes. His professorial chair was first filled by one of his weaker disciples, the former headmaster Gabler, whom Humboldt, full of contempt, called the *verhängnisvolle Gabel*, the "fateful fork."

By 1840, only nine years after Hegel's death, Schelling had been called to Berlin as the man capable of "combating the dragon-seed of Hegelian pantheism, of superficial sciolism and the lawless disintegration of domestic education, and introducing a scientific rebirth of the nation."[1]

Not only had Prussia turned away from Hegel; he was criticized widely in philosophical circles, indeed, reviled and mocked. Elegantly and temperately, but destruction bent, Berlin Professor Trendelenburg, in his *Logical Investigations*, criticized the core of Hegelian thought, the "dialectical method." But criticism did not stop with that. Hegel's whole mode of thought and especially his dialectic were unconscionably ridiculed. Schopenhauer, for whom Hegel was a "vulgar, dull, disgustingly repulsive, witless charlatan,"[2] talked about the "absolute galimatias [nonsense] of Hegelian dialectic."[3] Equally malicious were such epithets as the "dreary mill of dialectical thought" and "the sly formula according to which the Absolute Spirit moves in three-quarter time from thesis to antithesis to synthesis."[4]

"Behold, the feet of them which have buried thy husband are at the door, and shall carry thee out"; the words from Acts that Hegel quoted so often were hardly ever more apropos than when applied to Hegel himself. When Marx said that it had become the fashion to treat Hegel like a "dead dog," he was not exaggerating. Even if criticism should be directed at all scholarly effort, nonetheless the criticism visited on Hegel was a quite different thing, a matter of bad taste and underground sniping. Hegelian thought was assailed as if it were a heresy and it came into pestilential odor.

Thus the fight revolving about Hegel, for and against, showed all the signs, unusual in scientific argument, that are, however, familiar everywhere when political opinions, ideological directions, and religious movements are being contested, or when vital interests or emotional attitudes come up for debate. With Hegel the principle of total rejection or total acceptance was in force, and here, by way of reaction, what had been worshiped yesterday, today was harshly condemned.

Why, the thoughtful observer will ask himself, was it that such an about-face occurred. What was it that Hegel was really being condemned for, wherein had he failed? An examination of the motives that come to light in the criticisms shows them to be highly diverse. Some of the critics, above all technical philosophers like Trendelenburg and Schopenhauer, criticized the dialectical method on the basis of logical or methodological considerations. But the explanation quoted above of why Schelling was called to Berlin, accuses Hegel of pantheism, sciolism, and corruption. Indeed, it was quite often declared that Hegel had discredited philosophy as such.

Yet quite different is another kind of criticism, for example the kind associated with Kierkegaard and Marx. Marx did not dispute the fact that Hegel discovered the dialectic, and he himself made use of it, at the same time accusing Hegel of having used it to mystify. His criticism, therefore, was directed not against Hegel's philosophical method, but against its shallow and ideological application. Kierkegaard, on the other hand, attacked Hegel mainly for having corrupted philosophy. He, too, thought dialectically, but like Marx wanted to give dialectical thinking a completely new direction and meaning.

The more one dwells on the critical objections to Hegel, the clearer it becomes that the critics were united only in their sharp and passionate rejection, but disunited and split on what they were objecting to. By and large it seems as if one critic will accept what the other rejects, and vice versa.

From this it appears that this long accumulating rejection of Hegel must have had deeper reasons than a refusal to accept this or that idea or claim in the Hegelian philosophy. When Hegel's thought and Hegelianism were rejected at one fell swoop, it was mainly because Hegel was seen as representative of a mode of thinking that had come to be repudiated, outlawed, and indeed even regarded with horror.

In the introduction to the *Philosophy of Right* Hegel had declared that every philosophy represents "its own time caught in thought." He inveighed against those who believed that a philosophy could be extrapolated beyond its own day.

This Hegelian reflection is related to the proposition cited earlier that the rational is actual and the actual rational. However, while Hegel saw the task of philosophy to be a testing of the existing and the real for its rationality, actually he was attached to the great intellectual tradition of the Age of Enlightenment, a fact that he often proclaimed. For a long time, within this tradition, the belief had held sway that man was advancing toward better things in a slow but continuous evolution of the rational faculty.

From Kant came a famous definition of the Age of Enlightenment:

> Enlightenment is the emergence of man from his self-imposed immaturity. Immaturity is the inability to make use of one's understanding without another's guidance. The immaturity is self-imposed because the cause of it is not a dearth of understanding, but of decision and courage to be oneself without depending on another's guidance. *Sapere aude!* Have the courage to depend on your own understanding! This is the motto of the Enlightenment.[5]

For a long time man had shown this Kantian courage, grounded actually in an absolute trust in the capacity of reason. And even though Kant was also the one who, in his *Critique of Pure Reason*, showed the limits of theoretical thought, still he taught the slogan: Trust in reason. Basically he was only repeating what had been continuously taught and reiterated since the beginning of modern times, a sentiment summed up in what Gottsched had said in 1730: "Reason, gentlemen, reason is what had made man the king of animals."[6]

Hegel was also identified with this powerful belief in reason, for so long the idol of Western thought. The whole thrust of his thinking was an affirmation of absolute reason. With him, moreover, belief in reason was at the highest summit. In Hegelian thought it is not the scientific, technical, political, pedagogic or any other component of reason that determines the universe, but implicitly advancing Absolute Reason.

In closest connection with the belief in human reason was another powerful motivation, belief in progress. The theory of progress is that humankind on the whole is advancing, developing toward higher stages, traveling an ascending road in history. Just how strong this confidence in progress was is again shown by Kant, notwithstanding his second thoughts on the theoretical strength of reason. Kant was not basically an optimistic man and by no means a thinker who completely trusted the nature of man. Several statements can be found in Kant expressing his doubt about human capacities. On one occasion, for instance, he made the following cautious observation on man's nature: "How can one expect, however, that something perfectly straight could be carpentered out of such crooked wood?"[7]

The question as to whether man by nature was "good" or "bad," repeatedly discussed in this period in connection with Rousseau, was likewise very tentatively answered by Kant. As experience shows, man has a tendency to evil, but at the same time, thanks to his "intelligible" character, he has an "inborn tendency" toward the good.[8]

But once again it is the belief in reason, that is, in the human capacity to be intelligible, on which the tendency to be good is based. Thus, on the strength of his belief in reason, the aging Kant is still committed to the idea of progress.

As an old man he clung to the belief that mankind is slowly but steadily progressing. At the age of seventy-three, Kant wrote the following passage in an article called "It May Be Right in Theory, But That Does No Good in Practice":

I may assume, therefore: that since the human race is steadily advancing in respect of culture as a natural goal, it is also in process of advancing toward what is better in respect of the moral goal of its existence, and that this process, to be sure, may be interrupted from time to time, but is never terminated. I have no need to prove this assumption; those against it must disprove it.[9]

Hegel likewise adhered to this belief. For him, too, man was a creature who was "implicitly rational." Man had to "make his reason through the production of his self, by the emergence out of himself, but equally by building into himself," until he also became rational *für sich,* that is, in an explicit, actualized sense.

So, for Hegel, too, reason and progress are united, indeed, are raised to a synthesis in pursuance of which absolute reason, enthroned throughout the universe, is the determinant of man and the assurance of his gradual actualization. Man and mankind are moving forward, and world history is proof of this progress.

Yet having demonstrated that Hegel believed in the irresistible progress of the "spirit of the age," the question still remains whether Hegel believed in progress in a more literal, specific sense. For Hegel saw all development as dialectical. Development was not accomplished in a steady and only occasionally interrupted advance. Every development, while evincing the positive, was also forming the negative.

Progress, too, was dialectical. This much having been recognized, a very much different factor was introduced into the naive belief in progress advocated at the time. Whenever Hegel describes a dialectical evolution, the "negative" always appears along with the positive. When Hegel says in the *Phenomenology* that the life of spirit consists of being in disruption and enduring devastation, the same holds true for the progress of the spirit. The spirit prevails only by running the gauntlet of the negative and enduring it.

Between the lines, as it were, of Hegelian thought we see a glimmering of a different idea of progress. The absolute spirit, to be sure, is always moving forward, but in this progression always carries the "negative" along with it. And if one contemplates the first description of the self-developing spirit in the *Phenomenology*—a description that comes like a shock—it becomes abundantly clear what Hegel had in mind. Just before he evolves the last stage of the absolute spirit, the negative appears in its strongest form. Immediately before the "spirit sure of itself" comes the chapter on the self-estranged spirit.

The same sort of thing is indicated in Hegel's last work, the *Philosophy of Right*. Here the chapter on civil society is inserted before the one on the state, where the state is described as the "actualization of the ethical idea." This chapter on civil society, as earlier noted, shows the full scope of the negative. Civil society, we are told, is "the ethical life lost in its extremes."

Well, then, what kind of progress was it that engaged Hegel's belief? Certainly not a prudently slow, uninterrupted, and steadily advancing kind of progress. If Hegel had believed in that sort of thing he could neither have written the somber portrayal of the self-estranged spirit in the *Phenomenology*, nor his gloomy description of civil society. Had he believed in a simple, uncomplicated kind of progress he could never have displayed the spirit of devastating criticism and absolute bitterness in which these chapters are written.

All this might well be kept in mind when one reflects on Hegel's belief in progress. But neither the people of the period who admired Hegel nor the ones who criticized paid any attention to this aspect of Hegelian thought. On the contrary, both Hegel's followers and his critics took from his work only the end result, in which Hegel seemingly clung to a belief in progress despite everything.

And so it was that again and again Hegel's partisans as well as his detractors saw in him an optimistic and, in the last analysis, positive thinker. But whereas during Hegel's lifetime the intellectuals were fascinated by their notion of him as the great thinker who expounded a positive, albeit dialectical, metaphysic, in the reaction after his death it was just this ultimately positive trend of his thinking that was condemned.

Thus one of the main objections raised by Haym, in his critique, is to Hegel's "optimism and quietism." Haym repeats this reproach on several occasions and never forgets to remind us that this spirit made a reactionary of Hegel. Burckhardt made a similar judgment in a different context in his *World-Historical Observations*, again hitting pointedly at Hegel's optimism. He says that hitherto existing philosophies of history had divided history into longitudinal sections and in this fashion had tried "to arrive at a universal program of world development, mostly in a highly optimistic sense."

He accuses Hegel of imagining "that the upshot of history must (sic!) be a rational, necessary progress of the world-spirit." If the "sic!" inserted by Burckhardt expresses only doubt about such a claim, a subsequent and often quoted sentence asserts his complete incredulity: "But we are not privy to the goals of eternal wisdom and know them not. This impudent anticipation of a world-plan leads to errors, because it proceeds from false premises."[10]

All these reproaches of quietism and optimism, of "impudent anticipation" and the like do not in fact apply to Hegel at all. Anyone who knows him at all well is aware that the reconciliation of actuality and reason and the resulting fusion of the development of reason and history succeed only with great difficulty. The dialectical method is not least the product of the difficulties arising for him who, despite everything, would understand history as the evolution of absolute reason.

When all these rebukes were visited on Hegel, complaints which actually applied much more to the epoch he had brought to a close than to him, it showed how greatly the spirit of the age was in the grip of change.

It was one of those underground metamorphoses—a kind of sea change—which appears repeatedly in the history of mankind. There can be no doubt that humanity as a whole in all its configurations, like the single individual, is subject to this kind of change in mood and feeling. From time to time humanity feels itself to be on the way up to a high point, or even arriving at a peak, and looks confidently at the future, anticipates happiness, and marvels at itself. At other times humanity slips down into the valley, regards the future with anxiety, looks forward to all sorts of terror, and pities and despises itself.

History shows how moods come in waves, either lifting mankind to the heights of unbounded joy, or casting it down into the depths of profound despair. The reasons for one or the other mood seem to be numberless. Catastrophes, signs

such as a suddenly appearing comet, superstitiously interpreted, hysterics with great prophetic and suggestive power,
events both great and trivial, all can initiate a reversal of
mood. Such forebodings are about as trustworthy as the opposite. It is questionable whether mankind has any sort of sure
instinct for the future, or any real presentiment of it. As often
as man may seem to have this instinct, just as often will he
dance merrily on the edge of a smoking volcano, or be filled
with despair over some imagined evil.

This much being established, let it be applied to the particular and peculiar change of mood that took place between the
first and last quarters of the nineteenth century. Whereas
actually the whole century showed all the signs of economic
and technical advance, of progress in civilization and perhaps
in culture as well, nonetheless at the periphery of this continuum there were voices that threatened and warned. There
were not many of them, but they were influential and had far-
reaching effects. These Jeremiahs did not come from the tech-
nologists, politicians, or businessmen, but from circles devoted
to the life of the spirit. Four voices of this kind can be called
typical—Burckhardt, Marx, Kierkegaard, and Nietzsche—and
whereas all came from different camps, all prophesied gathering evil in one form or another.

In 1842 Burckhardt wrote: "Moreover, I anticipate extremely frightful crises, but humanity will withstand them,
and only then, perhaps, will Germany reach her truly golden
age."[11] If at this point it was only crisis which Burckhardt
warned about, in the future his outlook was to become gloom-
ier, year by year. In 1846 he said that the heralds of a social
Judgment Day were at the door and went on to note: "But I
cannot change it, and before general barbarism—for I see no
immediate prospect of anything else—breaks loose . . ."[12] In
1849 again he said: "I have no hope at all for the future:
possibly we may be allowed to have a couple of more or less
bearable decades, in the genre of Roman Imperial times. It is
my opinion, namely, that democrats and proletariat, even if
they make the most violent attempts, will have to yield to an
even harsher despotism."[13]

Burckhardt never lost this feeling and expressed similar sen-

timents again and again. In 1881 he said: "I feel in all my
bones that something is going to break out in the West, as
soon as Russia has been completely confused by further violent events. Then the day will come when all stages of top-
syturvydom must be lived through, until somewhere, after
naked, measureless violence, a real power is formed."[14] And
finally, in 1881, we are told: "Sometimes I am overcome by a
dread that Europe overnight may, so to speak, be stricken by
a sort of galloping consumption, visiting deathly weakness on
the forces now apparently sustaining us."[15]

Out of this same period, too, came the famous foreword to
Nietzsche's *Will to Power*, in which he wrote: "What I am
recounting is the history of the next two centuries. I am describing what is to come, and which can come in no other
way: the advent of nihilism. This story can already be told:
for here necessity itself is already at work. This future is already foretold in a hundred signs, this fate is being announced
everywhere; to this music of the future all ears are already
attuned. For a long time now our European culture has been
borne along by a tortured tension that increases from decade
to decade, as if headed for catastrophe: restless, violent, precipitate; like a river that is eager to reach the end, that no
longer stops to think, that is afraid of stopping to think."

Not only Burckhardt and Nietzsche had a vision of coming
disaster. Kierkegaard and Marx made the same pronouncement in a quite different vein. Thus Kierkegaard, in 1837, is
already writing in his *Journals*: "At the moment one is afraid
of nothing more than the total bankruptcy that Europe seems
to be facing, thereby forgetting what is far more dangerous,
the apparently inescapable bankruptcy in respect of the spirit
that stands at the door . . ."[16] From then on he returns constantly to prophetic proclamations of impending crisis. In 1846
he tells us: "All corruption comes ultimately from the natural
sciences."[17] In 1854 Kierkegaard described "the signs by
which it can be recognized whether a given condition is ripe
for decline,"[18] and finds these signs in his own times. And in
the same year he said: "It can no longer be a question of a
revolution once, in between, but of everything being founded
on a revolution that can break out at any moment."[19] What

Kierkegaard had in mind was by no means social or political revolution. Rather his despairing eye was fixed on Christendom, and the wrong track upon which Christianity had strayed. All-encompassing political revolution, the necessity and the unavoidability of the downfall of the existing world, these things Marx, meanwhile, had been predicting since 1843.

These four, as one voice, announced the coming destruction of their contemporary culture. This is all the more surprising in view of the fact that in point of departure, in the direction of their interest, in their viewpoint, and above all in the goals they set themselves, these thinkers had hardly anything in common and showed diametric differences.

To be sure, it would not be hard to find a whole chorus of minds opposed to this group of thinkers, people who predicted happiness for the century and times beyond. But that would constitute no objection. Obviously these powerful and, in their way, sensitive spirits already sensed a trembling in the foundations of existence of which the less clairvoyant were unaware. In any case, the events of our own history would seem to show that they were right. From the point of view peculiar to this group of critical thinkers, the sudden inversion of trust into mistrust was inevitable. The relative confidence and comfort with which the Age of Enlightenment and Hegel viewed the future vanished. The future was mistrusted, catastrophe expected. Yet evolution and development were never doubted. All of these thinkers recognized that things were in a state of rapid flux.

The main object of their dubiety was belief in progress. Advancing through change was still felt to be progression, but not progress in the sense of something gained. The picture visualized by these thinkers changed in every respect. Progress was no longer a matter of gaining something new, but of loss and peril.

As Burckhardt contemplated the swift developments all about him, he was fearful of a "sudden mortal weakening of sustaining and preserving forces." Kierkegaard saw a loss of Christianity in the agitation of his time. Nietzsche recognized the ineluctable decline of the existing culture as it moved toward "catastrophe." For Marx a radical transformation of the social and material foundations of events and the downfall of all existing things and of all existing order were in the process of fulfillment.

Thus the center of interest ceased to be the creation of a better new age and became primarily the decay of the present. As when twilight falls and night closes in, everything that in daylight had seemed bright and radiant turned dark, contemporary events took on a negative look. What only shortly before had been regarded as vital strength now showed signs of decay and destruction. An "inversion of values" began to appear, or, more accurately, hitherto existing values began to pass away.

And, as foreshadowed by these thinkers, a form of skepticism began to set in, in its consequences destructive of the status quo. The ensuing twentieth century was to make it clear that this mistrust remained in force.

Actually the critical spirit had from the first been the handmaid of modernity. It had shown itself in many guises: in Descartes' philosophy of doubt, in the Protestant critique of the Catholic Church, in the questioning of the authorities of antiquity, in the social order. Now this doubting spirit reappeared, raised its head anew with unbroken might. But with the difference that this time, through its spokesmen, it turned against that which it itself had created through the centuries.

In the critical storm that had ushered in modern thinking, ancient authorities, above all those of Christianity, were called into question, yet in the last analysis were still acknowledged. Now it could be asked whether the critical storm, currently in force, was not a far more radical thing, whether indeed its aim was not to sweep away *all* entrenched authority. It seemed as if one power alone was determined to hold sway: the power of analytical and critical thought.

The clearest indication of this is the fact that a strain of critical and destructive analysis entered even into the spirit of scientific thinking, for the time being the only uncontested authority. The times now emerging were to create a psychology that unmasked and destroyed and a physics applied to destruction. Literature and the arts delineated even more strongly the sinister and deformed.

Slowly but ineluctably the world changed. If Heg
taught that knowledge was "the only way to win scie
advance" and that the negative is likewise positive, these la
times followed a quite different, inverted prescription. The
positive was transformed into the negative. Light was turned
into darkness. What hitherto had been experienced as belief
was now regarded as superstition. Finally truth became untruth, reason unreason.

More than once Burckhardt described the positive spirit
from which, for him, his science of history derived. He put it
most beautifully in this letter:

> For me history is and will remain poetry on the largest
> scale; get it straight, I do not look on it at all romantically,
> fantastically, which would do no earthly good, but as a
> marvelous process of pupations and of new, forever new
> unveilings of the spirit. I remain standing at the rim of the
> world and stretch out my arms toward the primordial
> causes of all things . . .[20]

Meanwhile, in strange contrast to this attitude, another
spirit now appeared, at first sporadically, but soon gaining
strength. Beginning with Nietzsche and Marx, and carried
forward in history and psychology, a will to discover, in the
sense of unmasking, of debunking, began to go to work. There
was a reaching "behind" things. The beautiful surface appearance was destroyed. Nonculture was revealed behind culture,
disintegration behind synthesis, the bestial lurking in the
human psyche, etc. The lust to discover in the sense of wonderful revelations turned into a lust to tear the mask from the
face of history.

And there can be no doubt that the great realm which
Hegel had simply and comprehensively called the "Negative,"
now began to expand. But the negative which Hegel had seen
as the twin and satellite of the positive meanwhile became a
nothingness. A world of "negative essences" began to take
shape on a large scale. While it was expanding, the spirit of
accusation grew apace. It engendered that attitude, an attitude deeply permeating all human events, in which it is
clearly recognized that all being is closely related to nothing.

..vity and nothingness were not silent and
..ped to them was a significant and effective
..at could be described as a lust for the nega-
..ind of wild, demonic force. It was believed
..me from the negative, that decline was at
.. birth of the new. Thus once again that
.. shape which always manifests itself whenever history finds itself in such a mood.

Theories arose that were completely different in form but in
content all traceable to one essential idea. This was the idea
that by passing through the nothingness confronting humanity
the new could be born. Kierkegaard, Marx, and Nietzsche all
propounded this same notion, though to be sure in entirely
different ways. If our sketch of this development in its incipi-
ent stage is compared with what Hegel stood for, the gap
between him and his successors will become abundantly clear.
Hegel, too, had seen everything that imposes negative feelings
on man throughout his lifetime from first to last, the strongest
examples of which are death, loss, decline, and decay. But the
pride and pretension of the Hegelian kind of thinking was that
it took the negative likewise to be positive. Thus, despite
everything, Hegel was able to see the spirit as progressing by
way of contradiction. Although his own period and his personal life were not spared evil, Hegel stuck to his view of a
harmonious universe.

The period which now began was unable, however, to view
things this way. In the new mode of seeing things the negative
forced its way overpoweringly into the foreground. The present was riddled with signs of decline, the future seemed completely shrouded in darkness. The harmony of the absolute
spirit, even amid contradiction, in which Hegel had believed
now seemed like so much optimistic superstition, the synthetic-
universal Hegelian point of view so much pious lunacy. What
Hegel in the "strict process of dialectical thought" had passed
off as scientific philosophy had come to seem like grotesque
self-delusion.

While this self-delusion, as it was regarded, was falling to
pieces, an allegedly cooler, more temperate, and more critical

point of view was appearing, one that believed it had a sharper conception of truth. Not for the first time in human history a new spirit became operative.

It might be objected that this interpretation makes it seem as if only the human view of the world and not things themselves were changing. But this claim is not made, even if emphasis is placed on the powerful force exerted by this change of view. How much the general shift in outlook was enforced by a deeper and more ominous process of underlying change remains an open question.

The consequences, at any rate, are clear: they are shown in the decline of the Hegelian system, in the fact that he was granted only a brief reprieve during which his kind of thinking was to have the force of conviction. Now came a long period of thinking of a quite different kind. In it present and future changed color and what before had shone turned pale, and that which earlier had lain hidden in darkness was searched out and dragged forth into the light of day.

The twentieth century is still in the throes of this change. From generation to generation, in a continuous unfolding, the consciousness rearranges itself and suffers metamorphosis. In so doing, it has come to have the shape visible on all sides today—as much in political thinking as in social forms, as much in the general human attitude as in artistic expression.

In ensuing pages we shall dwell on the two thinkers who were the radical and extreme representatives of change—Kierkegaard and Marx. These two were certainly not the only exemplars. There were, in fact, many others in every department and sector of thought and action.

But these two stand out in the multiplicity of presences with a special, unique stamp of originality. Kierkegaard made his bid as the implacable, radical champion of the past. His intention was to annul the present in favor of the former Christianity. Marx stepped forward with the same implacability and radicalism, but with a contrary aim. For his part he advanced the ideas of evolution, change, and progress.

It has been the struggle between tradition and revolution which more than anything else has determined the character

of our century. And the nineteenth-century figures of Kierkegaard and Marx, so to speak, represent the extremes which the
twentieth century was to play out in action and suffering.

Both of these thinkers were decisively influenced by Hegel.
Each in his way made use of an intellectual instrument, the
dialectic, fashioned by Hegel. Thus, quite apart from all
metamorphosis and rearrangement, the stream of Western
thought flowed on and still flows, even if we do not know
where it is going.

# 17

## Søren Aabye Kierkegaard:
## Dates and Events

K ierkegaard was born in 1813, son of a merchant,
originally a hosier, but later a man of means.
He was one of several children, issue of his
father's second marriage. The mother seems to have been a
quiet, almost unnoticed woman; at one time she had been a
serving-girl in the father's employ.

The father, a devout, pietistic and, according to Kierkegaard's description, melancholy man, exerted a powerful influence on the son, from which Kierkegaard was never to escape.
The image of the father often appears in Kierkegaard's writings as a man who lived in close relationship with his son, but
who inculcated anxiety and despair. In his *Journals* (1848),
Kierkegaard said: "Personally, as a human being, I am a poor
fellow, an unhappy child who, out of love, made a sad old
man as unhappy as possible."[21]

In spite of, or because of this, the father emerges as a
strong, commanding figure, dominating Kierkegaard as long

as he lived. Kierkegaard lived in an almost mystical union
with his father. To him, Kierkegaard felt, he was indebted for
the two greatest things in his life, standing paradoxically side
by side: Christianity and despair. We see this in a passage in
the *Journals* from 1848: "From the beginning I have owed
everything to my father. This was his plea to me when, melancholy as he was, he saw me to be sad: See to it that you love
Jesus Christ well."[22] Kierkegaard never freed himself psychologically from his father and could not. Modern psychology is well aware of Kierkegaard's fate and has often investi-
gated it.

Psychological insight provides only partial access to the
larger Kierkegaard phenomenon. Even as he never got away
from his father, nor from the past that was his father's legacy,
neither did he ever break away from the larger and mightier
past of the Western world as embodied in Christianity. It was
Christianity that was the final goal of his life and thought.

Kierkegaard grew up in Copenhagen. He attended the middle school there and obviously was an odd, precocious boy. At
home he was nicknamed "the Fork" because once, when asked
what he would like to be when he grew up, he said "a fork," so
he could spear everything and be able to stick people who
bothered him.

Eventually he went to the University of Copenhagen. As a
twenty-two-year-old he debated what line of study he would
follow, and thought first of natural science but finally more of
theology, to which he then applied himself, and occasionally
he toyed with the idea of becoming a lawyer. But even while
thinking over these choices he supposed he lacked the ability
"to lead a completely human life."[23] He asked himself what
his destiny might be, what it was that God could have given
him to do. He explained that his aim in life was to "Find the
idea for which I will live and die."[24] All this sounds rather
grandiloquent, but in fact it was not, as Kierkegaard's later
development was to show.

After a protracted course of study, he earned his master of
arts degree with a dissertation *On the Concept of Irony*. Now
he was overcome by indecision again and could not make up
his mind on a profession. Off and on he considered becoming

a clergyman, since he had already passed the state theological examination. But he did not.

About 1840 he wrote: "My misfortune is mainly that at the time when I was pregnant with ideas I overlooked the ideal; on that account I gave birth to monsters, and on that account actuality does not accord with my burning desire . . ."[25]

From this time on, life began for him in earnest, but in a quite different way from what is usually meant by this expression. Henceforth Kierkegaard's life can be viewed as a fearful and scrupulous avoidance of any contact whatsoever with actual life, a life of solitude for its own sake lived, so to speak, behind drawn curtains. He immediately recoiled from every step that might have involved him with "real" life, that is, the life of the average middle-class person. Kierkegaard became engaged, but broke it off amid endless torments and outbreaks of despair. Nor did he ever make up his mind on a profession. It seems that he became a writer almost incidentally. Besides the religious writings that he called *Edifying Discourses*, he brought out a book under a pseudonym, supposedly a literary work which aroused notice as such. This book was in two parts and bore the title of *Either/Or*. The author's pseudonym was "Victor Eremita."

Kierkegaard's life was poor in external outlets and contacts. He had no regular job and sought none, he shunned every commitment, and after he had withdrawn or broken off from his first attempt at a betrothal, he never had another relationship with a woman. He lived on his own private income. With the exception of some small trips, among others one to Berlin, he never left Copenhagen. He also rejected any attempt to obligate him in any way. When a newspaper offered him a considerable honorarium for his collaboration, he immediately refused.

His wish was to live a sort of anonymous life, but he only partially succeeded. Although his writings appeared under a whole series of different pseudonyms, he was still well known to be an author even while he was anxiously avoiding all public contact. Copenhagen was well aware of him, a rather strange man to his contemporaries.

A Copenhagen humorous periodical, *The Corsair*, in part

because of his physical appearance, in part because he broke off his engagement, made him the butt of satirical comments. This hit home deeply with Kierkegaard and hurt him to the quick. How sensitive he was is shown by many statements, as when, for example, he said; "What, then, is the worse: to be executed or slow death by being trampled to death by geese?"[26]

To the Copenhagen of the period, then a small provincial city, Kierkegaard was a strange fellow who wrote books and kept strictly to himself. He was never seen at social gatherings and never came out in public. Twice the king invited him to a private conversation and he went, and now and again a review of one of his books would come out. But even this much Kierkegaard tried to avoid. Booksellers had to promise not to give away free copies to any newspaper, or in any other way to occasion a review.

Kierkegaard shunned all publicity. In the prefaces to his books he repeatedly let it be known that he placed no value on the "public." When he published a comprehensive two-volume work, his *Concluding Unscientific Postscript*, a sequel to *Philosophical Fragments,* he wrote in the preface of the latter:

> Seldom perhaps has a literary enterprise been more favored by fortune, or had a reception more in accordance with the author's wishes, than was the case with my *Philosophical Fragments*. Hesitant and reserved as it is my custom to be in connection with every form of self-appraisal, I dare nevertheless affirm one thing, and that with confidence, about the fate of the little book: it has created no sensation, absolutely none. Undisturbed, and in compliance with his own motto: "Better well hung than ill wed," the well-hung author has been left hanging. No one has asked him, not even in jest, for whom or for what purpose he hung. Better so, better well hung than by an unfortunate marriage to be brought into systematic relationship with all the world.[27]

But in fact Kierkegaard's very first book was a sensation. Moreover, Kierkegaard kept careful track of what was being said about his writings. If seldom publicly, he reacted in his

*Journals*, often very sensitively, to critical comment. Only rarely did anyone succeed in talking to Kierkegaard face to face, his own father and perhaps a few others excepted, but nonetheless he still paid close attention to public reaction. As already noted, the attack on him in *The Corsair* hurt him beyond all measure.

However poor in outer events his life may have been, by the same token Kierkegaard's inner life was of enormous importance. But with him these inner events occurred as behind drawn curtains. However, the *Journals* reveal the inner turmoil of conflict, fear, tumult, and sudden illuminations in which Kierkegaard lived. They show him to have been caught up in a powerful drama played out between himself, the world, and God.

That part of the drama which forced its way out into the open, meanwhile, was all dressed up, organized, and prepared with a particular purpose in mind. Part of it was that Kierkegaard wanted to mystify people. With some justification he was already saying in 1837: "Everyone has his revenge on the world. Mine consists in keeping my suffering and grief locked up in myself, while laughter is amusing everyone. If I see someone suffering, I pity him, comfort him as best I can, and listen quietly to him when he assures me that I am happy. If I can keep doing this to my dying day, then I am revenged."[28]

Yet why is it that Kierkegaard thinks he has to revenge himself on the world? What has the world done to him? With this question one comes up against a component of Kierkegaard's personality that is never quite absent from all his ingenious accomplishments. That Kierkegaard was excessively sensitive and easily offended, that he felt his life to be a torment, that subjectively he was heavily burdened by some sort of constitutional lack, some kind of "thorn in the flesh"—all these are facts that can be gathered from his work and the *Journals*. Was it, then, that Kierkegaard had to revenge himself because, so to speak, he had been shortchanged by life? Did he have to make the world pay simply because he existed?

Whatever the answer to this question, and it is not easily found, the fact of his lust for revenge remains. Yet in the last analysis this thirst for retribution has a metaphysical meaning.

His contemporary world, as Kierkegaard viewed it, was shattered, dedicated to destruction. Kierkegaard saw official Christianity as nothing but a great deception, the "modern" as so much "humbug."[29] It was at this inadequate world that his revenge was directed.

Himself shattered, Kierkegaard lived in a shattered world. This world merited his struggle and his revenge, but neither could be translated into words. His existence was thus transformed into suffering, which he stubbornly endured. All the energy that Kierkegaard had at his disposal went into describing his and the world's suffering.

His life flowed along uneventfully. It was more than taken up by his literary endeavors. His private means gave him enough to live on, and he never had the worry of making ends meet. With the years Kierkegaard seemed to withdraw more and more into his own world. At the same time he was conscious that no "single man" could help or save the age, and that he could only "express the fact that it is perishing."[30]

From about 1849 another idea began to stir in his brain. Statements like this began to show up in his *Journals*: "What with all the torment inside, and with the ascendancy I have had, and then with the treatment I have suffered, I have been brought to the point where very soon I may arrange a providence, an awakening, myself." Then suddenly we are told: "If God will make it possible for me to operate more humanly, so I shall not always need to make myself into the third person, so I can personally intervene in circumstance, then I shall be helped."[31]

But this was only a passing notion from which Kierkegaard drew back on the grounds that he was a "penitent from whom God can exact everything."[32] And so it seems this idea ended like so many other speculations about committing himself to an active calling.

Meanwhile matters suddenly began to come to a head for him. One of the few people with whom Kierkegaard had any contact, a man who had also been his father's friend, was the then Bishop Mynster. Kierkegaard wrote about him in his *Journals* in 1847:

Glory to Bishop Mynster. There is no one I have admired, no one living being more than Bishop Mynster, and it is a joy to me always to be reminded of my father. He is so placed that I see the difficulties more clearly than anyone who has attacked him. But what I have to say is of such a nature that it can be said very well without prejudice to him—*if only he himself does not make a blunder.* There is an ambiguity in his existence that cannot be avoided, because the state church is an ambiguity.[33]

Then in 1854 Bishop Mynster died. In a memorial address, the theologian Martensen, Mynster's successor in the bishopric, described the deceased bishop as a "witness to the truth." In December 1854 Kierkegaard published an article written earlier that year in February, titled "Was Bishop Mynster a 'witness to the truth,' one of the 'right witnesses to the truth'?—Is that the *truth?*"

Kierkegaard took formal exception to Martensen's claim. His article gave rise to a series of articles by others, some of them attacking Kierkegaard, some siding with him. The polemic continued, with Kierkegaard replying to his critics and sticking to his opinion. The little flood of articles developed into a storm, if perhaps no more than a storm in a teacup.[34]

Now it was as if the spell had been broken, as if the inner state of trance and isolation in which Kierkegaard had lived was collapsing. The battler in Kierkegaard came to life. About this time in his *Journals*, under the heading "To act catastrophically," he debated whether he should in fact seek to have a catastrophic effect.[35]

He actually made an attempt in this direction. From May to October in 1855 he published sharp and penetrating articles attacking official Christianity. The attack mounted from one article to the next. Finally, in the ninth piece, he came right out and in blunt language said that "clergymen are cannibals, and indeed of the most abominable sort."[36]

Kierkegaard was now obviously bent on starting a conflagration. Had he, by this means, at last found the meaning of his existence? Or had he gone beyond the mystery and the measure of it? Fate gave the answer. Before the last article came out ( No. 10), Kierkegaard died.

Kierkegaard went to his death as if he had been expecting it for a long time. In one of his last conversations he was asked by his friend Boesen whether all the "Moments," that is, all the articles that had appeared under this heading, were now published. Kierkegaard said they were and later, when Boesen remarked how much in Kierkegaard's life had been "wonderful," said: "Yes, I am very glad and very sad; for I can share joy with no one."[37]

Kierkegaard lived as a broken and penitential man in a world that he regarded as lost. Contemplating this suffering, one is tempted to write a Kierkegaardian pathology and interpret him within a pathological context.

This way of looking at Kierkegaard begins with the fact that he was a solitary. He had no partner and found no partnership during his whole life. His only companion was himself. He split himself up, so to speak, into parts and surrounded himself with the imaginary people of his pseudonyms. He talked to these figures and lived with them as if they were almost his intimates. He unbosomed himself more freely in the soliloquies of his *Journals*, however, than with his pseudonyms. But even in these soliloquies he was still mistrustful, and he repeatedly emphasized that he did not lay bare his final thoughts even in the *Journals*.

That Kierkegaard, to the extent one believes he can be understood in medical terms, was a neurotic may be taken for granted beyond a shadow of doubt. In fact, he described his melancholy, depressed, and anxious states with the meticulous exactitude of a psychologist or psychiatrist. The enduring theme of his *Journals* is the "cabin of melancholy," a forsakenness by God and man only occasionally broken by an enormous feeling of happiness.

Beyond this, in the *Journals* there are places where it is difficult to say whether Kierkegaard is describing poetic visions or psychotic images. It has been conjectured that he was schizophrenic, but this diagnosis cannot be confirmed unless new data are adduced.

The deep inner split in Kierkegaard's nature is obvious. He

himself described it again and again and knew all about it. For instance, he declared himself a "two-faced Janus"[38] and complained that his life was only "conjunctive." He said of himself: "While I declaim against others for not studying the sources, but compendia—I myself live a compedium. While I can conquer in any dispute, I have the ghost of my own fantasy on my back, and that I cannot dispute away."[39]

He hung suspended amid all things, committed neither to this nor to that. In the outer sense he could find no profession or calling, in the inner sense he was unable to find his way to the partnership of marriage. He was unable to attain the simple and primitive faith that he admired so much, yet could not be an unbeliever. In a real sense he could neither live nor die. "From my early childhood," he wrote in 1847, "the arrow of suffering has been planted in my heart. So long as it is there I am ironical—pull it out and I will die."[40] And long before this he had said: "The sad thing with me is that in one step right off the bat I use up the bit of joy and ease of mind that I have slowly distilled from the laboriously dyspeptic process of my life of thought."[41]

All this is factual and cannot be denied. It simply demonstrates that Kierkegaard was a sufferer and, in this sense, if you will, a "sick man." His weapon in defending himself against this sickness was a mighty strength of spirit. This spirit fended off existence with irony, looked imperiously and thoughtfully at the mystery of existence, and finally tried to see over and beyond it all. Kierkegaard's works are the documentation of this spirit.

# 18

# Kierkegaard's Concept of Irony

**B**efore we get into this documentation and, following Kierkegaard's directions, interpret the sequence and interrelatedness of his writings in terms of their final goal, let us discuss a work standing outside the overall Kierkegaardian plan and organization. This is Kierkegaard's master's thesis at the University of Copenhagen: *On the Concept of Irony, with Constant Reference to Socrates.*[42] This thesis, published under his own name, had, in Kierkegaard's opinion, no place in the total work. He clearly regarded it as a work of expediency, a means to an end, intended to be no more no less than a scholarly dissertation necessary to fulfill the requirements for a theological degree.

For us the work is more than this, although it is rarely accorded enough appreciation in the Kierkegaardian literature. It is related to Kierkegaard's later books in much the same way as Hegel's first work "On the Difference between the Systems of Fichte and Schelling" is to the Hegelian system.

Later themes are found *in nuce* in Hegel's youthful essay. Similarly, in the case of Kierkegaard it is fascinating for the observer to look back on this precursive work from the perspective of the subsequent production.

*On the Concept of Irony* can be briefly summarized as follows:

Its aim, first of all, is to draw a portrait of Socrates on the basis of the historical sources, that is, the reports of Xenophon, Aristophanes, and Plato. It is a critical study, demonstrating the ambiguity of the image of Socrates. It is also proof, as Kierkegaard saw it, that Socrates' essential nature can be defined as "irony." This proof Kierkegaard makes good mainly on the basis of the Platonic writings. This first chapter concludes with a summation setting the stage for further delving.

A second chapter again deals with the historic Socrates and advances the analysis. Now Kierkegaard turns to the mysterious Socrates who talks about his "daimon." Kierkegaard also addresses himself to the two accusations leveled against Socrates: that he did not recognize the gods of the state and that he corrupted the youth. He then goes on to write briefly about Socrates being sentenced to death.

So much for the historical presentation. While Kierkegaard takes great pains to be historically accurate, still he is not simply a historian. For example, Socrates' condemnation to death is described in only fragmentary fashion. Kierkegaard represents the event as if Socrates himself had chosen to die. In reality Socrates was first found guilty by only a narrow majority of votes. He had to respond to this condemnation and did so by petitioning to be publicly honored. On the urging of friends he finally declared himself ready to pay a fine. Only then was the condemnation to death made, this time by the greater majority of eighty votes.

Kierkegaard did not report these details. He had reached his true goal, a foregone conclusion to begin with. To the very end, as Kierkegaard saw it, the Socratic point of view remained ironic. Socrates lived ironically, taught ironically, and went to his death ironically. On this Socratic basis Kierkegaard defined the nature of irony in general. Irony, he said, was "infinite negativity." In his irony Socrates was negative about everything—the state, the Sophists, his favorite pupils. He hovered, as Kierkegaard put it, "in ironic satisfaction above all the determinations of the substantial life."[43]

Depicting Socrates, Kierkegaard depicted himself. He saw himself as Socrates and Socrates as a sort of Kierkegaard. Just as he, Kierkegaard, stood opposed to a world in decline, so had Socrates similarly confronted the world of his day. But Socrates had made his appearance before the arrival of Christianity. He had arrived on the scene in an age when the divine was becoming extinct, but during which the incarnation of the divine in the form of Christ was on the way. Socrates, therefore, had no choice but absolute negativity.

This was also Kierkegaard's own historical situation, as he himself defined it. He, too, lived in an age of religious decline, one in which religion was no longer a positive force. Thus Kierkegaard saw himself as one among a group of world historical individuals whom he described in many images. In one of these images in the *Journals,* which does not exactly fit Socrates because he was married, we are told: "Every time history is fated to take an essential step forward and make it through a difficult passage, immediately a team of regular relay horses appear: the unmarried, lonely men who live only for an idea . . ."[44]

For Kierkegaard, Socrates was a caesura, a turning point in world history. He said: "For the observer the life of Socrates is like a majestic pause in the course of history: one does not hear him at all; a deep stillness prevails until this is suddenly broken off by the discordant attempts of several different schools of disciples to trace back their origin to this hidden and mysterious source." He proceeds to develop this picture. "With Socrates the stream of the historical narrative plunges underground for a time like the river Guadalquivir." Socrates is "like a dash in punctuation," he is "the nothingness from which a beginning must be made."[45]

The argument is expanded in Part 2 of the thesis. After Socrates has been established as an ironist pure and simple, the embodiment of irony, the concept of irony as such and its treatment by Fichte, Schelling, Tieck, Sager, et al. is presented. Basic to all this supplemental discussion is the definition which Kierkegaard, so to speak, has posited as final: irony is infinite and absolute negativity.

With this presentation, again historically oriented, the argument is essentially closed, apart from a final brief chapter on "The Truth of Irony." At first glance this chapter does not seem to contain very much. Compared with the imposing claim that irony is infinite and absolute negativity, these final arguments seem very pale indeed. They involve a discussion of "irony mastered," which makes the poet and poetizing free. It is explained that only when irony is limited does it "acquire its proper significance and true validity."[46]

It almost seems as if these propositions, as if in a suddenly retractive balancing of accounts, take back half of what has been previously said. Kierkegaard is not at all convincing when he says that although irony can mislead as well as lead, nevertheless in his age it has to be "praised as a guide." One asks how the "truth of irony" is demonstrated by such propositions.

Nevertheless this chapter contains the very first indications of Kierkegaard's great problem. He feels himself to be an ironist. He has shown through Socrates the absolute power and significance of irony. He knows that irony both guides and misleads. How much he was aware of this last aspect of irony is shown in a passage of a quite different tone written in 1838 before his dissertation had been published. At this time he said: "Irony is an abnormal development which, like the abnormality of the livers of Strasbourg geese, ends up by killing the individual."[47]

If this comment is taken in the context of the definition of irony as absolute negativity, the connection becomes clear. Irony as negativity finally kills men, as it killed Socrates. Yet if this is the case, what connection does irony have with truth?

This is indeed the crucial point. The question is answered —at least for Kierkegaard—as soon as one accepts a proposition that also appears in this concluding chapter: "Irony is like the negative way, not the truth, but the way."[48] He goes on to make it clear that "Irony now limits, renders finite, defines and thereby yields truth, actuality and content; it chastens and punishes and thereby imparts stability, character, and consistency."[49]

Looking now at Kierkegaard's later works, we see that irony is a method that abrogates and chastises everything, a way that must be taken to arrive at truth. Thus it is the starting point, the point of departure, but not the end.

It was not for nothing that Kierkegaard chose Socrates and irony as the theme of his dissertation. From an early date Kierkegaard's weapons were wit and irony. He knew the power and superiority of irony, and at the same time its negativity. Moreover, from an equally early date depression was bound up with Kierkegaard's irony.

When Kierkegaard used Socrates in sketching a picture of irony, and in Socrates recognized the powerful and world historical effect of irony, in the guise of a theoretical treatise he was describing *in extenso* his own experience of existence: namely, that existence as such is ironic.

Also bound up with the power and superiority given by irony is yet another experience which Kierkegaard again described through the person of Socrates. If Socrates' existence was ironic, as Kierkegaard expressly said, it also made him "incapable of contracting any real relation with the existent (*Bestehenden*)."[50]

Kierkegaard described this circumstance on several occasions, as for example when he wrote: "The ironist, on the other hand, has advanced beyond the reach of his age and opened a front against it. That which shall come is hidden from him concealed behind his back, but the actuality he hostilely opposes is the one he shall destroy. Toward this he directs his consuming gaze, and concerning his relation to his age one may apply the words*: 'Behold, the feet of them who shall carry thee away stand already at the door.' "[51]

Thus irony is absolute negativity: it makes for estrangement. This, too, is portrayed through Socrates. Irony as negativity "no longer directs itself against this or that particular

---

* The passage, a favorite of Hegel's, comes from Acts 5:9. In the King James Version it reads: "Behold, the feet of them which have buried thy husband are at the door, and shall carry thee out."—*Tr.*

phenomenon, against a particular thing [*Tilvaerende*], but . . . the whole of existence [*Tilvaerelse*] has become alien to the ironic subject; he in turn has become estranged from existence [*Tilvaerelse*], and . . . because actuality has lost its validity for him, so he, too, is to a certain extent no longer actual."[52]

Here we hear a distant echo of what Hegel described as the "self-estrangement of the spirit." But the Hegelian concept of estrangement had nothing to do with irony. It was related to an epoch, or stage, of the spirit and with dialectical development or evolution. It had only one thing in common with the Kierkegaardian notion of ironic estrangement: a searching experience of the negative and the deactualization of the real. Thus Hegel describes it in one way, Kierkegaard in another— using Socrates and Socratic irony.

Yet on the other hand it is not by chance that Kierkegaard made frequent reference to Hegel in his dissertation on irony. The name of Hegel often crops up, quite apart from the quotations involving the Hegelian concept of irony and Hegel's interpretation of Socrates. Hegel is by no means as amicably and admiringly treated as Socrates. On the contrary, he is almost always spoken of satirically or even critically dismissed.

However, aside from the fact that Hegel was among the great contemporary philosophers, Kierkegaard could not pass him by for another reason. Inseparably bound up with the figure of Socrates is the pedagogical form of the dialectic peculiar to Socratic philosophy. Hegel likewise taught a dialectic, but one in its essence neither ironical nor pedagogic. Just how much Kierkegaard made the Socratic dialectic his own, and how completely he rejected Hegelian dialectic, will become evident later on.

Nonetheless he was impressed by one idea in the Hegelian dialectic. In Kierkegaard's chapter on the world historical validity of irony, he discusses, obviously leaning on Hegel, "a contradiction through which the development of the world occurs."[53] The given actuality of a certain age, he says, "is valid for a people and the individuals constituting that people." But because it is doomed to be superseded by another, approaching actuality, to that extent it is not valid. Thus "for the people contemporaneous with the Reformation, Catholicism was the given actuality, and yet it was an actuality which no longer had validity as such."

This is primarily the Hegelian idea of contradiction in history. But in taking it over Kierkegaard does not see it as signaling historical progress, only the tragedy of history. This was Socrates' situation in his age: he was surrounded by a world that still seemed valid, but which in fact was not. We can discern Kierkegaard's basic notion in this description: the ironist lives in an age which he has grown beyond. This being the case, Kierkegaard felt that he, too, had to become an ironist.

# 19

## The "Indirect Method" and the Indirect Life

Into this Kierkegaardian world of ideas, events intruded that were to have an enormous influence on his life. In 1837 Kierkegaard met Regina Olsen. In 1838 his father died. In 1840 he completed his theological examination, and about a year later his dissertation appeared. After finishing his examination Kierkegaard became engaged to Regina Olsen, but a year later broke the engagement.

Why Kierkegaard broke his engagement remains unclear. Only so much is certain, that he acted in response to a deeper necessity, perhaps related to some psychological or physical defect, the "thorn in the flesh." But Kierkegaard supplied no details about his move and boasted that no one would ever find out what the trouble had been. At the same time he constantly declared that he loved Regina Olsen. In 1841 he wrote in his *Journals*: "The only thing that consoles me is that I can lay myself down to die and in my dying hour confess the love that I cannot admit as long as I live. Which makes me happy and unhappy in the same measure."[54] From this point on similar passages appear in the *Journals*.

It seems impossible to find the root cause for breaking his engagement, the motivation for which Kierkegaard scrupulously concealed. By the same token it is all the more certain that with this step Kierkegaard made a final decision. For Kierkegaard the end of his betrothal had the character of a clean break with actuality.

Even while believing himself to be sinking into a profound depression, as he repeatedly recorded in his *Journals*, he came to a second decision. Kierkegaard began to produce. *Either/ Or* came out about a year and a half after he had broken with Regina Olsen. *Fear and Trembling* and *Repetition* were published that same year. Thereafter, year after year a whole series of works appeared, among others *Philosophical Fragments, On the Concept of Irony* and *Stages on Life's Way*. This means that during a period of something more than two years, a major portion of Kierkegaard's work, pouring forth in a steady stream, had been written and published.

Kierkegaard saw a connection between his productivity and breaking his engagement and the suffering that followed from this shattering actuality. In 1849 he wrote about the rupture of his betrothal to Regina in his *Journals* as follows: "The suffering was terrible; but melancholy as I was, I understood it as my own misery multiplied, as my misery multiplied by having made her unhappy—and then, then suddenly a richness broke forth in my soul, which makes me shudder when I look back on it.'"[55]

Many writers, like Goethe in his *Werther*, have poetized and made a literary work of their personal experience. There can be no doubt that in a number of publications Kierkegaard's basic material was provided by his encounter with Regina Olsen, the betrothal, and its being broken off. The experience also permitted Kierkegaard to see through all sorts of situations where deliberate deception is linked with a deeper truth in a most remarkable way. So it can be said that a large part of Kierkegaard's work is autobiographical, a mirroring of self.

Kierkegaard knew that the poet reflects what is in himself. Thus *Either/Or* begins with this passage:

> What is a poet? An unhappy man who in his heart harbors a deep anguish, but whose lips are so fashioned that the moans and cries which pass over them are transformed into ravishing music . . . And men crowd about the poet and say to him, "Sing for us soon again"—which is as much to say, "May new sufferings torment your soul, but may your lips be fashioned as before; for the cries would only distress us, but the music, the music, is delightful!"[56]

Accordingly, Kierkegaard understands his literary production, so far as it is poetical, as a singing of his torments. He succeeded in doing just this, for the first volume of *Either/Or* was received as a masterpiece of romantic poetry.

Meanwhile Kierkegaard was living a double and a triple life. Simultaneously with *Either/Or* he published another work, *Edifying Discourses*, written in a completely different style. These "discourses" are sermons in the literal sense of the word. They deal with such themes as "The High Priest," "The Publican" and "The Sinner." They begin with a prayer and cite a text from the Scriptures.

They reflect Kierkegaard's second existence, one clearly removed and separated from the first. Whereas the poetical works came out under pseudonyms—pseudonyms, to be sure, that were perfectly transparent—the *Edifying Discourses* were published without subterfuge under the name Kierkegaard.

Beyond this a third existence took shape and with it emerged a third plane of production, slowly developing out of the poetical. In ensuing years more poetical works in the vein of *Either/Or* and more edifying discourses continued to come out side by side. But in 1844 appeared a remarkable piece of writing that fell in between these two categories. It had the title of *Philosophical Fragments*, and it was followed in 1846 by a sequel called *Concluding Unscientific Postscript to the "Philosophical Fragments."*

Kierkegaard's total production, therefore, is confusingly

polyglot, as it were, and multivocal. He speaks in the language of the poet, the preacher, and the "unscientific" philosopher.

These writings in three different idioms continued until the year 1846, then they began to lessen. The essential seemed to have been said. Now the Christian-religious tenor of Kierkegaardian thought began to loom more and more. Kierkegaard took off his mask. The pseudonymous authors behind which he had hidden now disappeared. To be sure, one last pseudonym, "Climacus," suddenly appeared like a belated progeny.

But henceforth Kierkegaard the Christian stood forth for all to see, above all in *The Sickness unto Death*. At the same time he wrote the interpretative epilogue to his *The Point of View for My Work As an Author*. This book was published posthumously (1859) by his brother.

As a whole, this literary production is an unparalleled achievement, as is shown, for one thing, by the thematic breadth, which ranges from the poetic to the philosophical and into the religious. It is shown again in the actual execution: poetry of the greatest sensitivity and eloquence alternates with the language of the true preacher, while at the same time a sublime philosophy emerges.

Side by side appear the simple and pious thoughts of the Christian, and then Kierkegaard changes his tone and language and becomes a poet reflecting every differentiation and nuance, only again to exhibit tremendous speculative power in his philosophical works.

The many-sidedness of these works, a variety approaching the uncanny, the chameleonlike versatility which they demonstrate, still had an organized, planned character. Kierkegaard unfolded his literary production through a whole series of pseudonyms. There was nearly a dozen of them: Victor Eremita (*Either/Or*), Johannes de Silentio (*Fear and Trembling*), Constantia Constantius (*Repetition*), Vigilius Haufniensis (*The Concept of Dread*), Nicolaus Notabene (*Prefaces*), Johannes Climacus (*Philosophical Fragments*), Hilarius Bogbinder, William Afham the Assessor, Frater Taciturnus (*Stages on Life's Way*), Anticlimacus (*Training in Christianity*), etc.

They appear in appropriate works either singly or together and each speaks his part. They alternate with each other, sometimes they contradict each other, sometimes they appear united or support each other. They appeal to each other, or polemicize against each other. Each makes his confession directly or indirectly and then vanishes. Perhaps he will be evoked again, perhaps make only one appearance. But Kierkegaard holds the threads of the whole together. He himself is, and acknowledges himself to be, the director, the stage manager who organizes the whole. What at first glance appear to be scattered works come to have a cryptic unity and add up to an overriding idea. The figures are cunningly woven together, as in a novel or drama. Kierkegaard's individual works are also similarly interwoven.

What is the whole meant to be? A drama, a story, an epic? None of these. It is intended to be a theory, a doctrine that teaches. In a certain sense this doctrine offers nothing new. It merely repeats an old lesson: the lesson of Christianity. In a highly artistic way, using all the most modern technical and artistic means, it is simply intended to present what the Bible had already proclaimed.

Was Kierkegaard, then, a prophet, appearing in the guise of poet, philosopher, and preacher? Not even that. He did not feel himself to be sent and empowered by God. Rather he expounded his own lot and the lot of humankind. He bore fate as a sufferer, a stricken mortal, a Job of God.

It was in this manner, in any case, that he explained, commented on, and interpreted himself. If we did not know this from the thirteen volumes of his *Journals*, in which he continually reflected on himself and his work, we would have to infer it from the epilogues that he later wrote for the whole body of his writings.

Four years before his death, under the title of *On My Work As an Author*, Kierkegaard wrote a report intended to be a sort of "statement of accounts." Two years before this, under the similar title *The Point of View for My Work As an Author*, he had written a treatise described in its subtitles as a "Direct Report" and a "Report on History." The first work he published himself, the second appeared posthumously in 1859.

In the second report, brought out after his death, Kierkegaard provided a systematic arrangement of his works according to three categories: the poetical or, as he called them, the
"esthetic" writings; an interim body of work; and finally
the "completely religious" production. The total body of the
works, therefore, was listed in three "divisions." It is easy for
anyone who has read Kierkegaard to see that this articulation
of his work corresponds to his theory of three forms of existence, for he differentiated between "esthetic," "ethical," and
"religious" existence.

Kierkegaard partitioned his writings almost pedantically.
Under esthetic production he counted: *Either/Or* (1843),
*Fear and Trembling* (1843), *Repetition* (1843), *The Concept
of Dread* (1844), *Foreword* (1844), *Philosophical Fragments*
(1844), and *Stages on Life's Way* (1845). Remarkably
enough, he puts the eighteen *Edifying Discourses*, published
from time to time and inclusively in 1845, in the same category.

According to this same report the second division contained
only one two-volume work, published in 1846 as a sequel to
the *Philosophical Fragments* under the title of *Concluding
Unscientific Postscript to the "Philosophical Fragments"*. Thus
this work stands alone.

The third division comprises *Edifying Discourses in Varying
Tenor* (1847), *The Works of Love* (1847), the *Christian Discourses* (1848) and a work called *The Crises and the Crisis in
the Life of an Author* (1848).[57] At the time Kierkegaard was
dividing up and arranging his works in this manner, a number
of later writings had yet to appear. Most important of these,
*The Sickness unto Death* (1849), is therefore assigned no
place in the schema and so it must remain an open question
where it belongs.

Though this listing is obviously intended to impose a systematic arrangement by subject, it is also clear from the
chronological order that it reveals a certain historical sequence. The "esthetic" production lasted until about 1845, the
transitional work until 1846, and the "completely religious"
production until 1848. Consequently the systematic ordering

was at the same time genetic and temporal. It could be supposed that Kierkegaard developed from being a poetic writer through a second phase into a religious one. Finally, it could be imagined that Kierkegaard arranged the progression of his output according to the "stages" of his life.

But this was precisely what Kierkegaard did *not* wish. Though it is entirely possible that a certain temporal development actually is reflected in the arrangement, as Kierkegaard himself believed, this is of only secondary significance. As he himself would have it, Kierkegaard did not develop in such a biographical or psychological sense. And he is right when he claims this to be the case, because purely religious writings, namely, the *Edifying Discourses*, appeared in the period of poetic or esthetic production.

It is not a question of a sequence in which Kierkegaard dramatically and autobiographically acted out, as it were, the three forms of existence, but rather a question of juxtaposition. What might appear to be development and sequence, and what indeed is such in a certain sense, Kierkegaard wanted to have understood as an inner and simultaneous continuity. He had not presented and played out the three existential roles one after the other, but all at the same time, in one dimension containing the opposition, the unity, and the correlation of human existence.

It is now that the definitive, distinguishing mark of his work suddenly appears, a characteristic which does not permit Kierkegaard to be labeled as a "poet," "philosopher," or "Christian thinker." To understand this unique feature one must turn to Kierkegaard's "indirect" methods.

We know that Kierkegaard wrote alternately under his own name and under pseudonyms. The pseudonyms appeared until the very last, with the exception of such militant and provocative articles as "The Moment" of the final years. At the same time that Kierkegaard was at the peak of his esthetic production he was also writing the *Edifying Discourses* under his own name.

Kierkegaard explained why he wrote in these double and triple modes in the "balance sheet" that he himself published under the title *On My Work As an Author*. There he said:

The movement which my literary activity describes is this: *from* the poet—from the esthetic, *from* the philosopher—from the speculative out *to* the suggestion of the deepest intensification; from the *pseudonymous "Either/ Or" through the "Concluding Postscript,"* which was labeled *with my own as well as with the publisher's name, to* the "Three Discourses at the Communion on Fridays," of which two were given in the Church of Our Lady. This movement is *uno tenore*, written or accomplished, if I may say so, in a single breath, so that my literary work regarded as a *whole* is a religious one from beginning to end, which anyone can see and must see, if see he will.[58]

The zeal and emphasis with which Kierkegaard formulated these sentences and presented his final statement serves to show that he saw himself in his own mind not as a sort of chameleon but as consistently one and the same person. But was he *actually*? Such a doubt can and must be raised after reading the *Journals*.

If this question is left aside, and if Kierkegaard's own prescriptions are followed, then his work, in its many tonalities of language and wealth of authorship multiplying under the pseudonyms, does represent an internal unity. But this inner unity is "indirect," not "direct."

The truth, Kierkegaard believed, could no longer be taught directly. The age had lost the organic capacity to apprehend the truth, had *basically* lost it. The true could be shown to you only by leading you to it against your will, as it were, or by "tricking" you into it. Thus the game with the pseudonyms, and the work as a whole, presented through a diversity of changing, dramatically executed figures, is intended to convey the truth, convey it, that is, indirectly. This presupposes that each of the figures says *something* true, proclaims a part of the truth. None of the constituent figures tells the whole truth, nor do any of the pseudonyms say what is true for Kierkegaard.

In consequence, Kierkegaard is even able to claim that "in the pseudonymous writings there is not a single word" by himself. It is never he whom the pseudonymous writer represents. He is always the "secretary of what author it may be, at the same time, ironically enough, a dialectical reduplication of the same author as poet."[59]

If the techniques of this indirect method are now examined, it becomes clear immediately that it is modeled on the Socratic dialogic experience as described by Plato. However, this imitation suffers from one fundamental defect. Unlike Socrates, Kierkegaard does not look for dialogical partners. He has none and wants none, and in the last analysis it may be doubted that he could have conversed with one had he had him. Kierkegaard has no young men whom he loves. He pulls back from any contact, he has no desire to talk, only very much to write. Therefore, in the end he must talk only to himself and to his fantasy world.

Springing from this defect and complication came a singular curiosity and an accomplishment like none other in world literature. Kierkegaard's intellectual drama was performed on a stage where the author, the director, and the producer were Kierkegaard himself, not to mention commentator, critic, and audience.

Thus a continuous dialogue unfolded from one publication to the next. It began with the first volume of *Either/Or*. Even in this first work the second volume acts as an adversary to the first. This sort of thing continues in all the later writings. The dialogue is carried on by shadow figures, Kierkegaard being their "reduplication as poet." Kierkegaard is here, there, and everywhere. Standing off in the background, he holds all the threads. When the pseudonyms talk to and against each other, Kierkegaard adds new pseudonyms to the company in the guise of commentators. He also speaks out under his own name. But when he does so, he speaks in a religious manner, as if he knew nothing about the other matters.

To use Martin Thust's apt phrase, "Kierkegaard directs a puppet theater."[60] The content of the different pieces played in this puppet theater, pieces which collaborate dialogically, is taken from Kierkegaard's existence and the existence of his age as he saw it. He himself remains in the shadows. And the ultimate prompter is lost entirely in the dark: he is God, in whom Kierkegaard believes.

Kierkegaard believed that he was speaking in God's name.

Yet he spoke only in negatives; in his *Journals* he wrote: "I am not an apostle, who brings something from God and this with authority. No, I serve God, but without authority. My task is to make room so that God can come."[61]

Socrates wanted to be the midwife to truth, to help bring it to birth maieutically through dialogue. Kierkegaard asserted that his indirect method had the same goal. But in keeping with its peculiar esthetic, the Kierkegaardian method was to truth as the theater is to actuality. There is no actuality on the stage; it is only played. The dramatic truth of the piece is dramatically borne out by the actors. In the same way, Kierkegaard believed, his literary productions, so far as they were pseudonymous, played out the drama of "existential truth."

During his lifetime Kierkegaard made fun of "systems," above all of the Hegelian system. Whenever the subject of the Hegelian system came up, Kierkegaard heaped on it all the vials of his wrath and scorn. He made not only the Hegelian idea of system but also the Hegelian dialectic the butt of his criticism.

In the *Journals* he gives this biting description of the dialectic: ". . . the Hegelian process of rumination with three stomachs: first the immediate, then regurgitate it, then down again with it. Perhaps a subsequent master will be able to try it with four stomachs, etc., down again, then up again: I do not know whether the master understands what I mean."[62]

In the *Concluding Unscientific Postscript*, where we find the real quarrel with Hegel, this criticism becomes clearer: ". . . a system of existence cannot be given." Existence, to be sure, is a system, Kierkegaard says, but not for an existing spirit, only for God.[63]

Thus at first glance it may seem strange that one should think of Kierkegaard in terms of a "system of thought." On reflection, however, this is indeed possible, and even necessary. Kierkegaard builds up the body of his work by the "indirect method," following a definite pattern, which means systematically. Step by step in the pseudonymous works he methodically develops his basic argument, and from book to book moves toward his goal, now going forward, now reaching backward.

So, while there is no system per se, nonetheless there is a system of thought. The thought process never actually crystallizes into a system, never reaches this stage of completion. It proceeds according to a systematic arrangement, however, which perforce it must follow. We recall that with Kierkegaard the order or arrangement arises from what the pseudonyms expound. These pseudonyms provide a partial and fragmentary truth, which gradually advances toward final truth.

The systematic order that is followed, as is yet to be more precisely demonstrated, is in the nature of a peculiar *movement*. It moves step by step in a gradual process of disclosure, even if at the end there is no closed and final truth. In a certain sense, too, it is not a positive forward movement, but tends toward the negative.

The fact remains, however, that—leaving out of account the content disclosed along the way—an ordered way of thinking is always present. This order as an order of movement Kierkegaard calls "dialectical."

The real sense of this dialectic can be shown only in the presentation of the individual works. But anticipatively, at least, this dialectic as an operative method can be described in terms of its contradistinction to the Hegelian method.

When we speak about an operative dialectical method, Hegel at once comes to mind, for he, too, used an operative dialectic, out of which the universe of the Absolute Spirit arises. As the Hegelian dialectic proceeds, opposites unfold, cancel each other, and allow syntheses to emerge. Each new step in the dialectical movement paves the way for a new synthesis. The operative spirit of the age, in a positive, constructive process, works through the constant canceling out of negatives which always point the way to positives.

Here we see how completely different was the dialectical system of Kierkegaardian thought. Instead of a positive construction there is a negative one. Formally expressed, Kierkegaard does not, like Hegel, in his *Logic*, proceed from "being" to "nothing" to "becoming." He does not begin with the self-evident truth of being, but with the negative of untruth and partial truth as presented by the pseudonyms.

He sees himself confronted by a shattered and disunified existence, as he experienced it in himself and in the world. His thinking begins with the unfolding of an immanently contradictory world. His own life marched in step with this negativity. It began with a sad youth, fell apart with the breaking of his engagement, and proceeded even further to a break with all current actuality that led to a "catastrophic result."

The musical accompaniment to this life and experience is the reflective commentary which Kierkegaard gave to his writings. This commentary constitutes the essence of the Kierkegaardian dialectic. With him the dialectic did not function as a constructive building up of actuality, as Hegel saw it, but as a destructive dissolution. The point of view changed. Whereas for Hegel the world was entire, a universality, now the world, in total gloom, is fragmented and headed for destruction.

The system of ideas changes in keeping with this change in the basic assumption. While for Hegel actuality and its concepts are understood as a dialectical succession, for Kierkegaard there is a succession of fallacies and negative concepts. The world of the "negative" is now at hand, of "negative essences," the world of nothingness.

Remarkably enough, Marx also reversed the dialectical method in the same sense, "stood it on its head," as he put it. Albeit in another realm than Kierkegaard's, he too would dialectically unfold a world of negative events.

The trick, basically simple enough, by which the dialectic was changed was this: If Hegel had taught that everything negative is just as much positive, from the new point of view everything positive was just as much negative. Kierkegaard undertook to demonstrate this to be true in human existence, Marx in human society. Thus the train of positive and constructive thinking took a turn in the opposite direction toward the destructive and negative.

# 20

## The Pseudonymous Works

Kierkegaard himself, as already noted, described how his work was built up and gave instructions how it was to be read. He arranged his writings in a sequence, assigning both those appearing under his own name and those under pseudonyms their specific places, thus setting up a binding order.

If we only conditionally follow this arrangement in the following discussion of Kierkegaard's works, let us point out how our development of the subject departs from the Kierkegaardian prescription. We develop, generally following Kierkegaard, the totality of his work in terms of the outstanding writings. That is, we start with *Either/Or* and next go into *Fear and Trembling*. After this comes *Concluding Unscientific Postscript*. We end with *The Sickness unto Death*.

This sequence, to be sure, does not provide a detailed account of all the works, and so is vulnerable to a criticism of this choice. Nonetheless it does follow Kierkegaard's basic idea as he himself described it: from *Either/Or* through the *Concluding Postscript*. It does not, however, as Kierkegaard said at this point, put a stop to the sequence at *Three Discourses at the Communion on Fridays*, but takes the real concluding work to be *The Sickness unto Death*.

For Kierkegaard his literary production ended with *Three Discourses at the Communion on Fridays*, which appeared in 1851 and thus later than *The Sickness unto Death*. As he saw it, his work wound up with a positive and unequivocal profession of Christianity. But leaving aside the fact that this affirmation had been present from the beginning, and appeared in all the early *Edifying Discourses*, the actual end of Kierkegaard's literary production came with the publication of the ten articles under the title "The Moment."

These, too, are a profession of Christianity, even if they do take the form of a radical attack on official Christendom and Christianity. At the very end of his life Kierkegaard was speaking in terms of attack. The basis for this assault had long since been prepared. The real background for it is shown in *The Sickness unto Death*, and for this reason we conclude with this book.

The overthrow of existing Christianity, which Kierkegaard demanded and expected, did not come to pass. Developments occurred in theology that in many respects were in line with Kierkegaardian ideas, let us say as worked out in "dialectical theology," but his demand for the abrogation of official, established Christendom did not take place.

But another Kierkegaardian influence had far-reaching effects. Kierkegaard is the father of all modern existentialist philosophy, to the extent that his great theme of "existence" has also become the essential theme of this philosophy. So far as Kierkegaard has remained alive, he lives on in a philosophical capacity.

Our presentation, therefore, will not only reflect Kierkegaard as he was in his day, not only show his thought as he thought it, but come to an understanding of him in terms of his place in history and his continuing influence into present time.

Kierkegaard's first work (if we disregard his master's dissertation) came out under the title of *Either/Or*. This work breaks down into two parts which are totally divergent, not so much in content as in style and technique, this in line with and justifying the fact that two pseudonymous authors figure in the work.

In the preface Kierkegaard has the alleged editor, Victor Eremita, tell how by chance he found two manuscripts. One of them was a collection of essays in a legible, elegant, and often hastily written script, the other in a "clear, somewhat spreading, uniform and even handwriting . . . apparently that of a businessman."[64] The editor calls one manuscript "A's papers." Who this "A" is remains in the dark, but because the manuscript contains a series of "esthetic essays," he is called the esthete. The author of the second manuscript is more clearly identified. He is a magistrate and he is at least given a surname, "William."

So goes the introductory fable. It already tells us that we will be dealing with two different kinds of figures, thus justifying the different modalities of the book's two parts. Kierkegaard carries out this differentiation with the greatest artistry.

Whereas the second volume is a sort of closed report, the first seems to be almost an omnium-gatherum or potpourri. Aphorisms, an essay on the "musical-erotic" and a similar one on the tragic alternate with ironic essays, and end with the "Diary of a Seducer." The whole volume seems like a badly executed combination of heterogeneous parts, though all, to be sure, are written in one and the same spirit. This first volume is romantic literature in the highest sense. It is as if it were written in a spirit of light and undecided irony, in which, to be sure, the "negativity," the uncommittedness, and the ultimate lack of viewpoint of the author shimmer through.

It starts out with the aphorisms, or "diapsalmata," as Kierkegaard calls them. They go like this:

"Old age realizes the dreams of youth: look at Dean Swift; in his youth he built an asylum for the insane, in his old age he was himself an inmate."[65]

This malicious and ironically bitter tone returns again and again: "To be a perfect man is after all the highest human ideal. Now I have got corns, which ought to help some."[66]

Behind the virulent mockery lurks a no less virulent and biting critical faculty. Thus of philosophy Kierkegaard says: "What the philosophers say about Reality is often as disappointing as a sign you see in a shop window, which reads: Pressing Done Here. If you brought your clothes to be pressed, you would be fooled; for only the sign is for sale."[67]

This irony opens up the dark side of the world. Kierkegaard tells us: "It happened that a fire broke out in a theater. The clown came out to inform the public. They thought it was a joke and applauded. He repeated his warnings, they shouted him down. So I think the world will come to an end amid general applause from all the wits, who believe that it is a joke."[68]

Indeed, everything that Kierkegaard touches on in these aphorisms becomes ambiguous—half-serious, half mocking. For example, he says: "I prefer to talk with children, for it is still possible to hope they may become rational beings. But those who have already become so—good Lord!"[69]

Or again: "The social striving and the beautiful sympathy which prompts it spread more and more. In Leipzig a society has recently been formed whose members are pledged, out of sympathy for old horses, to eat their flesh."[70]

But Kierkegaard also turns his irony on himself: "The disproportion in my build is that my forelegs are too short. Like the kangaroo I have very short forelegs, and tremendously long hind legs. Ordinarily I sit quite still; but if I move, the tremendous leap that follows strikes terror in all to whom I am bound by the tender ties of kinships and friendship."[71]

As a rule there is more in these aphorisms about Kierkegaard himself than meets the eye, as when he says: "Alas, the doors of fortune do not open inward, so that by storming them one cannot force them open; they open outward, and therefore nothing can be done."[72]

The ten or so pages of these brightly checkered aphorisms serve, so to speak, as the prelude to the book. This curtain raiser pursues a definite goal, reached particularly by means of the diction, the style of the writing. Like most aphorisms, these too are mostly in the form of a paradox. Thus we are told: "Time flows, life is a dream, people say, and so on. I do not notice it. Time stands still, and I with it . . ." Or: "When I get up in the morning, I go straight back to bed again . . ."[73] Toward the end of the diapsalmata this paradoxical line is carried to extremes. There now comes a longer passage with the heading "Either/Or: An Ecstatic Lecture." Since the title of the book is *Either/Or* this "lecture" must contain the leit-motif, as it were, of the whole. It starts out like this:

"If you marry, you regret it; if you do not marry, you will also regret it; if you marry or do not marry, you will regret both; whether you marry or do not marry, you will regret both." The same theme is applied to other examples in the same rhythmic form, and in the first instance concludes with: "Hang yourself, you will regret it; do not hang yourself, and you will also regret that; hang yourself or do not hang yourself, you will regret both; whether you hang yourself or do not hang yourself, you will regret both. This, gentlemen, is the sum and substance of all philosophy . . ."

This "ecstatic lecture," particularly since it is titled the same as the whole book, might be thought of as a sort of table of contents. This is right, in fact, because from first to last, again and again the "either/or" theme is repeated like a kind of refrain. It must also be said that this either/or, according to Kierkegaard's underlying purpose, is indeed the leading theme, nonetheless it is constantly changed, and in such fashion that although Kierkegaard at first presents it in a playful way, handles it jestingly and ironically, he makes it progressively more serious and inescapable as the book progresses.

But at this introductory point in the work, the either/or idea is mockingly intended. Thus in the middle of the "lecture" Hegelian philosophy is plainly ridiculed:

But for those who can follow me, although I do not make any progress, I shall now unfold the eternal truth, by virtue of which this philosophy remains within itself, and admits of no higher philosophy. For if I proceeded from my principle, I should find it impossible to stop; for if I stopped, I should regret it, and if I did not stop, I should also regret that, etc. But since I never start, so can I never stop; my eternal departure is identical with my eternal cessation. Therefore I find myself in excellent shape. Experience has shown that it is by no means difficult for philosophy to begin. Far from it. It begins with nothing, and consequently can always begin. But the difficulty, both for philosophy and philosophers, is to stop. This difficulty is obviated in my philosophy; for if anyone believes that if I stop now, really stop, he proves himself lacking in speculative insight.[74]

The philosophy meant in this description is the Hegelian philosophy, if only because of the fact that in his *Logic* Hegel once said that in a certain sense philosophy begins with "nothing." The ridicule is directed above all at the Hegelian dialectic, which is understood as the illusion of movement, but which in reality is marking time in place. As Kierkegaard sarcastically put it: "I have only one principle, and I do not even proceed from that."

This first volume is kept in a peculiar state of indecision. It changes at will from irony to seriousness. In the middle of the volume are strewn pieces on music and tragedy, that is, on real esthetic themes. Later comes a piece called "The Unhappiest Man: An Enthusiastic Address before the Symparenekromenoi . . ." Then, somewhat further along still, comes another called "The Rotation Method." A sample is:

. . . and boredom is the root of all evil. The history of this can be traced from the very beginning of the world. The gods were bored, so they created man. Adam was bored because he was alone, so Eve was created. Thus boredom entered the world and increased in proportion to the increase of population. Adam was bored alone: then Adam and Eve were bored together; then Adam and Eve and Cain and Abel were bored *en famille*; then the population of the world increased, and the peoples were bored *en masse*. To divert themselves they conceived the idea of constructing a tower high enough to reach the heavens. This idea is itself as boring as the tower was high, and constitutes a terrible proof of how boredom gained the upper hand . . .[75]

At the conclusion of the first volume appears the "Diary of a Seducer," a piece which has been regarded by some as a high point in the art of romantic literature. The material for this diary comes from the story of Kierkegaard's own love and betrothal. But this experience, according to Kierkegaard's own testimony, filled with sadness and despair, is here couched in a different vein. Kierkegaard describes the Don Juan type, whose love ends the moment it has achieved its purpose. Thus the argument, presented in the form of letters, is built up. All stages of being in love are dramatically portrayed. At the climax the action suddenly breaks off. The seducer says: "I will have no farewell scene with her; nothing is more disgusting to me than a woman's tears and a woman's prayers, which alter everything and really mean nothing. I have loved her, but from now on she can no longer engross my soul . . ."[76]

With this the first volume ends and the second begins. In the second part Kierkegaard changes tone and style, form and content, characters and *mise en scène*. The second volume consists of four segments: "Esthetic Validity of Marriage," "Equilibrium between the Esthetic and the Ethical in the Composition of Personality," "Ultimatum" and "The Edification Implied in the Thought That As Against God We Are Always in the Wrong."

This second volume is easier to describe, its contents easier to reduce to a formula. Again it is written only in the form of two long letters. The alleged author is married and defends marriage against his friend, obviously the author of the first part of the book. While defending marriage, at the same time he attacks his friend's attitude toward life and his existential position.

Such is the action of this second part of the book, to the extent that it has any action at all. In it nothing really happens except that an attempt is made to persuade the author of the first volume that he is living in a world of despair. As a result, the whole reads in a rather didactic way, and this may well be the reason why it had far less public success than the first volume.

A few passages will serve to suggest the character and intention of the second volume. On the surface the book is sim-

ply an argument establishing the necessity of marriage, manifested both as a moral necessity and an actuality in human
beings. Yet this argument is not pursued in the usual sense of
showing that it is divinely, socially, or biologically ordained.

All these arguments, to be sure, are brought into play at the
appropriate place. But the intention of the proof goes beyond
this. Behind the scenes set up for our viewing, the general
theme of the book, that of "either/or," is debated. Thus, in the
middle of the volume, at the beginning of the section called
"Equilibrium between the Esthetic and the Ethical in the
Composition of Personality," we are told:

> What I have so often said to you I say now once again,
> or rather I shout it: Either/or, *aut/aut* . . . And now as for
> you, this phrase is only too often on your lips, it has almost
> become a byword with you. What significance has it for
> you? None at all. You, according to your own expression,
> regard it as a wink of the eye, a snap of the fingers, a *coup
> de main*, an abracadabra. At every opportunity you know
> how to introduce it, nor is it without effect; for it affects
> you as strong drink affects a neurasthenic, you become
> completely intoxicated by what you call the higher mad-
> ness. It is the compendium, you say, of all practical wis-
> dom, but no one has ever inculcated it so pithily (like a
> god in the form of a puppet talking to suffering humanity)
> as that great thinker and true practical philosopher who
> said to a man who had insulted him by pulling off his hat
> and throwing it on the floor: "If you pick it up you'll get a
> thrashing; if you don't pick it up, you'll also get a thrash-
> ing: now you can choose." You take great delight in "com-
> forting" people when they have recourse to you in critical
> situations. You listen to their exposition of the case and
> then say, "Yes, I perceive perfectly that there are two pos-
> sibilities, one can do either this or that. My sincere opinion
> and my friendly counsel is as follows: Do it/or don't do
> it—you will regret both." But he who mocks others, mocks
> himself, and your rejoinder is not a mere nothing, but a
> profound mockery of yourself, a sorry proof how limp your
> soul is, that your whole philosophy of life is concentrated

in one single proposition: "I say merely either/or . . ." Life is a masquerade, you explain, and for you there is inexhaustible material for amusement; and so far no one has succeeded in knowing you, for every revelation you make is always an illusion; it is only in this way you are able to breathe and prevent people from pressing importunately on you and obstructing your respiration. Your occupation consists in preserving your hiding-place, and that you succeed in doing, for your mask is the most enigmatic of all. In fact you are nothing; you are merely a relation to others, what you are told you are by virtue of this relation. To a fond shepherdess you hold out a languishing hand, and instantly you are masked in all possible bucolic sentimentality. A reverend spiritual father you deceive with a brotherly kiss, etc. You yourself are nothing, an enigmatic figure on whose brow is inscribed: Either/Or.[77]

This list of reproaches continues, always with the same purpose in mind: to expose the writer of the first part of the book, to tear off his masks and uncover the essence of the person behind. The next objection raised is that despite all the seeming playfulness and all the esthetic perfection portrayed in the first volume, all of it adds up only to "despair." And so we are now told: "Behold, my young friend, this life of yours is despair. Hide this if you will from others, from yourself you cannot hide it, it is despair. And yet in another sense this life is not despair. You are too frivolous to despair, and you are too melancholy not to come in touch with despair."[78]

Behind the desire for an unqualified enjoyment of life which the seducer preaches, Kierkegaard wants to show the melancholy that is the real author of despair. But for Kierkegaard melancholy is not something to be excused. On the contrary, it is a sin: "But melancholy is sin, really it is a sin *instar omnium*, for not to will deeply and sincerely is sin, and this is the mother of all sins. This sickness, or rather this sin, is very common in our age and so it is under this all young Germany and France now sigh . . ."[79]

It is fairly evident that when Kierkegaard holds a mirror up to the "seducer" he is also holding one up to himself. In spite of all Kierkegaard's protestations that he, personally, is not identified with the pseudonyms, in a certain sense all his writing is autobiographical. Indeed, this self-depiction is written with a systematic purpose in mind. It is autobiographical to the extent that any presentation of this kind is naturally filled with subjective, personally experienced material, but at the same time the concern here is to elevate the material into the universal and ethical.

The broadly executed and greatly elaborated basic idea of this second volume, its didactic purpose, so to speak, is to bring about a confrontation between ethical and esthetic-dialectical existence. The author of volume one is a seducer, the esthetic-romantic man, whose existence is the constant pursuit of pleasure and having more and more. According to Kierkegaard this existence is comprised of the appetences and the intrigues of the seducer's life, which eventually must lead him to melancholy, despair, and nothingness.

The author of the second volume, like the author of the first, expounds his maxims and rules for life. This Kierkegaard II, in polar opposition to Kierkegaard I, draws his own didactic conclusions and systematically develops them.

The inferences are evolved in terms of the fundamental either/or idea of the whole, for either/or is the leitmotif common to both authors. In the first volume of *Either/Or* an attitude is developed which basically is neither/nor. According to Kierkegaard, this connotes giving oneself up to the moment and its mood, seizing the opportunity and seeing what happens, living in the flux of the apparent and evanescent. At the same time, this means avoiding any real choice, taking no stand, wanting everything and being nothing. Therefore this kind of existence must end in despair, melancholy, and nothingness.

On the other hand, the second volume teaches the necessity of making a committed choice. Now for the first time the either/or situation makes its appearance, namely, as the compulsion to come to a decision. This decision, as Kierkegaard sees it, can be formulated only dialectically: choose or do not choose, in either case you have chosen. If you do not choose, then you are nothing and have given up. Only when you make up your mind and declare a choice have you begun to be something.

Quite obviously the ethical man is the higher type for Kierkegaard, the developed man who possesses the real fullness of existence. The following will bear this out:

> Every esthetical view of life is despair, it was said. This was attributed to the fact that it was built upon what may be and may not be. Such is not the case with the ethical view of life, for it builds life upon what essentially belongs to being. The esthetical, it was said, is that in a man whereby he immediately is the man he is; the ethical is that whereby a man becomes what he becomes. By this I do not intend to say that the man who lives esthetically does not develop, but he develops by necessity not by freedom; no metamorphosis takes place in him, no infinite movement where he reaches the point from whence he becomes what he becomes.[80]

This contrasting of the ethical and the esthetic forms of existence consists first of all in differentiating between an "immediate" and a "mediated" existence, to express the matter in Hegelian terms. And though Kierkegaard never admits his dependence on Hegel and treats him with angry contempt, here his dependence is quite plain to see. It is simply a dependence on that form of movement characteristic of dialectical thought. Even Kierkegaard cannot escape this Hegelian notion of progression.

All dialectical thinking, so to speak, climbs step by step upward and forward. It always moves from a first stage to a second one, a third one, etc. It also moves only by way of contrast. Whatever the new level may be, it is not reached by any sort of direct, and in this narrower sense logical, development, but by way of contradiction.

Therefore for Kierkegaard, too, ethical existence is a contradiction of esthetic existence: "He who chooses himself ethically has himself as his task, and not as a possibility merely, not as a toy to be played with arbitrarily. He can choose himself ethically only when he chooses himself in continuity, and so he has himself as a task that is manifoldly defined."

But what does this mean, choosing oneself? Kierkegaard interpreted it to mean just what is indicated in the paragraph cited above. The ethical person makes himself his task. The instructions given by Kierkegaard for doing this appear in the following passage:

> The principal difference,* and one on which everything hinges, is that the ethical individual is transparent to himself and does not live *ins Blaue hinein* [thoughtlessly] as does the esthetical individual. This difference states the whole case. He who lives ethically has seen himself, knows himself, penetrates with his consciousness his whole tangible self, does not allow indefinite thoughts to putter about within him, nor tempting possibilities distract him with their jugglery; he is not like a witch's letter from which one sense can be got now and then another depending on how one turns it. He knows himself . . .[81]

If this theory here expounded by Kierkegaard is viewed in the light of traditional ethical theory, it will be found to have something missing. A traditional ethic, to be sure, describes an overall ethical attitude, but it also always lays down commands and strictures appropriate to the attitude. In a traditional ethic, norms are established in a formal or material way that the ethically living person must obey and fulfill.

Kierkegaard gives only fleeting attention to this problem. He advocates an ethical attitude or way of thinking. He expressly asserts:

> . . . In the matter of ethics it is not a question of the multifariousness of duty, but of its intensity . . . The chief thing is not whether one can count on one's fingers how many duties one has, but that a man has once felt the intensity of duty in such a way that the consciousness of it is for him the assurance of the eternal validity of his being. I, therefore, by no means extol a man for being a man of duty, any more than I could commend him for being a bookworm, and yet it is certain that the man before whom duty has never revealed itself in its whole significance is

---

* i.e., between an ethical and an esthetical individual.—*Tr.*

quite as poor a sort as is the scholar who thinks like the foolish inhabitants of the village of Mol that learning comes to one *mir nichts und dir nichts.** Let the casuists be absorbed in discovering the multifariousness of duties. The chief thing, the only saving thing, is that in relation to his own life a man is not his uncle, but his father.[82]

The second volume, like the first, has a remarkable concluding section. Oddly enough it is in the form of a sermon and has the title "The Edification Implied in the Thought That As against God We Are Always in the Wrong."

In a certain sense, to be sure, it is perfectly understandable that the stage manager of the whole, Kierkegaard himself, should close this part of the work with a sermon. For the author of the second volume makes himself out to be a brave, honest, sober man, who while certainly not a limited person, at the same time is by no means a man of boundless wisdom. And in the picture of this man as drawn by Kierkegaard belonged an honest and simple relationship to the religious.

However, this second volume of *Either/Or* has a dark underlying sense, as had the first. That is, the dialectical play, the dialectical drama of existence, has yet to be acted out to the end. The first two acts have been performed. Only now will Kierkegaard develop the third.

In his *"Journals"* Kierkegaard commented on the development thus far: "What the whole *Either/Or* is especially concerned with, is that the metaphysical meaning underlying the whole, and which throughout leads everything into dilemma, be made very clear . . ."[83] This means, then, that only an apparent conclusion has been reached in the second volume. In view of the fact that the passage in the *"Journals"* just cited was written in 1841, before *Either/Or* was published, it is apparent that already Kierkegaard had it in mind to develop only one great dilemma in it, namely, the dilemma of esthetical and ethical existence. This is tantamount to letting us know beforehand that the real solution is not reached in the work at hand.

* The German phrase means "without further ado" or "without so much as a by-your-leave," etc.—*Tr.*

# 21

## The Religious and the "Pathos" of Dread

The same year that *Either/Or* appeared, Kierkegaard also published two smaller pieces, both of which came out on the same day. As can be inferred from Kierkegaard's own intimations, both these works were in the nature of an "indirect" message, correctly surmised by the German translator Schrempf as having been directed at Regina Olsen.[84] Perhaps *Fear and Trembling*, in which the rejection of Regina Olsen is represented as a religious sacrifice, was intended to show Kierkegaard's real reason for breaking off the engagement, whereas *Repetition*, which deals with a love story like the "Diary of a Seducer," was meant to let Regina know of his eternal love.[85]

These inferences are borne out by the choice of pseudonyms. The author of *Fear and Trembling* is Johannes de Silentio, the real Johannes being Kierkegaard himself, who is bound to silence. Author of *Repetition* is Constantia Constantius, the tried and true, if one may so understand the pseudonym.

In the whole sweep of Kierkegaard's writings, *Repetition* is to be taken as just what it says it is, a repetition of the experience of love. However, in *Fear and Trembling* the religious theme makes its first appearance in full panoply. In contrast to *Repetition*, where no new theme is introduced, *Fear and Trembling* introduces a new subject which carries forward the two subjects discussed in *Either/Or*. This is the theme of religious existence, now presented for consideration after the esthetical and ethical forms of existence appearing in *Either/Or*.

For contemporaries who saw Kierkegaard primarily as a poet and man of letters, *Fear and Trembling* must have been a new variant. Now, eschewing irony altogether, Kierkegaard suddenly turned his attention to a great religious figure: he described Abraham when commanded by God to sacrifice his son Isaac.

With this Kierkegaard came to grips with one of the most remarkable episodes in the Old Testament, the story of Abraham's temptation at the hands of God himself. Johannes de Silentio begins by recounting the tale in the words of the Bible, then proceeds to repeat and vary it, while describing what Abraham and Isaac could have felt. Then comes a panegyric of Abraham, the content of which is summed up in the Biblical statement: "No one is so great as Abraham! Who is capable of understanding him!"

Following this is a third section under the heading of "Problemata," in which Abraham is viewed from all sides: ethical, moral, human, and religious. Such problems as these are discussed: Can the ethical commandment "Thou shalt not kill" be abrogated? Is there such a thing as absolute obedience to God? Did Abraham have a right to keep silent about what he was going to do to Isaac and others?

The purpose of God's command to kill, unqualified obedience to God, the obligation to remain silent and Abraham's secrecy—all are subjected to discussion. From a personal point of view, it is as if Kierkegaard were cloaking what he had done to Regina Olsen in the guise of a religious sacrifice. For he, too, he felt, had committed a crime on higher command, and was thereafter pledged to silence about it.

Both parts of *Either/Or* and the existential forms of esthetic and ethical man were undoubtedly fashioned out of personal material, and the same procedure was followed in *Fear and Trembling*. Religious man and religious existence appear in the form of Abraham. But Kierkegaard lurks in the shadows behind Abraham, just as he did in *Either/Or* behind Poet A and Magistrate B.

The glorification of the religious existence is unmistakable, beginning with the sentence "none is so great as Abraham." Abraham is not an "esthetic," "tragic" or an "ethical" hero. He is a knight of the faith. He is great, great in his incomprehensibility.

Abraham is great because he believes. At the same time Kierkegaard will not concede that he is beyond understanding. He is not to be understood only by those who do not understand faith. Abraham stands at the pinnacle of belief, yet his faith is not a simple, but a paradoxical, phenomenon. It is ". . . a paradox which is capable of transforming a murder into a holy act most pleasing to God, a paradox which gives Isaac back to Abraham, which no thought can master, because faith begins precisely where thinking leaves off."[86]

Kierkegaard subtitled this work "A Dialectical Lyric." This is intended to mean that his reflections do not really take place in the dimension of rational thinking, but in another "lyrical" and ecstatic realm. At the same time the lyricism is dialectical, fulfilling itself as a movement and a passionate idea.

The "paradoxon" again makes its appearance, this time as a definition of faith, the same paradox continuously evoked in *Either/Or*, particularly in the first part. There it was a matter of ironic paradox, the run of the mill kind, so to speak, mere esthetical paradox, but now the whole tenor of the writing shows that Kierkegaard wanted to invest it with more weight and seriousness in its religious application.

In *Either/Or* Kierkegaard made it abundantly clear that two opposed forms of existence were at work in his nature. As unmistakably expressed in the very title of the book, Kierkegaard let it be known he was dealing with a schism and a contradiction.

As the reader of *Either/Or* cannot fail to gather, Kierkegaard is bent on presenting this schism with all possible sharpness. Whereas the esthetical man uses paradox as an existential game and makes the most of life in paradox, in the second part of *Either/Or* this discord has already become a more serious matter. Paradox no longer looms as a dialectical game, but as the necessity of making a decision.

Yet the reader of *Either/Or* can scarcely foresee that behind either/or, thus far described as two disparate forms of existence, there stands a neither/nor. This becomes clear in *Fear and Trembling*, that is, the fact that *neither* the esthetic form of existence *nor* the ethical one is the essential existence. The essential existence is the religious form.

There is no proof available of a hierarchy of existence as defined by Kierkegaard. He resigns himself to this fact and, through his pseudonym, avers that "one cannot understand Abraham." Yet nonetheless there is obviously a dialectical way of arriving at this claim, namely, the one which Kierkegaard calls "dialectically lyrical."

Critically examining this lyrical approach, we get an idea what this dialectical movement is. We might suppose, after what had been shown in *Either/Or*, that we now have a positive synthesis in the Hegelian sense of the dialectic. The religious form of existence might be imagined as a synthesis of the esthetic and ethical. Yet not for a moment did Kierkegaard have this in mind.

Rather, the religious is deduced throughout from negative categories: from the crime, the breach of the ethical and universal commandment, and from the silence regarding it all. These are all external attributes of Abraham. And while this negative movement of thought is being carried out, in the darkness faith as a destructive event takes shape.

This kind of negative progression and negative dialectical movement, as carried forward to completion from *Either/Or* to *Fear and Trembling*, Kierkegaard was to demonstrate in ever new variations. The indirect dialectical path followed here is basically the model for all of Kierkegaard's work.

Later, in his *Journals*, Kierkegaard said of *Fear and Trembling*: "Oh, when I am dead, then *Fear and Trembling* alone will be enough to give me the name of an immortal author.

Then it will be read, then it will be translated, too, into foreign languages. People will almost shudder at the frightful pathos of the book . . ."[87]

And indeed, after the ironic pathos of the first part of *Either/Or* and the ethical pathos of the second part, now religious pathos suddenly appears as a lyric of dread. Kierkegaard knew exactly what he was doing when he chose from the Bible the story of a cruel and jealous God, the story in which Abraham is the hero.

In *Repetition,* which came out at the same time as *Fear and Trembling,* Kierkegaard once again changed his theme. He turned back. *Repetition* repeats the love story theme already treated in the "Diary of a Seducer." Falling in love and then abandoning the loved one is described a second time—ergo, *Repetition.*

Kierkegaard had the great poetic gift of being able to color everything with a positive or negative melody of experience and feeling. At his command was the ability, which only a true poet can have, to impart the tonality of a subject as if in a musical composition. This artistic essence pervades all his thinking.

This same artistry determines his production and gives it its peculiar rhythm. Kierkegaard's entire body of work can be regarded as a musical composition in which certain basic themes appear again and again, but in ever new variations and tonal colors.

In this sense the basic theme reiterated in *Repetition* has now been given a quite different form. Tonality and events have been altered. What in the "Diary of a Seducer" was described in romantic, soaring movement, is now, so to speak, presented enigmatically and in its tragic aspect.

In the "Diary of a Seducer," the main figure, the "Seducer," acts out his part with the melodic cheerfulness of a Don Juan, but in *Repetition* the lover appears as "the unhappy one." He is introduced by his "confidant," to whom he writes letters about his unhappiness. In his role of the unhappy one he recites his sufferings, and through his letters he comes to life before the reader's eyes. The confidant observes and meditates on what transpires. He regards what is going on as an experiment, and therefore the book's subtitle is "An Essay in Experimental Psychology."

The play within a play unfolds in the letters written by the "unhappy young man" and in the meeting between him and the "confidant." The unhappy young man falls head over heels in love. But this love seems to be a misunderstanding and the girl becomes a burden to him. At the same time the unhappy young man is awakened to a period of intense poetic activity. The commentator and confidant says: "Now everything became clear to me. The young girl was not his beloved, only his muse . . ."[88]

It is only too evident that Kierkegaard is writing about an aspect of the story of his own engagement. Regina Olsen also became a burden to him, one that he could not bear. He, too, as expressly reported in the *Journals*, was similarly aroused to poetic activity.

In addition, the commentator indicates that behind these events a second series of events is occurring. As he puts it: "The idea is in motion." Exactly what idea is in motion, as so often with Kierkegaard, remains obscure. The plot, recounted in letters, continues to unfold, the "unhappy young man" wavers, torn this way and that. At one time he wants to run away, at another to commit himself to marriage. The dilemma is resolved—as it was when Kierkegaard resolved it—by the girl marrying another man.

With this the story ends. The "unhappy young man" feels free: "When the idea calls I forsake everything. . . . When the idea beckons to me I follow. . . . I grieve nobody by being faithful to my idea. . . . The chalice of inebriation is again held out to me. . . . Long life to the high flight of thought, to moral danger in the service of the idea . . ."[89]

The whole argument ends with a letter from the author, Constantia Constantius, addressed to the reader, a letter which, incidentally, establishes an indirect relationship between *Repetition* and *Fear and Trembling*. In the letter Constantia Constantius meditates on the "unhappy young man." He understands him as a poet, and to that extent as an "exception." But he reproaches him with having lacked a religious background, poet though he may have been. Had he had this religious background, he would not have been an unhappy person, but would have understood everything in religious fear and trembling. For: "A religious individual, on the contrary, reposes in himself and disdains all the childish pranks of reality."[90]

The extraordinarily involved events of the story, events constantly being reflected in a new dimension, beyond doubt depict Kierkegaard himself in his own involvements with love, marriage, and finally, the religious existence. At the end, as with all of Kierkegaard's pseudonymous works, we are left, so to speak, psychologically hanging between irony, cheerfulness, and depression.

Nevertheless a basic tone unmistakably pervades the whole, a tone that stands out and cannot be ignored. When the "unhappy young man" is describing his existence in his letters, he reveals the dread and nothingness of existence. At one point he tells us:

> I stick my finger into existence—it smells of nothing. Where am I? What is this thing called the world? Who is it who has lured me into the thing, and now leaves me here? Who am I? How did I come into the world? Why was I not consulted, why not made acquainted with its manners and customs, but rather thrust into the ranks as though I had been bought from a slave dealer?[91]

The question of the meaning of existence, therefore, is posed movingly and with the greatest urgency. It is expressed in a tone of doubt and at the same time accusingly. The situation is framed quite differently from the simple song:

> *Ich komme, ich weiss nicht woher,*
> *ich gehe, ich weiss nicht wohin,*
> *mich wundert, dass ich so fröhlich bin.*

> ( I come, whence I do not know,
> I go, whither I do not know,
> It surprises me I am so gay.)

When Kierkegaard poses these questions, he does so with a different emphasis: strange, that I should be so sad. Just as strikingly as the meaning of existence was put to question, now suddenly appears a description of dread, or anxiety. In the same letter it says:

> At other times I am quieter. Then I do not read, I sit shrunken together like an ancient ruin and gaze at everything. Then it seems to be as though I were a little child who goes pottering about the room or sits in a corner with his toys. I have a strange sensation. I cannot understand what it is that makes the grown folks so passionate, I cannot understand what they are quarreling about, and yet I cannot help listening. Then it seems to me that it was bad people who gave Job all that affliction, that it was his friends who now sit and bark at him. Then I weep loudly, a nameless dread of the world and of life and of men and of everything wrings my heart.[92]

Kierkegaard describes his own anxiety in almost the same words in the *Journals*.[93] *Repetition*, meanwhile, gives a clue as to how he understood this dread. It is metaphysical anxiety, nothing more nor less than fear in the face of existence. It is, moreover, an anxiety given of God, wherefore the "unhappy young man" compares himself to and identifies with Job, the religious sufferer. Indeed, when the letters to the confidant are not reporting on the young man's unhappiness, they are repeatedly describing Job.

Disregarding for a moment the fact that Kierkegaard is continually talking on different levels and in different tones, we can get at the essence of the whole performance: anxiety and despair over the nothingness of existence. Finally, beyond this, Kierkegaard describes this quintessential factor of anxiety several times in his *Journals*. One of these descriptions might be cited. A year before he died he wrote in his *Journals*, under the heading "Of Life's Arrival and Departure":

> Hear the cry of the parturient mother at the hour of giving birth, see the struggle of the dying at the last moment: and say then whether that which begins and that which ends like this can be designed for pleasure.

True enough, we human beings do everything to get by

these two points as speedily as possible, we hasten, as fast as we can, to forget the birth cry and to turn it into pleasure over having given a creature life. And when someone dies, straightway it is: he dropped off to sleep softly and easily, death is a sleep, a quiet sleep—all of which we say not on account of the deceased, but on our own account, in order not to lose any of our joy in life, to change everything so that it will serve to increase our pleasure in life between the birth cry and the death cry, between the mother's cry and the child's repetition of the same cry when the child some day dies. Supposing there were a colossally magnificent hall where everything had been done to produce sheer joy and splendor—but the entrance to this hall was a disgustingly filthy henhouse-ladder and it were impossible to go up it without soiling oneself with filth, and the admission were paid by self-prostitution, and when day dawned pleasure was all over and it ended with being thrown out with a kick—but all through the night everything would be done to keep up and intensify the pleasure and the joy!

What is meant here? To consider well these two questions: how did I get into this and how do I get out of it again, how will it end? What is thoughtlessness? To do everything to drown our entrance and exit in forgetfulness, to explain around or explain away what lies between the cry of the newly-born and the repetition of the cry when he was newly born to breathing his last in his death-throes.[94]

Behind the mask of pseudonymity in one year—in *Either/ Or, Fear and Trembling,* and *Repetition*—Kierkegaard had covered what for him were the given actualities. He had described this seeming actuality as life-dividedness, as the nothingness of existence, and as fear and trembling. A systematic ground plan had been clearly laid down, the permutations of "esthetic," "ethical" and "religious" existence demonstrated.

These forms of existence had not been presented in juxtaposition, but in a succession. But whereas the direction of the "esthetical" and "ethical" forms of existence seems plain enough, a certain ambiguity lingers about the religious mode.

And so again using a pseudonym, a year later Kierkegaard published a work called *The Concept of Dread*. The alleged author is called Vigilius Haufniensis and the subtitle reads: "A simple psychological deliberation oriented in the direction of the problem of original sin."

Whereas in earlier pseudonymous publications there were tales within tales in which other imaginary characters advance the argument and other commentators besides the alleged editor crop up from time to time, in *The Concept of Dread* there is for the first time only one pseudonym. In the preface the author says about himself: "So far as concerns my humble person, I admit with all honesty that as an author I am a king without a country, but also that in fear and much trembling I am an author without pretensions."[95] Once again, then, we have the catch phrase "fear and trembling." Thus we already have an indication, as further announced in the subtitle, that we are dealing with a religious problem and presumably the problem is to be dealt with psychologically. Kierkegaard spells out his theme in the introduction: "The mood of psychology is the dread corresponding to its discovery, and in its dread it delineates sin, while again and again it is alarmed by the sketch it produces."[96] Thus quite openly it is stated that psychology is a sort of offshoot of dread and that it, as it were, delineates sin.

So it goes throughout the course of the whole investigation which, practically speaking, expounds the far-reaching metaphysic of dread or *Angst* repeatedly dealt with in existentialist philosophy. However, what is special in the Kierkegaardian version is his correlation of "dread" and "knowledge."

This is remarkable indeed. Through his pseudonym Vigilius Haufniensis, Kierkegaard teaches us that all knowledge is dread and springs from dread. Before knowledge there was unwitting innocence. "Innocence," Kierkegaard declares, "is ignorance." In his innocence man is not determined as spirit but is spiritually determined in immediate unity with his natural condition. "Spirit is dreaming in man." And for proof of this proposition Kierkegaard calls on the Bible and the doctrine of original sin. He then goes on to say:

In this state there is peace and repose; but at the same time there is something different, which is not dissension and strife, for there is nothing to strive with. What is it then? Nothing. But what effect does nothing produce? It begets dread. This is the profound secret of innocence, that at the same time it is dread. Dreamingly the spirit projects its own reality; but this reality is nothing; but this nothing constantly sees innocence outside of it.[97]

These few sentences, interwoven with the highest dialectical skill, can be interpreted and elaborated in various ways. Dread points the way to nothingness. Dread is given along with innocence, thus directing it toward nothingness. But at the same time nothingness is what is generated by dread. And finally—from the dogmatic point of view—dread leads to nothingness, namely, to sin.

In these and similar reflections Kierkegaard's coupling of dread and nothingness as interchangeable first makes its appearance. Real dread is not the fear of something definite, but the fear of nothingness—and this "nothing" in turn generates those extreme forms of anxiety found above all in the realm of the pathological.

But to all this Kierkegaard adds a religious interpretation. In further expositions of dread, the relationship with original sin is described. In this context dread is depicted as the result of a lack of consciousness of sin, and finally  is conceived as a directive toward religion, as a "means toward redemption." The whole thrust of the argument is defined in one aspect by the following words at the beginning of the book: "Everything turns upon dread coming into view."[98]

On the other hand the book is also in fact a theory about humankind based on dread. Thus in the last chapter we are told: "If a man were a beast or an angel he would not be able to be in dread. Since he is a synthesis he can be in dread, and the greater the dread, the greater the man."[99] In these expositions it must not be forgotten just what specific and ultimately impenetrable dread it was that Kierkegaard had in mind.

For this kind of dread, obviously, was for him the basis for the human condition in general. As he saw it, dread is closely bound up with the very nature of the spirit. This is made clear when Kierkegaard tells us that it is related to itself as dread. And, remarkably enough, for Kierkegaard spirit is born out of dread: "The spirit cannot do away with itself; nor can it grasp itself so long as it had itself outside of itself. Neither can man sink down into the vegetative life, for he is determined as spirit. He cannot flee from dread, for he loves it; really he does not love it, for he flees from it."[100]

Kierkegaard is the preceptor and harbinger of dread. Dread is his all-dominant, fundamental theme, and the pseudonymous productions are, above all, dedicated to it. Dread appears under the most diverse guises, as "melancholy," as "sin," as "despair." But always the issue at hand is to remember that "everything turns upon dread coming into view."

Sometimes in the pseudonymous writings dread is completely in the foreground, as in *Fear and Trembling*, where Kierkegaard expounds on the pathos and suffering of dread. It is likewise a fundamental theme in *The Concept of Dread* and *The Sickness unto Death*.

The other writings, too, are only roundabout ways of dealing with the subject of dread. The work that made Kierkegaard's literary reputation represents such a detour. For however much the joy of life may seem to be taught in the first volume of *Either/Or*, in the second volume the theme of despair is developed, and there is a demonstration that *joie de vivre* is only a disguise for despair.

Still another pseudonymous work followed the same line, *Stages on Life's Way*, which came out in 1846, supposedly published by the bookbinder Hilarius. In this work are assembled, as if to say good-by, almost all the pseudonyms that had hitherto appeared. Altogether there are five of them, gathered at a dinner party: Johannes the Seducer, Constantia Constantius, Victor Eremita, the "Unhappy Young Man" and a new one, the "Fashions Dealer." All the established ones play the roles they have played before. They speak the same kind of lines, ironically, mockingly, romantically.

They repeat the themes of the first volume of *Either/Or*: joy of life, seduction, woman, etc. The reiteration then moves ahead. Adjoined to the description of the dinner party is a lengthy dissertation called "Divers thoughts on marriage against objections; by a husband." Once again, as in the second volume of *Either/Or*, the happiness and necessity of marriage are proclaimed.

After this comes a "story of suffering" titled "Guilty? Not Guilty?" related by Frater Taciturnus as a "psychological experiment." Obviously this story is intended to be an indirect message to Regina Olsen, Kierkegaard's erstwhile betrothed. This is indicated, among other things, by the fact that into it Kierkegaard put his final letter to Regina, word for word.

There can be no doubt that this book contains a great deal of autobiographical material. Kierkegaard's father's experience is described under the heading of "Quiet Despair." As so often with Kierkegaard, he confesses his own melancholy in the book and sees himself as a "frontier guard" who "day and night has to fight against all the attacks of an inborn melancholy."[101]

Beyond this the book is certainly also a self-justification directed at Regina Olsen: "All the heroes who occupy my fantasy have suffered deep affliction, into which they could admit no one, nor would want to. I do not want a woman just to shift the burden of my melancholy onto her."[102]

Whether the book was intended to be primarily a message to Regina Olsen, or to a larger public, it goes through all the "stages" that Kierkegaard himself had traversed. He describes the "demonic" existence he has led and justifies it by his vocation for religion. The stages on life's way are listed: the romantic life-feeling and the esthetic existence, marriage and the ethical existence. More and more the essence of things is laid bare: melancholy, despair, and suffering. However, the story of suffering, told in diary form, concludes as follows: "Here for the time being the diary ends. It deals with nothing. Yet not in the same sense as Louis XVII's diary, which from day to day is said to have read: Went hunting, nothing; went hunting, etc. It contains nothing. But according to Cicero the easiest letters are those that deal with nothing: so sometimes the most difficult life is that which deals with nothing."[103]

As always, now follows a commentary by the pseudonymous editor, Frater Taciturnus, who interprets the preceding story of suffering. And finally Frater Taciturnus, in an ambiguous and mocking manner, spells out the role which Kierkegaard ascribes to himself:

> You, however, who stand in time and live with time, do you not observe how existence is quaking at its very foundations? Do you not hear the trumpet calling you to battle? Do you not see how decisions are falling all over each other in breathless haste? Where do this hissing and roaring come from if not from the boiling depths? Whence this frightful travail if the times are not pregnant? Do not believe him on that account! Do not listen to him at all! What does he, in his sarcastic garrulity, intended to be Socratic, really have to say to you? That from travail one may not directly infer birth, that the ostensible travail could also be mere flatulence; that a taut, heavy body does not unconditionally prove pregnancy, or even something quite different, what Suetonius certainly had in mind when he said of a Roman emperor: *Vultus erat nitentis*. Therefore do not let yourself be confounded by him! Pay no attention to him at all! He has not been able to legitimize himself as plenipotentiary of the age . . .[104]

Kierkegaard himself certainly felt that this book was a kind of repeat performance. This can be gathered from his diary comment on the "relationship between *Either/Or* and the *Stages*." In this note in the *Journals* he explains that *Stages* is different from *Either/Or* in three respects. In *Stages* the esthetic-sensuous has been suppressed, and the didactic magistrate who defends marriage in *Either/Or* had become a disputatious, combative person. The third point of difference that he mentions is undoubtedly the most important. In the *Stages* the religious becomes a "demonic approximation (the *quidam* of the experiment), humor as its prerequisite and its incognito (Frater Taciturnus)."[105]

Yet the demonic in religiosity had been described much earlier, in *Fear and Trembling*. Thus in fact it had only returned, one of that dark circle of concepts which can be subsumed under the common denominator of "dread." If at the

end one asks what dread really is and what kind of dread
Kierkegaard actually had in mind, it is clear that for him
dread was something metaphysical. And although he portrayed the terror and gruesomeness of dread in all its variations, and though he described the nothingness of dread again
and again, it is also clear that dread as such has only a negative content.

This other, elusive side of dread, however, was described by
Kierkegaard in his *Journals* as cleverly as it was mysteriously.
In 1849 he said: "Dread is the first reflex of possibility, a
shimmer and yet a fearful enchantment."[106]

# 22

## The Philosophical Writings

We now come to Kierkegaard's philosophical writings or, to put it more precisely, to those writings that were the precursor of existentialist philosophy. The author intentionally designates these works not as directly philosophical, but as *Philosophical Fragments* and *Concluding Unscientific Postscript*.

In both works he admits that he does not really consider himself to be a philosopher and certainly not one with a "scientific philosophy." And in fact Kierkegaard does not follow the style of philosophical thinking as it had developed through the centuries, and even less inherited tradition. He cannot be ranked with such names as Plato, Aristotle, Descartes, Leibniz, Kant, etc.

However, as a philosopher he might be compared with many thinkers of the Middle Ages and also to Pascal—that is, with thinkers whose primary concern was religious and for whom philosophy was of secondary consideration. But this

analogy can be made only with qualifications; for Kierkegaard, unlike the medieval thinkers, is not indebted to any
specific religious theory expressed in dogma, a fact that also
distinguishes him from Pascal. As much as he feels himself to
be a Christian, he feels equally that he is a revolutionary and a
reformer of existing Christianity.

Kierkegaard's philosophy can be partially approached on
the basis of these qualifications, but on the other hand there is
also the peculiarity of his style of thinking, which is difficult to
interpret in terms of traditional distinctions. Kierkegaard had
shown in the pseudonymous writings that he was really a poet.
He is a poet, in all events, insofar as impressions and passionate visions are his true métier. The power of language at his
disposal, the power of imagery at his command, his sensibility
of feeling and much else lend his performances poetic power.

Intermingled is that visionary and proclamatory passion
that carries the poet beyond the representation and the poetizing as such into the prophetic. The prophetic gift, on the other
hand, is the acute power of discernment that Kierkegaard en-
joyed.

Kierkegaard's capacity to discern is limited to relationships
and connections. In a deeper sense his thinking is erratic; it
moves from one kind of thought and one kind of perception to
another.

It is also characteristic of Kierkegaard's poetic work that it
should verge on the aphoristic. *Either/Or* is introduced by
aphorisms, to which essays are appended, followed by the
"Diary of a Seducer," written for the most part in the form of
letters. Thus the whole is essentially developed rhapsodically;
as is *Fear and Trembling* and all the other writings poetic in
character.

Whenever Kierkegaard abandons this style, as for instance
in the second volume of *Either/Or*, his execution immediately
becomes more halting, more didactic, and more complicated.
The genuine philosopher's way of presenting ideas and relationships between ideas in a clear and simple fashion, as in the
case of Descartes, was a gift that Kierkegaard did not have.
He always remained rooted in a figurative, empathic, and

prescient kind of thinking, mixed with a penetrating perceptiveness.

Therefore the presentation of a philosophical theory as such must not be expected of *Philosophical Fragments*[107] and the *Unscientific Postscript*.[108] Instead we find them to be something quite different, as shown by a mere glance at the table of contents and chapter headings. The themes seem to stand side by side almost unrelated, without any recognizable continuity. The *Philosophical Fragments* starts out with an outline of a "Project of Thought." But then comes a chapter on "The God as Teacher and Savior," in turn followed by one on "The Absolute Paradox." The *Concluding Unscientific Postscript* proceeds in the same way. It, too, begins with an apparently systematic intent, with the "objective" and the "subjective problem" of Christianity. However, this gives way to a long chapter on Lessing, and this in turn to another in which the "subjective problem" is solved.

The second volume explores "actual subjectivity," but in the fourth chapter there is a sudden switch back to the *Philosophical Fragments*. Then—a complete surprise, at least for anyone expecting to be oriented by means of the headings —come new themes: "The Pathetic," "Existential Suffering" and "Humor." The end of the book is no less astonishing. A concluding chapter has the heading "B: The Dialectic," whereby A is meant to be "The Pathetic."

When one actually begins to read, one finds the same sort of thing repeated on a different plane; Kierkegaard is constantly shifting from propositions that are entirely or halfway didactic to ironic passages, to invective, to figurative representations. Anyone who, simply reading along, gives way to the magic of this flying off in all directions will be gripped by it. But anyone expecting a systematic development or even a textbook discussion will soon become uneasy.

Kierkegaard does not teach; he imparts information. But he does not impart directly, that is, *not* everything presented in what appears to be a perfectly serious tone is in fact seriously intended. Sometimes the irony is immediately evident, as when Kierkegaard mocks "system":

Once or twice I have been on the verge of bending the knee. But at the last moment, when I already had my handkerchief spread on the ground, to avoid soiling my trousers, and I made a trusting appeal to one of the initiated who stood by: "Tell me now sincerely, is it entirely finished; for if so I will kneel down before it, even at the risk of ruining a pair of trousers (for on account of the heavy traffic to and fro the road has become quite muddy),"—I always received the same answer: "No, it is not yet quite finished." And so there was another postponement—of the System, and of my homage.[109]

Devoid of systematization, in part humorous, then again with deep irony, in part didactic and sometimes passionately eruptive, the whole moves in devious ways toward the goal set by the author. Anyone who knows nothing about Kierkegaard may, as he reads, feel trapped in a labyrinthine movement. For Kierkegaard, however, the form and content of his presentation is *dialectical*. It is a methodical process running through the work from beginning to end.

It is out of the question to reproduce the train of thought and the content of *"Philosophical Fragments"* and *Concluding Unscientific Postscript* in abbreviated form.

Yet it seems necessary to provide some sort of table of contents to prepare the reader for what is coming. This can be done only by picking out the many catch phrases recurring periodically in Kierkegaard's dialectical thought. In this way an idea of the whole can be gained, though an idea which does not really reflect the living, glittering, and mobile argument, but which is only a kind of framework.

In *Philosophical Fragments* Kierkegaard presents "A Project of Thought" as the first chapter. The commentary on the title page reads: "Is an historical point of departure possible for an eternal consciousness; how can such a point of departure have anything but a merely historical interest; is it possible to base an eternal happiness upon historical knowledge?"[110]

We have three questions, then, questions which themselves may be questioned as to whether they are seriously or merely ironically intended. To underscore this ambiguity, Kierkegaard has also put a "Propositio" at the beginning of this first chapter, which reads: "The question is asked in ignorance, by one who does not even know what can have led him to ask it."[111]

It cannot be expected of Kierkegaard that he will answer his question with a yes or no. This is not his method of teaching. Whenever Kierkegaard poses a question, he does not regard it as an interrogation which can be answered simply and unambiguously, but rather as a springboard. In this case, however, the question posed gives him a jumping-off point, bringing him to an old key term in a new formulation.

In the third chapter, "The Absolute Paradox: A Metaphysical Crotchet," and the fourth chapter, "The Case of the Contemporary Disciple," the subject of paradox is discussed. Proceeding from the question, itself actually paradoxical, whether an eternal consciousness can be reached from a transitory historical point of departure, that is, whether Christianity as eternal truth can have a temporal beginning, a formulation is made of "absolute paradox."

This absolute paradox appears in different forms, sometimes as the "paradoxical passion of Reason," always pushing from the known into the unknown. But what is the unknown? Says Kierkegaard: "It is not a human being, insofar as we know what man is; nor is it any other known thing. So let us call this unknown something: *the God*. It is nothing more than a name we assign to it . . ."*

Kierkegaard rejects proofs of the existence of God. "For if the God does not exist it would of course be impossible to prove it; and if he does exist, it would be folly to attempt it . . ."[112]

In this train of thought Kierkegaard perfects the peculiar dialectical game already familiar from *Either/Or*. Nothing is *proved* dialectically, as with Hegel, nor is anything dialectically disputed, as with Kant. As Kierkegaard zigzags dialectically about the idea, he merely shows that there is not, and cannot be, any proof of God, but that meanwhile the question of God's existence does independently exist.

---

* In Kierkegaard's Danish it is *Guden*, "the God," not "God."—*Tr.*

Out of an analogous dialectical process Kierkegaard arrives at a positive statement which says: there is paradox. Immediately attaching itself to this conclusion is this question: "Can such a paradox be thought?"

Once again it cannot be expected that Kierkegaard will answer a question like this with a straight yes or no. In still another leap Kierkegaard reaches a new position. Now he turns back to his "project of thought," and answers the question to the extent that the following conclusion can be deemed an answer. Only one thing is possible: *to believe.*

This conclusion, however, is cloaked in an idea that is once again dialectical in form. Thus we are now told:

> But in that case is not Faith as paradoxical as the *Paradox*? Precisely so; how else could it have the Paradox for its object, and be happy in relation to the Paradox? Faith is itself a miracle, and all that holds true of the Paradox also holds true of truth. But within the framework of this miracle everything is again Socratic, yet so that the miracle is never canceled—the miracle, namely, that the eternal condition is given in time.[113]

With this the theme of *Philosophical Fragments* has been treated essentially, though actually the dialectical analysis continues for some time longer. It moves in circles and recapitulates the "Project of Thought."

If the *Philosophical Fragments* is to some extent summed up in the first chapter, "The Project of Thought," it made good sense when Kierkegaard gave the title of *Concluding Unscientific Postscript* to the next and by far more comprehensive work. The two volumes of this *Postscript* are indeed just that, a postscript or meditative commentary. But the word "commentary" must not be taken to mean that Kierkegaard merely provided a body of annotation. Rather the whole problem is discussed in a new and broader way, and the consequences of the basic theme, "paradox," are elaborated. With this, as the facts described in the pseudonymous writings are deepened, a series of concepts now take shape. The most important of these are: existence, subjective thinker, subjective truth, and

others are joined to these. Proceeding on the basis of the negative dialectic which Kierkegaard constantly taught and demonstrated, the "existing" is developed in respect of its unknow-
ing and "pathetic" content. This "existing" is for Kierkegaard
condensed in such concepts as "existence as pathos," and as
"suffering" and "guilt." While Kierkegaard is evolving, eluci-
dating, and describing these concepts, the peculiar mixture
already familiar from the poetical and pseudonymous works
again declares itself. We are given a kind of sublimated, intro-
spectively digested and thought out autobiography of the
man. Kierkegaard all along is talking about himself and, in a
certain sense, only about himself.

Yet he does not talk about himself in terms of his merely
adventitious experience. Rather, he deduces experience in
general out of the generality of his own experience but he
does not do this didactically.

Everything imaginable crops up in this remarkable potpourri: descriptions of people and of social milieus of all
kinds, stories, anecdotes and experiences, historical presenta-
tions, casual commentaries, topical criticisms, and much more.
Often Kierkegaard seems only to be playing with words. But
this is an illusion, for every time, after such passages, immediately a penetrating and often extremely concentrated intellectual formulation will suddenly appear.

Summations like this spring forth with telling effect from
the plethora of kaleidoscopically changing images, even when
Kierkegaard does not emphasize them. Often it is only the
tone that sets them apart. At such times Kierkegaard drops
irony and, against his usual custom, speaks out seriously,
sometimes dictatorially, and even ominously.

If the decisive key terms are pulled together to abstract the
essential from the wealth of accessory material, the dialectical
thrust carrying the argument forward will be recognized at
once. By way of introduction in the *Concluding Unscientific
Postscript* there is another analysis of the problem already
posed in the *Fragments*—"Is an historical point of departure
possible for an eternal consciousness?" The problem is divided
into its "objective" and "subjective" aspects. Whereas the first

aspect receives relatively brief treatment, the second is dealt
with at length. Indeed, this second discussion takes up the
larger part of the first volume and the beginning of the second.

It becomes apparent that for Kierkegaard the "objective
problem of the truth of Christianity" is only introductory in
nature. At this preliminary stage, Kierkegaard speaks not
without a certain respect about the "historical point of view,"
about the Church, the Holy Scriptures, "the proof of the centuries" of Christianity. Yet this respect is deprecatory. Between the lines the message comes through that, for Kierkegaard, a Christianity which legitimizes itself historically is
dead. This judgment may be clarified using his own words:

> When the question is treated objectively, it becomes im-
> possible for the subject to face the decision with passion,
> least of all with an infinitely interested passion. It is a self-
> contradiction, and therefore comical, to be infinitely inter-
> ested in that which at its maximum still always remains an
> approximation. If in spite of this, passion is nevertheless
> imported, we get fanaticism. For an infinitely interested
> passion every iota will be of infinite value. The fault is not
> in the infinitely interested passion, but in the fact that its
> object has become an approximate object.[114]

This means that Christendom has lost its object, exchanged
it for an "approximation." In these passages we already begin
to get an idea of what Kierkegaard will assign as the content
of the "absolute paradox"—namely, passion. But before Kierkegaard takes up this theme, he once again delineates what it
is he is after. He secures his perimeter, so to speak, from
misunderstandings arising on the one side from conventional
Christianity, on the other from speculative Christianity.

He describes contemporary Christianity with undisguised
scorn:

> If a man were to say quite simply and unassumingly
> that he was concerned for himself, lest perhaps he had no
> right to call himself a Christian . . . people would say:

"How tiresome to make such a fuss about nothing at all; why can't he behave like the rest of us, who are all Christians?" . . . And if he happened to be married, his wife would say to him: "Dear husband of mine, how can you get such notions in your head? Are you not a Dane, and does not geography say that the Lutheran form of the Christian religion is the ruling religion in Denmark? For you are surely not a Jew, nor are you a Mohammedan; what can you be if not a Christian? . . ."[115]

And speculation is treated just as ironically:

But perhaps philosophy will say: "These are popular and simple reflections, which theologians and popularizing philosophers are fit to expound; but speculative philosophy has nothing to do with such things." How terrible to be excluded from the superior wisdom of popular philosophy! . . .[116]

Kierkegaard's real theme suddenly comes to light again in the first volume in the second book, or segment, with a chapter on Lessing called "An Expression of Gratitude." One particular statement by Lessing had a special fascination for Kierkegaard: "If God held all truth in his right hand, and in his left hand held the lifelong pursuit of it, albeit with the proviso that forever and a day I would be doomed to stray, and if God spoke to me, saying, 'Choose,' with humility I would choose his left hand and say, 'Father, let me have that! Pure truth is for you alone.'"

The full force of Kierkegaard's anger toward Hegel and the Hegelian system can be appreciated when one reads his commentary on this Lessing quotation: "When Lessing wrote these words the System was presumably not finished; alas! and now Lessing is dead. Were he living in these times, now that the System is almost finished, or at least under construction and will be finished by next Sunday; believe me, Lessing would have stretched out both his hands to lay hold of it . . ."[117]

All along, in the background of these as yet preliminary

reflections, the real Kierkegaardian propositions and themes have been lurking. Now suddenly they appear with almost didactic clarity: "A logical system is possible; an existential system impossible." And from this point on Kierkegaard limits himself to the real theme, starting here and ending in the second book. It is the theme of "existence." This same theme has been explored at length in modern existentialist philosophy, in part dependent on Kierkegaard, in part proceeding from another descriptive-phenomenological position. At the same time, Kierkegaard's concept of existence has been trivialized. That is, its really vital nucleus, the dialectical unfolding, has been removed.

However, this unfolding or unrolling is the distinguishing feature of the existential concept as Kierkegaard uses it. The concept cannot be understood once the dialectical part has been abstracted and existence derived descriptively from dread, from "going to pieces," or whatever. Above all, the Kierkegaardian concept cannot be grasped unless it is borne in mind that Kierkegaard derives existence immediately from the "paradox."

Hand in hand with this goes the fact that throughout wide stretches of the *Concluding Unscientific Postscript* Kierkegaard repeatedly treats run-of-the-mill, conventional knowledge of existence ironically. In the chapter on "The Task of Becoming Subjective" we are told:

> For example, the problem of what it means to die: I know concerning this what people in general know about it; I know I shall die if I take a dose of sulphuric acid, and also if I drown myself, or go to sleep in an atmosphere of coal gas, and so forth. I know that Napoleon always went about with poison ready at hand, and that Juliet in Shakespeare poisoned herself. I know that the Stoics regarded suicide as a courageous deed, and that others consider it a cowardly act. I know that the tragic hero dies in the fifth act of the drama, and that his death has an infinite significance in pathos, but that when a bartender dies death does not have this significance. . . . I know further what the clergy are accustomed to say on this subject, and

I am familiar with the general run of themes treated at funerals. . . . Nevertheless, in spite of this almost extraordinary knowledge or facility in knowledge, I can by no means regard death as something I have understood.[118]

And Kierkegaard continues to mock and be ironic. Masterfully, he treats everything ironically, even himself. It is this process alone, according to him, that gives rise to the truth of the Paradox.

I had been a student for half a score of years. Although never lazy, all my activity was nevertheless like a glittering inactivity, a kind of occupation for which I still have a great partiality, and for which, perhaps, I even have a little genius. . . . So there I sat and smoked my cigar until I lapsed into thought. Among other thoughts I remember these: You are going on, I said to myself, to become an old man, without being anything. . . . Here my soliloquy was interrupted, for my cigar was smoked out and a new one had to be lit. So I smoked again and then suddenly this thought flashed through my mind: You must do something . . .[119]

But all of this, however much spun out, is no more than background, so much destructive and equivocal irony leading to an abrupt emergent thesis. With all common and apparently objective truth destroyed, this thesis states: "*An objective uncertainty held fast in an approximation-process of the most passionate inwardness is the truth,* the highest truth attainable for an *existing* Individual."[120]

At this point, the movement of ideas again flows into the great dialectical process. It is tied in with the first dialectical thesis of paradox. First, belief is paradox. Positive Christianity, the truth of conventional Christianity and objective truth have now been destroyed. This kind of truth has been shown to be ironical and ambiguous. Thus the way has been cleared so *another* truth can make its appearance. This is dialectical truth, as Kierkegaard understands it. It has nothing to do with certainty, but instead it is objective uncertainty passionately held fast.

At the same time, the Kierkegaardian notion of dialectic is made clear. It is simply "becoming," and by no means objective but subjective becoming. For Kierkegaard dialectic is a living process moving toward fulfillment, a truth that is never finished and closed. Dialectic as thought is the act of sympathizing and empathizing with an unattainable consummation that always proceeds out of paradox and always returns to it. This dialectic, which seeks the truth, does not believe in certainty; it holds passionately fast, on the contrary, to uncertainty. The "subjectively existing thinker" is one who does not live in the delusory actuality of an outer world fashioned in a conventional way, but in the inwardness of uncertainty.

Curiously, in this dialectical thought process truth is transformed from a "something" into a "nothing." This nothing is demonstrated by objective uncertainty, its content is paradox, its actuality, existence.

Not until the second book of the *Concluding Unscientific Postscript* does this theme achieve its full effect. The concept of existence grows out of the Kierkegaardian definition of "subjective truth" as uncertainty in the Socratic sense. Now Kierkegaard can say: "Existence involves a tremendous contradiction."

In the course of this advancing train of thought—so far as this kind of dialectical thinking does advance rather than circle about—Kierkegaard returned to paradox, his original point of departure. Objective uncertainty and its truth have developed out of the paradox of belief, and out of them, in turn, existence.

For the hallmark of existence is objective uncertainty, in which the subject lives suspended amid endless movement. "Existence, like movement, is a difficult category to deal with; for if I think it, I abrogate it; and then I do not think it. It might therefore seem to be the proper thing to say that there is something which cannot be thought, namely, existence. But the difficulty persists, in that existence itself combines thinking with existing, insofar as the thinker exists."[121] It is Kierkegaard's old experience, which he had described poetically in

*Either/Or,* in *Fear and Trembling,* in *The Concept of Dread* and all his writings. It becomes evident that objective and logical thought can never grasp the fact of existence.

That which exists does not of itself permit being thought, but nonetheless the existing individual thinks: "When it is impossible to think existence, and the existing individual nonetheless thinks, what does this signify? It signifies that he thinks intermittently, that he thinks before and after. His thought cannot attain to absolute continuity. It is only in fantasy that an existing individual can be constantly *sub specie aeternitatis.*"[122]

While Kierkegaard is tirelessly describing this contradiction, he develops the task of the "subjective thinker":

> There is an old saying that *oratio, tentatio, meditatio faciunt theologum* (prayer, temptation, meditation make the theologian). Similarly there is required for a subjective thinker imagination and feeling, dialectics in existential awareness, together with passion. But passion first and last; for it is impossible to think about existence in existence without passion. Existence involves a tremendous contradiction, from which the subjective thinker does not have to abstract, though he can if he will, but in which it is his business to remain.[123]

In this passage it becomes clear, among other things, that for Kierkegaard dialectic, in a simple sense, is a sinking down into the unfathomable. Thought's peculiar task, as the subjective thinker functions, appears to be thinking the incomprehensible. Objective thinking, however, is a denatured kind of thought, removed from its real object. It has ceased to be vital thought. One might almost say that it is thought grown old and weary. Thus Kierkegaard can repeatedly refer to Socrates and Greek philosophy as "the youth of philosophy."

The second volume of the *Concluding Unscientific Postscript* is given over to a presentation of existential reality. The theme is carried along analogously.

Existence is only partially thought. Beyond this it is pathos, suffering, and guilt. What Kierkegaard has really been looking for all along now becomes visible. He restates his theory of the three stages of existence: the esthetic (in the passion for the secular world); the ethical (in the passion for the universal); and the religious (in the passion for absolute indeterminateness), all enduring forms of human existence.

With this it becomes clear how existence for Kierkegaard is more a question of suffering than it is of action. Only God is fitted for action in the strict sense of the word. Such is the sense of the following passage: "God does not think, he creates; God does not exist, he is eternal. Man thinks and exists, and existence separates thought and being, holding them apart from one another in succession."[124]

Man is denied real creation; it is reserved for God. Man lives in the duality of existing and thinking, in a hybrid state, and not in unity. And now, remarkably, the old proposition that man is fashioned of finiteness and infinitude has been turned around here into the proposition that he is a mixture of existence and thought.

We shall skip over the long expositions which Kierkegaard tacks onto his basic definition of existence, that is, the detailed description of what he calls the "pathetic." We will dwell only on the basic effort. Using every means at his disposal, Kierkegaard tries to show dialectically that the essential content of "existential pathos is guilt."

With this the work ends. There is one last large section under the heading of "The Dialectical." Anyone expecting to find in it a methodological description of the dialectic will be disappointed. Instead the "dialectical" is described as the central point, the focus of existence, which is to say that it is to be inferred as the upshot of what has been described. Actually, the dialectical is a simple thing, or at any rate can be reduced to a simple formula. According to this formula existence is the "dialectical contradiction . . . which is the breach (with immanence.)"[125] Meanwhile the fact remains that there is an "absolute incongruity between the eternal truth of Christianity and any attempt to give it an historical basis." However, the existential result of this situation is "heightened pathos," an "absolute consciousness of sin."

Herewith *this* investigation has reached its dialectical end.

Yet this is not to say that Kierkegaard has spoken his last word. The dialectical movement continues. In an appendix, "For an Understanding with the Reader," the pseudonymous author says: "The undersigned, Johannes Climacus, who has written this book, does not give himself out to be a Christian; he is completely taken up with the thought how difficult it must be to be a Christian."[126]

# 23

## The Final Stages

Kierkegaard's completely pseudonymous and poetic writings continued until 1845. They closed with *Stages on Life's Way*, a work which is, as it were, a symposium of the Kierkegaardian pseudonyms. When Kierkegaard later looked back on this body of literary, poetic work, he saw it as a "richness" which "made his flesh creep."

After this came the half-pseudonymous production known to us as Kierkegaard's philosophical works. These compositions are marked by the fact that although the alleged author is given the name of J. Climacus, Kierkegaard himself is openly listed as the publisher. Moreover, Climacus no longer writes in a poetic vein. In the subtitle of *Concluding Unscientific Postscript* the book is described as "A Mimetic-Pathetic-Dialectic Composition" and "An Existential Contribution."

As Kierkegaard himself admitted, the philosophical works represented a "turning point" in his literary activity. As publisher he assumed part of the responsibility for what he wrote.

And now esthetic contemplation turned from demonstrative dramatics to the inner existential question of "How does one become a Christian?"

But the road he had covered so far, as Kierkegaard saw it, had been a dialectical one. In all the poetic works, feeling, acting, suffering, operative individuals had been introduced on the stage and made to perform. While fulfilling their dramatic purpose, only to fade from sight upon its completion, they had been subjected to commentary and judgment. The esthetic had been condemned, the ethical man recognized as of intermediate status, the religious man seen as a mystery and as the paradox of existence.

The poetic production ended when it had been established that the religious is incomprehensible yet nonetheless excellent. To the extent that these ideas were the result of what had gone before, the philosophical works resumed the theme and examined the paradox of existence and the "pathetic" in its various forms.

Now Kierkegaard half abandoned his pseudonymous guise. To be sure, he did use a new pseudonym, but by this time Kierkegaard's true identity could be seen shining through it. Then, remarkably enough, there was still one more pseudonymous author, a straggler who appeared, in 1849, as the alleged writer of *The Sickness unto Death*. His name was "Anti-Climacus," with Kierkegaard's name on the title page as publisher. When assigning a place for this book in his "statement of accounts," he said:

> Later indeed a new pseudonymous author did appear: Anti-Climacus. However, that he is pseudonymous means just what the name (Anticlimacus—anticlimax) indicates, that he, turned backwards, comes to a halt. All the earlier pseudonymity is at a lower level than that of the edifying writer, the new pseudonym is a higher pseudonymity. It is just because of this that a halt is made: something higher is indicated, and it is just this that forces me back within my limits, passes the judgment on me that my life does not measure up to so high a claim, and so the communication is a poetical one.[127]

In the *Journals* there is a second comment on the pseudonym Anti-Climacus, which goes: "So, then. Now the *Sickness unto Death* is coming out, but pseudonymously with me as publisher. . . . The pseudonym is Johannes Anti-Climacus, in contrast to Climacus, who says he is not a Christian. Anti-Climacus is the opposite extreme: a Christian to extraordinary degree—assuming that I, myself, can make it to the point of being simply a Christian at all."[128]

Well, then, is this Anti-Climacus a Christian in an extraordinary sense, but perhaps not a "simple Christian"? This remains unclear. All that is certain is that this piece of writing, according to its subtitle, is intended to be "A Christian Psychological Exposition for Edification and Awakening."

According to this stage direction, which in fact is not simple at all, *The Sickness unto Death* is a sort of final transitional work. Kierkegaard does come to a halt, as he himself said he would. He looks back. At the same time he passes judgment on what has gone before. Climacus had been one who "stood on the summit." He was a man who found himself, so to speak, at the pinnacle of thought. Now his place was taken by Anti-Climacus, who abandoned this lofty position yet at the same time represented a "higher one."

The actual content of the book corresponds to these directives. It describes "despair as sickness unto death." Kierkegaard expressly makes it clear that here he does not mean temporal, but eternal death. It is not a question, then, of earthly, worldly despair, but of another form.

In the treatise itself the various forms of despair are portrayed. For Kierkegaard the concept of despair widens step by step. Only in a brief, introductory way is it referred to in the sense usually understood, that is, as despair over mundane and pragmatic events. This kind of despair is not the real thing, or at most is only a prelude to it.

Mortal despair, in the Kierkegaardian sense, only begins when it threatens the loss of the "self." Yet this despair is already beginning to appear when man gives himself over to worldliness, piling up money, pursuing worldly affairs. All the time he is doing these things he is working toward the loss of his own self and so lives in despair.

Whereas this despair is, as it were, an unconscious thing because the person in question does not realize that he has a self, this is not the case in a succeeding stage: "Despair at not wanting to be oneself." This is the despair of weakness, as Kierkegaard describes it. This stage, in turn, is followed by the despair of defiance, in which man despairingly asserts a claim to self.

The second section of the book shifts the preceding psychological observations into a religious context. To the extent that "sin" is described in this second part, the argument advances the idea of the "existential pathos" of suffering and guilt as dealt with at the end of *Postscript*. The second section starts off with Socrates and the Socratic definition of "sin as ignorance." Socrates himself, of course, had not used the Christian term "sin." Kierkegaard leans on those passages in Socrates where he says that injustice can be traced back to ignorance or to imperfect knowledge.

As the work moves along, it turns more and more toward a Christian contemplation of sin, finally ending with an exposition of the sin against the Holy Ghost. According to Kierkegaard this is the sin of declaring Christianity to be an untruth, which represents sin potentiated, the highest form of despair.

It is noteworthy that by this time Kierkegaard has already gone far toward abandoning the style of the pseudonymous productions, and that in many passages *The Sickness unto Death* speaks to us in a Christian way in the immediate sense. To be sure, the religious is still developed, as Kierkegaard puts it, out of the psychological, out of the psychological approach.

That is, at the start despair is mainly understood as a phenomenon residing in the self, the I, the ego, of man. Quite evidently despair is seen as an incongruity between the I and the I, as a faulty relationship between self and self. This despair, which Kierkegaard clearly thought of as a sickness of his times, is a sickness of the spirit. The spirit as I and self is the sign of man. But the spirit is not master of itself and it is only through the mediation of a higher agency that man is helped to become himself. If this relationship is thrown into disarray, the consequence is despair. The composition is oriented from the start in terms of this definition of spirit, that is to say, because this conception in turn is based on the definition of man. Kierkegaard describes it as follows: "Man is a synthesis of the infinite and the finite, of the temporal and the eternal, of freedom and necessity. A synthesis is a relation between two factors. So regarded, man is not yet a self."[129] Kierkegaard then goes on to say that man achieves selfhood only when he arrives at the right relation between the finite and the infinite. To the extent that the argument explores this right relationship, it is done from the viewpoint, and according to the negative proof offered by it, of despair resulting from the non-relationship of self to self.

There is an important reference to Anti-Climacus in another context. By 1848 Kierkegaard had written an essay which, after long hesitation, he brought out in 1850 under the title of *Training in Christianity*. We shall forgo trying to paraphrase it and confine ourselves to what Kierkegaard himself said about this essay. In his *Point of View for My Work As an Author*, Kierkegaard felt that *Training in Christianity*— written under the pseudonym Anti-Climacus—was an attempt to "give that which exists a point of view that will afford it an ideal footing." Has Kierkegaard, then, undergone a change; does he now have it in mind to save the existent? If *Training in Christianity* was actually meant to be an attempt of this kind, such an intention was recanted in the preface of the second edition. In this preface we are told that "I have had this dissertation republished in a completely *unchanged* edition, because I regard it to be an historical document." Kierkegaard then goes on to say he has "arrived at the conviction" that "the existent, understood from a Christian point of view, is untenable."

This was Kierkegaard's last, great position, as already described. Henceforth he became a militant and agitator. He published pamphlets, attacked the Church and, in the most trenchant way possible for him, took a stand against official Christianity. During this struggle he died.

A strange life had come to an end. Had he reached his goal? Had this great body of work, planned and developed under such ingenious direction, achieved what its creator had intended?

What Kierkegaard had wanted, a religious awakening and reform, he did not bring to pass. Something else has endured: that portrayal of nothingness, of negative knowledge, that description of a world of negative shadows and essences which Kierkegaard returned to again and again.

However, the most ingenious of these formulations appears on the last pages of the *Journals*, written in 1854. What they show is the world that Kierkegaard had lived in: the night of the unconditioned, of nothing, of a negative God. The passage, headed "The Night of the Unconditioned," goes:

> Man has a natural dread of going into the dark—small wonder, then, naturally, that he should dread the unconditioned, dread yielding to the unconditioned, of which it holds true that no night and no darkness is half so black as this darkness and this night, where all relative goals (the common milestones and signposts), where all means (the lanterns with which we ordinarily help ourselves), where the tenderest and most intimate feelings of surrender are extinguished, for otherwise the unconditioned is not unconditioned.[130]

Remarkably, too, this vision is correlated with the image of God and Christianity which Kierkegaard outlined in a few words the year before he died. The little passage, under the heading "All-Nothing," proceeds in this lapidary fashion: "God creates everything out of nothing—and everything that God will use he first reduces to nothing."[131]

This somber picture of God is completed in another Kierkegaardian description of Christianity from about the same time, called "Unrest." Here he says:

> Like the fisherman who, when he has cast his net, makes a noise in the water to drive the fish his way and so catch more; like the hunter who, with a gang of drivers, surrounds the whole terrain and scares up the game galore toward the place where they are to be shot: so does God, who wants to be loved, hunt for man with the help of unrest.
>
> Christianity is the most intensively strong, the greatest

possible unrest, none greater can be imagined. It desires
(such was the effect of the life of Christ) to unsettle
human existence down to its deepest depths, blow up
everything, break everything.

. . . Where there would be a Christian, there must be
unrest; and where a Christian has come into being, there
will be unrest.[132]

Kierkegaard, to be sure, had often said that God is love. But
opposing this image of God as love is the other one: God as
the fisherman who catches men and as the hunter who shoots
them. It is a dark and almost implacable image of divinity that
has arisen here: a God who creates everything out of nothing
and who wants nothing because otherwise he would not catch
men.

# 24

## Kierkegaard's Dialectic

The inimitable identity of work and life, greater in the case of Kierkegaard than with any other thinker, was not a matter of happenstance. It sprang from a planned and purposefully executed design, a design realized by coupling literary production and life-fulfillment in a unique way.

On the one hand, the literary production was the documentation of an experience in which Kierkegaard saw himself as a sort of God's actor and stand-in. On the other, the same documentation also evaluated, judged, and criticized experiences and forms of experience as they appeared. Thus a sort of hierarchy of three forms of existence was arrived at. In this sense, the literary production, whether pseudonymous, half-pseudonymous, or direct, also serves to guide and direct.

The *Journals* served the purpose of keeping Kierkegaard's life and work always geared together. In the literary or poetic works Kierkegaard resorted to another means of keeping things geared together. Here the imaginary authors stand in intimate relationship with each other. They point at one another, comment on and elucidate each other. They relate to one another in such fashion that while appearing as pseudonyms on the stage they are also carrying on a conversation behind the scenes.

This dialogue never ceases. Again and again Kierkegaard found a way to keep it going. How the different pseudonyms of the poetic writings carried on this conversation is illustrated in part in the single works themselves, in part when they are brought together as a group in *Stages on Life's Way*.

The conversation continues even in the philosophical and half-pseudonymous works. Between the first and second volumes of *Concluding Unscientific Postscript* is found an appendix in which "contemporary efforts in Danish literature" are discussed in detail. Here the author, Climacus, writes:

> What happens? Just as I sit here, out comes *Either/Or*. Here was realized what I myself had proposed to do. . . . But things went from bad to worse; for step by step, just as I was about to realize my resolve in action, out came a pseudonymous work which accomplished what I had intended. There was something curiously ironical in the entire situation; it was fortunate that I never talked to anyone about my resolve, that not even my landlady had noticed anything, for otherwise people would doubtless have laughed at my comic predicament, as it is indeed droll enough that the cause to which I had devoted myself prospered, though not through me. And that the cause did prosper I convinced myself from the fact that every time I read through such a pseudonymous work, it became clearer to me what I had intended to do.[133]

In this imaginary story the idea is to let the reader of the philosophical works know "indirectly" that Climacus's meditative and theorizing point of view is in partnership with the poetical writings of the other pseudonyms. Climacus goes on to comment on the earlier poetical writings of the other pseudonyms, which ranged from *Either/Or* to *Stages on Life's Way*. There is no better illustration of what the dialectic and the indirect method meant to Kierkegaard. The ring which, toward the middle of this appendix, Kierkegaard places around all the pseudonymous writings—with the exception of the straggler, *The Sickness unto Death*—is intended to bind together the two planes of poetical and philosophical presentation. Whereas the poetical pseudonyms play out their roles dramatically, as seducer, as husband, as the unhappy man, etc., the philosophical writings speak to us as a thinking commentary; whereas the philosophical thought is developed in a dimension of "concrete" thinking, the poetic works represent the drama complementary to it. This was what Kierkegaard intended. Simultaneously he projected a poetical experience on one plane while, on the philosophical plane, directing and following up the drama in the dimension of thought.

Many attempts have been made to explain what Kierkegaard understood by existential thinking. But none of these elucidations is valid unless it clearly demonstrates that here "thinking" is not what is usually conceived by the term, for the reason that it is dramatized thinking. As such it has no "object" in the usual sense of the word. Nor does it arise as the result of an objective effort. Rather, it has its origin in a passionate experience and begins to be thinking only when it describes passionate fulfillment. But for Kierkegaard this means thinking "subjectively."

Again, the terms "subjective thinking" and "subjective thinker" can be correctly understood only when there is a recognition of the manner in which the objective reference has been abolished. For Kierkegaard the thinker without passion is "a mediocre fellow." Yet thinking passionately in his sense does not mean clinging passionately to its object. Passionate thinking begins only when, in passionate fulfillment, the object, as it were, is dissolved, and becomes "inwardness," that is, "subjectivity."

Included in this process, to be sure, is the assumption that from the start the subjective thinker confronts the "object" negatively and rejectively, and that his goal cannot be objective thinking. According to this proposition, there is no objective truth, since for the subjective thinker subject and object, in this context, are immaterial.

If this critique of objective knowledge is viewed without prejudice, its ideological background is perfectly clear. Kierkegaard rejects the preoccupation of Western man and Western thought with the objective world. He fears the externalization of man, the loss of inwardness. When he says that in days to come all sorts of misfortune will come from the natural sciences, his intention is to characterize this state of affairs.

Whether such a claim is accepted or rejected, Kierkegaard's basic epistemological idea is significant above and beyond this attitude. This epistemology stands or falls on dialectical thinking and on the way that Kierkegaard uses dialectic. For him dialectic is not an "objective cognitive expedient" and not the scientific method that Hegel had claimed it to be.

Nonetheless it has a lasting methodological value, though this value does not rest on the fact that it can delineate objects. Thus it is that Kierkegaard mocks Hegel's attempt to comprehend the objective, historical world, or the realm of logic dialectically. Nor is dialectic for him, as for Kant, a way toward proving that certain questions are theoretically unanswerable.

But his dialectic does raise the claim of being able to apprehend living events in process of fulfillment. For Kierkegaard this also means that existence and the existential appear in the process of dialectical cognition. Moreover, this realm can be grasped no other way but dialectically.

In the sense of the cognitive critique thereby assumed, Kierkegaard's underlying idea can be developed from another angle, too. Every act of thought or cognition directed at an object is obliged, in this process, to rule out all subjective factors calculated to qualify—better, disqualify—the object as object. As in psychology, the subjective becomes an object of cognition; here, too, a similar kind of objectivity must be attained. In experiment, again, the experimenter's personal factors must be excluded if objectivity is to be attained.

Still to be considered in such a procedure is a final subjective component of cognition which may not be allowed to manifest itself because it falsifies objectivity. Kierkegaard believed that he was able to demonstrate this component by means of his dialectical thinking. What he wanted to do, in effect, was to apprehend a realm of events which, though to be sure it never reaches full objectivity, nonetheless can be indicated and reasoned out. Kierkegaard understood the procedure which he developed to be a means of indirect communication, because it does not assume the form of a positive, direct theory. Here, similarly, one can speak in terms of indirect investigation. This kind of analysis does not arrive at its objective by coming directly to grips with it, that is, by the method of direct description. Instead it sets an investigatory event in motion, which then takes on changing forms. This technique Kierkegaard used as a sort of self-experiment.

Yet a parallel between Kierkegaard's method and modern psychological procedure comes strongly to mind: the procedure, for example, used more and more in the analytical techniques of depth psychology. In psychological analysis, as in Kierkegaard, the subject is made to talk, to present himself in the flux of his different life situations, of his ideas and his objective and subjective relations. The fact that Kierkegaard's work throughout can be regarded as self-analysis in a comprehensive form is enough to show how closely Kierkegaard comes to depth psychology.

Beyond this, later developments in analytical procedure, as for instance in so-called "existential analysis," have a clear connection with Kierkegaard's thinking. All dialectic, whether it stems from Hegel, Kierkegaard, or Marx, has its starting point in antithesis, contrast, contradiction, etc.

As a model of such a statement we can take Socrates' proposition, when he says: "I know that I know nothing." From the standpoint of formal logic such a proposition is a "contradiction."* But the condemnation of propositions of this kind running through the whole history of Western thought has nonetheless not prevented their repeated utterance.

If we think of such proverbs as *Einmal ist keinmal†*—and of the jokes often based on such paradoxes, of the countless *bon mots* in the category of La Rochefoucauld's "Anyone who

* For if you know at all, it would seem you must know something, and not nothing.—*Tr.*

† Literally, "Once is never," but actually used as meaning "Once doesn't count" or "The exception proves the rule."—*Tr.*

lives without foolishness is not as wise as he thinks," of such propositions as Hegel's "The way to the spirit is the round-about way," then a glance will suffice to recognize that existing alongside the dimension of noncontradictory statement is an equally large dimension of contradictory statements. These propositions do not always take the form of sharp and logically comprehensible contradictions. Statements of this sort vary. They progress from a point where contrast is only lightly defined, to antithesis just beginning to become more clearly logical in nature, to the heightened form of self-contradiction represented by full-blown paradox. The classic model might be the paradox "All that I say is a lie," or the Cretan Epemenides' assertion that "All Cretans lie." Without getting into the question that immediately arises of the validity of such propositions, let it be merely repeated that such inherently contrasting statements are the breeding ground of dialectic. Thus Kant developed his transcendental dialectic out of antithetical propositions of metaphysical origin and to it adjoined his critique of metaphysics. The Platonic Socrates evolved the technique of contrasting statements in the form of dialogue. Hegel's dialectical technique was also characterized by this same procedure, and this is to name only the most memorable examples.

Meanwhile, the dialectical technique does not begin with the kind of contrasting statements we quite correctly use in describing a flag as black and white. Here the statement that the flag is both black and white merely means that two diverse phenomena are united in one object. The kind of contrasting statement permitting dialectical development requires something more than this.

Socrates' proposition "I know that I know nothing" *simultaneously* expresses the fact that he knows both nothing and something, while also stating that he knows neither something nor nothing. Therefore, the true paradox does not unite differences and opposites in one object, but in the same proposition denies and affirms, negates and makes positive. The genuine paradox cancels itself out, annuls itself.

Kierkegaard's pseudonymous production began with *Ei-*

*ther/Or*, that is, with a contrasting of two forms of existence. So far as we can speak at all here of "antithesis," we have yet to arrive at the acute form of the paradox, yet everywhere evident is a tendency in this direction. From the start the description and exposition are deliberately designed with this in mind.

The esthetic existence is portrayed as neutralizing itself, canceling itself out. This is demonstrated by the pseudonymous author of the second volume of *Either/Or*. But at the same time, at the conclusion of this second part the ethical existence is also represented as canceling itself out.

When Kierkegaard now turns to a description of the religious existence, he describes it as absolute paradox, as he does the religious in general. The whole impression left here, and in every succeeding description of the religious in the framework of the pseudonymous production, is that Kierkegaard is striving to make it clear that the religious, viewed logically, is paradoxical, unintelligible, and self-contradictory.

All dialectic, as we have said, begins with showing contradiction. Yet in the foregoing reflections it has been made clear that mere contrast or antithesis is not enough to meet the demands of a kind of antithesis making dialectic possible. Only when oppositions have reached the sharpest form of the paradoxical and self-neutralizing contradiction can real dialectical movement begin.

On the other hand, in a second stage, every dialectical technique is characterized by an *unfolding* of contradiction. A couple of examples may serve to show how different are the ways in which this is possible. The Platonic Socrates unfolds contradictions by means of dialogue in which there is a confrontation of opposed opinions. Kant unfolds the contradictions of pure reason by setting metaphysically provable, but at the same time mutually exclusive, statements over against each other.

However, it was Hegel who first tried to endow contradiction with a universal function. A comprehensive reality was ascribed to the antithetical process, and it was extended to all areas of thought. The real seat and source of contradiction was the "Spirit." Thus Hegel unfolded the Spirit, from the *Phe-nomenology* through the *Logic*, the *Philosophy of Nature, The History of Philosophy*, etc.

Kierkegaard's great hostility toward Hegel was that of an unfriendly brother. However much Kierkegaard rejected and ridiculed Hegelian universalism, nonetheless antithesis and its explication was for him, too, the universal key.

He started by showing the contradictoriness of human exis-tence. He went on to unfold the paradoxicalness of existence. Ultimately he even carried paradox into religion. And even though he did not admit it, in the end the image and idea of God as Kierkegaard projected them are just as paradoxical as his conception of existence.

The second step in any dialectic, the one leading to the presentation, unfolding, and extension of contradiction, de-termines what form the dialectic will take. In consequence, one dialectic is never the same as another. In any given in-stance it gets its more precise form from the way it is applied, rather than from the goal toward which it strives.

Yet generally, characteristic forms can be distinguished in the dialectical technique. Each technique is committed to un-fold contradiction in a certain limited sphere. Socrates chose to demonstrate contradiction within the context of dialogue and the counterposition of opinions. Kant unfolded contradic-tion in the realm of pure reason, beyond the bounds of experi-ence. Hegel developed contradiction in the stages of the Ab-solute Spirit.

Thus dialectic is an instrument that cuts many ways. It evolves differently when used by Socrates in his search for truth than when used by Kant in a critique of pure reason. It assumes still another form when Hegel uses it as a means of showing the process of Absolute Spirit. Up to a certain point, moreover, dialectical technique is also determined by the goal at hand. In the case of Hegel, for example, his specific tech-nique is a synthetic dialectic, in which any given higher level of phenomena is determined by the contradiction of the one preceding. Simultaneously, this new phenomenon, as it achieves synthesis, once again evolves from contradiction and thus conditions the succeeding phenomenon. The whole of the

Absolute Spirit, in accordance with this process, appears as a succession of unities proceeding out of contradictions, which again and again dissolve into new ones. Ultimately Hegel's dialectical technique consists in constantly changing his gaze as he feels his way along through history, scanning it, now seeing actuality as antithetical, now as unified. Herein lies the peculiar uncertainty of the Hegelian logic: though such a shifting of focus may be possible in every historical consideration, it becomes extraordinarily difficult when applied to concepts which, as means of thought, are fixed unities. Hegel gets around this by stipulating the "self-movement of concepts."

At the outset, Kierkegaard uses another technique to allow one and the same phenomenon to be shown first as unity, then as contradiction. In his pseudonymous poetical works he demonstrates a unity fashioned after this or that actuality, say of the romantic or the ethical man. He then shifts his point of view and unmasks what he has just shown to be unity so as to reveal it as contradiction. Thus in the second volume of *Either/Or* the apparent unity of the esthetic man is unmasked from the viewpoint of the "Husband" and the "Magistrate."

However, no *positive* synthesis is achieved in the next step, which leads to the religious. Religious existence, to be sure, is expressly designated to be a higher form, yet it is not characterized as the unity of the preceding esthetic and ethical forms of existence.

On the contrary, contradiction is now driven even deeper. The pseudonymous author "Johannes de Silentio," who describes religious existence through the person of Abraham, understands it as absolute paradox. In the commentary on this embodied in *Philosophical Fragments* and *Concluding Unscientific Postscript*, the same view is again taken. If the absolute paradox is presented existentially in the poetic works, it crops up again in a philosophical context in the *Fragments*.

In the last work, paradox is glossed with the subtitle "A Metaphysical Crochet." With each succeeding step, paradox is deepened and widened. The *Concluding Unscientific Postscript* in particular is a treatise on the "absolute paradox."

Thus Kierkegaard's dialectical technique involves a progressive expansion of paradox. At the beginning, in the first part of *Either/Or*, paradox is ironically described, in the second seriously and didactically, in the third instance, in *Fear and Trembling*, it is described in terms of the pathos of dread. This sense of paradox is demonstrated again in the *Postscript*, where the absolute existential paradox is identified with the pathos of guilt and suffering.

Earlier, on occasion, we have characterized Kierkegaard's dialectic as destructive. This description may now be pointed up. Kierkegaard first destroyed human existence, then objective thought. He did this by expanding and intensifying contradiction at given moments. At each step that Kierkegaard took, contradiction became more trenchant and unconditional.

In keeping with this progression, it was not until the end of the pseudonymous works that existential contradiction appeared in full panoply at its greatest intensity, whereafter it led to the "night of the unconditioned" and to a God who creates everything out of nothing only to foredoom everything he fashions to nothingness.

Every dialectical technique must work with what Hegel called *Aufhebung*. By this he meant any transition from positive to negative and from negative to positive. For him this peculiarly German term, which combines the senses of "canceling out," "nullification," and "sublimation," connotes development together with the dissolution of what went before. As in the simple example provided earlier, the blossom "cancels out" or "sublimates" the bud; similarly in the development of the Absolute Spirit each step forward nullifies and sublimates what has gone before.

For Hegel, however, the process of *Aufhebung* is always an emergence into a next and higher stage, and so a constructive act. But with Kierkegaard the process of canceling out is radicalized. To be sure, with him, too, the process means a passing over into a next stage. Thus the esthetical existence described in the first part of *Either/Or* is canceled out by the ethical existence described in the second part. Then, in turn, the ethical form of existence is similarly nullified by religious existence. But with each step this nullification process gains in scope and intensity.

Kierkegaard conceived his task to be the abrogation of the

existing as a phenomenon, as something having a historical origin, to bring out paradoxicalness. He ultimately expressed this as "making room so that God can come."

It is not until this point that a sort of synthesis makes its appearance as a kind of vision of the future. Kierkegaard did not feel he was qualified to spell out his vision in detail. He could only show that his contemporary world had crucified Christ a second time. In this sense his existence had, as it were, paved the way for the dialectical leap, but not yet taken it. This was not altered by the fact that in the closing days of his life Kierkegaard wanted to work "catastrophically," only to be prevented by death from taking this final step.

# THE MATERIALISTIC DIALECTIC
## OF KARL MARX
## AND HIS HISTORICAL MATERIALISM

# 25

## A Sketch of the Life of Karl Marx

The life of Karl Marx is not a simple matter, even if one sticks to the catchwords and clichés. It covers a relatively easy childhood and youth, a period of some twenty years spent in Trier. Thereafter came a few more untroubled years of study in Bonn and Berlin. From then on the struggle began, and forty years of hard times followed, a bitter and unremitting struggle for his daily bread. Not until he had grown old did Marx achieve a more or less adequate living standard. It was not only the struggle to earn a bare living that made Marx again and again beseech his friend Engels for pitifully small sums of money. Three of his children died, and perhaps would not have had he had the means to take better care of them. How much these children meant to him is told by the letter to Lasalle in which he said the death of his third child had shaken him "heart and brain."[1]

Marx was born the son of Heinrich Marx, who stemmed from an old rabbinical family. His father's real name was

Herschel Levi, but immediately after the birth of his son Karl he became a Christian and took the name of Heinrich Marx. The father was a delicate and gentle man, anything but a fighter. But he worked his way up in the world and the rabbi's son became a lawyer. He grew away from orthodox Jewry, and for him the baptismal certificate was indeed, as Heinrich Heine put it, an "admission ticket to European culture."[2]

Heinrich Marx was well regarded in his home town of Trier. He had a legal practice and later got the title of a councilor of justice. For his climb up the social ladder he certainly had to thank the fact that for a long period Trier (Trèves) was under Napoleonic rule. Not until the Napoleonic Code came into effect were Jews permitted to engage in trade or the professions. However, when Karl Marx was born, the Rhineland had been Prussian again for four years.

Even under these new conditions Karl Marx's father was able to manage. He was anything but a revolutionary and was timid by nature. He was able to do what his son could not, adapt himself in all respects, and finally even became an ardent Prussian patriot. He was an admirer of Voltaire, Lessing, and Kant; he revered the Prussian king, Frederick the Great. Thus he lived in harmony with himself and with the world and raised his children in the spirit of a liberal Protestantism. He loved his son Karl tenderly, but was distressed by his totally different nature. If the father had had his way—as so often is the case—something quite different would have become of his son. Once when the student Karl Marx was thinking about writing a play, the father recommended that he take some famous high light of Prussian history as his subject. Nothing was more typical of the father than when he wrote his son: "Your opinions on right are not without truth, but very much calculated, if made into a system, to stir up storms, and you know how violent scholarly storms are. If what is objectionable in the matter cannot be entirely removed, at least the form should be toned down and made pleasing."[3] He was spared from ever knowing that his son raised not only scholarly storms, but a hurricane that swept the world. Instead he lived in the belief that his son Karl was to go far in the bourgeois world, and cherished the hope that his son's name one day would be held "in high esteem." Yet now and then he did have gloomy misgivings: "My heart swells sometimes, thinking about you and your future, yet sometimes, too, I cannot rid myself of ideas that arouse sad foreboding and fear. . . . Is there any place in this vale of tears for mundane but softer feelings so vitally consoling to the sensitive man? Since the future obviously is animated and governed by a daimon not given to all men, is this daimon of a heavenly or of a Faustian nature?"[4]

Whether it was because of a prescient heart, or out of the deeper insight of an unquestionably wise older man, in all events he regarded his son with growing concern. This becomes apparent above all in his letters to the Marx of the student years. Up to that time the young Marx seems to have given his father little trouble. He had attended the *gymnasium* in Trier and his mother considered him to be a "child of fortune." At seventeen he got his diploma. Thanks to his talents he had been able to translate difficult passages in the classics and had made a name for himself for the wealth of ideas shown in his Latin essay.

Then he went to the University of Bonn and lived the free student life. Whether this life, as his father once wrote, really was a "wild upheaval,"[5] or whether he just overdid his high-spiritedness in the first semesters cannot be determined for lack of other witnesses. He enrolled as a law student, but never became drawn to the law, let alone engrossed in it. When he went back from Bonn to his home town he became engaged to Jenny von Westphalen, daughter of a high Trier government official. This engagement of the eighteen-year-old Karl, which actually had to be kept secret, may have seemed to Marx's father a promise that his son would climb the ladder of bourgeois society. Young Marx himself was wildly infatuated and clung to his betrothed, who was sensible and the "prettiest girl in Trier," with glowing love.

Next, when the young man was eighteen he went to Berlin to study, and we have a long letter from him to his father about the first two Berlin semesters, in which he made a sort of confession and statement of accounts. The letter is filled with tenderness, the youthful Marx on the whole seeming to

have been a gentle person. The conclusion of this letter is both
affectionate and moving:

> In the hope that the clouds besetting our families will
> gradually pass over, that I myself will be privileged to
> suffer and to weep and perhaps to show you face to face
> the deep sympathy, the boundless love that so often I have
> been able to express only badly, in the hope that you, too,
> dear, ever beloved father, reflecting on the often confused
> make-up of my spirit, forgive me when the heart has often
> seemed to err while deafened by the struggling spirit, that
> soon you will be completely well again so that I can press
> you to my heart in person and speak out my whole mind.
> Your everloving son, Karl. [A postscript follows in which
> he says:] Be so kind as to give my best to my sweet, lovely
> Jenny. Her letter is beautiful, already read through by me
> twelve times and I am still discovering new charms. It is in
> all respects, even stylistically, the finest letter that I can
> think of from a lady.[6]

Berlin decided the fate of Karl Marx. Or, more accurately,
Prussia and Hegel decided it. At the beginning he was electri-
fied by the atmosphere of the University of Berlin. It was
perhaps less the professors than the spirit of Hegel still living
on at the university. Dutifully he listened to the jurists Savigny
and Gans. The first was a fanatical antiliberal, the second a
pupil of Hegel and editor of Hegel's *Philosophy of History*.
But Gans was a progressive and all along had combined disci-
pleship with a critical spirit toward Hegel. For the rest, however, the university was dominated by a collection of mediocre
Hegelians who did not look beyond the Hegelian system.

The Hegelian school of thought was split into a Right and a
Left wing. It was a cleavage that had necessarily had to come.
The aging Hegel, who had declared his faith in the Prussian
state, had left behind apart from this legacy his theory of the
eternal and ceaseless movement of history. Even while rejecting liberalism, he had proclaimed that the progress of mankind resided in the progress of the consciousness of freedom in
man.

This bifurcation for posterity of necessity became an ambiguity. And while the orthodox followers of Hegel were doing what mediocre people do in all ages, making a rigid dogma out of living theory, the Hegelian Left wanted to follow not the letter but the spirit of the master.

Marx very quickly came under the sway of these opposition Hegelians. He joined the "Doktorclub," an organization of young academics. This encounter was decisive for him. Bruno Bauer, Max Stirner, Friedrich Köppen and others belonged to the group. Marx kept up his connection with them until one day, with his typical radicalism, he pulled away.

Young Marx's intellectual development moved rapidly, but he did not become a lawyer. Quite the contrary, this field of study retreated more and more into the background, and Marx finally earned his doctorate with a philosophical thesis in 1841. He also graduated from Jena, not Berlin. The reason for this was that he had no connection with the Berlin professors and, too, graduation was much simpler at Jena. It could even be carried out *in absentia*. At this time Marx was certainly planning to qualify for a philosophical career. His friend Bruno Bauer had already left Berlin and was teaching at the University of Bonn. There Marx could qualify for a university lectureship and, Bauer hoped, with him would create a center of antireactionary thought: "If you come to Bonn this hole-in-the-wall will perhaps soon become the object of general attention and we can precipitate crisis at the most opportune time."[7]

Marx was now a doctor of philosophy, and meanwhile his father had died. He moved to Bonn. But there, too, things had come to a critical head. In 1842, because of his sharp and almost atheistic critique of the Gospels, Bruno Bauer was removed from his teaching post. In Berlin, too, the curve of reaction was on the rise. After the death of Frederick William III, his son, Frederick William IV, had acceded to the throne and, all romantic inclinations notwithstanding, basically followed in his father's footsteps, clinging to the idea of the divine right of kings. The Prussian police apparatus and the omnipotent censor were harder at work than ever. Germany was not a stronghold of freedom but a state strictly governed, for the most part, by police methods. While all over Europe kings and princes were striving to restore rights diminished and shaken by Napoleon, this goal was most successfully pursued, perhaps, by emergent Prussia.

But Marx had opposed this social idea. He was an intellectual, attached to the Hegel who had conceived freedom to be the principle of world history. He was against reaction, against the bourgeoisie, against the Establishment as represented by the state, church, and police. He fought against philistinism and his heart was with the revolutionaries who, in the last analysis, were fighting for civil freedom against an absolutist government.

Coming events were to impel him further in this direction. In spite of what appeared to be a mild edict against censorship, in practice censorship was intensified. Thus the *Hallischen Jahrbücher* ("Halle Annals"), for which Marx was to write an article on the censorship problem, was put under pressure by the censor, and the editor, Ruge, wrote to Marx that it was impossible to publish the article because everything that "smells of Bauer, Feuerbach, and me" would be turned down by the censor.

Marx then got acquainted with the publicist Moses Hess, who invited him to collaborate on the *Rheinische Zeitung*. For three-quarters of a year he was a contributor to, and from October 1842, editor of this publication. It was in this period that he became a propagandistic writer, commenting on and criticizing policies of the day. A Marx was now revealed who won over others to his learned style. All the articles that he wrote for the *Rheinische Zeitung* already showed that sharpness of pen, that uncompromising quality in his thinking, and the enormous propagandistic power which henceforth were to appear again and again in his writings.

At first the readership of the newspaper increased. It became recognized and famous, but this did not last long. The censor intervened, and in 1843 Marx left the editorial staff. A brief notice in the issue of March 18, 1843, read: "The undersigned gives notice that on account of current censorship conditions he has resigned from the editorial staff of the *Rheinische Zeitung*. Dr. Marx."[8]

A short time later Marx married his betrothed, and a new chapter in his life began in a double sense. For now, practically speaking, the period of emigration began. In November Marx moved with his wife to Paris. There, together with Ruge, he put out a periodical, which was given the title *Deutsch-französische Jahrbücher*, or "German-French Annals." Only two issues of this magazine were published, then the Engels' backing dried up. At the same time differences had arisen between Ruge and Marx. Once again Marx was out of a job.

The Prussian government, which had been displeased with this periodical, now arranged with the French government for the deportation of a number of writers and émigrés, one of whom was Marx. In 1845 he had to leave Paris within twenty-four hours and French territory within three days.

He again went into exile, this time in Brussels. Even as he arrived he had to sign a document obligating himself not to print anything in Brussels on the politics of the day. In 1848, after the publication of the *Communist Manifesto*, he was again banished, but concurrently was invited by the French revolutionary government to return to Paris from Brussels. As it turned out, he stayed in Paris for only a short time. Meanwhile revolution had spread throughout Europe and Marx went back to Cologne. There, in 1848, the *Neue Rheinische Zeitung* came out under the editorship of Karl Marx and soon became the most famous newspaper of that year of revolution. But soon the revolution collapsed, and shortly afterward Marx was once again deported from Germany. He had gone off on an attempt to raise money for the paper and was greeted by the deportation order upon his return to Cologne. He arranged his financial affairs as best he could, pawned his wife's silver to have something to live on, and this time left Germany for good.

At first Marx went to Paris. However, when the French government denied him permission to settle there and ordered him to go to the Department of Morbihan in Brittany if he wanted to live in France, he went to London. He was now thirty-one years old and hereafter London was to be his home. The *Neue Rheinische Revue* was founded while he was in

exile in London. For obvious reasons it was ill-prepared finan-
cially and editorially. After a few issues had come out there
was one more double issue, and then it folded.

Now began the increasingly bitter years, during which Marx
and his family had to get by on what little he could earn from
writing articles. This pittance was far from enough to live on.
Without his friend Engels, who was well off and who again
and again sent small sums of money, Marx and his family
would have literally starved to death in London. A constant
struggle to get his daily bread commenced: if he did get his
hands on a tiny sum, most of it had to go to pay the debts he
had run up at the baker's and butcher's. Marx, as earlier
noted, lost three of his children, and for obvious reasons: hunger and no money for a doctor and medicine. After the death
of his third child Marx wrote that he could not get over her
loss: "My child's death has deeply shaken me in heart and
brain, and I feel the loss as much as I did on the first day. My
poor wife is completely broken up."

The years passed in indefatigable activity. Some of this activity was political, but for the most part Marx worked in the
British Museum. He wrote and wrote and would not capitu-
late, and his wife stuck by him with a steadfastness that beg-
gars description. His fame grew, but he still had to keep
asking Engels to send him a few pounds.

So the years sped by in struggle and misery and yet in the
constant hope of a world revolution soon to come. Marx's
private life did not ease until his friend Engels was able to
send him a yearly stipend.

But in between were the years of frightful poverty, during
which he wrote that he could not call the doctor for his sick
children because he had "no money for medicine," and had to
feed his family for days on bread and potatoes, to a point
where he was not sure they could stick it out another day.
Now and then there would be a little ray of light, as when for
a time he was writing a series of articles on the European
situation for a New York newspaper. When this source of
income dried up in 1860, in his extremity Marx even got himself a job on the railroad as a ticket seller. But neither his
appearance nor his clothes were suitable, and he was let go.[9]

Only an iron constitution, psychological and physical, could have stood up under this existence—a life which, as far as material circumstance went, for forty years was worse than that of many a proletarian. But Karl Marx lived to be almost seventy-five years old, meanwhile having lived through the death of his wife and his oldest living daughter. He finally died of a lung abscess while asleep in an armchair in his workroom.

# 26

---

# A Sketch of the Personality

The older Marx wondered whether there was room in his son's heart for the ordinary but softer feelings so consoling to a man in this vale of tears.[10] He early recognized that his son was gifted with a demonic genius. However, the year the father wrote to this effect, the particular career that Karl Marx was to follow had not yet become evident.

In a progress report he wrote to his father, the nineteen-year-old student is indeed revealed as an astonishing person. First of all, obviously, he is filled with an insatiable thirst for knowledge and a powerful drive to act. Yet it seems that his heart did indeed have a place for "softer" feelings, when he reported on the three copybooks of poems with which he had launched his studies. Apparently these poems were utterly dreadful, and even their titles—"Song of the Elves," "Song of the Gnomes," "Song of the Sirens"—are highly unpromising. Mehring says that "they are formless in every sense of the word."[11] Marx himself criticized them with that pitiless trenchancy he later so often turned on others:

> Everything real is blurry and this blurred state knows no bounds, attacks on the present, feeling in broad and form-less strokes, nothing natural, everything constructed out of moonshine, the complete opposite of what is out there and what ought to be out there, rhetorical reflections instead of poetical thoughts, though perhaps a certain warmth of feeling and striving for verve characterize all the poems of the first three volumes, which I have sent Jenny and she received.[12]

The whole sweep of a longing that knew no bounds found an outlet in all sorts of forms and made *dichten* into *breiten*.*

It is curious, the sharpness and clearsightedness and cool-ness with which Marx, only a year later, criticized these effu-sions. But by now, if his later reports are to be trusted, poetry had become the least of his activities. But this time the ac-counting had become: "I had to study law and above all felt a strong impulse to come to grips with philosophy."[13] Now it was everything at once. He read Reimarus and Thibaut, he translated the first two books of the Roman Pandects, read Lessing, Solger, Winckelmann, histories of art and of Ger-many, he translated Tacitus and Ovid, he began to learn En-glish and Italian from grammars, read in the literature of the law—Savigny, Feuerbach, Grolmann and others—he trans-lated Aristotle's *Rhetoric* and after that reread Bacon and Hegel, etc.

The young Marx, like the mature Marx, must have had an astounding capacity to absorb information; there was a place in his head for everything. When he was over sixty years old Marx was learning Russian and after six months mastered the language well enough to be able to read it. His hunger for books grew rather than lessened with the years. Along with this went a tremendous capacity for work. Marx took ten

---

* A play on words. *Dichten* generally means to write poetry or compose something. But it can also mean to make tight or watertight. *Breiten* means to spread or flatten out, to extend, and so is antonymous to *dichten* in its second sense—*Tr.*

hours of work a day for granted. Even in his later years he rose at seven, read and wrote till two, after lunch again worked until dinnertime and, after an evening walk, again went back to his study and worked until two and three in the morning.

Even as a young man it was characteristic of Marx to put the huge amount of material that he devoured to productive use immediately. He read and assimilated incessantly, he thought and wrote endlessly. From his reports to his father on his two Berlin semesters we learn that besides all his reading he wrote his own "Philosophy of Right" which, so he said, covered 300 sheets of paper, and a dialogue running to twenty-four pages called "Cleanthes, or Concerning the Point of Departure and Necessary Progress of Philosophy."

This passion for work and reading, as we have said, was not merely an occasional thing. From all that we know it continued all his life. Ruge described his fellow editor, Marx, as a worker of "uncommon intensity," who was forever dropping everything to plunge "once again into an endless sea of books," and who, if possible, was "even more on edge and violent . . . when he had worked himself sick and had not been to bed for three or even four nights in a row."[14]

It seems to have been one of the man's basic traits that he repeatedly taxed himself to the limit, whereupon a brief collapse would ensue, obviously a physical reaction to his over-exertion, and then immediately thereafter work would resume in the same old style. Even in the early Berlin period he reported on an "indisposition" of this kind. He said later he got up from his bed, burned what he had written, and again plunged into his work.

Marx drove himself hard not only in work. The demon his father had wondered about was in fact of neither a heavenly nor a Faustian nature. Marx, young and old, was the instrument of an enormous and driving passion that exploded in all directions. The same intense passion that made for such tender devotion to his parents and later his wife and family, also took the form of a raging, intractable capacity for work, and again could be a boundless wrath, ready to erupt at any moment, against everything that he despised.

And it must not be forgotten that it was in the last analysis this same driving force which led him to espouse the cause of the poor and wretched. Burckhardt's observation, to the effect that "passion is the mother of all great things, that is, real passion, which wants something new and not merely the downfall of the old," applies to few so aptly as to Marx.

Karl Marx, endowed with passion to such a great degree, thus was destined to lead anything but a tame life. He hated everything that constricted him. He simply overran every obstacle that threatened to impose limits on him. At the outset of his university years he broke through the limits of the field of law which he was supposed to be studying. He flung himself at once into a sea of thought and knowledge. Later, in a second bursting forth, he raged against the Prussian state. But this was a storm that never subsided. It grew into not only the battle against capitalism, which is his greatest work, but even reached the point where he declared war on his own followers once they appeared suspect to him.

His outstanding characteristic was a unique combination of passion and reason. Marxist reasoning is anything but cool and calculated. For this sort of thing he had no gift. His diplomacy was bad, his practical calculations a failure; he really always worked with his imagination. However, his reasoning faculty was razor-sharp. His strength lay in this critical faculty.

His critical power was based on the vast fund of knowledge which he uninterruptedly collected and evaluated. His erudition and judgmental capacity were the qualities that impressed everybody who met him. Even when he was only twenty-three years old his friend Köppen wrote to him: "Look at you, you're a storehouse of ideas, a workhouse, or, to put it in Berlinese, a regular *Ochsenkopf* [blockhead] of ideas."[15] And decades later the Englishman Hyndman wrote:

When we left Marx my companion asked me what I thought of him. I think, I said, he is the Aristotle of the nineteenth century. Only hardly had I said this than I realized this comparison did not quite fit. Of all things it is impossible to imagine his ever having been a courtier of Alexander the Great. Besides, Marx has never—although the opposite has been claimed—so isolated himself from immediate human interests as to be able to tackle facts and their relationship in that cold, dry way that is so characteristic of the greatest philosopher of antiquity. There can be no doubt that with Marx hatred of exploitation and wage-slavery was not merely intellectual and philosophical, but passionately personal as well.[16]

Hyndman was right, except for forgetting that all his life Marx strove to write a rational and, as it were, cold, dry theory that would justify his revolutionary attitude. After all, the fifteen years spent working out *Capital* show that he made an effort to produce a sober and scientific argument for his notions.

However, when at first glance Hyndman pronounced Marx to be a philosopher, he was not the only one who had the same impression. Many years before, Moses Hess described Marx in a letter as follows: ". . . you can be prepared to meet the greatest, perhaps the only living, philosopher . . . who, however, will deal the last blow to medieval religion and politics; he combines the deepest philosophical seriousness with the most cutting wit . . ."[17]

Both Hyndman and Hess clearly felt the peculiar combination of passion and reason that was Marx's special hallmark. Their definition of Marx's character is equally borne out by his work. Marx—not unlike Kierkegaard—was a remarkable mixture of the constructive, speculative philosopher and the rational empiricist. On one side, to the extent that he was governed by his critical understanding, he was the skeptical critic of human society and of mankind. On the other side he was an impassioned utopian who, like all of his kind, dreamed of paradise on earth. Whether the latter aspect of his nature became more cautious and less in evidence with advancing years is a moot question.

It was unavoidable that such a pronounced, opinionated, and glowingly passionate personality should have been seen very differently by different people. Not many ever saw the Marx whose sensitivity aroused his father's concern, or the man whom Jenny Marx and the children knew as the "Moor" or "Old Nick," and about whom one visitor during the last years said: ". . . (he was) a well-bred, highly educated German-Englishman . . . a man full of zest thanks to comfortable financial circumstances . . ."[18]

It was a quite different impression that he made on most people. In a famous article that appeared in 1880, in the Russian review *The European Messenger*, the author, Anienkow, described his meeting with Marx in 1847. He visited Marx bearing a letter of introduction from a Russian landowner admired by Marx. His reception was friendly, and he was invited to attend a meeting of Marx, Engels, and Weitling the following day. First of all he described Marx:

> He himself represented the type of man who is made of energy, will power, and unbendable conviction, a type also highly striking in outer appearance. On his head a thick, black mane, his hands covered with hair, his shirt crookedly buttoned up, he nonetheless had the look of a man who had the authority and power to command respect, even though his outer appearance and actions may have seemed strange. His movements were awkward, but bold and self-confident, his manner contrary to all accepted social forms. But it was a proud manner, with a trace of contempt, and his sharp voice with a metallic ring accorded remarkably with the radical judgments on people and things that he let fall. He spoke only in imperatives brooking no opposition, the effect of which was additionally sharpened by the almost painfully moving tone pervading everything he said. This tone expressed the firm conviction of his mission to rule minds and prescribe laws for them. Before me stood the embodiment of a democratic dictator such as might materialize in one's mind in a moment of fantasy.

Thus the impression left on Anienkow, perhaps not so much on the occasion of his initial meeting as on the second day of the discussion. The "communist" Weitling, a labor leader in the *Bund der Gerechten* ("League of the Just") was certainly a confused ideologue, in whom revolutionary Christian ideas were intermingled with muddled theories. While the four men, according to Anienkow's description, were sitting together—the tall, English-looking Engels; Weitling, who looked like a traveling salesman, though he was actually a journeyman tailor; Marx and himself—Weitling began to speak. He had not been talking long before Marx interrupted him with a direct and hostile question as to how he justified the agitation he was causing with so much clamor, and particularly how he justified having robbed so many workers of their bread by it.

Weitling tried to reply but Marx got angrier and angrier. Again he interrupted, accused Weitling of making useless propaganda, ran him down as an absurd apostle who preferred his audience to be made up of asses who would listen to him with their mouths hanging open. With hardly a pretense at being polite, he pointed at his Russian visitor and said: "Here with us is a Russian," and perhaps in his country there might be a place for a combination of "absurd apostles and absurd young men."

When Weitling now became excited himself, Marx pounded the table hard, jumped up and took his measure. "Never," he said, "has ignorance been of any use to anyone." With that the conversation was over. Weitling had been ticked off like a schoolboy, Marx paced stormily back and forth, and Anienkow took his leave.[19]

Anienkow was not the only one to describe Marx in this manner. There were many who experienced the Marx who glowed with anger and got to know his wildly eruptive temperament. And beyond these impressions one has only to take a look at Marx's *Collected Letters* to discover here, too, the same explosive and at all times irritable spirit, ready at any moment to pour forth torrents of abusive argument.

This mixture of passion and reason, of constructive philosophy and empiric observation, of utopianism and keen factual analysis distinguished not only the Marxian personality but Marx's writings as well. Within the historical context it was a remarkably effective mixture. The times were critical and enlightened; men lived in the consciousness of the power of exact scientific thinking, and a merely utopian socialism had really small prospect of any broad success.

The scientific socialism taught by Marx scarcely showed any sign of the utopian element. This bloomed in secret. The side of Marx turned to outward view was that of a rational, scientific, and politico-economic champion of the necessity of a socialized economy. Behind the critique of the present loomed the theory of history, no less laying claim to being scientific.

It was under this sign of science that Marx was able to recruit his believers. A numerous contingent, then, believed in Marx's erudition. Yet on the other hand his scientific socialism, in its prophecy of a classless society and a communist society, also provided adequate nourishment for people of a more credulous and less scientific turn of mind.

Thus, out of these two roots grew a mighty movement which on the one hand fed belief and an almost religious striving, and which on the other hand could pass as a critical, scientific point of view based on empirical observation.

In the final analysis the secret of Marxian communism's phenomenal success is rooted in this mixture of the passionate and the rational. Marx could not have known just how successful such a mixture would be, but ever since its birth Marxism has lived from two sources: its prophecy of utopia and its scientific methodology. Thanks to these qualities it has been able to resist and overcome all the difficulties that any mass movement is bound to encounter.

# 27

# The Development of Marxian Thought

I t seems that the young Marx was not much concerned with scholarship during his first two semesters at Bonn. His father, at any rate, obviously felt this to be the case and later reminded his son about his "wild roistering" at Bonn. He found fault with his son for spending so much and once inquired whether "dueling really has so much to do with philosophy."

The young Marx did not like listening to lectures. His father wrote: "I know, of course, that you don't attach much importance to lectures . . ." On the other hand it cannot be imagined that he was completely given over to the usual student life of the period, and after all his father did warn him again and again of "studying too much." He was aware of his son's proclivity for throwing himself into a subject and then working the night through, oblivious in a fury of concentration.

In Berlin, too, it was not the lectures and the narrower university activities that attracted him. However, he did enjoy listening to the historian Savigny and had a high opinion of the jurist Gans. The first was an antiliberal, but Gans, who, as Hegel's pupil, had published the master's *Philosophy of History*, was of a progressive mind and, indeed, had polemicized against the aging Hegel and his repudiation of liberal thought. In any case, during Marx's nine semesters at Berlin, he attended nine lecture courses, most of which were in the law.

Of decisive influence on him was the *Doktorclub*, which he had already joined by his second semester. This was a club of young intellectuals who spent the evening in beer-cellar discussions. An array of gifted, intelligent, and antireactionary people belonged to it. Among them were Bruno Bauer, long associated with Marx, and besides him Kaspar Schmidt, who under the pseudonym of Max Stirner became known through his work *The Ego and His Own*. Other members of the club were Rutenberg, whom Marx, in a letter to his father, described as his intimate friend, Karl Friedrich Köppen and others. It was a company of highly talented young people, typical intellectuals who lived in protest against the government, the church, and bourgeois philistinism.

Singly and as a group they were at odds with the reactionary climate that had prevailed in Prussia since Hegel's day and which was growing more reactionary all the time. Almost all of them paid a price for their dissent. Bruno Bauer, then *Privatdocent* of theology, as already noted, was forced to give up his teaching post. Max Stirner was a teacher at a girls' school. His *History of Reaction*, written in 1852, aroused little notice, but his defiantly skeptical *The Ego and His Own* became famous. He finally turned to journalism. Karl Friedrich Köppen was also a schoolteacher and remained one to the end of his life. He was mainly a historian and earned praise with his *Introduction to Nordic Mythology* published in 1837. Köppen was considered to be an excellent teacher who could stimulate and inspire his students, one of them later reported. But none of these obviously talented men could get into the universities or stay there if they did. The prevailing political climate was against them. After the downfall of Napoleon and the end of the Napoleonic wars, all the kings and princes of Europe were striving to restore former social conditions. Prussia, then in the process of ascendancy, showed this tendency most of all.

And yet Berlin was just the place where dissent flourished. This kind of thinking was connected with Hegel and represented an attempt to update him. To be sure, the older Hegel had been antiliberal and had wanted to have nothing to do with war and revolution, and the orthodox Hegelians stood as far to the right and were as loyal to the government as he had been. But the so-called Hegelians of the Left, who boasted that they were carrying forward the living spirit and not the letter of the master's thought, had identified themselves with the other, opposite tendency in Hegelian thought, as expressed in the *Philosophy of History* with its notion of progress in world history as the advance of the consciousness of freedom.

Thus it was with this group of Hegelians who gathered in the *Doktorclub*. Yet they did more talking and reasoning than actually going out to fight for their ideas, and that was the reason why Marx parted company with them in a highly critical spirit. However, at this earlier date the thinking and attitudes of the group must have had an extraordinary influence on the young Marx. Here he found what he was looking for: intelligence and passionate interest in free and critical thought.

Also decisive for Marx was his contact with Hegelianism. His reaction was ambivalent, for he was as much repelled as drawn by the philosophy of Hegel. In a long letter of intellectual reckoning to his father he wrote: "I have read fragments of Hegelian philosophy whose grotesque melody of the crags [*Felsenmelodie*] were not to my liking."[20] What did he mean by *Felsenmelodie*? Was Hegel's thought fashioned too much out of square-hewn stones for his taste, or did he take offense at the "melody" of the dialectic?

However it may have been, quite clearly Marx felt an uneasiness with Hegel that was never to leave him. Ultimately he took up arms against the "mystifying" tendency for which he later condemned Hegel. But despite this—or perhaps, indeed, on this very account—Hegel's philosophy in good measure determined Marx's intellectual fate. Marx without Hegel is unthinkable.

However, in this early period in the company of the Hegelian Left whom he met in the *Doktorclub,* he got to know a living Hegelianism that impressed him profoundly. He had direct contact with disciples of Hegel to whom, as he later wrote in his dissertation, Hegelian theory was not a "consecrated science" to which one surrendered oneself with "naive, uncritical trust." Rather these were people who clung to the master because for them his teachings were "in a state of becoming, in which to its outermost periphery his most intimate spiritual heart's blood pulsed on."[21]

So he, too, became a disciple of Hegel, although with uneasiness and reluctance. The conflict in him between adherence and antagonism is reflected in his first account of this relationship. In the same letter where he spoke about the "grotesque melody of the crags," there were quite different passages. He had written, he said, a dialogue, "Cleanthes, or Concerning the Point of Departure and Necessary Progress of Philosophy." Referring to this, he said:

> . . . like a hale and hearty pilgrim I set about the work itself, about a philosophical-dialectical development of divinity, as manifested as an implicit concept, as religion, as nature, as history. My last proposition was the beginning of the Hegelian system, and this work, to effect which I made myself to some degree acquainted with natural science, Schelling, and history, which caused me endless brain-racking, and which is so commonly (*kommun*) written (since actually it is intended to be a new logic) that I myself can hardly think my way back into it again, this, my dearest child, fostered by moonshine, like a false siren delivers me into the hands of the enemy.

It is easy to see that the young Marx in his Cleanthes dialogue retraced and shortened the road that Hegel had followed for a lifetime. In any case, the program as Marx developed it contained certain basic traits of the Hegelian system; the way via the concept to nature and history, the unfolding of divinity in a philosophical and dialectical manner.

Now for the first time Marx seemed to get closer to Hegel, that is, during the time when he was overcome by an "indisposition." As a result, he said: ". . . I am chaining myself ever faster to the current world philosophy I had thought to escape from . . ." It was to be a long while before Marx freed himself from Hegelian philosophy and, in a certain sense, he never did escape from it.

But now the idea that he himself should follow a university teaching career seemed to become more and more fixed in Marx's mind. To be sure, he continued to keep law under consideration and to attend lectures in it, but here, again, he was thinking of getting a professorship. However, he got his doctoral degree in 1841. His dissertation was a philosophical work called "The Difference between Democritean and Epicurean Natural Philosophy."

The circumstances surrounding his matriculation are not entirely clear, but it appears that certain difficulties stood in the way of getting his degree at Berlin. Therefore he graduated from Jena. His friend Bauer had long been urging him to take the "miserable" exam and come to Bonn. There he would qualify for university lecturing, as already described.

The doctoral dissertation, the original of which is lost, has been preserved in a transcript that Marx made himself. Some fragments that he added show Marx's position on Hegel at that time, if perhaps not in detail at least sketchily. As already noted, Marx spoke of the master as one to whom *science* (Wissenschaft) was a "becoming," a developing thing. In a long passage he discussed Hegel's position on the proof of God, the theme of one of Hegel's last lectures. He was of the opinion that Hegel had "completely distorted the theological evidence, that is, cast it aside, in order to justify it (his position)." He said: "What must it be like for clients whose lawyer can do nothing to spare them the death sentence except kill them himself?"[22]

However, the dependence on Hegel is unmistakable. It comes out in the style, in the typically Hegelian turns of phrase. Marx spoke in the master's voice about the "philosophers of hair-, fingernail-, toenail-clippings and excrements." He drew pictures like those found in Hegel's letters. An example: ". . . the multitudes of subordinate, carping, unindividualistic constructions, which either hide behind a philosophical giant of the past . . . or behind which stands a Lilliputian, armed with bifocal glasses . . ."[23]

At the same time, in these fragments, in a few words here and there and in cross-threaded dialectical propositions, a problem crops up which was also always latent in Hegel. It is the problem of reconciling theory and practice, the question of how theory works or does not work, how theory and practice are related.

Hegel had two opposite opinions on this question. The young Hegel took the view that idealistic theory as to how things ought to be would set the world in motion. The older Hegel rejected this notion. According to him, the realm of ideas develops only when a life-form has matured.

From the few sentences that Marx devoted to the matter it cannot be determined whether they conform with the thoughts of the old Hegel as they appear in the preface to the *Philosophy of Right*. But in one passage his own feeling on the subject stands out quite clearly: "It is a psychological law that the critical spirit that has become implicitly free becomes practical energy, and, issuing forth as *will* out of the shadowy realm of Amenthes, turns against the worldly actuality existing without it (will)." This means that the theoretically emancipated spirit, having achieved clarity, turns against actuality, critically and even militantly as well. "What was inner light becomes consuming flame that turns outward."

It shows a first adumbration of Marx's later revolutionary theory, but in its further unfolding the idea becomes dialectically confused. Marx asserts that "the philosophization of the world is at the same time a secularization of philosophy, that its actualization is also its loss. What it does battle with externally is its own inner lack, and it is precisely in battle that it succumbs to the very evils which on the other hand it is combating as such. And these evils are only annulled by becoming subject to them."[24]

If this is the "objective" side of philosophy, then, according to Marx, there is also the "subjective" side, the relationship between the philosophical system being actualized and its spiritual advocates or bearers. Again an analogous argument is unfolded, in which the ideas turn in negative circles. Marx

distinguishes between a "liberal party" and "positive philosophy." "Each of these parties does just what the other wants to.
do and which it cannot do itself," etc.

This much is clear: Marx has mastered the dialectical play
of the idea which, as it cancels itself out, spirals upward. It is
also to be assumed that in this description he had completely
concrete opinions and directions of thought in mind, but he
does not say what they are. Finally, it is clear, too, that
everything he says is basically related to Hegelian philosophy,
which as a "system" cannot be "actualized" in its present form.

The thought glimmering here in a vague, indeterminate dialectic, two years later found lucid and definitive expression in
Marx's essay *Contribution to the Critique of Hegel's Philosophy of Right*. When this occurred, the Marxian theory of
*revolution* had been born in principle.

# 28

## The Dialectic in the Youthful Writings

During the years 1842–1847 Marx experienced a development which made a socialist thinker and social revolutionary out of the young philosopher who had been influenced by Hegel. In point of practical development, these same years made the twenty-three-year-old doctor of philosophy who had planned to settle down as a *Privatdocent* into a militant journalist.

At the same time, Marx's inner development was perfected, as witnessed by the fact that whereas the doctoral thesis offered at Jena in 1841 dealt with Epicurus, at the end of this period in 1847 came the *Communist Manifesto*, a socialist and communist document of worldwide historical importance.

His financial circumstances had also suffered a considerable change. As a student, generously supplied with funds by his father, Marx had lived like any young bourgeois, the kind of small, fixed-income existence dependent on first of the month remittances. Now Marx was on his own and in addition had taken over the responsibility for a growing family while in a job situation offering no unconditional middle-class security.

As a free-lance contributor and later as editor of the *Rheinische Zeitung*, he was confronted by hitherto completely alien tasks and came into contact with circles unknown to him before. He got to know the machinations of politics, and he gained insight into the economic difficulties of running a newspaper. As a student he had spoken and written freely, but now he felt the weight of the censor. If the newspaper was to provide him with a living, he had to watch out for its existence and raise money for it. But even this life, which at least provided a certain stable framework, was of short duration. It ended with his resignation from the editorship of the *Rheinische Zeitung*. Marx left Germany and entered into the insecurity of emigration.

Under the pressure of this development, Marx's personality had to change accordingly. During his student career Marx was a budding scholar whose milieu was theory. Yet Marx's disposition was that of a battler, a political journalist, and agitator. Mixing scholarship and daily journalism is never a simple thing, so different are the demands of the two. Marx chose an intermediate situation, one which was in a certain sense to continue for his remaining days. He became both a scholar and an agitator, a theoretician and a practitioner of politics.

Arnold Ruge, who with Marx published the shortlived *Deutsch-französische Jahrbücher* ("German-French Annals") in Paris, described Marx, with whom he had a falling out, as follows: "Then he has a peculiar nature, completely suited for learning and writing, but quite unfitted for journalism . . . With his scholarly disposition he belongs entirely to the German world, but with his revolutionary way of thinking he is excluded from it."[25]

This description sums up in a perceptive fashion the dilemma in which Marx found himself. Ruge not only saw the intermediate situation between scholar and journalist but also grasped the specific inner sense of this émigré existence. Marx had grown beyond his national homeland, Germany—which Hegel, for example, had never left—or at any rate been kicked out of. From here on he was to live as an émigré in France and London, between nationalities—that bitter existence of an "international" who must dwell in strange countries, beset by homesickness and contempt for the country from which he has come.

But Ruge, who to be sure very clearly saw the division of this situation, failed to recognize the enormous energy with which Marx ruthlessly worked and lived, against himself and others. It also has to be doubted whether Ruge realized just how much Marx was cut out for both vocations. There is no question, in any case, that Marx was successful as a journalist. His work on the *Rheinische Zeitung* alone is proof. Certainly, some later critics have asserted that all Marx published in this newspaper were "longwinded, scurrilous attacks on the Prussian censor, on the Bundestag and on the big landowners in general."[26] But it cannot be denied that these articles, long-winded and theoretical though they might have been, repeatedly showed brilliant formulations and strikingly apt images and similes, and were above all penetratingly written.

Certainly the man who wrote these pieces was half philosopher and half something else again. Thus in one article he wrote:

Philosophy, above all German philosophy, has a hankering for loneliness, for passionless self-contemplation which to begin with is alien to the trigger-happy, quotidian character of a newspaper, which rejoices only in communication. Philosophy, understood as systematic development, is unpopular. Its secret weaving within itself looks, to the profane eye, like an activity as eccentric as it is impractical; it is viewed as a professor of the magical arts, whose incantations sound solemn because they are not understood. [But this scolding is followed by these words of appreciation:] Philosophers do not grow like mushrooms out of the earth, they are the fruits of their time, of their people, whose most subtle, precious and invisible juices circulate in philosophical ideas. The same spirit builds philosophical systems in the brain of philosophers that builds railroads with the workers' hands. Philosophy does not stand outside the world any more than the brain is outside man because it is not located in the stomach; but in fact philosophy is in the world with the brain prior to actually setting foot on earth, while many other human spheres long stand fast-rooted in the earth and gather in the fruits of the world with their hands before suspecting that the head is also of this world, or that this world is the world of the head.[27]

Certainly this style and delivery was too high-flown for the average simple newspaper reader. Marx was never to master the completely simple and primitive style of the demagogue, though gradually he did simplify his thinking to a point where the clarity of the presentation and the strong impact of the imagery made it accessible to less sophisticated minds.

Since Marx stood between philosophy and practical politics, it was to his advantage that he was able, as Ruge said, to work himself into practical matters with an obsessive capacity for toil. As Ruge says, he threw himself in a "sea of books" and, thanks to the agility of his thinking and his quickness of grasp, in short order he acquired whatever knowledge he had been lacking. Superficial orientation had never sufficed for Marx. As an émigré he immediately learned French and studied the French journalists intensively, while working his way more and more into the literature of social science. How exact his knowledge of this literature became with the years is witnessed by the four thick volumes which Karl Kautsky compiled from Marx's literary remains and published under the title of *Theories of Surplus Value*.

Out of this period came that group of Marx's writings that have been called the *Jugendschriften*, or "Youthful Writings." Part of this work is in the form of occasional articles published by Marx himself, as in the "German-French Annals"; some, like *The Holy Family*, were independently published works written in collaboration with Friedrich Engels, and still another portion of them were never published by Marx at all, but appeared posthumously almost a hundred years after his death.

The most important writings can be listed in sequence as

follows. In 1844 a piece called *Contribution to the Critique of Hegel's Philosophy of Right* appeared in the "German-French Annals." A collaborative work by Marx and Engels, *The Holy Family, or a Critique of Critical Critique* followed a year later. The "Critique of the Hegelian Philosophy of the State," which had to do with some passages in a section of Hegel's *Philosophy of Right,* cannot be definitively dated. In Rjazanow's opinion it was not written before March 1843, but according to other representations (v. Landshut and I. P. Mayer), it was already written by 1841–42.[28]

A manuscript of a fragmentary nature allegedly written about 1844 has been given the title *Economic and Philosophic Manuscripts of 1844* by editors Landshut and Mayer.[29] This comprehensive work, written together by Marx and Engels and already sent to the publisher with the intention of having it come out in print, is supposed to have originated in 1845–46. However, publication never went through and this work, too, did not appear until brought out by Rjazanow eighty-six years after Marx's death.

These writings, to which must be added the articles on the Jewish question that also came out in the "German-French Annals" in 1843, today make it possible for us to provide a more precise description of Marx's ideological development. This evolution clearly shows a break from Hegel, but no less clearly a dependence on him. It becomes evident that Marx was much more strongly bound to Hegel than those interpreters who see Marx as having grown out of his philosophical swaddling clothes during this early period would like to have it.

But above all it must be emphasized that in this period Marx sketched out a dialectical theory of revolution that evolved out of his having come directly to grips with Hegel. Because in this theory revolution is necessary and because the working class is recognized to be its instrument, Marx hit on the conception of a "material" basis for revolution. This he recognized and expressed in his *Contribution to the Critique of Hegel's Philosophy of Right.* As he put it: "Revolutions stand in need, namely, of a *passive* element, a *material* basis."[30]

Take note here, too, though it has been overlooked by many

interpreters of Marx, that the material basis of revolution is regarded as passive in nature. The theory, advanced in the *Communist Manifesto*, and thereafter to become ever more apparent, that the "advance of production" and material development actively compel revolution and pave the way for it, is still not present here, and evolved later.

The dialectical movement in terms of which Marx developed his idea of the economic necessity of revolution out of his original revolutionary theory is exhibited in the fragment *Economic and Philosophic Manuscripts of 1844*. We speak here of a dialectical movement because the first theory of revolution, as can be shown more precisely, starts with the idea that revolutionary doctrine and theory, brought to bear on the masses, will cause them to revolt. However, the later concept has it that the material conditions of the masses permits no other way but revolution.

Marxism, above all in its final development, combined these two ideas. It advanced the thesis, in a certain sense self-evident, that whereas economic circumstances without fail propagate revolution, it should not by any means be left out of account that agitation and revolutionary activity are also indispensable. Practically speaking, this is the key idea which has guided all Marxist revolutionaries since Marx himself.

However, before such a synthesis could be arrived at, the conception predicating revolution as necessitated by material circumstance also had to have its other side, the idea that revolution proceeds immutably in terms of a "natural law" of evolution. In the total picture of Marxian theory, this means proving that revolutions are naturally necessary phases of human history and evolution.

These two concepts stand side by side in the Marxian essay on the subject. Philosophical considerations in part conforming with Hegel and in part critical of him mingle and crisscross and again alternate with economic reflections. On the one hand Marx is opposed to the Hegelian theory that history follows the law of the spirit, on the other he demonstrates the imperfection of current economic theories. It is very curious to see how Marx infuses a philosophy derived from Hegel into basic economic ideas and, conversely, undertakes to make economic insights the basis of the same philosophy.

By 1844 the newly sprung synthesis suddenly made its appearance in *The Holy Family*. Here it emerged as a brilliant and ingeniously formulated description of the dialectic of capitalism and the proletariat.

This youthful development, which ran its course in the short space of three or four years, was rounded out by the last work of the series, *The German Ideology*. By now Marx had completely freed himself from Hegel and developed his own theory of history.

He had now found his theory of "historical materialism," a theory allowing an essentially simpler, virtually primitive interpretation of history. It can be described in one short sentence: It is not consciousness that makes history, but history that produces consciousness. However, since human history is known to be primarily a matter of the evolution of economic forces, the Marxian contention ultimately reads: Economic evolution determines history and history consciousness.

By now, however, Marx is not a primitive but a dialectical materialist. This is best demonstrated by a passage from *Theses on Feuerbach*: "The materialistic theory of changing conditions and education forgets that conditions are changed by men and that the educator must himself be educated. This doctrine, therefore, has to divide society into two parts, one of which is superior to society. The synchronization of altering conditions and human activity or self-changing can only be conceived and rationally understood as *revolutionary practice*."[31]

These sentences leave no doubt that notwithstanding the correctness of the proposition according to which material conditions are determinative, for its part revolutionary practice does and must change these conditions.

# 29

## The Theory of Revolution

If this development, so far presented in an abbreviated form, were described step by step in more detail, first of all would come the article called *Contribution to the Critique of Hegel's Philosophy of Right*. The title would lead one to believe that the treatise contained a criticism of Hegel's *Philosophy of Right*, and to be sure it does occasionally figure in the argument. But the fact remains that the piece really never gets down to a discussion or criticism of the alleged subject.

Rather, the theme of the piece is the German political situation, which is critically surveyed as to the possibility of a revolution. In this connection Marx does raise the question of German philosophy, but this is the only passage where Hegel's name appears, other than in the title. In this passage Marx outlines his theme, explains the title of the essay, and asserts:

> This critique of the *German philosophy of the state and the right*, which found its most consistent, richest and final

rendering through Hegel, is two things, a critical analysis of the modern state and the actuality associated with it as well as a decisive denial of the whole hitherto existing *mode of German political and legal consciousness*, the most eminent, most universal and scientifically elevated expression of which is none other than this speculative philosophy of right itself.[32]

Here at least it is made clear why the *Philosophy of Right* has been brought into play in the first place. Marx's argument is that this aspect of Hegelian philosophy is an expression of "German history standing *al pari* with the official modern present."* The critique of the *Philosophy of Right*, then, is at the same time a critique of Germany. Admittedly, in the essay the actual content of the *Philosophy of Right* is not critically analyzed at all. But since the piece was subtitled "Introduction," we can assume that a critique more to the point was to have appeared in later issues of the periodical.

As it was, Marx very quickly got into his own, basically much larger critical theme, the actual German situation, which he described as the "war of German conditions . . . a flagrant contradiction of generally recognized axioms," in that they abrogated the very philosophy which had defended and justified them. That is, actual German life annulled Hegelian philosophy. But since this Hegelian philosophy was at the same time written in the name of freedom and historical progress, Marx came to this dialectical conclusion: "You cannot annul the philosophy without actualizing it."[33]

This last sentence indicates how much Marx admired Hegel despite everything. Yet the same dialectical formulation also has a deeper meaning. It reaffirms the idea already expressed in the dissertation that the spirit, having found freedom, dialectically transforms word into deed.

With this begins the peculiar dialectic of revolution which is the real meat of the article. Hegelian philosophy, Marx gives us to understand, had taught the idea of freedom, had lived on it, even though it had applied the idea falsely to the actuality

---

* That is, Hegel had written what amounted to an apologia for the then prevailing establishment.—*Tr.*

of Germany, which was in fact quite different and unfree. Freedom itself had to be actualized; Hegel's theory had to be put into practice, made into revolution. Thus were recognition and rejection of Hegel intermingled in Marx. This feeling toward Hegel was never to change. Even the mature Marx admired and scorned Hegel in the same breath.

Marx admired Hegel's accomplishments, but meanwhile recognized that Hegel had not, so to speak, practiced what he preached, and thus the whole problem of the relation between theory and practice arose for Marx. This issue proceeded from a critical philosophy that had been evolved especially by the Hegelian Left which had recognized that Germany was behind in all forms of development, had no revolution, whose political situation beggared description, and was underdeveloped as no other country, except intellectually, where it was overdeveloped. Among Hegel's disciples of the Left, in short, a comprehensive and trenchant critique of Germany had developed. But what use was this critique as long as it remained theoretical?

> The weapon of criticism can certainly never replace the criticism of weapons, material power must be overthrown by material power, and theory becomes material power only when it takes hold of the masses. Theory is able to grip the masses as soon as it is demonstrated to them *ad hominem*, and it is demonstrated to them *ad hominem* as soon as it becomes radical. Being radical is getting at the root of the matter. But for men the root is man himself.[34]

These four sentences fall like hammer blows. Their content is as clear as it is lapidary. It proclaims a formula that has been endlessly tested, which says: "Carry your criticism to the masses, bring the masses to a consciousness of how bad things are. Grip the very balls of their existence, radicalize their thoughts and feelings. Then they will furnish you the material strength to overthrow the existing situation."

In these passages is found nothing less than the basic operative principle of revolution that, in a certain sense, has been followed by all leaders of mass movements. Yet seldom has this principle been enunciated with such clarity. Still, the basic idea is perfectly simple. It acknowledges a principle that actually is *not* materialistic, to the extent that there is reliance on the power of thought and the radical word, which is the way it has always gone in history. Every revolutionary has projected and imparted to the masses the power of his word, his belief, his ideas and notions.

Whether this comes about by having half-confused ideas mysteriously react upon the crowd or through theory based on reasonable ideas, whether the crowd is imbued with dark and mythic notions or with concrete goals and promises, it always happens in the way described by the young Marx: an idea is conveyed to people in a radical form.

Marx, not yet thirty years old, with great foresight was aware of how to handle the *technique* of revolution. In these few sentences, the technical principle of revolution that from then on revolutionary Marxism was faithfully to follow is expressed with lucid conviction. Certainly others, Machiavelli for instance, had seen this relationship, but none succeeded like Marx in translating his operative principles of political practice into action.

Meanwhile the argument went beyond this. Marx was not content with showing the general operative principle of revolution. He actually wanted to apply it, to revolutionize Germany, to lead history to a "German day of resurrection." The next question along these lines was: How promote a *radical* German revolution? Marx now proceeded to develop the idea already noted that all revolutions need a passive element, a material foundation. Following this idea, for the first time Marx presents his class theory. The term "class," by the way, was current in the literature of political science in Marx's day and did not originate with him. It must also be surmised, although proof cannot be offered, that Marx was adapting Hegelian precedent in his theory of classes. In Hegel's *Philosophy of Right* is found the proposition that civil society generates a *class* which exists in "dependency and need" and which is condemned to an "incapacity for the feeling and enjoyment of the higher freedoms and especially the spiritual advantages of civil society."

Whether Marx knew this reference, whether he had read it

and forgotten it, or perhaps had never come across it at all, in all events he now gave the idea a new twist. His own description of class was like a detailed exposition of Hegel's brief notice. "Where then," he asked, "is the *positive* possibility of German emancipation?"

> Answer: In the formation of a class with *radical ties* [lit., *Ketten*, "chains"], a class of civil society which is no class at all, an estate which is the dissolution of all estates, a sphere possessed of a universal character through its universal suffering and which lays claim to no *special right* because no *special wrong*, but *absolute wrong*, is perpetrated on it, which can no longer challenge on historical but only on human sanction, which does not stand in one-sided opposition to consequences, but in complete opposition to German state affairs, finally, which cannot emancipate itself without emancipating itself from all other spheres of society and thereby emancipating all remaining spheres of society, which, in a word, is the complete forfeiture [*Verlust*] of man, in such fashion that only through the complete reconquest of man can selfhood be won. This dissolution of society as a special estate is the *proletariat*.[35]

Marx follows the Hegelian line of thought even further. For Hegel had already described the dialectic in consequence of which civil society, however rich it might be, is not rich enough to prevent the rise of the class that he had depicted. Marx extends and sharpens the Hegelian description. The proletariat represents the "dissolution of the world-order hitherto existing." The proclamation of this fact is the "secret" of the existence of the proletariat.

The dialectical argument concludes with Marx announcing that the "secret weapon" of the proletariat is philosophy, but that critical philosophy finds its "material weapons" in the proletariat and consequently this "critical" theory becomes the "material practice" of revolution.

It is a long, unbroken passage almost Hegelian in structure. Its content is derivative of Hegel, thought out as dialectically as Hegel would have thought it, but far more radically.

Marx repeated the same train of thought on another occasion in *The Holy Family*, which came out the same year. This time, however, he does not proceed on the basis of the idea that critical philosophy imparts a radical consciousness to the proletariat, on the strength of which it achieves revolution. Instead, in the following passage from *The Holy Family*, the dialectical process of civil society's dissolution is described:

> Proletariat and wealth are opposites. As such they form a whole. They are both formations of the world of private property . . .
>
> Private property, as wealth, is forced to maintain its own existence and therewith the existence of its opposite, the proletariat. Private property satisfied with itself is the positive side of the antithesis.
>
> The proletariat, conversely, as proletariat is forced to abolish itself and, with this, abolish the private property that is its conditioning antithesis and which makes it a proletariat. The negative side of the antithesis, the unrest in it, is private property dissolved and in process of dissolution.
>
> The possessing class and the proletarian class represent the same human self-estrangement. But the first class feels satisfied and sanctioned in this self-estrangement, knows estrangement as its own power, and in it possesses the semblance of a human existence; the second class feels itself annihilated in estrangement, in it sees impotence and the actuality of an inhuman existence.

Thus Marx again describes the dehumanization of the proletarian class. Now he falls back on Hegel, on his notion of "self-estrangement" found in the *Phenomenology*. From the *Phenomenology*, too, comes the term *Verworfenheit*—"baseness" or "depravity." The idea is then carried a step further, in this manner:

> In its *politico-economic* [author's italics] movement private property drives on to its own dissolution, but only by a development that is independent of and opposed to its will, unconscious, occurring because of the nature of the matter, simply because it engenders the proletariat as

proletariat, misery conscious of its spiritual and physical misery, dehumanization conscious of itself as such and, on that account, self-abolishing.[36]

A new idea appearing here only inconspicuously—actually only in one word, *nationalökonomisch*, "politico-economic"— was to be increasingly expanded and finally lead to dialectical materialism.

The next step, which saw Marx again moving a little further away from Hegel and nearer to dialectical materialism, was taken in the fragment called *Economic and Philosophic Manuscripts*. This piece, as the editors Landshut and Mayer thought, develops "economic" considerations that alternately oppose and interweave each other in a fragmentary way. The ideational bond holding the constituent elements together is that of an "estranged" world. This idea, taken from Hegel, is used, however, not in the Hegelian sense, but to work against it. The estranged world and alienation in general are conceived as a series of human conditions, economic and social. The idea of labor and of its historical evolution moves more visibly into the foreground and is already recognized as the leading principle of history.

When Hegel described the world of self-estranged spirit in the *Phenomenology* he conceived it as the "absolute and general perversion and estrangement of the Idea." But when Marx pursues the same theme using the same terminology it is not the world of *Bildung*—of Spirit forming, shaping, educating itself—that he describes, but a much more concrete and tangible actuality.

Marx had already described the god of money in the articles on the Jewish question published in the "German-French Annals." There he had said:

> Money is the jealous god of Israel, before whom no other god may exist. Money degrades all men's gods—and turns them into a commodity. Money is the universal *value* of all things, constituted for its own sake. On this account it has robbed the whole world, of man as of nature, of its

proper value. To man money is the estranged essence of his labor and his existence and this strange essence rules him and he prays to it.

This description is incisively elaborated:

> The god of the Jews has been secularized, he has become a worldly god. Exchange is the real god of the Jews. Their god is only illusory exchange ...
>
> Judaism reaches its peak with the perfecting of civil society; but civil society is consummated only in the *Christian* world. Only under the rule of Christianity, which externalizes all mankind's national, natural, moral and theoretical circumstances, was civil society able to separate itself completely from the state, to tear apart all generic human bonds and replace these generic bonds with egoism and selfish needs, dissolving the human world into a world of atomistic individuals, all inimically opposed to one another. Christianity sprang from Judaism and has been dissolved again into Judaism.[37]

Not by any means Judaism alone, then, but Christianity quite as much, and ultimately all religion, is depraved. Religion is an estrangement of man, because man, "as long as he is enslaved by religion, knows how to objectify his essence only by making it into a *strange* fantastic essence."[38]

Marx goes into this same theme again in the *Economic and Philosophic Manuscripts*.

> What is done for me through *money*, what I pay, that is, what money can buy, that is what I, myself, the possessor of the money, *am*. My strength is as great as the strength of the money. Money's characteristics are mine—the characteristics and essential strengths of its owner. That which I am and can do, therefore, is by no means determined by my personality. *I* am ugly, but I can buy myself the most beautiful wife. Therefore I am not ugly, for the effect of ugliness, its power to repel, is negated by money. Accord-

ing to my individuality I am lame, but money provides me with twenty-four feet, therefore I am not lame . . ." [And he continues:]

When I have no money for traveling, I have no *need* to travel, that is, no actual and self-actualizing need. If I have a vocation for study, but have no money, I really have no vocation for study at all, that is, no effective, no *true* vocation. Conversely, if I really have no vocation for study, but do have the will *and* the money for it, then I have an *effective* vocation for it . . .

In his description of the magic power of money, Marx makes money into a demonic godhead: "Money is the visible godhead, the transformation of all human qualities into their opposite, the general mixing up and perversion of all things, a close uniting of impossibilities. It is the universal whore, the universal pimp of men and peoples."

Emphasis is on the power of money to pervert all things: "The perversion and confusion of all human and natural qualities, the close unification of the impossible—the *godlike* power of money lies in its essence as the estranged, alienating and self-externalizing species being [*Gattungswesen*] of man. It is human capacity alienated."[39]

In connection with his portrayal Marx cites both Goethe and Shakespeare. But all socialist and communist thinkers had believed in this Luciferian god described by Marx in terms of Hegelian "estrangement." In the socialist *Utopia* of Thomas More, which appeared in 1516, there is a passage where the discoverer and chronicler of this happy isle says:

Howbeit, doubtless, Master More, to speak as truly as my mind moves me, wheresoever possessions are private, where money yields all influence, it is hard and almost impossible that there the commonwealth may be justly governed, and prosperously flourish. Unless you think that justice is there executed, where all things come into the hands of evil men; or that prosperity there flourishes where all is divided among a few; which few nevertheless do not live very richly, and the rest live miserably, wretched and beggarly.[40]

More, then, had already described the power of money to pervert, because it gives the best to the worst. Money is the root of all evil, mother of all injustice and enemy of the just. And not only money, but private property as the embodiment of money, is equally unjust. As Proudhon put it, property is "theft."

# 30

## The Transition to the Economic

A little later still, Marx again drew upon Hegel when he moved from his analysis of money and private property to an at first tentatively developed theory of labor. This description of labor and its distinguishing characteristics is the boundary line where Marxian philosophy begins to link up with politico-economic considerations.

Reflection on labor as a fact and a concept permeate the whole fragment. Even in the preface Marx says that the piece he is about to present will also deal with "the relation between political economy and the state, the law, morality, civil life" etc., and that its "results will be arrived at through an entirely empirical analysis based on a conscientiously critical study of the political economy."[41] And indeed, throughout, mention is made of authoritative authors on the subject of political economy—John Stuart Mill, Adam Smith, David Ricardo, among others. Yet in the main they are brought in as objects of criticism because in Marx's opinion they lacked a clear understanding of the essential nature of labor.

As Marx saw it, these political economists did not have a clear enough recognition that private property and the production of wealth arising from labor and the division of labor are an "estranged and alienated form of human activity as species activity."[42] Because they failed to grasp this fact, they had not penetrated to the primary and *radical* essence of the process, to man himself. Now Marx proceeded to develop a theory of man, a theory which initially leaned on Hegel:

> The greatness of the Hegelian *Phenomenology* and of its end result—the dialectic of negativity as the moving and generating principle—is simply that Hegel conceives the self-creation of man as process, objectification as loss of the object, as alienation and as transcendence of this alienation; that he thus grasps the essence of *labor* and comprehends objective man—true, because real man—as the outcome of man's *own labor*. . . . Let us provisionally say just this much in advance: Hegel's standpoint is that of modern political economy. He grasps *labor* as the *essence* of man—as man's essence in the act of proving itself; he sees only the positive, not the negative side of labor.

In the last part of this sentence, where Hegel is described as not having seen the negative side of labor, the Marxian critique, as yet not clearly enunciated, is already presaged. Before the critique is spelled out, a positive value is placed on the fact that Hegel had understood labor dialectically, as "*man's coming-to-be for himself* within *alienation*."[43]

Into this interpretation of Hegel, Marx now fits some of his own theory. While property is arising from the historical development of human labor and especially from the division of labor, the movement of history, in which man repeatedly creates himself anew, is being realized. At the same time, the act of creation is an act of estrangement, and private property is the "material, sensuous expression of *estranged human* life." Man, to be sure, becomes "objective," but at the same time feels himself to be a "strange and inhuman object."[44]

Man loses himself in the object: "Private property has made

us so stupid and one-sided that an object becomes *ours* only when we have it, that is, when it exists for us as capital or is immediately possessed, eaten or worn on our body by us, or lived in, in brief, when it is *used*."[45] With this step, estrangement replaces *all* physical and spiritual senses. The sense of "having" rises triumphantly above all others.

Even though Marx evolves this idea only in basic outline and by way of hints, it sounds as if he feels that man, in the course of his historical evolution, becomes bestialized. Man develops his five senses, to be sure, throughout his history, but the more he is governed by practical needs, the more limited he becomes.

The same idea is also implied in Marx's theory of man, according to which man living in terms of private property and capital is spiritually impoverished. Yet Marx does not dispute the necessity of this development. Man has to travel this road, has to acquire this stage of actuality, has to run the course of this process of alienation. Marx does not contend this: "The human being must be reduced to this absolute poverty, so that he will give birth out of it to his inner riches." By "absolute poverty" Marx naturally means, in this context, the state of the modern world, in which external wealth is accompanied by inner impoverishment.

Now, having gotten so far, Marx had to make an about-face. The dialectical development had to take a new turn. "Self-estrangement" had to be transcended. Communism is the "*positive* transcendence of *private property* . . . the complete *emancipation* of all human senses and qualities."[46] With communism man becomes a real human being.

In such pronouncements as these it is already clearly evident how strong a part is played in this theory of man by the time-honored belief in the "redemption" or "salvation" of man. But redemption in this context has ceased to be of a religious nature. Man is not to be redeemed by supernatural powers, but by himself, in the course of his historical development.

The next step is communism. It is extraordinarily interesting to note that at this point Marx obviously regarded communism as an intermediate stage. He wrote one passage of which no more is later heard: *"Communism* is the necessary pattern and the dynamic principle of the immediate future, but communism as such is not the goal of human development—which goal is the structure of human society."[47]

However, this does not alter the fact that Marx had a splendid vision of the new man as he would be in a communist society. The form that communism will take is described as follows: it will be a real conversion of the *human* essence through and for mankind, "the complete return of man to himself as a *social* (i.e., human) being":

> This communism, as fully developed naturalism, equals humanism, and as fully developed humanism equals naturalism; it is the *genuine* resolution of the conflict between man and nature and between man and man—the true resolution of the strife between existence and essence, between objectification and self-confirmation, between freedom and necessity, between the individual and the species. Communism is the riddle of history solved, and it knows itself to be this solution.[48]

Everything that Marx wrote, however angrily he may have scored the times he lived in, in the last analysis was impelled by a belief in the future. But no work that Marx ever wrote later was to portray and exalt the communist idea and communism so positively. The later Marx became much more cautious in his utterances along this line. The longer the delay in the revolution he had hoped to see consummated immediately, the more his gaze turned to the distant future and to concrete preparations for the great day.

There was another reason, however, why Marx became more careful with his pronouncements on the future. We have already noted how Marx's thinking was colored by a belief that man could work his own salvation. Now, Marx never lost this belief completely. This was impossible, since if he abandoned this belief he would have had to abandon his belief in revolution along with it. However, in the course of a steady evolution his redemptive belief took on another form.

That is, the more Marx became convinced that economic evolution and its laws determined the course of history, the more, in consequence, the dialectical materialism which Marx developed in this period took on an economic stamp and the more he had to make revolution dependent on economic evolution.

In the *Economic and Philosophic Manuscripts*, Marx was still writing in terms of a dialectical materialism of a philosophical character, but hereafter philosophical dialectic was to diminish in Marxian thinking. However, it did give him his point of departure, culminating in the recognition that the proletariat represented the "complete loss of man," to be transcended only by the "complete reconquest of man."

Marx continued to adhere to this thesis in these "fragments." Here there is a very forceful description of the man victimized by pleasure and wealth, as an "individual without essence, on the rampage," at whose side stands the proletarian as a man of "slave labor" and a "sacrificial nothing of a creature."[49]

This state of affairs is blamed on private property, under which "every person speculates on creating a new need in *another*," thereby "establishing over the other an alien power." In this "mutual swindling and mutual plundering" man "becomes ever poorer as man" and the more dependent on money the more "the *power* of money increases."[50]

Here are found the beginnings of the *economic dialectic* that increasingly invades and impregnates the philosophical argument. Relative to this development the theory of estrangement was to recede. Replacing it is a new insight, also first found in Marx's "1844 Manuscripts." This new perception is expressed in such passages as: "*Industry* is the *actual*, historical relationship of nature, and therefore of natural science, to man . . ."[51]

Marx describes his own position very precisely:

> In order to abolish the *idea* of private property, the *idea* of communism is completely sufficient. It takes *actual* communist action to abolish actual private property. History will come to it; and this movement, which in *theory*

we already know to be a self-transcending movement, will constitute *in actual fact* a very severe and long drawn out process. But we must regard it as a real advance to have gained beforehand a consciousness of the limited character as well as of the goal of this historical movement—and a consciousness which reaches out beyond it.[52]

Even though the year when this concept was formulated cannot be precisely determined, as presented in a fragmentary way in the "1844 Manuscripts," the point where it occurred in the development of the Marxian system is clear enough. The fragment came at that point where Marx was still a Hegelian, yet so critically at odds with Hegelian thought that he had to evolve his own dialectic. He already knew that this new dialectic was "materialistic" in nature, but he had yet to arrive at the point, due to come later, of separating it cleanly from the Hegelian model.

And so at this stage he developed a highly peculiar form of dialectic, which on the one hand leaned on Hegel and on the other pulled away from him. His initial point of departure was taken entirely from Hegel. It derived from the *Phenomenology*. Marx was obviously fascinated by Hegel's chapter on the "self-estranged spirit." Like Hegel, he, too, saw himself confronted by a whole world of self-estrangement.

Yet at the same time another point of view was becoming evident. In Marx's opinion Hegel had been correct in his recognition of the fact of self-estrangement, but incorrect in his explanation of it. Hegel, that is, had apprehended self-estrangement only as a state of consciousness. He could not think of it otherwise, since for him man, in the essential sense, was only self-consciousness. As Marx put it: "For Hegel the *essence of man—man*—equals *self-consciousness*. All estrangement of the human essence is therefore *nothing but estrangement of self-consciousness*."[53]

This spiritual theory of the nature of man, if one might so call it, was countered by Marx with another theory, which he later summed up in the formula: "Not consciousness, but being, determines life." At this juncture, however, in the manuscript at hand, he criticized Hegel for bypassing "man's *real* estrangement," and for not recognizing that what he, Hegel, meant by "estrangement" was only the surface appearance of a more deeply-lying phenomenon.

With this commitment Marx would have pulled back and turned away from Hegel, were it not that he still felt bound to him in another respect. For Hegel, as Marx saw it, had also repeatedly recognized that the essence of man lay in labor. He granted that indeed Hegel had comprehended "objective man . . . as the outcome of man's *own labor*."

But even here the basic difference can be seen. For Hegel man is ultimately not the product of his own labor, but the product of the Idea coming to be aware of itself. In the process of dialectical actualization, the self-establishing of man, to be sure, occurs, but in the last analysis it belongs to the Idea, and not to man as such.

In all events, it was Hegel who had applied the lever of a dialectic, in which technique Marx as yet was nothing but a neophyte. For Marx, too, the fundamental thing was the dialectical process, and when he spelled out this process, he did it, so to speak, in terms of the critical assumptions he brought to bear on Hegel.

He was at one with Hegel in the idea that man "externalizes" himself in the world of objects. He echoed Hegel's opinion that labor is the process by which man surrenders himself to objects, and that it is through labor that man "objectifies" himself. But for Marx this process was not of a spiritual, but a highly materialistic, nature.

Labor, therefore, is the real dialectical process. But man is shaped not by spiritual or intellectual labor, but by labor in its material aspect. Through labor man evolves and becomes the "result of himself."

Marx was to hold to this thought. It provided a basis for his later assertion that man's real history is not that of his consciousness and his ideologies, but of production of a material nature. Even now Marx could say: "If, therefore, industry is conceived as the *exoteric* revelation of man's *essential powers*, we also gain an understanding of the *human* essence of nature, or the *natural* science of man. In consequence, natural science will lose its abstract material—or, rather, its idealistic tendency . . ."[54]

The dialectical event as now described by Marx on the basis of these presuppositions has yet to acquire its later form. Beginning with *The German Ideology*, Marx recognized the driving force of his dialectic as seated in the antithesis and contradiction of "forces of production" and "conditions of production." (In *The German Ideology* he speaks of the "conditions of intercourse.")

Yet this basic dialectical contradiction is in fact already indicated in the *Economic and Philosophic Manuscripts*. Midway in the argument comes the dialectic of "man," modeled on Hegel. This dialectic is described from two sides. Uppermost is the idea, already noted, that man must be actualized in labor in order to experience development. This notion Marx found not only in Hegel but in contemporary political economy as well, and used it for his own purposes.

Man's actualization, then, is dialectical in nature. This means that man, who labors and who must labor, at the same time externalizes and estranges himself in labor. In this context Marx again and again returns to the fact that "the realm of strange essences to which man is subjugated" grows along with the "mass of objects" that are the fruit of his labor.

But now he linked another idea to the one taken from Hegel. He claimed that work is not merely an egotistic process serving the needs of individuals. He conceives labor as always being "social" in nature:

> Thus the *social* character is the general character of the whole movement: *just as* society itself produces *man as man*, so is society *produced* by him. Activity and mind, both in their content and in their *mode of existence*, are *social: social* activity and *social* mind. The *human* essence of nature first exists only for *social* man; for only here does nature exist for him as a *bond* with *man*—as his existence for the other and the other's existence for him—as the life-element of human actuality. Only here does nature exist as the *foundation* of his own *human* existence. Only here has what is to him his *natural* existence become his *human*

existence, and nature become man for him. Thus *society*
is the unity of being of man with nature—the true resurrection of nature—the naturalism of man and the humani-
zation of nature both brought to fulfillment.[55]

We cite this passage in all its detail and multiple repetitions
because it shows so clearly what the dialectic is driving at.
This goal is the "true" society, one where the individual has
become unified with it. And behind it all lurks utopia, the
ideal society which from time immemorial has haunted the
minds of socialistic and communistic thinkers.

Marx saw this ideal society in communism. This society is
conscious of itself as a "reintegration or return of man to himself" by way of a "transcendence of human estrangement."[56]
Further along, he enthusiastically describes the coming of the
communist movement: "When communist *artisans* associate
with one another . . . they acquire a new need—the need for
society . . . Company association and conversation, which
again has society as its end, are enough for them; the brother-
hood of man is no mere phrase with them, but a fact of life,
and the nobility of man shines upon us from their work-
hardened bodies."[57]

But neither now nor later on did Marx rest content with
simply describing communistic socialists, as social utopians
have done in all ages. More important and essential to him
was criticism of society in its present form.

To this end he had to show how, and through what kind of
dialectical evolution, contemporary "self-estranged" society
had come into being. From the start Marx made it clear that
the present society is not the real one, only its historical precursor. But how is this antecedent stage to be understood, and
wherein lay the necessity of its being formed at all?

At this point Marx introduces the politico-economic analysis
already described in its essentials. The basic cause of man's
self-estrangement and of society's estrangement is the division
of labor and, beyond that, private property. Marx says: "The
examination of the *division of labor* and *exchange* is of extreme interest because these are *perceptibly alienated* expres-

sions of human *activity* and of *essential human power* as a
*species* activity and power."[58]

Here, in contrast to utopian notions of the ideal socialized
man, is found a theory of man as *selbstisch*—"egoistic"—and
"self-estranged." This, too, had already been described. Division of labor, private property, money, capital and industry
are necessary through which man must proceed. Along this
road man becomes estranged from himself; he even loses the
awareness of his five senses as they become overwhelmed by
possessions.

According to Marx this development is not fortuitous, but
necessary. Man must travel this way: "Precisely in the fact
that *division of labor* and *exchange* are embodiments of private property lies the twofold proof, on the one hand that
*human* life required *private property* for its realization, and on
the other hand that it now requires the supersession of private
property."

With this the dialectical ring and chain of proof is closed,
the argument wherein the necessity of development up to this
point is tied in with the necessity of the "transcendence of
private property" and the establishment of a communist society. For Marx the refutation of Hegel is as important as the
proof of communist necessity. On this account the fragment
vacillates between politico-economic considerations and discussions of Hegelian philosophy.

In contrast to the dialectic of historical materialism as later
evolved, where the main emphasis is placed on economic dialectic, here we have a dialectic of an entirely different kind. In
this piece of writing Marx conceives the history of man as an
unfolding of his "essential strength" and perceives human society as losing itself dialectically in capitalism in the process of
self-estrangement and as "winning" itself back again dialectically in communism. But from now on this idea was to recede
more and more into the background.

It was the study of economic relationships that led Marx to
the conviction that the "anatomy of civil society," indeed, the
history of man, is to be "sought in political economy."

# 31

---

# The Critique of Hegel

In the preface to *Economic and Philosophic Manuscripts* Marx called attention to his announcement in the *Deutsch-Französischen Jahrbüchern* of a critique of Hegel's *Philosophy of Right*. While preparing this critique for publication, Marx said, it had become evident to him that here two themes were unsuitably intermingled: the critique of Hegel's "speculation" and the critical investigation of "law, ethics, politics," etc. On this account he planned to treat single areas of the general subject "in a series of distinct, independent pamphlets," then "in a special work to present them as a connected whole showing the interrelationship of the separate parts." At the same time he would provide a critique of the purely speculative aspect of Hegel.[59]

The fragment as we see it today can be regarded as a sketch in which the various independent parts are presented in outline form. But this outline, a huge thing in accordance with his ambitious plan, actually mingled together what had been originally conceived as independent pamphlets. Meanwhile the critique of Hegel is divided by subject, such as the critique of "morality," the critique of "private property," etc.

Ultimately this critique runs like an unbroken thread through the whole work. The inner necessity that drove Marx back to Hegel again and again is easily understood. Hegel had given Marx his catchwords: man's self-estrangement, the dialectical evolution of wealth, the negative description of civil society and much else. Indeed, he had pointed out the dialectic of labor.

In this sense, in Marx's opinion, Hegel had had at his disposal all means of access to an understanding of social actuality, and yet had not really grasped what it was all about.

This gave rise to the need for explanation, or, more precisely, for a critical discussion in which Hegel's mistake would be spelled out. To arrive at an understanding of Hegel's "double-mistake," Marx concentrated his critique mainly on the *Phenomenology*, which he thought of as the "birthplace of the Hegelian philosophy."

The gist of the critique can be summed up in a couple of sentences. Marx felt that Hegel, to be sure, had been aware of the essence of labor and its dialectic. To this extent he had stood on the solid ground of an actual political economy. At the same time, however, he had failed to understand the significance of the essence of labor, because he had "been cognizant of and acknowledged" labor to be no more than an "abstract spiritual" entity. In consequence he had been unable to comprehend the process of economic estrangement as it had actually taken place.

In his mind's eye Marx now saw a curious drama unfold. The great thinker, Hegel, who had conceived man's self-estrangement, himself became the victim of self-estrangement because he had failed to understand the actual nature of labor. "The philosopher (that is, one who is himself an abstract form of estranged man) sets himself up as the measuring rod of the estranged world."[60] Estranged in his ideas and in his actuality, he fulfills a similarly unreal movement.

The Hegelian dialectic, correct in methodological principle, runs its course in empty space. For "the man estranged from himself is also the thinker estranged from his *essence*—that is, from the natural and human essence." And Hegel's work is to be regarded in this light. "His thoughts are therefore fixed mental shapes or ghosts dwelling outside nature and man," says Marx. "Hegel has locked up all these fixed mental forms together in his *Logic*" and out of them made "an act of abstraction which revolves in its own circle."

Hegel indeed approached all of philosophy this way, that is, he summed up "hitherto existing philosophy in respect of its individual moments." But this kind of "thinking, revolving solely within the orbit of thought" is "sans eyes, sans teeth, sans tears, sans everything."[61]

Hegel's thought, in brief, engenders its own dissolution. From now on, Hegelian philosophy for Marx seems to have been no more than just another small example of the more comprehensive process of self-dissolution occurring in civil society.

In a subsequent stage of his thinking, Marx was to conceive Hegelianism, both that of the Young Hegelians and that of the Old, in terms of the epithet "putrescence of the Absolute Spirit." Following out this line of thought, which enabled him to understand the nature of "ideology," he was to come to the conclusion that "philosophy as an independent branch of activity" had lost "its medium of existence" and its right to exist.

# 32

## The Conclusion of the Developmental Period and the Youthful Writings: The German Ideology

**M**arx wrote *The German Ideology* in collaboration with Engels.[62] He later said of this work that it was intended "to elaborate the opposition of our point of view to the ideological in German philosophy in general" and to settle accounts with "our former philosophical conscience." When the finished work reached the publisher, but could not be actually brought out in print at that time because of changed political conditions, Marx and Engels said they "were all the more willing to give it over to the gnawing criticism of the mice" since they had accomplished their main purpose, "self-agreement."[63]

The importance of this comprehensive work does not lie within that part of the "self-agreement" indicated by the subtitle "Critique of most recent German philosophy as represented by Feuerbach, B. Bauer and Stirner and of the various prophets of German socialism." This part of the book is devoted to a bitingly critical and detailed discussion of these thinkers, one after the other. In this procedure there is no lack of such language as "this godfearing man has the shamelessness . . ." (Bauer), "the enormous credulity of our saints . . ." (Stirner), and "the inspired doctor is a spiritualistic charlatan, a pious fraud, a mystical swindler . . ." (Kuhlmann).[64]

The work is preceded by a relatively short section on Feuerbach that was conceived as an introduction to the whole. In his day Mehring had a presentiment that this introductory chapter would go down as "incomparably more interesting than the critique of Bruno Bauer or Max Stirner," though to be sure he assumed it had never been completed. No doubt he based this supposition on a statement by Engels, who, in his later work on Feuerbach, wrote that he had "dug up and looked over the old manuscript" of 1845–46, and then went on to say that "the section on Feuerbach was not completed. The finished part consists of an exposition of the materialist conception of history, which only shows how incomplete our knowledge of economic history then was."[65]

Engels may have been right, for in that period Marx's and Engels's knowledge of economics and research into the literature of economics was not nearly as comprehensive as it later became. Yet this did not prevent this exposition of the materialist interpretation of history from being, in its way, a definitive outline of the new economic and dialectical materialism. Later on it was altered in particulars, more cleanly formulated (*Critique of Political Economy*), or presented in a more popularly intelligible way (*Communist Manifesto*). But in view of the fact that neither Marx nor Engels ever wrote a real text of historical materialism, this outline has great significance.

It contains two basic and closely connected ideas. On the one hand the Marxist concept of "ideology" is developed, and on the other—presented only in a fleeting outline—history is apprehended as the result of the "contradiction between the powers of production and the form of intercourse."*

It is characteristic of this whole approach to the problem, an

---

* Here *Verkehr* is intended to mean social intercourse in its entirety, including commerce which is another, more limited meaning of *Verkehr*.— *Tr.*

approach henceforth to be quite different from what had gone before, that the notion of human estrangement and self-estrangement, earlier so passionately expounded, should now lose its pathos. Only occasionally do references to estrangement crop up and then in a rather deprecatory way. Thus at one point when Marx alludes to "estrangement" he adds parenthetically "to use a term which will be comprehensible to the philosophers."[66]

On another occasion, after Marx and Engels have demonstrated their notions of economic and historical evolution, they say: "The whole process was thus conceived as a process of self-estrangement of 'man,'* and this was essentially due to the fact that the average individual of the later stage was always foisted onto the earlier stage, and the consciousness of a later age onto the individuals of an earlier one."[67]

There is no indication here that Marx is recalling a conception that only shortly before he had espoused. This makes it all the clearer that the process of Marx's separation from Hegel has been completed. Marx no longer feels any proof is needed that Hegel himself was a self-estranged spirit. A simpler and at the same time more generally systematic explanation of Hegelian thought is presented in the theory of "ideology."

The term "ideology" did not originate with Marx, and the theory that ideas are dependent on their historical situation and social content also came before Marx. Napoleon I had used the expression "ideology" in a critical sense, and a series of writers before Marx (P. Gallupi, Destutt de Tracy, M. Gioja, among others) had discussed the ideological theme.[68]

But Marx sharpened and precisely defined the notion of the dependence of ideas on context by reducing it to a simple formula. Whereas ideas, to be sure, can be viewed as products of the human mind, "the production of ideas, of conceptions, of consciousness is at first directly interwoven with the material activity and the material intercourse of men, the language of real life."

However, in this statement the sharpness which Marx gave

---

* The subject here under discussion by Marx and Engels is how philosophers and others have made an abstraction of "man," thus inverting actuality.—Tr.

this idea is as yet not completely visible. Two subsequent sentences make it crystal clear what Marx had in mind: "Life is not determined by consciousness, but consciousness by life."[69] Then, further along: "Consciousness therefore from the very start is a social product and remains so as long as men exist at all."[70]

The main idea underlying these statements, the idea, that is, that life is not determined by consciousness, but consciousness by life, is definitive in Marxian thought. About fifteen years later he repeated it almost word for word in the preface to the *Critique of Political Economy*. There he said: "It is not the consciousness of men that determines their being, but, conversely, their social being that determines their consciousness."[71] And again, another fifteen years later, in the afterword to the first volume of *Capital*, while polemicizing against Hegel, he wrote: "With me, just the opposite, the ideal is nothing but the material transposed into man's head."

All these formulations express the relationship which Marx now proceeded to elaborate in catch phrases. Consciousness, he claimed, is above all language, but language arises from the "pressing need of intercourse with other men." He goes on to say that "consciousness is at first, of course, merely consciousness concerning the immediate sensuous environment," which first "appears to men as a completely alien, all-powerful and unassailable force." After this stage of consciousness, which takes the form, on the one hand, of "natural religion," on the other as "purely herd consciousness" or "sheep-like consciousness," come other stages, until finally a level of development is reached in which consciousness "can really flatter itself that it is something other than consciousness of existing practice . . ."[72]

The methodological conclusion which Marx draws from this argument is as simple as the argument itself. *All* "theoretical products and forms of consciousness, religion, philosophy, ethics, etc., etc." and all "formations of ideas" are explicable in terms of "material practice" and by this "means, of course, the whole thing can be shown in its totality (and therefore, too, the reciprocal action of these various sides on one another)."[73]

That Marx himself is thinking in terms of fundamentals and not of a schematic application of the principle becomes evident in his announcement of a new "positive" science. This science will not be a "recipe or schema . . . for neatly trimming the epochs of history. On the contrary, our difficulties begin only when we set about the observation and arrangement—the real depiction—of our historical material, whether of a past epoch or of the present."[74]

Any representation of the material content of the concept of ideology as here developed by Marx would not, however, be complete without some description of the mood in which it was evolved. This mood is most strikingly expressed in one blunt passage, which proceeds abruptly in this manner: "Moreover, it is quite immaterial what consciousness starts to do on its own: out of all such muck we get only the one inference that these three moments, the forces of production, the state of society and consciousness can and must come into contradiction with one another, because the division of labor implies the possibility, indeed the fact, that intellectual and material activity—enjoyment and labor, production and consumption—devolve on different individuals, and that the only possibility of their not coming into contradiction lies in the negation in its turn of the division of labor."[75]

One will not be far from the mark if the sense of this passage is directly taken to mean "consciousness on its own . . ." is only "muck." Marx has now made a clean break with the kind of idealistic philosophy dealing in consciousness, self-consciousness, and the like. Where in the *Economic and Philosophic Manuscripts* the theme of consciousness had been recognized by a critique which, though sharp, was unmistakably deferent, it now seems that the subject has been dismissed once and for all. Moses Hess, for instance, who in the *Economic and Philosophic Manuscripts* had been quoted favorably, now, like all the rest, Hegel and Feuerbach excepted, has become a "saint"* who "utters tautologies with an air of importance" and who, moreover, "plagiarizes" Hegel.[76]

---

* Marx refers to Hess as "Saint Max" both to suggest spurious authority and by way of animadversion to Saint-Simon, the French socialist.—*Tr.*

# 33

## The Materialistic Thesis: Production as the Motive Force of History

As the ideological theory was being developed in short and striking lines, the materialism which Marx hereafter advocated was likewise evolved in a few strokes. It is a dialectical materialism, which means that it is based on the *movement* of material events.

For Marx, the basic idea on which all others rest is that man "produces" through his labor. This production is threefold: satisfaction of needs, creation of new needs, and reproduction.

However, according to Marx the *first* historical act is "the production of the means to satisfy these needs."[77] All three levels of need work side by side from the beginning. The satisfaction of needs, the production of new needs, and the reproduction of life all constantly work together. Therefore the production and reproduction of life are possible only in social cooperation. Marx proceeds from the concept of men as socially bound in their labor, not from the fiction of a Robinson Crusoe making out on his own.

These considerations led Marx to make a fundamental distinction between "power of production" and "form of intercourse." Later on he was to speak in terms of the forces or means of production and the conditions of production. What he had in mind was this: labor can be viewed as to accomplishment, but also as to how it is organized.

Marx found his dialectical point of departure in this reciprocal relationship. He started off with a proposition that for him was a proven fact: the productive forces are constantly developing and are conditioned in their progressive development by the growth of population and thus of needs.

"The form of intercourse" and conditions of production represent for Marx a retarding factor in respect to this development. For Marx it is not true that the conditions of production change as a matter of course with the expansion of the forces of production. Rather, whatever productive conditions may be obtaining have a tendency to remain stable.

In this circumstance Marx finds a driving historical force operating in terms of dialectical "contradiction." He tells us that "in the development of productive forces there comes a stage at which productive forces and means of intercourse are called into existence which, under the existing relationship, can only cause mischief, and which are no longer productive but destructive forces (machinery and money) . . ."[78] The tension unavoidably arising out of, and indeed inherent in, the development of production generates "class conflict."

With this the basic schema of history, as Marx construed it, had been laid down. "Thus all collisions of history have their origin, according to our view, in the contradiction between the productive forces and the form of intercourse." Out of this fundamental contradiction arise all other contradictions, first and foremost the class conflict. Any ruling class, as principal beneficiary, is interested in preserving the prevailing conditions of production. Only the dominated class which does the mass of the labor can force the necessary transformation of the existing form of intercourse, and do it only through revolution. Thus the contradiction between productive forces and the form of intercourse must "necessarily on each occasion burst out in a revolution."[79]

Previous revolutions in the course of history, in Marx's view, were never able to do away with the fundamentals leading to the revolutionary event. Now, however, a stage had been reached where contradiction was at its most acute form. Recently evolved productive forces had become "forces of destruction." Since in all previous revolutions "the mode of activity always remained unchallenged and it was only a question of a different distribution of this activity, a new distribution of labor to other persons," the communist revolution would have to be "directed against the preceding *mode* of activity, do away with labor, and abolish the rule of all classes together with the classes themselves." He then goes on to say: "This revolution is necessary, therefore, not only because the ruling class cannot be overthrown in any other way, but also because the class *overthrowing* it can only in a revolution succeed in ridding itself of all the muck of the ages and become fit to found society anew." Meanwhile, to carry out this program an "alteration of men on a mass scale is necessary . . ."[80]

Much of what has been cited above is a repetition of ideas earlier elaborated by Marx. In general, the whole work can be viewed as a repetition and recapitulation of earlier insights and theses, were it not that the new dominant idea of the dialectic of production was to provide the main materialistic feature of Marx's dialectical interpretation of history.

# 34

## Theory and Practice

The German Ideology was written by Marx and Engels between the late summer of 1845 and the fall of 1846 in Brussels, where Marx had gone after his expulsion from Paris. After copying The German Ideology, Marx and Engels got busy with other plans. Engels planned to make preparations with Hess for a socialist monthly periodical, while he and Marx together had it in mind to publish a library of works by socialist writers, one that would have a "practical effect that will sink home with the Germans."[81]

The aim behind all these projects was clearly to spread the communist idea, not merely to engage in theorizing on socialism and its problems. Marx was to write his theoretical work while concurrently practicing revolution. The really basic Marxian work, especially on political economy, was in consequence to stretch out through many years. The outline of this project, *Critique of Political Economy*, appeared in 1859, but the first volume of *Capital* did not come out until 1867. Meanwhile, as early as 1845 Engels, in a letter to Marx, indicated that even at that time he was expecting the book as soon as possible.[82]

This clearly reveals Marx's attitude at this time toward theory; it was a means to an end in the struggle and had no value for its own sake alone. Thus theory was subordinated to and integrated with political activity.

The critical part of *The German Ideology* already showed that Marx and Engels had washed their hands of the literary spokesmen of German socialism. In Brussels followed the final break with Weitling, whose League of the Just had a considerable following. During the same period in Brussels, 1846/47, Marx wrote another book, under the title of *The Poverty of Philosophy*, which cut off his connection with Proudhon.

Meanwhile Marx and Engels were steadily at work building an organization to disseminate their ideas. Thus in a letter Marx reported that he and Engels had founded two public democratic societies, the German Workers Society and the Cosmopolitan Democratic Society. It was at the German Workers Association, founded in Brussels in 1847, that Marx gave his lectures on *Wage Labor and Capital*.

In 1845 Engels and Marx left Brussels for a six-week trip to England, where there was a League of Communists made up of a group of exiled revolutionary workers. In 1847 the central committee of this league commissioned Marx to draw up a manifesto, which has become world famous as the *Communist Manifesto*.

None of Marx's writings more clearly shows his ability to unite theoretical interpretation with political action. The manifesto begins with these words: "A specter is haunting Europe—the specter of communism." In Part 1 there is a brief theoretical discussion explaining that all history up to the present has been a history of class struggles. Two classes have always stood in opposition to one another, the oppressors and the oppressed. This is followed by a brief historical summary in which Marx develops his basic idea that the contradiction between "the means of production and exchange" and the "condition" generated by them created crises first in feudal and now in bourgeois society.

In Part 2 the communists are represented as the people who are most resolutely seeking the conquest of political power and the overthrow of the bourgeoisie. Their basic demand is the abolition of private property. Under the heading of "Socialist and Communist Literature," Part 3 describes three forms of socialism: "reactionary," "conservative or bourgeois socialism," and "critical-utopian socialism." All of these are subjected to criticism, particularly the category of "reactionary socialism," with its subforms of "feudal," "petty bourgeois," and "German or 'true' socialism."

The fourth and concluding part is an open declaration of war. Communists want the "forcible overthrow of all existing social conditions." Then the manifesto goes on to say: "Let the ruling classes tremble at a communist revolution." After this is sounded the clarion call to arms that is still ringing in our ears over a hundred years later: "Workers of the world, unite!"

This manifesto has become a great world-historical document. Pondering the source of its effectiveness, one may say that its power derives in part from its convincingly presented and intelligibly formulated theoretical judgments. But in no small measure the effectiveness of this piece of writing rests on something else, too. While the manifesto is seeking to inoculate the opponents of the bourgeoisie with the belief that this class is doomed to historical extinction, it also gives the worker —to the extent that he commits himself to communism—a consciousness of being a member of an elite to whom the future belongs. This thought is expressed in the famous passage near the end of the manifesto: "The proletarians have nothing to lose but their chains. They have a world to win."[83] As it turned out, this promise of world dominion was to bind generations of revolutionaries to the Marxian idea.

Central to Marx's and Engels's thinking, now as before, was the idea of revolution. They awaited the moment to strike. At this point, as just noted, Marx also broke off his relationship with Proudhon, with whom in the Paris period he had spent long nights in discussion. In a letter to Marx, in which Proudhon invited Marx to collaborate in a communist correspondence, Proudhon declared himself to be an enemy of all "dogmatic fanaticism." It was dogmatism above all, Proudhon said, that he wanted to destroy. He did not want, by great expenditure of "excommunications and anathemas . . . to soft-soap the people with doctrines." He stood for, he said, the policy of a "wise and far-seeing patience." He rejected revolution and declared that "therefore we may not represent revolutionary action to be a means of social reform, because this alleged means would be an appeal to force, to arbitrary action, in brief, a contradiction."[84]

Marx answered him in *The Poetry of Philosophy* (1847), in his characteristic way: looking down his nose, cutting, pitiless. He tore Proudhon's economic deliberations apart by undertaking to prove, as he had said he would in the preface, that Proudhon had no understanding at all of either philosophy or political economy.

This work, in the main devoted to politico-economic considerations, again concluded with an avowal of radical revolution. It acknowledged that the coming struggle will result in the "clash of man against man." The time for "social revolution" had not yet come, and would not come until new social forms had been created. Until that happened the final word had always to be: "Fight or die; bloody war or nothing. Thus the question is implacably posed."[85] With this quotation from George Sand the work concludes.

Marx himself expected revolution and waited for the "final encounter." He was to spend his whole life waiting for the great day. At this particular juncture, the time to move into action seemed to be near. In February 1848, revolution broke out in Paris. The time that Marx had prophesied in 1843 in his dissertation on Hegel's *Philosophy of Right* seemed to have arrived, for in it he had written: "When all internal conditions are right, the German day of resurrection will be heralded by the smashing of the Gallic cock."

The *Communist Manifesto* had appeared in 1848 on the eve of the revolution of that same year. On the strength of this coincidence Marx and his family were expelled from Belgium. Almost simultaneously came an invitation from the French revolutionary regime to return to Paris.

And now it might have seemed that a glorious time for revolutionaries had dawned, for revolution reached down into

Italy, and Germany and Austria came into its grip. German émigrés living in Paris organized a "German Legion." Marx watched all these happenings with mistrust. He was in a quandary. There was nothing he wanted more than revolution, but he saw that the time for the kind of revolution he was looking forward to had not yet arrived. Marx particularly felt the time was not yet ripe in Germany, which had not yet had a bourgeois revolution. Yet he did not want to stand off to one side, doing nothing. So he went back to Germany and founded the *Neue Rheinische Zeitung* as a sort of sequel to the former publication.

All the articles that Marx (and Engels) wrote for this newspaper show the inadequacy of the current revolution as measured against the kind of revolution they had in mind. By June they had already disavowed the French revolution.[86] On June 28, after the retreat of the radical members of the French government and the June revolt, Marx announced that the "last official remains of the February revolution . . . had melted away like a misty apparition."[87] And on New Year's Day, 1849, he made this somber prediction: "Revolutionary uprising of the French working class, world war—that is the table of contents for the year 1849." Later that month the same message was repeated: "The next world war will not only cause reactionary classes and dynasties to vanish from the face of the earth, but whole reactionary peoples as well. And that, too, will be progress."[88]

In May the *Neue Rheinische Zeitung* was banned. Marx was hailed into court in Cologne and charged with sedition. After making a speech in his own defense, he was finally released, but the Prussian government ordered him out of the country. What was left of his assets was used up in the liquidation of the newspaper. After a brief stopover in France, Marx went on to England, for what was to be a final emigration of long duration.

With him he took the firm conviction that only a comprehensive revolution could save mankind, and the absolute certainty, stronger than ever, that his and only his teachings were right. His scorn for and rejection of all other theories became, if anything, greater than before. At the same time he continued to believe that real revolution would break out at any moment.

Thus the battle was lost, but the theory remained correct. The claim to authority raised by Marx in coming years was to be ever more widely recognized. Marx was to become the highest theoretical court of appeal, the theoretical conscience of the socialist movement.

# 35

## Recapitulation and Formulation of Historical Materialism in the Critique of Political Economy

The creator of historical materialism, to put it bluntly, was not much of a historian. That "principal phenomenon of history . . . which fluctuates this way and that, free and unfree, in a thousand forms, complexly, in all imaginable guises, now speaking through masses, now through individuals, now optimistic in mood, again pessimistic . . . ,"[89] that is, history's changing face as such really had no interest for Marx.

He was interested in the past as the precursor of the future, though on the other hand his main interest lay in the present. Usually the man wrapped up in the present sees the past as its forerunner and the future as its sequel. But Marx, when he looked at the present, already saw the future in it. His was always a futurist interest in the present, and it was equally true for him that the future was vitally and visibly prognosticated by the present.

This has always been characteristic of the revolutionary, to summon to revolution with eyes fixed on the future. Only from this point of view can there be a determination of what Marx's interest in history was like. It had nothing to do, as he himself said, with "interpreting" the world; it was a question of "changing" the world.[90]

But in order to change the world, one must understand the laws of change. Once this preparatory labor is accomplished, the way will be cleared for meaningful action. When Marx found historical and dialectical materialism, for him the general riddle of history had been essentially solved.

The solution consisted merely in coming up with a workable formula summing up the *basic movement* of history, that is, its repetitive transformations. Marx was thoroughly aware that at issue was a way of thinking, an intellectual model. To be sure, it had to contain the conditions and essential mode of historical movement. But at the same time he was aware, as he said, that his historical materialism was no *passe partout* that would open up every door. If this thought-model or formula was to be put to work in the investigation of a specific historical period, by the same token it had to be filled out with content and phenomena.

Marx had discovered his formula in the short space of three years, 1843–46. He was so little historically minded that he had not even bothered to probe past epochs. What little he did in this direction, he did superficially, as in *The German Ideology* and the *Communist Manifesto*.

Once enunciated, the intellectual model as such remained unaltered. It was not corrected, improved, or changed at all. Characteristic is the fact that thirteen years after *The German Ideology* appeared, the same formula was transcribed almost unchanged in the preface to *Critique of Political Economy*.

In this famous passage we are told that a critical review of the Hegelian *Philosophy of Right* had led to an investigation. This investigation resulted in the conclusion that the "conditions of the law and forms of the state cannot be understood in terms of themselves, nor of the general evolution of the human spirit," but that they are "rooted in the material conditions of life," in consequence of which "the anatomy of civil society is to be sought in political economy."

While alluding to the fact that from this time on he continued his investigation of political economy, once again he repeated the basis of this analysis, that is, the thought formula or model of historical materialism. Again we are told almost word for word what he already had formulated for us in *The German Ideology*:

> It is not the consciousness of men that determines their being, but, just the opposite, their social being which determines their consciousness. At a certain stage of its evolution, society's material powers of production come into conflict with existing conditions of production, or, what is only a juristic expression for the same, with the conditions of property within which they have hitherto moved. These conditions break the fetters of the developmental forms of the productive forces out of which they arise. An epoch of social revolution then ensues. With the change in the economic foundation the whole monstrous superstructure sooner or later topples down.

This is a repetition of a recapitulation of ideas developed in *The German Ideology*, reproduced virtually unchanged. The only difference is that the term "conditions of production" suddenly appears instead of "form of intercourse."

Other ideas, too, remain essentially unchanged. Before Marx gets to this passage, he emphasizes that the basis of historical events is the production of life. As he puts it:

> In the social production of their lives men accede to certain determined, necessary conditions independent of their will, conditions of production that correspond to a definite state of development of their material forces of production. The totality of these conditions of production constitutes the economic structure of the society, the real basis on which a juristic and political superstructure is raised and to which certain social conditions correspond.[91]

Here again the train of thought found in *The German Ideology* is repeated, though now, to be sure, the concept of conditions of production, which in their totality constitute the basis and economic structure of society, has been more sharply

defined. This time, too, substructure (or basis) is more clearly
differentiated from superstructure. The juristic, political conditions, the forms of social consciousness, indeed ultimately
the "social, political, and intellectual life-process in general,"
are superstructures in the Marxian sense, arising out of the
fundament.

When revolution comes, the basis for it is economic change.
"With the change in the economic foundation sooner or later
the whole monstrous superstructure topples down," and while
the conditions of production "have changed and continue to
change it comes to the point of change in the superstructure,"
in ideological forms. The sharp distinction made here between
the ideological forms of revolution and the material revolution
of the conditions of production had already been established
in *The German Ideology*. However, it may be doubted that
the distinction is actually as sharply put in the earlier work as
it is here by the conceptual separation of "forces of production," "conditions of production," and finally "ideological
forms." That is, if one reads very attentively, it becomes clear
in reexamining the separate formulations that what Marx
called the conditions of production are *partially* determined
by the forces of production, but *partially*, too, by the ideological forms.

Here a certain change and complication of the earlier, simpler formula have become evident. It comes to light in the
tripartite division of productive forces, productive conditions,
and ideological forms. That is, if the conditions of production
are determined both by the productive forces and the ideological forms, it is, after all, conceivable that the productive conditions and finally the productive forces are also changed by
ideological influence. With that, the productive forces would
be robbed of their power really to lead and determine. As is
obviously the case, a revolution would be possible on the basis
of ideological change.

But Marx and Marxism would not acknowledge this possibility. Ideological forms are seen as passive and only through
them men can fight economic conflict. Marx adhered scrupulously to the belief that ideological forms are only sequels and
offshoots of the economic basis. For him this strict differentia-

tion became a guiding methodological principle. He said expressly that "in viewing such revolutions one must constantly distinguish between the revolution in the economic conditions of production that can be verified as true by natural science, and the juristic, political, religious, artistic or philosophic forms wherein men become aware of, and fight, this conflict."[92]

With this the leading role of productive forces has been sharply defined. It is these forces that give rise to the conditions of production and, beyond that, to the ideological forms. Every change in history and every revolutionary movement is preceded by a change in productive forces. The conditions of production and the ideological forms lag behind, and any change in them is dependent on the productive forces.

Marx was to stick fast to this thought model. Related to this is the fact that from now on he was only incidentally interested in ideology, and no longer concerned about its investigation. His real effort was directed at the examination of economic forces. From this time forward and to the end of his life it was the investigation of the economic structure of his times that consistently engaged his central interest. The result was *Capital*.

# 36

## Capital

When the first volume of *Capital* appeared in 1867, Marx was both famous and infamous and above all feared. He had long since become a public figure, ever since the revolutionary period of 1848. He might even have been a legendary personality had he not, very much in the flesh, from his London vantage in particular, followed out and critically observed the steadily growing labor movement.

Beyond this he was a commanding figure at the First Internationale, founded in London in 1864, and before which he gave the opening address. The German Workers Alliance founded by Lasalle in 1863 also leaned on Marx. Lasalle regarded Marx as his theoretical mentor, though Marx mistrusted him greatly. When the Social Democratic Workers Party was founded in 1869, it was based on international socialism and the class struggle.

The idea of class struggle as formulated by Marx was very

widely known. For many this shibboleth alone sufficed, and many were content to busy themselves with the historical theory of classes as developed by Marx. Meanwhile Marx and his followers saw to it that the "specter" of a communist revolution did not disappear.

During this period, however, day after day Marx sat in the reading room of the British Museum, writing his newspaper articles and collecting material for the work on political economy that was to have appeared as early as 1845, but the first outline of which did not come out until 1859.

Finally, in 1867, the first volume was published. It was slow to achieve public recognition and a second, revised edition did not come out until 1873, whereupon its victory march began and it was translated into all languages.

The whole work was never completed. But the first volume was a comprehensive effort and the two succeeding volumes which Engels compiled from Marx's literary remains were to prove not inferior to the first. How basic and carefully conceived the whole work is, is shown by the fact that it was intended to cover the "process of production," the "process of circulation" and the "total process of capitalistic production."

The whole book shared the fate suffered by so many definitive works written throughout a lifetime: it is incomplete and breaks off in chapter 52. Engels, whose painstaking efforts are to be thanked for the fact that the second and third volumes were published, himself said that the volumes which he edited were far less finished than he had supposed. Engels intended to bring out a fourth volume, which would have contained a "detailed critical history of the core of political economy, the theory of surplus value."* But this fourth volume did not, as it turned out, appear in this form. Kautsky later made three volumes out of the material and published them under the title of *Theories of Surplus Value*.[93]

The work done in preparation for the manuscript of *Capital* was gigantic. The vastness of this research effort extending over decades can be appreciated by first looking over the three

* *Mehrwert*=surplus value. This peculiarly Marxian term means the ratio between work necessary to fill the worker's needs and work producing profit for the employer.—*Tr*.

volumes of *Capital* and then realizing that critical preparations for *Surplus Value*, which obviously was related to the
*Critique of Political Economy* that came out in 1861–63,
and which itself was written in 1861–63, ran to 1,472 quarto
pages.

At the same time it will become clear how tirelessly Marx
thought through and formulated his material, again thought it
through, and again formulated it in a new order. In contrast to
the earlier writings, which were often written more or less in
haste and often hastily published, *Capital*, even if it was never
entirely finished, has the splendor of a truly mighty piece of
work, figured out to the last detail with painstaking care.

*Capital* was really the climax of Marx's labor. In another
sense, too, it rounded out his theoretical and scientific effort.
For however autonomous and specialized it may seem to be,
it is nonetheless an application and interpretation of that intellectual formula, that thought model, which Marx called dialectical and historical materialism. From this standpoint *Capital*
is historical materialism empirically concretized. It is the dialectical and historical interpretation of the epoch of history in
which Marx lived.

Marx now fulfilled his promise to apply his formulation of
general dialectical thinking to history. The primary result
which he sought with his labor was to show that the actuality
and movement of a historical period could be revealed by an
analysis of the productive process then prevailing, that is, by
an analysis of existing productive forces and conditions. *Capital* was to do this. The work was limited to an analysis of
production, but naturally spilled over repeatedly into the
superstructure, that is, into the political, legal, and moral dimension, in other words into the ideological.

Anyone losing sight of this relation is liable to regard the
book as a "remarkable mix of economic theory, history, sociology and propaganda,"[94] not to be assigned to any of the usual
categories of scholarly effort. But a mere mixture was not at all
what Marx had in mind. The universal frame that he gave the
work was conceived as something much greater than that.
And whereas his intention in *Capital* is to limit himself to the
detailed politico-economic evidence, this does not prevent

him from pulling back repeatedly to cast a sweeping gaze over the all-encompassing whole, the basic event, which is actually the "production process."

The result of all this is to impose a peculiar difficulty on the reader as he toils his way through the welter of pages and chapters. While he is struggling to get a grip on all the detail and particulars, he is only too apt to lose sight of the forest because of the trees. All too easily he is apt to forget that superimposed as a leitmotif on the special economic interpretation of a certain historical epoch is a general theory of dialectical materialism. Marx himself recognized this difficulty. In the epilogue to the second edition of the first volume of *Capital* he alluded to the basic direction of his thinking and complained that his method was little understood.

Connected with this complaint is the fact that *Capital* can, in fact, be understood—and also criticized—in two ways: either as an explicitly closed piece of work resting exclusively on certain factual economic evidence, or as a part of the general thought formula of dialectical and historical materialism. Anyone presuming complete understanding has to use both approaches, however, since insight into the book's more limited, factual aspect presupposes the wider horizon, and vice versa.

At the same time this basic difficulty gave rise to a peculiar advantage of which Marx was well aware. He never forgot that he was writing a theoretical work designed to serve immediately the purposes of political action, and not one that was merely neutral and scientific. From this arose the necessity of bringing facts and proofs to bear that in the last analysis would be immediately recognizable and easily grasped. In consequence, the whole work can be boiled down to several convenient, directly convincing, and immediately accessible ideas. Some have done just that. With a certain justification the total content of the work has been reduced to such formulas as theory of surplus value, theory of capitalistic accumulation, theory of capitalistic concentration, pauperization theory, and crisis theory.

These main ideas having been abstracted, they signify the following. The theory of surplus value, as Marx himself indicated, is the central concept of the whole. By surplus value Marx means an incremental value which the worker creates by the product of his labor, a value over and beyond what the worker himself needs, but which is taken away from him by the capitalists and entrepreneurs.

The analysis by means of which Marx evolves the concept of surplus value is long and searching. At the very beginning of *Capital* he established the "two-fold character" of labor. He proceeds on the basis of the concept of "commodity" and of the wealth of capitalist society, which he represents as an "immense accumulation of commodities." He demonstrates the dual character of commodity value, which sometimes takes the form of "use-value," and again of "exchange-value."

What, then, is the use-value of labor power which, in the modern process of production, the worker provides the entrepreneur as a sort of commodity? With this question, according to Marx, it turns out that the entrepreneur does not buy from the worker the product of his labor. This product is the property of the capitalist, the entrepreneur. It is the use-value of his labor power that the capitalist buys from the worker. This use-value is less than the value of that which the worker creates. The surplus value thus resulting is the capitalist's profit, and is dependent on the extent to which he is successful in exploiting the labor power of the worker.

Capitalistic production, however, has another key characteristic. The worker must labor in order to live. The capitalist also keeps his pot boiling by profit, but above all must try beyond this to increase his capital. If capital no longer worked profitably, buying labor power would no longer make sense to the capitalist. However, if the worker is faced with the choice of working or not working, then his life process, the very continuance of his existence, is threatened.

When does this situation arise? According to Marx it has to arise in the capitalistic process of production for a variety of reasons. With increasing production, as occurs with the development of productive forces—for example, machines—less labor power is necessarily required for the creation of a commodity. Under these circumstances a smaller amount of labor power, and with this fewer workers, is needed.

However, since the laborer must labor, and in competition with other labor powers, he must now offer his labor power more cheaply. This necessity arises above all when, as a consequence of competition, the entrepreneur must lower the price of his product. The victim is the worker, as long as a glut of labor power obtains.

Here begins the so-called "theory of pauperization." Marx showed that increasing production creates an excess of commodities, which, under certain circumstances, cannot be disposed of. Simultaneously there is an oversupply of labor. This means that there is an ever present danger that the price of labor power will be depressed and the worker will earn wages insuring him only a minimal existence.

In the capitalistic mode of production, Marx says, this process must go on ceaselessly, and inevitably leads to the pauperization of the proletariat. Great legions of unemployed, ultimately willing to work at any price, stand face to face with workers who do have employment.

This process is unavoidable, because the law of capital dictates that the entrepreneur is interested in production only when it yields a profit and makes for surplus value.

From the standpoint of the proletariat, pauperization is irresistible. Paralleling this process is another which Marx called the accumulation of capital. The surplus value exploited out of the worker is converted into capital. Part of surplus value is consumed or expended by the capitalist, but the remainder he "makes use of or accumulates as capital."

This process continues without stop. The more capital an entrepreneur has, the greater his chance of accumulating capital. This situation is not altered by the fact that individual capitalists fail and lose their capital. Generally speaking, the accumulation of capital proceeds steadily.

Marx himself said that these three facts—the difference between use-value and exchange value, the surplus value arising therefrom and the "irrational manifestation" of wage-labor— were basic to the first volume of *Capital*. And indeed from what Marx called his three basic sets of facts, are derived the three theories of surplus value, pauperization, and accumulation of capital.

Whereas the first volume is mainly devoted to a description of surplus value, of the characteristics of wage-labor, and a demonstration of capital accumulation, in the second volume Marx launches into an investigation no longer limited to this cycle, but aimed at arriving at an understanding of the "historical tendency of capitalistic accumulation." The description of the conditions and the cyclic process of capitalistic production is followed by a prognosis. Marx discerns a basic tendency in this system. It strives to liquidate the private property of the immediate producer, that is, the worker. This occurs for one thing because of the "general, absolute law of accumulation," according to which the poverty of the workers must increase in consonance with the increase in the "industrial reserve army."

At the same time, however, the competitive struggle and the superiority of large-scale capital make increasingly for a concentration of capital, until at last capital, on the one hand, is concentrated among a few, while on the other, in opposition to these few stands a host of proletarians grown endlessly numerous. This development is nourished by periodic crises, which bring about the downfall of smaller capitalists while at the same time augmenting the industrial reserve army.

Unavoidably this form of production drives on toward final and total crisis, a crisis which will bring the whole development to full stop. In the course of mounting expropriation ("one capitalist always kills off many"), with the resulting growth of misery, of spoliation and dehumanization, the "monopoly of capital becomes a shackle on the mode of production, which has sprung up and flourished along with, and under, it." Centralization of the means of production and the socialization of labor reach a point "where they become incompatible with their capitalistic integument." This integument "is burst asunder. The knell of capitalistic private property sounds. The expropriators are expropriated."[95]

The phenomena described here—the ever greater centralization of capital, the concentration of capital in the hands of a few, the growth of the proletariat and at last the final crisis—all these events, in the Marxian view, arise of absolute necessity from the very nature and working method of capitalistic production. Thus the Marxian analysis of the capitalistic mode of production of Marx's day ends with a proof of its inevitable evolution. Insofar as the present is an indicator of the future and of the mounting antagonism within the capitalist structure, its manifestations of decay and dissolution herald the end of the system.

# 37

# The Method of Capital

Reducing *Capital*, as we have just done, to its basic ideas and theories gives only a skeletal notion of the work. And quite apart from this, the book is an immense storehouse of facts. Anyone undertaking to understand Marx as primarily a theoretical, constructive, or even speculative thinker, as might easily occur, should never forget that he also provides an abundance of facts to give his work an empirical foundation.

As already noted, during his whole life Marx was a voracious reader, and toward the end of his days this mania for reading increased to a point where he never got around to writing at all. His almost unlimited capacity for absorbing masses of material day after day was combined with an ability to digest and reproduce what he had read. Accordingly there is an extraordinary amount of "processed" matter from the literature in *Capital*. These facts are by no means drawn from scientific works alone. Marx found his material in all sorts of places: in newspapers from all over the world, in reports past and present, in official reports, etc.

Seen in this light, *Capital* is a piece of work built up fact by fact, stone by stone. The reader is given an irrefutable picture of what was in actual fact a ruthless and cruelly inhumane exploitation of the working man. Whatever the subject under discussion—the fifteen-hour working day of adults, the ten- and twelve-hour working day of children, the merciless destruction of people to get grazing lands for sheep, the horrible persecution of the poor who had been driven to beg—Marx gives a documented picture of the period which only a few people living today are aware was the real thing only a hundred years or so ago. This must be appreciated if one is to understand Marx's anger and hatred.

The aim of *Capital* was to incorporate a huge mass of supportive factual material into Marx's intellectual conception. And this task, of having a theory of history long since perfected arise anew out of the actuality of the economy of his century, was all the more of a problem for Marx because what he had in mind here was something more than a mere *description*. Of this difficulty Marx was himself aware.

In the famous afterword to the second edition of the first volume of *Capital* he complains that his method has "been little understood." As proof he cites judgments of his method appearing in various discussions of the book. The first critic thought that Marx had "treated economics metaphysically," the second claimed that Marx used "the deductive method of the whole English school," the third classed Marx among "the most important analytical minds." A Russian critic found his method of inquiry to be "severely realistic," but his method of presentation "idealistic and German-dialectical." With one critic, however, Marx did agree. This one declared that Marx primarily wanted "to find the law of phenomena," not only the law in force at the moment, but the law as showing the variation and development of phenomena, that is, the law "of their transition from one form into another, from one series of connections into another."

It is understandable that Marx should have taken his hat off to this critic, for he had really grasped Marx's special methodological problem. Marx goes on to describe this problem in his own words:

> Of course the method of presentation must differ in form from that of the inquiry. The latter has to appropriate the material in detail, to analyze its different forms of development, to trace out their inner connection. Only after this work is done can the actual movement be adequately described. If this is done successfully, if the life of the subject-matter is ideally reflected as in a mirror, then it may appear as if we had before us a mere a priori construction.[96]

This description spells out with great clarity the peculiarity and goal of the Marxian method. At the same time it reveals, no less, the form which the dialectical method had by this time taken in Marx's adaptation.

The famous lines which now follow have been often noted and cited. In them he distinguishes between his and Hegel's dialectical method. He accuses Hegel of having regarded the "Idea" as the "demiurge of the real world," of having used the dialectical method for "mystification" and thus transfigured "the existing state of things." Although Hegel had recognized the dialectical laws of movement, he had misapplied them.

As clear in themselves as these objections directed against Hegel may be, there is a danger of misconstruing them if one does not carefully think through the preceding section. For it is not in the catchword assertion that he, Marx, has turned Hegel's dialectic right side up again (since it had been "standing on its head"), or in his claim that with him, Marx, "the ideal is nothing else than the material world reflected by the human mind, and translated into forms of thought" that one will find what is characteristic in the Marxian method. Rather, this distinguishing characteristic is found in Marx's foregoing remarks.

To be sure, in Marx's view this movement follows a general dialectical formula and *form* of motion, as Hegel had shown. But much more important is proving and tracking down the individual dialectical steps by which the general form of movement is fulfilled and realized.

When this has been done, the dialectical method undergoes a highly definitive change. What had been a universal conceptual formula has now become a tool, an instrument of inquiry. In its new guise the dialectic no longer decreed contradictions a priori and then resolved them according to a formal dialectical schema. Rather it sought first to recognize actual contradictions and their tensions, tried to discover from where they really came, and then from this information deduce the tendencies by virtue of which they had come into being.

While Marx was applying this procedure for the first time, using the dialectical method as an instrument that defined, brought together, and impressed order on a body of empirical material, he was, to be sure, following the same road that Hegel had taken. Yet he had the right to claim that his mode of procedure differed basically from Hegel's for the reason that the general intellectual formula of the dialectic had been transformed into a methodological process for the precise investigation of actuality. It was this process that was Marx's creation, by virtue of which, among other things, he became the founder of modern sociology.

When Marx's various critics accuse him, conflictingly, of operating "realistically" or "idealistically," "deductively" or "analytically," in all cases they are merely characterizing the peculiarity of his method. The weakness of this method, but also its greatness and efficiency, lies in the fact that out of the fullness of a historic continuum (*Geschehen*), manifested in and described by facts, he undertook to prove the validity of "ideal" laws.

# 38

## The Utopian in Marx

A dialectical process that a whole epoch searched thoroughly for contradictions, seeking to apprehend their severity and tension, a process that moreover sought to understand how men would prospectively behave in this situation, beyond question had the character of a truly diagnostic investigation. It was Marx's intention to use dialectical thinking this way—so far as he felt himself to be a scholar and scientist.

Nonetheless Marx never intended to restrict himself to research or scholarship, and carried over into all his investigations the conviction, long since hardened, of the necessity of revolution. He never denied that in this sense theory was for him only a means to a practical end. And *Capital* was dedicated above all to the proof that revolution was unavoidable.

Following this premise, the dialectical method, in all the careful elaboration that it underwent in Marx's hands, became an instrument serving prophecy. Marx anticipated a future which, he believed, just as necessarily had to be prefigured in thought as it necessarily had to come.

This differentiates Marx from all other utopian thinkers. He strongly rejected all utopian socialism and, in keeping with this rejection, he and his followers chose to understand their communism as scientific and not utopian.

The distinction seems clear: from the first, utopian thinkers have described a better state or a better society. They have depicted these utopias as conceivable and possible (for example, Plato), or even as already realized and actually existing somewhere, as in the case of Thomas More's island. But these thinkers skip over the matter of how these utopias got that way, leaving open the question of how it all came about.

Marx took a quite different tack. He did not proceed on the basis of describing a better future society, nor in any way project the forms the new society would assume. The whole weight of his description falls on the inadequacies of existing society and on the demonstration of the forces that are destroying it. The utopians also criticized existing society, if only by way of contrasting it with their picture of a better one. With Marx, however, the critical discussion took every precedence over utopian description. To the extent that future society is described at all, it is not done in terms of a positive utopian image, but is constructed, so to speak, out of the negatives of utopia.

However, an anticipation of the future still exists. Therefore the question can be asked whether this anticipation contains utopian elements, that is, whether it proceeds from a preconception of a better and more beautiful future. Now there is no doubt that, by and large, Marx's thinking was directed toward a better future with a classless society, but this prospect lay hidden behind the veil of the present. With Marx the idea of a better future is constantly bound up with the image of a self-destructing present.

Marx, therefore, was certainly no utopian in the usual sense of the word, and in his works are found only isolated and extremely infrequent references to what a future communist society will actually be like. In *The German Ideology*, however, this almost naive piece of description suddenly crops up:

> For as soon as labor is distributed, each man has a particular, exclusive sphere of activity from which he cannot escape. He is a hunter, a fisherman, a shepherd, or a critic, and must remain so if he does not want to lose his means of livelihood; while in a communist society, where nobody has one exclusive sphere of activity, but each can become accomplished in any branch he wishes, society regulates the general production and thus makes it possible for me to do one thing today and another tomorrow, to hunt in the morning, fish in the afternoon, raise sheep in the evening, criticize after supper, just as I have a mind, without ever becoming hunter, shepherd, or critic.[97]

At this time Marx also promised that in a communist society there would be perfect freedom of action and living, because the social organization would go a long way toward eliminating the compulsion to work. In other youthful writings, too, indications can be found of what Marx imagined communist society would be like, some of them frankly enthusiastic.

In the essay *Contribution to a Critique of Hegel's Philosophy of Right*, Marx explains that from the "complete loss" of man in existing society must come the "complete restoration of man" in the society to follow. In the *Economic and Philosophic Manuscripts* are found passages already cited implying that in the future society a new man will come into being, a man who will regain his original meaning. Communism is described as "humanism consummated," as a society in which there is no conflict between "man and nature," and in which all contradictions have been resolved.

But later on these undoubtedly utopian projections were to retreat into the background. The older Marx became increasingly more hesitant and cautious about making such statements. Only one basic idea retained its nuclear form, to be discovered again in the well-known passage at the end of the third volume of *Capital*. Here Marx speaks about the "true realm of freedom" which will be realized in the coming communist society. However, there is no longer any mention of complete freedom of action. Now it goes like this: "The realm of freedom begins indeed only when labor that is determined by external need and expediency ceases to be; it lies, therefore, in the nature of things beyond the sphere of actual material production."[98]

And once again Marx formulated the unique qualifications for the emergence of such a realm of freedom: "Freedom in this region can only consist in having socialized men, the associated producers, rationally regulate, bring under their communal control, this, their exchange of material with nature, instead of being ruled by it as by a blind power."

Here, to be sure, we can recognize a repetition of the idea in *The German Ideology* to the effect that a communist society regulates the general production. But before this Marx had already said by way of qualification, as if wishing to warn against too great optimism: "As the wild animal must contend with nature in order to satisfy his needs, in order to maintain his life and reproduce, so must the civilized person, and this he must do in all social forms and under all possible methods of production." This remains forever a "realm of necessity" and only on the basis of a form of production as rationalized as it can possibly be can the realm of freedom, that is, that "development of human forces which amounts to an end in itself," be constructed.

If Marx became ever more cautious about making positive statements of the kind that had a utopian ring in his earlier writings, at the same time he grew less positive about the coming revolution. In the youthful writings we find a dark and menacing image of revolution. In the *Poverty of Philosophy* we are told that the revolution will occur as a struggle of "man against man," as a "bloody war." This threatening notice grew stronger just after the revolution of 1848, at the time of the demise of the *Neue Rheinische Zeitung*. At this point Marx proclaimed there was only one way to "cut short the murderous death throes of the old societies, to simplify, to concentrate," namely, by "revolutionary terrorism." It was plainly put: "We are merciless, we ask no mercy from you. When our turn comes, we shall not be sparing with terrorism."[99]

It should not, of course, be assumed that the older Marx regarded revolution as child's play. But the more deeply he studied revolutionary tactics and the history of revolution, the more we find at least occasional intimations of the possibility of a more moderate sort of revolution. For instance, as is well known Marx once said that in England the otherwise unavoidable revolution might be carried out by peaceful and legal means, thus admitting at least one exception to the rule. And in *Capital* there is at least one passage in which Marx says that the process of transforming scattered private property arising from the labor of individuals into capitalist property "is naturally a process incomparably more protracted, violent and difficult than the transformation of capitalistic private property, already practically resting on socialized production, into socialized property." In the first process, Marx goes on to say, "it was a question of the expropriation of a mass of people by a few usurpers; in the latter we have the expropriation of a few usurpers by the mass of the people."[100]

If utopian notions are perhaps still discernible in the early writings, Marx nonetheless drew away from them the more sober and realistic he became. It is precisely this objectivity which gives Marx's thought the great persuasive power which we associate with "scientific socialism."

Yet this does not alter the fact that the main strength of Marxism derives from these two notions: one, the concept of a better human condition; two, the concept that this more desirable classless society can be achieved only through the destruction of existing society. These two ideas are inseparably bound together, and they simplify, guide, and support the Marxist political movement.

# 39

## The Formal System of Dialectic in Marx

When, in the afterword to *Capital*, Marx expressly committed himself to the dialectical method, he praised Hegel in this connection as the one who was "the first to present its general form of working in a comprehensive and conscious manner." He thus admitted unequivocally that there are general forms of dialectical movement which Hegel was the first to understand.

Meanwhile Hegel himself never got beyond intimations of the development of a general dialectical system. Even in his *Logic* he primarily developed the dialectic of logical categories, but not a dialectical formalism. It may in any case be doubted whether such a formalism can be developed at all. Be that as it may, no formal system of dialectic exists, such as has long been known, for instance, in formal logic, both in the older type of logic and in the modern symbolic types.

We know of no such comparable dialectical formalism. Our knowledge of the formal character of this kind of thinking—

however applied, or whether applicable at all—is limited to
the few familiar passages that can be quickly counted off and
which yield no more than a few basic principles.

That is to say, any dialectical thinking begins with phenomena defined as contradictions, or even as antitheses. To
this initial idea a second is added, namely, that contradiction
necessarily brings into play the process which Hegel called
*Aufhebung*—transcendence, sublimation, sublation, abolish-
ment, annulment of contradiction, as the term is variously
translated. Every contradiction contains a dialectical *Span-
nung*, or tension, which compels its resolution. This leads to a
third basic notion. The new given arising out of the resolution
of contradiction again evolves into contradiction, whereupon
the *Aufhebung* process just described is repeated.

Contradiction, resolution of contradiction, a new unity that
itself develops into a new contradiction—this is the fundamental rhythm of the dialectic, summed up in the formula "thesis,
antithesis, and synthesis."

But in this formula there is much that remains unclear. How
does contradiction come about? What do the transcendence
and resolution of contradiction really mean? To what extent is
a new unity formed? Why and how does a new contradiction
arise, only to be resolved as before?

These are only a few of the questions which immediately
spring to mind. These basic questions have to be answered,
even if we discount the additional ones which spring up the
minute the dialectical thought process is confronted by formal
logic. In a word, the formal character of dialectical thinking
has to be made clear, and, moreover, there must be a demonstration of where this kind of thinking stands in respect to the
principles of so-called formal logic.

To the extent that Hegel ever went at all into such problems, he came up only with statements to the effect that the
dialectical method is the only true one, that it alone is capable
of comprehending the "whole" whereas formal logic is obsolete, etc. Thus it is not to be wondered at that Hegel has been
accused of having a tendency to talk his way around questions
he could not, or would not, answer.

Other dialecticians more or less followed the Hegelian

precedent. Neither Kierkegaard nor Marx, any more than Hegel, ever addressed himself to the question of a formal system of dialectic. For Kierkegaard no such system could exist in any case, because for him dialectical thinking is not an objective thought process at all. On the contrary, the main aim of the existential dialectic is to transcend the realm of validity as represented by objective truth and systematic argumentation.

But this was not Marx's view at all. With respect to objectivity, unlike Kierkegaard he was not opposed to Hegelian thinking on the matter. Rather he saw dialectical thinking as a means of comprehending objective fact. His objection to Hegel lay in his contention that whereas Hegel had, to be sure, recognized the general forms of movement of dialectic, he had used them in a false and mystifying way. As for the rest, he never wasted a moment's thought on the question of how these "general forms of movement" actually come into being. It was enough for him that Hegel had recognized them.

So it is that the dialectic as a method remains today basically no more complete than when Hegel first outlined it. It has, of course, been mercilessly criticized, and even characterized as one colossal error. But the adherents of dialectic, like Kierkegaard and Marx, never worried their heads about this. They simply continued to think dialectically, and what they thought continues to spread to this day.

If this fact is borne in mind, and if, beyond this, the great practical consequences of their thinking is taken into consideration, it is impossible not to appreciate that, if nothing else, dialectic is an effective mode of thought. At the same time it also becomes clear that each dialectical thinker went only his own way, with the result that the dialectic arrives at different ends in each case. One again recognizes here the peculiar state of affairs already described. The end result of dialectical thinking in general is what in each case it started out with in the first place—a contradiction. Each dialectical system and thought form contradicts the other. None is comparable to the other in predisposition, development or goal.

Now, if dialectical thinking is so liable to modification that as a tool it can function quite differently depending on who is using it, the question has to arise as to whether there are "general forms of movement" at all. At least the question must be asked where this variability comes from, and what it signifies. If general dialectical forms of movement are assumed, then it has to be shown why they are so flexible.

The immediate answer is not hard to find. Dialectical thinking changes according to how the basic phenomenon, the contradiction, is defined. It varies further according to the way the contradiction initially laid down is developed. It changes a third time according to the goal of the particular dialectic.

It is easy enough to see, to make only the simplest demonstration, that Hegel, Kierkegaard, and Marx defined "contradiction" quite differently. For Hegel there was one universal and ever demonstrable contradiction, that of the "positive" and the "negative." This contradiction springs up throughout the whole world of concepts and everywhere in thought. For Kierkegaard there was one single and absolute contradiction, that of existence. For Marx, on the other hand, it was social contradiction that stood out above all else, a contradiction lying in men's social relationships, in labor, the division of labor, and history.

Finally, behind whatever development of and approach to contradiction may be chosen, different aims must be recognized. Hegel had it in mind to understand and elucidate the world in its totality, to find the truth of the actual whole. Precisely the opposite, Kierkegaard wanted to dissolve the truth of science and objective thinking and destroy what Hegel had built up. On the whole he was not so much concerned with the resolution of contradiction as such, but with deepening and widening the dissolving process in the service of religion. Marx, finally, for his part was concerned with developing social contradiction historically, to show its current workings and to transcend or cancel it out by revolution.

In this context of goals the three dialecticians are absolutely opposed. Hegel wanted to explain the world and come to a conciliatory understanding of it. Marx, in consequence, accused him of mystifying and of transfiguring what actually exists. Kierkegaard's purpose was to show the endless contradictoriness of existence and the world and so lead the way to

God. For Marx, to whom religion was the "opium of the people," any such enterprise was sheer nonsense and no less erroneous than Hegel's mystification. He, too, completely destroyed the present, but meanwhile showed that beyond the present world lay a better world, and thus his final goal resulted—in revolution.

With each additional step taken in these diverse directions, the differences among the three become more glaringly evident. And at the same time the question as to "general forms of movement" becomes more pressing. One has to ask whether the differences appearing so clearly between the existing dialectic teachings may not also obtain in dialectical thinking as a formal structure.

This question can be answered, as will be done in the next chapter in the case of Marx, only if the *formal* idiosyncrasies of dialectical thinking are thoroughly explored, the peculiarities particularly characteristic of this mode of thinking. Our aim will be to show that general dialectical forms of movement change with any given system. This change is certainly determined by the approach and the goal in mind, and it can be shown to spill over into the formal structure as well.

To prove this, let us proceed in terms of the generally recognized characteristics of dialectical thought. This kind of thinking at the outset 1) posits an initial contradiction, which 2) develops, creates a tension, and finally breaks through to release and resolution, and in this fashion 3) strives to reach a goal. Thus we distinguish three components in the general structure of dialectical thought: 1) the initial dialectical proposition; 2) the dialectical development or process; and 3) the dialectical goal.

# 40

## The Dialectical Approach in Marx

Like every dialectician, Marx, too, began with the phenomenon of contradiction, which he saw as having two forms. The first, formulated early in his youthful writings, is the contradiction between two classes, the haves and the have-nots. It is a social contradiction, coming to light in the fact of property, which in Marx's time was expressed in the discrepancy between proletariats and capitalists. In his philosophical conception this contradiction is manifested as man's "self-alienation" or "self-estrangement," and leads to loss of self or identity.

Marx generalized this contradiction as class conflict. Class conflict permeates all past history and is not only represented in the contradiction between those who own property and those who do not, but even more between those who oppress and those who are oppressed. To Marx's way of thinking this last is an independent fact of social life.

In the youthful writings, a second contradiction takes the place of the one involving class conflict, and was specifically formulated for the first time in *The German Ideology*. It is understood as a contradiction independent of and underlying the development of consciousness. It is rooted in the necessity of human labor and in the contradiction between productive power and the form of economic intercourse as propagated by social development. Later on it is also understood as the contradiction between productive forces (the forces of production) and the conditions of production.

To this point Marx followed the general laws of the movement of dialectical thinking, beginning with the phenomenon and a characterization of its basic contradictions. But even at this stage a typical transformation of these forms of movement had begun to appear. That is to say, for Marx these basic forms are not of equal value. There is a ratio of interdependency which at times appears to be a ratio of causality. The *leading* contradiction, and the one which gives rise to all others, is the opposition between the forces of production and the conditions of production, and the feared one flowing out of it: the contradiction represented by class conflict. Human society, by virtue of the division of labor, in any given contradiction between productive forces and productive conditions, is split asunder, and it is *out of this circumstance* of economic-social contradiction that any class conflict is generated. The process may be shown schematically as in the illustration.

When Marx set up this group of binding relationships, he gave priority to the material contradiction inherent in the lawfulness of economic development. The universal fact and the universal form of contradiction are narrowed down for him to a phenomenon which, as he saw it, is material in nature. The multiplicity of all phenomena of contradiction stems back to the productive force of men impelled by the need to satisfy wants.

This situation, moreover, provides the materialistic basis for the development of contradiction. Because material production has first say and leads the way, history follows in train, as likewise does the development of a consciousness of economic

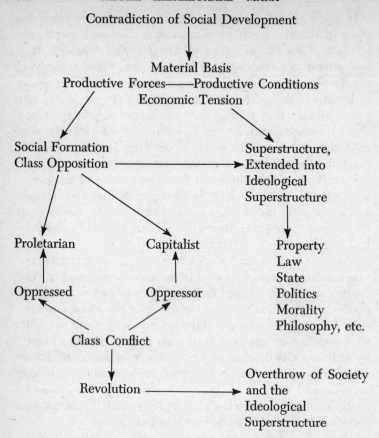

evolution. Because of this point of view, any dialectic of consciousness explored by Marx was for him of secondary importance.

On this account, Marx has always been accused of giving a one-sided definition of history. Once the proposition that material events play the leading role is extended to a point where economic production is seen as giving rise, to put the matter plainly, to events of a spiritual or intellectual nature, we have in any case arrived at a primitive materialism.

Marx clearly rejected this criticism. Even so the danger of a one-sided interpretation of history remains. The undeniable fact that intellectual events deeply influence history, the equally undeniable fact that the evolution of the forces of production is impossible without intellectual activity and much else besides are enough to indicate that assigning the leading role to economic events must be handled with extreme care. Otherwise distortions and simplifications arise, of which there are in fact more than a few.

# 41

---

# The Dialectic Process

The central notion about which Marx from the start grouped his theoretical efforts was that of a revolution bound to come. It can be said without hesitation that it was on this very account and none other that Marx seized on the dialectical method, since to him it seemed to be the ideal instrument for showing the necessity and ineluctability of revolution.

The dialectical method seemed to be the accepted means of choice because every revolution, first of all, is characterized by radical change, by the overthrow and abolition of what exists. This basic event of "revolution" is also basic to dialectical thought. The main concept in Hegel's dialectical schema is *Aufhebung*, that is, transcendence, sublimation, supersession, annulment of existing contradiction, and thus in the broad sense a kind of revolution. According to his theory, the movement leading to sublimation is already given in the fact of contradiction, that is, by the existence of "positive" and "negative."

Hegel laid down the formal schema of *Aufhebung* in one brief proposition. Because the "negative is equally positive" every contradiction evolves into a new and higher unity. Hegel applied this intellectual form to all evolution whatsoever. He taught that the bloom supersedes or "sublimates" the bud and the fruit supersedes the bloom, and that in historical evolution later events represent a transcendence or annulment of those preceding. As we have shown, Hegel was certainly not uninfluenced in developing this intellectual schema by his experience of the French Revolution.

It may now appear as if Marx simply appropriated the Hegelian intellectual schema. However, this was not the case. With Marx the Hegelian model experienced a demonstrable formal change. This change is bound up, as has already been described, with the initial Marxian approach, his choice of attack.

The economic contradiction between productive forces and conditions is for Marx a dialectical opposition which must necessarily be transcended. In this antithesis the conditions of production—that is, the capitalism of Marx's day—are the negative and limiting element. But sublimation by no means proceeds directly out of these conditions.

The resolution of the conflict between the forces and conditions of production, rather, is a complicated thing. In a first stage it operates in such a way that newly emergent forces of production, under the pressure of existing conditions of production, assume the form of "forces of destruction." Thus, for instance, the invention of machines does not immediately serve to ease working conditions. The capitalist who uses the machines as new sources of profit, quite the contrary, depresses working conditions by means of them.

The forces of production, evolving in this fashion, sharpen the opposition between classes and compel class conflict. Under the pressure of an ever mounting danger of complete disorganization of economic life, a climax of violent overthrow is finally reached. Thus Marx explains past revolutions and from the same conditions infers the one to come.

Spelling out this process schematically, we see the following:

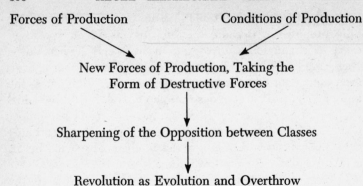

Forces of Production        Conditions of Production

New Forces of Production, Taking the
Form of Destructive Forces

Sharpening of the Opposition between Classes

Revolution as Evolution and Overthrow

This schema shows how, according to the Marxian notion, revolution as the overthrow of existing conditions of production at the same time sets the stage for the possibility of a positive development of productive forces. It shows, more than anything else, that Marx visualized a chainlike dialectical process wherein economic contradiction continually grows. But, as he saw it, the real villain was inhibiting action of "conditions of production," until finally there had to be a violent revolution.

At this point, Marx has really parted company with the Hegelian model. In the Marxian dialectical process there is a constant positive factor, the forces of production, and a constant negative factor, the conditions of production. This leads to sudden alterations and revolution because ultimately the inhibiting conditions of production must be transcended.

In this manner Marx narrowed down the dialectical process which Hegel had seen as totally comprehensive to a material phenomenon, that is, to the interplay between productive forces and conditions. For him basically there is only one dialectic, which is economic in nature, and any other dialectic, for example the ideological one, is of secondary significance. Actually, however, Marx was not quite consistent in this respect, since he was also convinced of the driving force of ideological propaganda.

# 42

## The Dialectical Goal

Hegel used the dialectical method to understand the historical process as far as it had then run its course. For Marx the dialectical method was the instrument by means of which history yet to come could be predicted. This prediction went so far as to prophesy the total revolution that would abolish existing civil society.

It might now be assumed that Marx believed the dialectical process would continue in force after the revolution. This can be argued on the basis that in the postrevolutionary situation the productive forces would have to be organized anew under new conditions of production. Once this happened there would be a nucleus of a new economic contradiction. Even now the new conditions of production would still have to play the same role of highest court of resort, inhibiting further development.

There is no apparent reason at all why the dialectical process should suddenly come to a standstill. If, as Marx tells us, it worked in the past, it has to be assumed it will keep on working in the future. As the generations are superseded in the evolution of the human race and traditions change, it might be imagined that new productive forces and correspondingly new productive conditions would dialectically replace the old at any given point.

Hegel did not in any way project his dialectical notion into the future, but nonetheless it can be assumed from the whole direction of his dialectic that he never thought of it as not continuing. However, he has been accused of regarding his own historical period as the culmination.

To return to Marx, first of all we can say that the dialectical process, as he saw it, would not in fact continue after the revolution. With world revolution it would come to an end as known in its previous form. Once there was world revolution, the dialectic as hitherto experienced would be transcended, and with this man's prehistory would be over.

Marx justified this prediction as follows: once a communist revolution had occurred, entirely doing away with private property, the very basis of the economic dialectic would be wiped out. Thereafter the distinction between haves and have-nots would cease to exist because property would then be in the hands of everybody. As a consequence, the opposition of classes would be abolished and a "classless society" would replace the previous class society. The "true realm of freedom" could then begin, based on a mode of production henceforth controlled and free of contradiction.

Whether Marx seriously believed that all contradictions would be thrust aside in this manner, and whether he expected a classless society to be a final situation purged of conflict, may be left an open question. As already noted, he was very sparing with statements on what the coming communist society would be like, though beyond any doubt he expected it would represent a great advance over everything that had gone before.

The advance ending man's previous history would rest on the abolition of economic contradiction and in the advent thereafter of a definitive, final economic organization of society. As a result, the dialectic previously in force would also come to a close. Whether it would be replaced by a new one Marx never said.

The dialectical form of development that Marx read into past and future history was different from Hegel's. Hegel saw the developmental process as continuous: new syntheses would constantly arise out of ever new antitheses and contradictions. But for Marx one single, mounting antithesis was to persist throughout the whole "prehistory" of mankind. This opposition flowed out of property and the correlative tensions between productive forces and productive conditions. At a certain point, that is, when world revolution intervened, this particular contradiction and the dialectic bound up with it would be completely annulled. The classless society would be the synthesis and the concluding step in this phase of human development.

Again we have to ask just how many utopian elements did in fact creep into the sober and realistic kind of thinking to which Marx was otherwise so attached. The answer depends on the degree to which the classless society can be regarded as a utopia. Actual facts seem to show that every society establishes an order of rank. In this sense a classless society, one without any hierarchical arrangement whatsoever, is obviously impossible.

Yet on the whole our analysis of Marx and our occasional comparison of him with Hegel show that the two thinkers are separated by more than the difference between an idealistic and a materialistic mode of thought. Over and beyond this, there are highly significant differences in the definition of the general forms of movement of the dialectic.

However, so far as these underlying forms of movements are used in dealing with actuality, they tell us as much or as little about actuality as do the forms of syllogism. No truth resides implicitly in dialectical thought, nor does the use of dialectical formulas in any way guarantee knowledge.

We have also shown, moreover, that in every case where dialectical thinking has been applied, the general forms of movement can be modified almost at will and made to conform to the goals at hand. The comparison of Hegel with Marx and of the two with Kierkegaard has shown that there is not *one*, but many ways of looking at things dialectically, and that the way dialectic is used is always situationally determined.

# Sources, Quotations and Supplements

In general the quotations from Hegel are taken from the Glockner Jubilee Edition in twenty volumes of *Georg Wilhelm Friedrich Hegels Sämtliche Werke* ("Georg Wilhelm Friedrich Hegel's Collected Works"), here shortened to "Hegel's Works." Where quotations have been taken from other editions they have been marked accordingly.

Quotations from the works of Kierkegaard and Marx come from various editions.

(In listing the sources for Hegel and Marx, the German title of the work in question will be given once with its English equivalent, and thereafter only the English equivalent. In the case of Kierkegaard, since the author worked from German translations of the Danish and does not list the original Danish titles, only English equivalents will be listed.—*Tr.*)

## PART I. Hegel's Dialectical System

1. *Hegels Werke*, vol. 2, *Phänomenologie*, p. 14 ("Hegel's Works," vol. 2, *Phenomenology*)

2. In a letter dated September 21, 1798, Kant wrote to Garve: "In skimming through the same [Garve's book, *Übersicht der vornehmsten Prinzipien der Sittenlehre*, or "Survey of the Most Eminent Principles of Moral Philosophy," Breslau, 1789] I happened on the note on page 339: in view of which I must protest.—My point of departure is not the investigation of God's existence, of immortality, etc., but the antinomy of pure reason: The world has a beginning—: it has no beginning, etc., to the fourth: There is freedom in man—as opposed to: There is no freedom, but all in man is natural necessity: it was this that awoke me from dogmatic slumber and drove me on to the *Critique of Pure Reason* itself, so as to do away with pure reason's apparent self-contradiction."

3. Kant, *Kritik der reinen Vernunft* (*Critique of Pure Reason*), 2nd edition, p. 353 et seq.

4. "Hegel's Works," vol. 4. *Wissenschaft der Logik* (*Science of Logic*), p. 54

5. Ibid., p. 13

6. Ibid., p. 46

7. Søren Kierkegaard, *The Journals*, in two volumes, selected and translated into the German as *Die Tagebücher* by Theodor Haecker, 1923, vol. 2, p. 351 et seq.

8. *Dokumente zu Hegels Entwicklung* ("Documentation of Hegel's Development"), edited by J. Hoffmeister, 1936, p. 428

9. *Briefe von und an Hegel* ("Letters to and from Hegel"), edited by J. Hoffmeister, letter to Niethammer, vol. 2, p. 272

10. Ibid., vol. 1, p. 374

11. Ibid., vol. 1, p. 314

12. Ibid., vol. 1, p. 219

13. Ibid., vol. 1, p. 120

14. Ibid., vol. 2, p. 28

15. Ibid., vol. 2, p. 86

16. "Documentation of Hegel's Development," p. 352

17. "Hegel's Works," vol. 2, *Vorlesungen über die Philosophie der Weltgeschichte* ("Lectures on the Philosophy of World History"), p. 557

18. "Hegel's Works," vol. 2, *Phenomenology*, p. 453

19. "Hegel's Works," vol. 1, *Rechtsphilosophie* (*Philosophy of Right*), p. 331

20. "Hegel's Works," vol. 1, articles from *Der kritische Journal der Philosophie* ("Critical Journal of Philosophy") and other writings from the Jena period, p. 44

21. "Hegel's Works," vol. 2, *Phenomenology*, p. 404. The whole passage reads: "The dismemberment of consciousness, in its self-awareness and self-expressiveness, is laughing at existence; as well as the confusion of the whole and oneself, to scorn; at

the same time it is the fading away, still self-aware, of this whole confusion."

22. "Hegel's Works," vol. 7, *Philosophy of Right*, p. 264. Cf. R. Heiss, *Hegel und Marx* ("Hegel and Marx") in *Symposion*, a philosophical annual, 1949, pp. 169–206, and *Die Dialektik bei Hegel und Marx* ("The Dialectic in Hegel and Marx"), Bremen, 1961

23. "Hegel's Works," vol. 7, p. 263

24. "Hegel's Works," vol. 7, p. 319

25. Karl Marx, Afterword to the second edition of "Capital," 1873

26. "Hegel's Works," vol. 2, "Phenomenology," p. 34

27. "Hegel's Works," vol. 4, "Logic," p. 51; cf. Robert Heiss, *Wesen und Formen der Dialektik* ("Essences and Forms of the Dialectic"), Cologne, 1959, p. 142 et seq.

28. "Hegel's Works," vol. 7, "Philosophy of Right," p. 268

29. R. Haym, *Hegel und Seine Zeit* ("Hegel and His Period"), 1857, p. 17

30. "Documentation of Hegel's Development," p. 9

31. Ibid., p. 8

32. Ibid., p. 37

33. Ibid., p. 53

34. W. Dilthey, *Die Jugendgeschichte Hegels* ("Story of Hegel's Youth"), in Wilhelm Dilthey's collected works, vol. 4, p. 13

35. "Documentation," p. 431 and 433

36. Ibid., p. 428 et seq.

37. R. Haym, "Hegel and His Period," p. 17

38. Ibid., p. 17

39. Theodor Haering, *Hegel: Sein Wollen und Sein Werk* ("Hegel: His Intention and His Work"), 1929, p. 49

40. After a statement made by Hegel's sister, cf. "Documentation," p. 394

41. "Hegel's Works," vol. 2, "Lectures on the Philosophy of History," p. 557 et seq.

42. "Documentation," p. 430

43. "Letters to and from Hegel," vol. 1, p. 23

44. Ibid., vol. 1, p. 42

45. Quoted after Haym, "Hegel and His Period," p. 484

46. In the first outline of *Verfassung des Deutschen Reichs* ("Constitution of the German Empire"), 1789/90. Printed in "Documentation," p. 283. Cf. *Die Verfassung Deutschlands* ("The German Constitution"), on the basis of the ms. in Hegel's literary remains, edited by Dr. Heller, 1922

47. "Letters," vol. 1, p. 24

48. Ibid., vol. 1, p. 59 et seq.

49. Printed in Nohl's *Hegels Theologische Jugendschrifte* ("Hegel's Youthful Theological Writings"), Tübingen, 1907, pp. 345–351

50. *Jenenser Logik, Metaphysik und Naturphilosophie* ("Jena Logic, Metaphysics and Natural Philosophy"), edited by G. Lasson, Leipzig, 1923

51. Cf. J. Hoffmeister's account in his introduction to Hegel's "Phenomenology," 1937, pp. XXVIII et seq., and Theodor L. Haering's *Die Entstehungsgeschichte der Phänomenologie des Geistes* ("History of the Genesis of the Phenomenology of the Spirit"), in the proceedings of the Third Hegel Congress, 1934, p. 118 et seq.

52. S. Kierkegaard, "The Journals," vol. 1, p. 71

53. Nietzsche's collected works, Musarion Edition, vol. 14, p. 313, *Aus dem Nachlass* ("From the Literary Remains")

54. Ibid., vol. 14, p. 366

55. Ibid., vol. 14, p. 58, *Götterdämmerung* ("Twilight of the Idols")

56. "Hegel's Works," vol. 12, p. 49, Introduction to the "Phenomenology"

57. Ibid., vol. 2, p. 620, Conclusion of the "Phenomenology"

58. In J. Hoffmeister's "Documentation," pp. 351, 353, 360 and 370

59. Ibid., p. 364 et seq. (This and the some fifty-eight Jena fragments cited were taken by Hoffmeister from *Georg Friedrich Wilhelm Hegels Leben* ("The life of Georg Friedrich Wilhelm Hegel") by K. Rosenkranz, pp. 537–555.) The whole fragment reads as follows:

"God, having become Nature, had extended Himself into the magnificence and the mute cycle of formations, become conscious of the expansion, of the lost punctuality, and grown angry about it. The anger is this shaping, this gathering into the empty point. He finds Himself as such, and His essence is poured out into unquiet, restless eternity, where there is no present, only a wild going outward, always becoming as fast as transcended. This anger, while He is this rushing outward, is the destruction of Nature. The going beyond His creations is at the same time an absolute going into Himself, a growing into a central point. In so doing His anger devours His formations into Himself. Your whole realm of extension must pass through this central point; by it your limbs are crushed and your flesh mashed until it becomes part of this fluidity.

"God's anger with Himself in His otherness, the fallen Lucifer, here established, rises against God, and its beauty makes him arrogant. Conscious of its form, Nature puts it on display, and in it takes pleasure in itself. But this explicit being or its being as consciousness is not being as an ever peaceful notion of itself, such that the idea is only a secondary thing, empty, inactive space receiving its content, rather this consciousness is immediately absolute activity—it is anger itself, inflammation, an inflammation of anger in this being that rises up and tears apart its arrogant splendors. Nature thus rent apart ascends into a new, ideal form as a shadow-realm that has lost its first life, into the phenomenon of Spirit after the death of its (first) life. This new form is also the conquest of evil, the having held out in the glow of pain in the central point, where, now purified, it has left behind all its dross in the crucible, and become a residuum that is pure nothingness. It lifts itself up as free Spirit, which in Nature now sees only this, its transfiguration.

"Such myths, such intuitions are the intuitions of *barbarism*. The form of these intuitions, or rather in this case the rage against this Absolute that has become and endured, annihilates the individual. For the individual counts for nothing in it. He does not perish, but is undone, and such an intuition must undergo still another process to be absolute. This is the science or the recognition that every imagining of oneself into one's self is that course of God's life out of which knowledge itself flows; awareness that Nature in its essence is not the otherness about the Spirit, in its lostness, becomes enraged, but in its intuition of itself is Spirit. The individual as such is himself Nature, and the intuition of the divine essence is a natural thing, though its content is like the Spirit. The individual takes the same course (as God) in the consuming of himself or in science, for in the latter the natural essence of the subject is destroyed. And it is not only a case of elevating the individual thereto or a cultivation of the same; it is not merely a way of looking at it from his (the individual's) side, a relating to it; but it is the second circle of the Absolute itself, which, having become Spirit, as such, as Spirit born forth, as consciousness, enters into pain, so that the Spirit as consciousness generates its own self-realization (. . . *so dass der Geist als Bewusstsein jenes sein Werden ein ihm selbst als einem gewordenen erzeugt.*—The aforesaid intuition of religion is universal religion and is this only as science. It is not a question of reliving something, of producing in oneself that first way as an intuitively experienced cycle; rather science lifts itself above belief and its intuition, gives itself up to Spirit and realizes itself as Spirit. The cultivation, the scientific development of this intuition, consists in its always remaining Spirit, that it does not lose Spirit and as Spirit that does not lose itself becomes something else and finds itself again. Knowing makes each moment of the intuition, each moment being explicitly an impenetrable, definite form which does not disclose its innerness but goes forth, acts and vanishes through another acting on it, into a process implicit in itself or into a spiritual Nature."

60. "Hegel's Works," vol. 4, "Logic," p. 46

61. Ibid., vol. 19, *Vorlesungen über die Geschichte der Philosophie III* ("Lectures on the History of Philosophy III"), p. 303
62. Ibid., vol. 1, p. 45
63. "Letters," vol. 1, p. 113
64. Ibid., vol. 1, p. 161
65. Ibid., vol. 1, p. 161
66. "Hegel's Works," vol. 2, "Phenomenology," p. 44 et seq.
67. Ibid., vol. 2, p. 45
68. Ibid., vol. 2, p. 39
69. Ibid., vol. 2, p. 48 et seq.
70. Ibid., vol. 2, p. 14
71. Ibid., vol. 2, p. 14
72. Ibid., vol. 2, p. 24
73. Ibid., vol. 2, p. 25
74. Ibid., vol. 2, p. 35
75. Ibid., vol. 2, p. 34
76. Ibid., vol. 2, p. 30 et seq.
77. Ibid., vol. 2, p. 419
78. Ibid., vol. 2, p. 172
79. R. Haym, "Hegel and His Period," p. 238
80. Ibid., p. 239
81. "Hegel's Works," vol. 2, p. 377
82. Ibid., vol. 2, p. 374
83. Ibid., vol. 2, p. 400
84. Ibid., vol. 2, p. 404
85. Ibid., vol. 2, p. 451 et seq.
86. Ibid., vol. 2, p. 453 et seq.
87. Friedrich Engels and Karl Marx, *Die heilige Familie, oder Kritik der kritischen Kritik* ("The Holy Family, or Critique of Critical Critique"), 1845. Reprinted in: *Aus dem literarischen Nachlass von Karl Marx und Friedrich Engels* ("From the Literary Remains of Karl Marx and Friedrich Engels"), three volumes, edited by F. Mehring, fourth edition. The passage quoted is found in vol. 2, p. 132.
88. "Hegel's Works," vol. 2, p. 399
89. Friedrich Julius Stahl, *Was Ist die Revolution?* ("What Is Revolution?"), 1852, and *Die gegenwärtigen Parteien im Stat und Kirche* ("Contemporary Parties in Church and State"), lectures from the year 1850, published in 1863
90. "Letters," vol. 1, p. 161
91. Ibid., vol. 1, p. 136
92. Ibid., vol. 1, p. 193
93. Ibid., vol. 1, p. 223
94. Ibid., vol. 1, p. 240
95. Ibid., vol. 1, p. 187
96. Ibid., vol. 1, p. 138

97. Ibid., vol. 2, p. 28 et seq.
98. Jakob Burckhardt, *Weltgeschichtliche Betrachtungen* ("Views on World History"), in the complete edition of collected works by Oeri and Dürr, vol. 7, 1929, p. 2
99. "Letters," vol. 2, p. 85 et seq.
100. Ibid., vol. 1, p. 253 et seq.
101. Ibid., vol. 1, p. 331
102. R. Haym, "Hegel and His Period," p. 505 et seq.
103. "Letters," vol. 1, p. 390
104. Ibid., vol. 1, p. 418 et seq.
105. "Hegel's Works," vol. 3, *Philosophische Propädeutik* ("Philosophical Propaedeutic"), p. 82. It is interesting that Hegel should develop an almost modern conception of "drive" on pp. 39/40. His distinction between man and animal, which he later repeated and elaborated above all in Section 190 of "Philosophy of Right," rests on this definition of drive.
106. "Hegel's Works," vol. 3, p. 111 et seq.
107. Ibid., vol. 3, p. 142
108. "Letters," vol. 1, p. 393
109. Ibid., vol. 1, p. 196
110. "Hegel's Works," vol. 4, "Logic," p. 51
111. Ibid., vol. 4, p. 50
112. Ibid., vol. 4, p. 48
113. I. Kant, *Kritik der reinen Vernunft* ("Critique of Pure Reason"), preface to second edition, B VIII et seq.
114. "Hegel's Works," vol. 4, p. 87 et seq.
115. Ibid., vol. 2, p. 12
116. Ibid., vol. 4, p. 51 et seq.
117. Ibid., vol. 4, p. 46
118. Ibid., vol. 4, p. 52
119. Ibid., vol. 2, p. 38 et seq.
120. Ibid., vol. 4, p. 45
121. Ibid., vol. 4, p. 51
122. "Letters," vol. 1, p. 392
123. Ibid., vol. 2, p. 107
124. Ibid., vol. 2, p. 73
125. Ibid., vol. 2, note to letter 290, p. 408
126. Ibid., vol. 2, p. 167
127. "Hegel's Works," vol. 6, *Heidelberger Encyklopädie* ("Heidelberg Encyclopedia"), first edition, 1871, p. 4 et seq.
128. G. F. W. Hegel, *Encyklopädie der philosophischen Wissenschaften im Grundriss* ("Encyclopedia of the Philosophical Sciences in Outline Form"), reedited by Lasson, second edition, Leipzig, 1920, p. 7. The Lasson edition is based on the second, 1827 edition, not on the first, 1817 edition. All quotations from this version have a different form in the first edition.

129. Ibid., Lasson edition, p. 13
130. Ibid., p. 15
131. Ibid., p. 43
132. Ibid., p. 105
133. Editors Henning, Michelet and Boumann followed the idea that the "Encyclopedia" represented Hegel's real system when, in the first edition of Hegel's works (1832–1887), on the basis of literary remains and by the addition of various lectures by Hegel, they expanded it into an Hegelian "System of Philosophy" in three volumes: Part 1, "Logic"; Part 2, "Natural Philosophy"; and Part 3, "Philosophy of Spirit." (In the Glockner facsimile edition, vol. 8–10.)
134. "Hegel's Works," vol. 9, "Philosophy of Nature," p. 49. This passage is found only in the version of Hegel's "Philosophy of Nature" edited by Michelet, which was compiled from various transcripts of Hegel's lectures made by colleagues. Even though there is no doubt that Hegel did actually say this, or something like it, nonetheless it is worth noting that in the three editions of the "Encyclopedia" which Hegel himself attended to, nothing exactly corresponding can be found. To be sure, there, too, the problem is constantly coming up that Nature as the "Idea in the form of otherness" (*Anderssein*, lit., "other being") is the "negative of itself or itself *externalized*." ("Heidelberg Encyclopedia," § 192, as in § 247 of the second edition.) In the Jena natural philosophy ("Jena Logic, Metaphysics and Natural Philosophy," edited by Lasson, p. 195) already we find the following: "This idea of Nature, in its general determinateness, is opposed to the Spirit as the otherness of the same; but it is implicitly the reflection in itself of the transition of otherness into Spirit. Its relation to Spirit, or that it is the other of Spirit, is inherent in itself. Only in its first moment is it pure Nature and in itself opposed to this or to the process of becoming otherness, and its other moment is immediately the positive beginning of this, its change." The notion that Nature is the "other" and the "otherness" of the Idea persisted with Hegel. Occasionally it reached a point where it became the notion that Nature is the self-estranged Idea. And on one occasion ("Hegel's Works," vol. 9, "Philosophy of Nature," p. 50) we are told right out: "Nature is self-estranged Spirit, which in Nature only *runs wild*, a bacchantic god who does not curb himself or keep himself in hand; in Nature the unity of the concept lies hidden."
135. "Hegel's Works," vol. 9, p. 48
136. "Letters," vol. 2, p. 169
137. Cf. in "Letters," vol. 3, p. 202 and especially the note to this letter on p. 422
138. "Hegel's Works," vol. 16, *Vorlesungen über die Philosophie*

*der Religion* ("Lectures on the Philosophy of Religion"), vol. 1, p. 281

139. Ibid., vol. 16, p. 307
140. "Letters," vol. 2, p. 218
141. Ibid., vol. 2, p. 182
142. Ibid., vol. 2, p. 154
143. Heinrich Gustav Hotho, *Vorstudien für Leben und Kunst* ("Preliminary Studies for Life and Art"), 1835, p. 383 et seq., quoted after H. Glockner, "Hegel," vol. 1, p. 441 et seq.
144. K. Rosenkranz, *Von Magdeburg bis Königsberg* ("From Magdeburg to Königsberg"), 1873, p. 300
145. Cf. "Letters," vol. 3, p. 211 et seq. and especially the note to the letter by Hegel on p. 424 et seq.
146. "Letters," vol. 1, p. 374
147. Ibid., vol. 1, p. 314
148. R. Haym, "Hegel and His Period," p. 364
149. "Hegel's Works," vol. 2, "Lectures on the Philosophy of History", p. 568
150. "Letters," vol. 2, p. 367
151. "Hegel's Works," vol. 2, p. 19
152. Ibid., vol. 2, p. 45 et seq.
153. Ibid., vol. 2, p. 61
154. Ibid., vol. 2, p. 111
155. Ibid., vol. 2, p. 129
156. Ibid., vol. 2, p. 561
157. Ibid., vol. 2, p. 562
158. Ibid., vol. 2, p. 566
159. Ibid., vol. 2, p. 564
160. Ibid., vol. 2, p. 562 et seq.
161. In Karl Marx, *Der historische Materialismus, Die Frühschriften* ("Historical Materialism, The Early Writings"), edited by S. Landshut and J. P. Mayer, two volumes, 1932, vol. 1, pp. 20–187
162. "Hegel's Works," vol. 8, p. 31 et seq.
163. "Letters," vol. 2, p. 242
164. "Hegel's Works," vol. 7, *Grundlinien der Philosophie des Rechts, oder Naturrecht und Staatswissenschaft in Grundrisse* ("Basics of the Philosophy of Right, or Natural Law and Political Science in Outline"), p. 26 et seq.
165. Ibid., vol. 7, p. 32 et seq.
166. Ibid., vol. 7, p. 35
167. Ibid., vol. 7, p. 36 et seq.
168. Ibid., vol. 7, p. 84
169. Ibid., vol. 7, p. 50
170. Ibid., vol. 7, § § 4–28
171. Ibid., vol. 7, § § 22–24
172. Ibid., vol. 7, p. 54 et seq.

173. Ibid., vol. 7, p. 56
174. Ibid., vol. 7, p. 63
175. Ibid., vol. 7, p. 71
176. Ibid., vol. 7, p. 74
177. Ibid., vol. 7, pp. 63, 272
178. Ibid., vol. 7, p. 237 et seq.
179. Ibid., vol. 7, p. 238
180. Ibid., vol. 7, p. 247
181. Ibid., vol. 7, p. 261
182. Karl Marx, *Zur Kritik der Politischen Ökonomie* ("Contribution to a Critique of Political Economy"), edited by K. Kautsky, 11th edition, 1930, p. LIV
183. "Hegel's Works," vol. 7, p. 263 et seq. (§ 183)
184. Ibid., vol. 7, p. 265 et seq. (§ 185)
185. Ibid., vol. 7, p. 263
186. Ibid., vol. 7, p. 266
187. Ibid., vol. 7, p. 273
188. Ibid., vol. 7, p. 275 (§ 194)
189. Ibid., vol. 7, p. 273 (§ § 190 and 191)
190. Karl Marx, in the posthumous ms. *Nationalökonomie und Philosophie* ("Political Economy and Philosophy"), quoted after the Landshut/Mayer edition in *Der historische Materialismus* ("Historical Materialism"), vol. 1, p. 314
191. "Hegel's Works," vol. 7, pp. 315, 314 (§ 238)
192. Ibid., vol. 7, p. 318
193. Ibid., vol. 7, p. 318 (§ 243/244)
194. Ibid., vol. 7, p. 319 et seq. (§ § 245–247)
195. S. Kierkegaard, "The Journals," vol. 1, p. 62
196. S. Kierkegaard, "Concluding Unscientific Postscript," Part 1, translated into the German by H. M. Junghans, 1957, p. 99

## PART II. Kierkegaard's Existential Dialectic

1. Quoted from L. Noack's *Philosophie-geschichtliches Lexikon* ("Dictionary of the History of Philosophy"), Leipzig, 1879, p. 782
2. A. Schopenhauer, *Fragmente zur Geschichte der Philosophie* ("Fragments Contributing to the History of Philosophy"), in *Parerga und Paralipomena* ("Parerga and Paralipomena"). Taken from Schopenhauer's collected works, edited by Hübscher, vol. 5, 1946, p. 102
3. A. Schopenhauer, *Anhang zur Skizze einer Geschichte der Lehre vom Idealen zum Realen* ("Supplement to a Sketch of a History of the Ideal to the Real"), "Parerga and Paralipomena." From Schopenhauer's collected works, vol. 5, p. 31. Cf. Schopenhauer's essay *Über der Universitätsphilosophie* ("On University Philosophy"), "Parerga and Paralipomena."

4. L. Gumplowicz, *Der Rassenkampf* ("The Race Conflict"), Innsbruck, 1883, p. 10 et seq.

5. I. Kant, *Beantwortung der Frage: Was Ist Aufklärung?* ("Reply to the Question: What Is Enlightenment?"), 1784, in I. Kant's "Works," edited by Cassirer, vol. 4, 1913, p. 169

6. Gottsched, *Drei kleine Reden zur Verteidigung Gottes und der Vernunft im 1730. Jahre der vertrauten Rednergesellschaft gehalten von Gottsched* ("Three Little Talks on the Defense of God and Reason in 1730. Annals of the Confidential Speakers Society, Given by Gottsched"). Appearing in Gottsched's translation of Pierre Bayle's "Dictionary," vol. 4, p. 271 et seq.

7. I. Kant, *Die Religion innerhalb der Grenzen der blossen Vernunft* ("Religion within the Limits of Bare Reason"), I. Kant's "Works," vol. 6, p. 245

8. I. Kant, *Anthropologie* ("Anthropology"), in Kant's collected works, vol. 8, p. 218 et seq.

9. I. Kant's collected works, vol. 6, p. 393

10. Jakob Burckhardt, Complete Edition, vol. 7, edited by Oeri and Dürr, p. 2

11. J. Burckhardt, *Briefe* ("Letters"), edited by Kaphahn, 1935, p. 57

12. Ibid., p. 148

13. Ibid., p. 185

14. Ibid., p. 442

15. Ibid., p. 448

16. S. Kierkegaard, "The Journals," selected and edited by Th. Haecker, in German translation, vol. 1, p. 58

17. Ibid. vol. 1, p. 284

18. Ibid. vol. 2, p. 367

19. Ibid., vol. 2, p. 357

20. J. Burckhardt, "Letters," edited by Kaphahn, p. 61

21. S. Kierkegaard, "Journals," vol. 1, p. 402

22. Ibid., vol. 2, p. 387

23. Ibid., vol. 1, p. 30

24. Ibid., vol. 1, p. 28

25. Ibid., vol. 1, p. 154

26. Ibid., vol. 2, p. 143

27. S. Kierkegaard, "Concluding Unscientific Postscript," Part 1, translated into the German by H. M. Junghans, 1957, p. 3

28. S. Kierkegaard, "The Journals," vol. 1, p. 83

29. Ibid., vol. 2, p. 115

30. Ibid., vol. 2, p. 33

31. Ibid., vol. 2, p. 73 et seq.

32. Ibid., vol. 2, p. 75

33. Ibid., vol. 1, p. 355 et seq.

34. Cf. A. Dorner and Chr. Schrempf, *Søren Kierkegaards Angriff auf die Christenheit* ("Søren Kierkegaard's Attack on Chris-

tianity"), (*Agitatorische Schriften und Aufsätze 1851–1855*, or Propagandistic Writings and Articles 1851–1855), Stuttgart, 1896, p. 91 et seq.

35. S. Kierkegaard, "The Journals," vol. 2, p. 400 et seq.
36. Dorner-Schrempf, "Søren Kierkegaard's Attack on Christianity," p. 362 et seq.
37. S. Kierkegaard, "The Journals," vol. 2, p. 415
38. Ibid., vol. 1, p. 84
39. Ibid., vol. 1, p. 74
40. Ibid., vol. 1, p. 338
41. Ibid., vol. 1, p. 139
42. Translated into German by Wilhelm Kütemeyer, *Der Begriff der Ironie mit ständiger Rücksicht auf Sokrates* ("The Concept of Irony, With Constant Reference to Socrates"), München, 1929
43. S. Kierkegaard, "The Concept of Irony," p. 225
44. S. Kierkegaard, "The Journals," vol. 1, p. 324
45. S. Kierkegaard, "The Concept of Irony," p. 205
46. Ibid., p. 334 et seq.
47. S. Kierkegaard, "The Journals," vol. 1, p. 99
48. S. Kierkegaard, "The Concept of Irony," p. 339
49. Ibid., p. 338
50. Ibid., p. 183
51. Ibid., p. 269. The sentence "Behold, the feet of them which have buried thy husband are at the door, and shall carry thee out" was also often quoted by Hegel. It comes from Acts 5:9. (Tr.: The equivalent from the King James Bible has been used here. The rendering in German is somewhat different: "Behold, the feet of them who shall carry thee away are at the door.")
52. S. Kierkegaard, "The Concept of Irony," p. 266
53. Ibid., p. 267 et seq.
54. S. Kierkegaard, "The Journals," vol. 1, p. 158
55. Ibid., vol. 2, p. 100
56. S. Kierkegaard, *Entweder/Oder* ("Either/Or"), translated into German by Chr. Schrempf, vol. 1, 1922, p. 17. In an earlier translation by O. Gleiss of "Either/Or, A Fragment of Life," second edition (no year given), the passage is more literally rendered. In English it goes, more or less: "What is a poet? An unhappy man who in his heart harbors a deep anguish, but whose lips are so fashioned that the moans and cries which pass over them are transformed into ravishing music. His fate is like that of the unfortunate victims whom the tyrant Phalaris imprisoned in his brazen bull and slowly tortured over a steady fire; their cries could not reach the tyrant's ears so as to strike terror into his heart; when they reached his ears they sounded like sweet music. And men crowd about the poet and say to

him, 'Sing for us soon again'—which is as much as to say, 'May new sufferings torment your soul, but may your lips be fashioned as before; for the cries would only distress us, but the music, the music, is delightful.' and the critics come forward and say, 'That is perfectly done—just as it should be according to the rules of esthetics.' Now it is understood that a critic resembles a poet to a hair; he only lacks the anguish in his heart and the music upon his lips. I tell you, I would rather be a swineherd, understood by the swine, than a poet misunderstood by men."

57. Dorner-Schrempf, "Søren Kierkegaard's Attack on Christianity," p. 390.
58. Ibid., p. 4 et seq.
59. S. Kierkegaard, "A First and Last Explanation," 1846, from the Dorner-Schrempf translation of "Attack on Christianity," p. 372 et seq. Cf. the translation in the German by M. Junghans in "Postscript," vol. 2, 1958, p. 339 et seq.
60. Martin Thust, *Die Marionettentheater Soren Kierkegaards* ("Søren Kierkegaard's Marionette Theatre"), in *Zeitwende*, 1925, p. 18 et seq.
61. S. Kierkegaard, "The Journals," vol. 2, p. 398 et seq.
62. Ibid., vol. 1, p. 51
63. S. Kierkegaard, "Postscript," translated into German by Martin Junghans, vol. 1, 1957, p. 111
64. S. Kierkegaard, "Either/Or," vol. 1, translated into German by W. Pfleiderer and Chr. Schrempf, p. 6
65. Ibid., vol. 1, p. 18
66. Ibid., vol. 1, p. 24
67. Ibid., vol. 1, p. 29
68. Ibid., vol. 1, p. 27
69. Ibid., vol. 1, p. 17
70. Ibid., vol. 1, p. 30
71. Ibid., vol. 1, p. 34
72. Ibid., vol. 1, p. 21
73. Ibid., vol. 1, p. 23
74. Ibid., vol. 1, p. 34 et seq.
75. Ibid., vol. 1, p. 255 et seq.
76. Ibid., vol. 1, p. 396
77. Ibid., vol. 2, (Part 2, "B's Papers"). From the German translation by W. Pfleiderer and Chr. Schrempf, 1922, p. 131 et seq.
78. Ibid., vol. 2, p. 174
79. Ibid., vol. 2, p. 159. This passage does not begin with the statement that melancholy is "sin," but first says: "What, then, is melancholy? Nothing else but hysteria of the spirit."
80. Ibid., vol. 2, p. 191 et seq.
81. Ibid., vol. 2, p. 221

82. Ibid., vol. 2, p. 228 et seq.
83. S. Kierkegaard, "The Journals," vol. 1, p. 172
84. From the afterword to the German translation of "Fear and Trembling," by Ketels, Gottsched, and Schrempf, third edition, 1923, p. 126
85. S. Kierkegaard, "Fear and Trembling; The Repetition," translated into German by Ketels, Gottsched, and Schrempf, third edition, 1923, p. 126
86. Ibid., p. 50
87. S. Kierkegaard, "The Journals," vol. 2, p. 89
88. S. Kierkegaard, "Repetition," translated into German by Ketels, Gottsched, and Schrempf, third edition, 1923, p. 126
89. Ibid., p. 200
90. Ibid., p. 206
91. Ibid., p. 183
92. Ibid., p. 188
93. Cf. this passage in "The Journals," vol. 1, p. 131: "All of existence frightens me, from the smallest fly to the mysteries of incarnation; everything is inexplicable to me, mostly I myself; all of existence is polluted for me, most of all I myself . . ."
94. S. Kierkegaard, "The Journals," vol. 1, p. 394 et seq.
95. S. Kierkegaard, "The Concept of Irony," translated into German by Chr. Schrempf, 1912, p. 1 et seq.
96. Ibid., p. 9
97. Ibid., p. 36
98. Ibid., p. 38
99. Ibid., p. 156
100. Ibid., p. 38
101. S. Kierkegaard, "Stages on Life's Way," or as sometimes rendered, "Stages on the Road of Life," subtitled "Studies of Different Kinds, Collected, Brought to Press and Edited by Hilarius Buchbinder." Translated into German by Chr. Schrempf and W. Pfleiderer, 1922, p. 173
102. Ibid., p. 175
103. Ibid., p. 363
104. Ibid., p. 457 et seq.
105. S. Kierkegaard, "The Journals," vol. 1, p. 223 et seq.
106. Ibid., vol. 2, p. 91
107. S. Kierkegaard, "Philosophical Fragments, or A Fragment of Philosophy, by Johannes Climacus," published by S. K., translated into German by Emanuel Hirsch, 1952.
108. S. Kierkegaard, "Concluding Unscientific Postscript to the Philosophical Fragments," Parts 1 and 2, translated into German by H. M. Junghans, 1957/58
109. Ibid., vol. 1, p. 99 et seq.
110. Ibid., vol. 1, p. 1
111. S. Kierkegaard, "Philosophical Fragments," p. 7

112. Ibid., p. 37
113. Ibid., p. 62
114. S. Kierkegaard, "Postscript," vol. 1, p. 27
115. Ibid., vol. 1, p. 47
116. Ibid., vol. 1, p. 48
117. Ibid., vol. 1, p. 98 et seq.
118. Ibid., vol. 1, p. 156
119. Ibid., vol. 1, p. 176 et seq.
120. Ibid., vol. 1, p. 194
121. Ibid., vol. 2, p. 9
122. Ibid., vol. 2, p. 31
123. Ibid., vol. 2, p. 54
124. Ibid., vol. 2, p. 35
125. Ibid., vol. 2, p. 281
126. Ibid., vol. 2, p. 331
127. Dorner-Schrempf, "Attack on Christianity," p. 4 (footnote)
128. S. Kierkegaard, "The Journals," vol. 2, p. 71
129. S. Kierkegaard, "The Sickness unto Death: A Christian Psychological Exposition for Edification and Awakening." Translated into German by Ingeborg Frieser, 1949, p. 16
130. S. Kierkegaard, "The Journals," vol. 2, p. 339
131. Ibid., vol. 2, p. 366
132. Ibid., vol. 2, p. 379
133. S. Kierkegaard, "Postscript," vol. 1, p. 245

## PART III. The Materialistic Dialectic of Karl Marx and His Historical Materialism

1. This son of Marx's, nicknamed "Musch," fell sick in March 1855, and died in April. Marx wrote at this time: "I am tired as a dog from the long night watches, since I am Musch's nurse." Three days later he wrote: "My own heart is bleeding and my head is burning, though naturally I have to put up a brave front. During his illness the child did not for a moment behave contrary to his original, goodnatured, and at the same time self-reliant character." About a week later he reported the child's death to Engels, and on April 12 wrote him as follows: "The house naturally is quite desolated and destitute since the death of the dear child who made it come to life. It is indescribable how we miss the boy at every turn. I have lived through all kinds of adversity, but not until now did I know what unhappiness really is . . . " Cf. *Briefwechsel zwischen Friedrich Engels und Karl Marx, 1841–1850* ("Correspondence between Friedrich Engels and Karl Marx, 1841–1850"), edited by A. Bebel and Ed. Bernstein, vol. 2, 1926, p. 71 et seq.
2. From Franz Mehring's *Aus dem literarischen Nachlass von Karl Marx und Friedrich Engels, 1841/1850* ("From the

Literary Remains of Karl Marx and Friedrich Engels, 1841/
1850"). Three volumes, fourth edition, 1923, vol. 1, p. 4.
Further references in Auguste Cornu's "Karl Marx and Friedrich Engels: Life and Work," vol. 1, 1818–1844, East Berlin,
1954. Quoted from Heinrich Heine, "Works," two volumes,
1962, edited by Martin Greiner, vol. 2, p. 921.

3. Letter from the father, Heinrich Marx, to his son, Karl, in
   December, 1836. Quote from "Literary Remains," vol. 1, p. 14.

4. Letter from Heinrich Marx to Karl Marx, March, 1857. From
   "Literary Remains," vol. 1, p. 14

5. During this period the father once asked his son: "Is dueling,
   then, so very much interwoven with philosophy?" From
   "Literary Remains," vol. 1, p. 7.

6. Letter from Karl Marx to his father, November, 1837. Published in the *Neuen Zeit*, vol. 6, no. 1, p. 6 et seq.

7. Letter from Bruno Bauer to Karl Marx, dated March 31, 1841.
   From "Literary Remains," vol. 1, p. 32 et seq. Also cf. p. 59
   et seq.

8. No. 77 of the *Rheinische Zeitung*, March 18, 1843. From
   "Literary Remains," vol. 1, p. 207.

9. The endlessly desperate financial straits in which Marx and
   his family lived for many years, a situation in which Marx
   lived through sickness, the death of his children, unremitting
   daily want, and tormenting anxieties about eking out enough
   money to keep body and soul together, become devastatingly
   clear in the correspondence between Engels and Marx. These
   letters express the misery of it better than all descriptions and
   reports. A short abstract from the letters may show what we
   mean.

   Thus, for instance, on April 24, 1852, Marx wrote to Engels:
   "During the past week I've been through a hideous business
   you can't possibly imagine. On the day of the funeral (Marx's
   daughter Franziska had died) none of the money promised
   from all sides showed up, so that finally I was forced to run
   to some of my French neighbors to pay for the burial expenses." Then, on July 13, it went like this: "My wife is in bad
   shape, getting thin and has a cough." Seven weeks later, in a
   letter to Engels: "My wife is sick, little Jenny is sick, Lenchen
   has a sort of nerve fever. I was not able, nor am I yet, to call
   the doctor because I have no money for medicine. For eight
   or ten days I've been feeding the family on bread and potatoes,
   which it is doubtful I can raise today. This diet naturally is
   not helpful under the present climatic conditions . . ."

   Again and again Engels sent money, sometimes five, sometimes two, then again ten pounds, as much as he had to spare.
   Almost regularly Marx's letters to Engels begin with words of
   thanks for sums received. But since these contributions were

only a drop in the bucket, the need continued. On March 10, 1853, Marx wrote: "The five pounds received. This week I came within a hair of dropping out. An inflammation of the lungs, that is, or at any rate something close to it. It's hereditary in my family. My older boy died of it." About five weeks later Mrs. Marx wrote to Engels: "It's horribly embarrassing for me to have to write you about money matters. You've already helped us only too often. But this time I am at my wit's end, I don't see any way out. . . . Could you send us something? The baker has given notice he's shutting off the bread on Friday . . . "

This misery had no end. It reached another climax in 1857. On January 20 of that year Marx wrote: "I've completely run aground, therefore, in a tenement where I've stuck my few bare essentials, and where it is impossible to grind it out from day to day, as in Dean Street, with no prospects and growing family expenses. I don't have the least idea what I ought to do, and indeed am in the same desperate situation as I was four years ago. I thought I had been through the worst. *Mais non.* Worst part of it is, this isn't a temporary crisis. I don't see how I'm ever going to work my way out of it."

The cool and almost cheeky (*schnoddrig*) tone of the letters shows that sentimental lamentations did not lie in Marx's nature, that it was real need which drove him to acknowledge his plight. Again on March 24, 1857, we are told: "I'm very sorry to have to put the squeeze on you for the time being, since the reverses into which I've fallen have reduced me to a point where everything pawnable has been pawned. You will understand that even the most equable people—and I do, indeed, have a lot of calm in this rotten business—will lose their patience from time to time and turn against their friends especially."

Repeatedly, then, he had to beg for money. Engels was constantly helping him with small remittances—more than which he could not give, since his father as it was thought he was spending too much money. Marx was constantly in hot water up to his neck. Every now and then he would come apart: "Indeed, if this situation continues I'd rather lie a hundred fathoms under the ground than keep on vegetating this way. Always to be a burden on others and along with it to be plagued with the most trivial kind of crap, in the long run is intolerable. I, personally, work off misery through my strong preoccupation with universal matters. My wife, naturally, has not got the same resources," etc. (January 28, 1858).

And again the situation became critical. In a letter dated July 15, 1858, Marx wrote: "I beseech you, first of all, not to be dismayed by the content of this letter, since it is absolutely not an appeal to your already excessively abused cash box. On the other hand we must mutually consider whether some sort of way can be found out of this situation, for it is absolutely no longer bearable." He goes on to say that he is wasting time "running around making useless attempts to raise money." He comments on his "rundown physical condition" and the "domestic woe" caused by the fact that his wife's "nerves are shattered by all this crap." She should be sent on a trip to get her health back, but this would do no good, even if it were possible, "as long as she is harassed by the daily pressure and the ghost of an unavoidable final catastrophe."

This situation—more accurately, this hell—lasted for more than a decade. In January 1857 Marx wrote that he was "completely on his uppers" and in March 1867: "First of all I must get back my clothes and watch that are in the pawnshop. I can also hardly leave my family in the present situation, *sans sou* and with the creditors growing more shameless every day." Sometimes bill collectors laid siege to the house so that Marx repeatedly spoke of a "storm of creditors." "For two months now I have been living on nothing but the pawnshop and there with daily dunning demands, ever more unbearable, heaped on me." (Letter of July 31, 1865.) It seems inconceivable that pressure like this could have been endured for so long, though it was. Even earlier, on July 18, 1862, Marx had written: "My wife tells me every day that she wishes she were lying with the children in the grave, and I can't really blame her, for the humiliations, torments and fears that have to be borne in this situation are in fact indescribable." If Marx's letters contain endless complaints about poverty, sickness, and misery, still these laments are extremely brief and constitute the smallest part of the whole letter. The principal content of this correspondence is given over to discussions of political events, to happenings in general and the common goal, and to the work on "Capital," still laboriously in progress amid all the worries. In all of world history no piece of writing was ever more desperately wrought in sheer defiance of fate and with endless tenacity and sacrifice than was "Capital." That it should have progressed at all and to some extent been completed was nothing short of a miracle.

10. Letter from the father, Heinrich Marx, to Karl Marx in March, 1837. From "Literary Remains," vol. 1, p. 14
11. "Literary Remains," vol. 1, p. 26
12. Ibid., vol. 1, p. 16, letter to the father dated November 10, 1837
13. Letter to father, November 10, 1837
14. Letter from Arnold Ruge to Ludwig Feuerbach on May 15, 1844. From "Literary Remains," vol. 2, p. 14

15. Letter from Friedrich Köppen to Karl Marx on June 3, 1841. From "Literary Remains," vol. 1, p. 33.
16. From H. Böll's *Karl Marx: Ein deutscher Jude verändert die Welt* ("Karl Marx: A German Jew Changes the World"), in *Porträts deutsch-jüdischer Geistesgeschichte* ("Portraits from German-Jewish Intellectual History"), edited by Thilo Koch, 1961, p. 63. Marx himself had a different opinion of H. H. Hyndman, founder of the Social-Democratic Federation, and soon broke with him. Of Hyndman he wrote: "Hyndman's political mission is of a problematical nature. The man deserved to be bored by your little letter, all the more since his impudence toward me assumes that I cannot compromise him on propagandistic grounds." (Letter to Engels, March 8, 1882.)
17. Letter from Moses Hess to Bertold Auerbach. Quoted in Erich Thier's introduction to his edition of Marx's youthful work "Political Economy and Philosophy," 1950, p. 58 et seq. The friendship between Engels, Hess, and Marx did not last long. On January 15, 1847, Engels wrote to Marx: "It was very nice of you to let me know about Moses. The fine fellow came to call on me, didn't find me in, and I wrote to him that he should arrange an appointment. Which took place yesterday. The man has changed a lot. Youthful locks well about his head, a pretty little beard gives his sharp chin some grace, a girlish red stains his cheeks, *la grandeur déchue se peignait dans ses beaux yeux* ("Lost grandeur (lit.) 'combs its hair' in his lovely eyes") and a strange modesty has come over him. Here in Paris I've got accustomed to a very shameless tone, for putting on the dog is part of the game and with it one makes out with many a bird. But this ravishing exterior on the one-time world-shattering high flyer Hess just about got me down. However, the heroic deeds of the true socialists, of his young people (Whereof below) and his own unchanged essential self gave me courage again. Enough. I treated him so coldly and contemptuously that he will have no desire ever to come again."
18. The Russian sociologist Maxim Kowalewsky, whose name gets occasional friendly mention in the letters of 1876–1879. Quoted from Isaiah Berlin's *Karl Marx, Sein Leben und Sein Werk* ("Karl Marx, His Life and Work"). Translated from the English by I. Fetscher, 1959, p. 293.
19. This description was translated and printed in the *Neuen Zeit*, first year, Stuttgart, 1883. It was reprinted in Karl Marx's "Historical Materialism. The Early Writings," edited by S. Landshut and J. P. Mayer, vol. 2, p. 532 et seq.
20. Letter of November 10, 1837
21. From "Literary Remains," edited by Mehring, fourth edition, 1923, vol. 1, p. 113

22. Ibid., vol. 1, p. 117
23. Ibid., vol. 1, p. 116
24. Ibid., vol. 1, p. 114 et seq.
25. Ibid., vol. 2, p. 14 (Letter from Arnold Ruge to Ludwig Feuerbach, May 15, 1844).
26. Isaiah Berlin, "Karl Marx," p. 85
27. Reprint of some of Karl Marx's articles in the *Rheinische Zeitung* in "Literary Remains," vol. 1, p. 259
28. Cf. Landshut/Mayer, *Die Frühschriften* ("The Early Writings"), p. XIX et seq.
29. Besides the version of this manuscript in "Early Writings" edited by Landshut/Mayer, there is a better one in the historico-critical edition of Marx's collected works, *Marx-Engels-Gesamtausgabe* ("Marx-Engels: Complete Edition"), Frankfurt-Berlin-Moscow, first section, vol. 3. Another version is found in Erich Thier's *Karl Marx, National Ökonomie und Philosophie* ("Karl Marx, Political Economy and Philosophy"). Cf. arrangement of the text and critique in this edition, p. 6 et seq.
30. Landshut/Mayer, "The Early Writings," vol. 1, p. 273
31. Karl Marx-Friedrich Engels, *Die deutsche Ideologie* ("The German Ideology"), edited on behalf of the Marx-Engels Institute by V. Adoratskij, 1932, p. 534 ("Theses on Feuerbach").
32. Landshut/Mayer, "Early Writings," vol. 1, p. 271
33. Ibid., vol. 1, p. 270
34. Ibid., vol. 1, p. 272
35. Ibid., vol. 1, p. 278 et seq.
36. From Friedrich Engels-Karl Marx's *Die heilige Familie, oder Kritik der kritischen Kritik* ("The Holy Family, or Critique of Critical Critique"). Subtitled *Gegen Bruno Bauer und Konsorten* ("Against Bruno Bauer and Consorts"), in "Literary Remains," vol. 2, p. 132
37. Landshut/Mayer, "Early Writings," vol. 1, p. 260 et seq.
38. Ibid., vol. 1, p. 262
39. Karl Marx, "Political Economy and Philosophy," from the Thier edition, p. 228 et seq.
40. Thomas More's "Utopia," translated into the German by Gerhard Ritter, 1922, p. 38
41. Karl Marx, "Political Economy and Philosophy," p. 131
42. Ibid., p. 217
43. Ibid., p. 242 et seq.
44. Ibid., p. 182
45. Ibid., p. 187
46. Ibid., p. 188
47. Ibid., p. 199
48. Ibid., p. 181
49. Ibid., p. 213

50. Ibid., p. 199 et seq.
51. Ibid., p. 193
52. Ibid., p. 210
53. Ibid., p. 245
54. Ibid., p. 193 et seq.
55. Ibid., p. 183 et seq.
56. Ibid., p. 180
57. Ibid., p. 211
58. Ibid., p. 224
59. Ibid., p. 224
60. Ibid., p. 240. However, philosophy shares this fate with other intellectual disciplines: "It is rooted in the nature of estrangement that each sphere should impose another and opposed standard on me; in one case as to morality, again as to political economy . . . " p. 206.
61. Ibid., p. 263 et seq.
62. Friedrich Engels-Karl Marx, "The German Ideology," edited by Adoratskij, p. 15 et seq.
63. Cf. introduction to "The German Ideology" by Adoratskij, p. XI. The passage quoted is found in the preface to Marx's "Contribution to a Critique of Political Economy," Karl Kautsky edition (the 11th), 1930, p. LVI et seq.
64. Cf. "Literary Remains, 1841–1850," edited by F. Mehring, fourth edition, 1923, vol. 2, p. 346
65. Friedrich Engels, *Ludwig Feuerbach und der Ausgang der klassischen deutschen Philosophie* ("Ludwig Feuerbach and the Close of Classical German Philosophy"), edited by H. Duncker, 1927, p. 14
66. Engels-Marx, "The German Ideology," Adoratskij edition, p. 24
67. Ibid., p. 59
68. Cf. Karl Mannheim, *Ideologie und Utopie* ("Ideology and Utopia"), 1929, especially p. 25 et seq. Also, Hans Barth, *Wahrheit und Ideologie* ("Truth and Ideology"), 1945, especially the first section on Destutt de Tracy.
69. Engels-Marx, "The German Ideology," Adoratskij edition, p. 16 et seq.
70. Ibid., p. 20
71. Karl Marx, "Contribution to a Critique of Political Economy," Kautsky edition, 1930, p. LV
72. Engels-Marx, "The German Ideology," Adoratskij edition, p. 20 et seq.
73. Ibid., p. 27
74. Ibid., p. 16 et seq.
75. Ibid., p. 21
76. Ibid., p. 92 et seq.
77. Ibid., p. 18. For Marx "the first prerequisite of all human

existence" and also of history was that people should keep alive, that is, have "food and drink, shelter, clothing and other things as well." History actually begins only "when the first satisfied need itself, the act of satisfying and the newly gained instrument of satisfaction leads to new needs." (p. 18). Here lies the primordial dialectic and the root source of history. The satisfaction of need creates new needs. This idea is similar to the one developed by Hegel in "Philosophy of Right" on the difference between animal and human needs. (Hegel, "Philosophy of Right," §§ 190 and 191.)

78. Engels-Marx, "The German Ideology," Adoratskij edition, p. 63. Cf. a passage of like tenor in "Contribution to a Critique of Political Economy," Kautsky edition, p. LV. "At a certain level of its development labor's material forces of production come into conflict with the existing conditions of production . . . ", etc.

79. Engels-Marx, "The German Ideology," Adoratskij edition, p. 63.

80. Ibid., p. 59 et seq.

81. Cf. "Literary Remains," edited by Mehring, fourth edition, 1923, vol. 2, p. 329 et seq. The passage is quoted from a letter from Engels to Marx dated March 17, 1845. Engels ventures the opinion in the letter that the library of socialist writings then being planned should contain only "such things whose positive content at least for the next few years will have current application."

82. Letter from Engels to Marx, January 20, 1845: "Make sure you finish your book on political economy . . . we must strike while the iron is hot . . . The time is now ripe. Therefore, make sure you are finished *before* April . . ."

83. Karl Marx, "The Communist Manifesto," eighth authorized edition by Karl Kautsky, 1921, p. 56

84. Cf. "Literary Remains," vol. 2, p. 335

85. Karl Marx, *Das Elend der Philosophie: Antwort zu Proudhons "Philosophie des Elends"* ("The Poverty of Philosophy: Reply to Proudhon's 'Philosophie of Poverty'"), German by E. Bernstein and K. Kautsky, with preface and notes by Friedrich Engels, 1895, p. 164.

86. *Die Neue Rheinische Zeitung,* article in issue of June 13, 1848. Reprinted in "Literary Remains," vol. 2, p. 97.

87. *Neue Rheinische Zeitung,* article on French and English class conflicts, reprinted in "Literary Remains," vol. 3, p. 115

88. Ibid., article on Hungary, January, 1849. Reprinted in "Literary Remains," vol. 3, p. 233 et seq.

89. Jakob Burckhardt in "Views of World History," complete edition of Burckhardt's works, edited by Oeri and Dürr, vol. 7, p. 5

90. Karl Marx, "Theses on Feuerbach," in "The German Ideology," Adoratskij edition, supplement, p. 535
91. Karl Marx, "Contribution to a Critique of Political Economy," Karl Kautsky edition, the 11th, 1930, p. VIV et seq.
92. Ibid. p. LV
93. Karl Marx, *Theorien über den Mehrwert* ("Theories of Surplus Value"), edited by Karl Kautsky, three volumes, vol. 1, *Die Anfänge der Theorie vom Mehrwert bis Adam Smith* ("Beginnings of the Surplus Value Theory up to Adam Smith"); vol. 2, "David Ricardo"; and vol. 3, *Von Ricardo zur Vulgarökonomie* ("From Ricardo to Common Economy"), fourth edition, 1921.
94. Isaiah Berlin, "Karl Marx," 1959, p. 251
95. Karl Marx, *Das Kapital: Kritik der politischen Ökonomie* ("Capital: Critique of Political Economy"), vol. 1, Marx-Engels Institute popular edition, 1932, p. 803
96. Ibid., p. 17 et seq.
97. Engels-Marx, "The German Ideology," Adoratskij edition, p. 22
98. Karl Marx, "Capital," book 3, chapter 48: "The Trinitarian Formula."
99. *Neue Rheinische Zeitung*, "Summons to the Workers of Cologne," reprinted in "Literary Remains," vol. 3, p. 268
100. Karl Marx, "Capital," vol. 1, Marx-Engels Institute popular edition, p. 804

# Index

Abraham, 245–48

Absolutes, in Hegelian philosophy

Freedom, 75–76

Idea, 84, 92, 96, 101, 106, 117–18, 138, 142, 162, 164–66; criticism of, 378

Knowledge, 48, 61, 96, 106

Reason, 190–91

Spirit, basic operative thought, 4, 5; as contradiction, 16–17, 200, 288–89, 290; criticism of, 188; cycle of, 41–44; evolution of, 132; and history, 101; image of, 38, 40; and truth, 53

"Absolute Freedom and the Terror," in *Phenomenology*, 64

Accumulation, theory of, 371, 372, 373–74

*Acts of the Apostles*, quote, 158, 188, 216, 216n.

Actuality; in Hegelian philosophy, 4, 5, 82, 161, 164; and dialectic, 37, 182–83; and education, 64; example of, 90; and reason, 155–56, 190; and thought, 142; and irony, 217–18; as nothingness of existence, 252

"Aesthetics," (Hegel lectures), 123–24

Anienkow, 309–10

Animals, compared with man, 166–67, 170, 175

Antinomial theory, 7, 9

Antiquity, classical, 5

Antithesis, 331, 343, 399

"an und fur sich," 13–14, 55, 138, 163, 183

425

Appearance, Hegelian concept of, 50–51

Aristotle, 36, 87, 138

Bacon, Francis, 87

Baillie, J. B., 51

*Bamberger Zeitung*, 71–72

Baure, Bruno, 299–300, 313, 349–50

Becoming, in Hegel, 55, 82; in *Logic*, 88–89, 91; Kierkegaard's subjective, 270

Being, in Hegelian philosophy, 14, 83, 85, 88–89, 91, 112; Marx on, 341

Belief, in Kierkegaard, 264, 269

Böhme, Jakob, 42

Boredom, Kierkegaard on, 236

Bourgeoisie, overthrow of, 359

Burckhardt, Jakob Christoph, 76, 307; critic of Hegel, 193–97

*Capital* (Marx), 308, 357–58, discussion of, 368–375; empirical basis of, 376–77

Capitalism, 176

*Christian Discourses* (Kierkegaard), 224

Christianity: In Hegelian thought, 42, 99–100; influence on H., 5, 63; and freedom, 138; For Kierkegaard: betrayal of, 182; deception of, 208; destruction of, 196–97; influence on K., 204, 222–23; opposition to, 209, 232, 262, 278–79; paradox in, 263, 266–67, 272, 273, 277–78, 279–80; Marx on

Christianity and money, 333

Civil society, 15, 150–153; as negative in dialectic, 158, 168–69; Hegel on, 171–78; Marx on, 329–331

Class theory, 329–331; conflict, 355–56, 368–69, 390–91, 395

Classless society, 381, 384, 398–99

*Cleanthes, or Concerning the Point of Departure . . .* (Marx), 306, 315

Climacus, (Kierkegaardian pseudonym), Anti-, 275–76, 278; Johannes, 273–74, 276, 282

*Collected Letters* (Marx), 310

Commodity *See* Surplus value, theory of

Communism, 340–41, 343–45, actuality of, 381–83; as salvation, 338–39

*Communist Manifesto* (Marx), 301, 319, 324, 350; quotes from, 358–359

Communists, 358–59

*Concept of Dread* (Kierkegaard), 224, 253–55

Concepts, of formal logic, 89–90, 94; in *Logic*, 85, 88–92, 94

*See also* Self-movement of concepts

Conceptualism, as component of Hegel. thought, 42; 82

*Concluding Unscientific Postscript* (Kierkegaard), 180, 206, 221, 224, 226, 228, 231–32, 274, 289; discussion of, 259, 261–273, 282

Consciousness, Hegelian, in history, 37, 58–59, 84, 103;

and self-consciousness, 48, 82; self-consciousness in love, 169–70; Kierkegaard's eternal, 263, 265; Marx on consciousness and society, 351–53, 365

Constantia Constantius (Kierkegaard's pseudonym), 244, 249, 255

Contradiction, theory of, 7–8, 16, 46; in concept of right, 163–64; in dialectic, 241, 285–88, 386; and existence, 270, 272, 288; influence on Kierkegaard, 217–18; in logic, 104–106; in Marxian thought, 350, 355–56, 358, 390–92, 395, 398–99
See also Negativity

Contribution to the Critique of Hegel's Philosophy of Right (Marx), 323, 326; theme of, 360

Cosmopolitan Democratic Society, 358

Crises and the Crisis in the Life of an Author (Kierkegaard), 224

Crisis theory, 371, 374

Critique of contemporary world, by Hegel, 62, 142–46, 156, 171; by Marx, 134, 172, 174, 343–44; in general, 195–201

Critique of Hegel, 128, 130–31, 140–42, 143–47, 151–52, 154; after death, 188–90, 193–94; by Kierk., 142, 158, 180, 189, 266; by Marx, 172, 188, 327–28, 346–48, 378

Critique of the Hegelian Philosophy of the State (Marx), 323

Critique of Political Economy (Marx), 350, 352, 357, 370

Critique of Pure Reason (Kant), 7–9, 36, 51

Cronus, 39

Culture, Kierkegaard on, 191; unmasking of, 199–200; as self-estranged spirit, 15

Cycle of the Absolute, 41–44, 55–56
See also Self-movement of concepts

Dante, Divine Comedy, 61

Death, Hegel on, 56–57; Kierkegaard on, 268–69

Descartes, René, 87, 198, 260

Despair, 204–05, 239, 255–56, 276–77

Destruction, theme of; Kierkegaard on, 182–83, 230, 388; Marx on, 182–83, 195–200, 384, 395

Deutsch-französische Jahrbücher (German-French Annals), 301, 320, 332, 346

Development, idea of, 81–82; as dialectical, 192

Dialectic, 8–9, 36, 385–89, 399–400
In Hegelian philosophy: and actuality, 142, 150, 157–58; ambiguity of, 101, 107, 131, 133, 141–42, 178, 181, 183–84, 288; assumptions, 131–32; criticism, 89, 141–42, 188–90, 378, 386–87; in Encyclopaedia, 114–

Dialectic (*cont'd.*)
116; essential to, 34, 36, 38; as experience, 182; explication of, 90–94, 96–107; and French Revolution, 24–25; goals of, 117–18; and God, 121; and history, 66–69, 73, 76, 99, 101, 130, 397; influence, 181–84; in Jena fragment, 43–44; in *Logic*, 88–89, 99; and man, 167; in *Phenomenology*, 48, 50–57, 62, 90; in *Phil. of History*, 137, 142–44; in *Phil. of Right*, 147, 150–51, 157–58; value of, 140–41

Kant: 7–8

Kierkegaard: compared with Hegel, 217–18, 229–30, 286–91; criticism of Hegel's dialectic, 228; existential dialectic, 268, 275, 387; as movement, 241, 246–47

Marx: 318, 323–25; of revolution, 327–330; as investigative tool, 379, 380–81

Dialectic materialism, 325, 332, 364, 370, 371; discussed, 336–345, 390–93, 395–99
*See also* Historical materialism; Revolution

"Diary of a Seducer," *Either/Or* (Kierkegaard), 233, 237, 248

Diderot, *Rameau's Nephew*, 61n.

*Difference between Democritean and Epicurean Natural Philosophy* (Marx), 316

Dilthey, Wilhelm, 20, 22, 25

Disunion, 133

Doktorclub, 299, 313–14

Dread, concept of, 253, 254–55, 257–58

Drive, 165–66, 173

Duboc, Julius, 136

*Economic and Philosophical Manuscripts* (Marx), 323–24, 332–34, 340–41, 343–44, 346, 353

Economic conditions, 332, 344, 365–66
*See also* Civil Society

Economic process, in Marxian thought, 329–45, 354–67, 371

*Edifying Discourses* (Kierkegaard), 221, 224, 225

Education, 63–64, 68, 170

Ego, 63

*Ego and His Own* (Stirner), 313

*Either/Or* (Kierkegaard), 205, 220, 224, 231–32, 244–45, 252, 255, 257, 260, 263, 282, 286–87, 289–90; discussed, 221, 226–27, 233–43, 246–48

*Encyclopaedia of Philosophic Sciences* (Hegel), 81, 148, 164; basic construction, 160; discussed, 110–121; Hegelian system in, 112; parts of, 113, 123–25

Engels, Friedrich, 301–02, 309–10, 322–23, 349–50, 357–58, 369

Enlightenment, Age of, 64–65, 190, 197

Esthetical existence, 224, 241–43, 246, 252, 271–72, 287

Estrangement, 347, 351; ironic, 216–17; and society, 174,

331–34; theory of, 337–45; transcended by communism, 344
*See also* Self-estrangement, Spirit of

Ethical existence, 224, 241–43, 246, 252, 271–72, 287

Ethics, 242; in *Phil. of Right*, 159–60, 163–64, 168; state as fulfillment of, 171; Kierkegaard on, 241–43

Ethos (*Sittlichkeit*), 62n. *See* Ethics

Eugen, Karl, 21

Existence, 225, 227–28, 230, 257; nothingness of, 250–53; paradox, 268–70; "pathetic," 272; three forms of, 224

Existential dialectic, 5, 268, 270–72, 284, 286, 387

Existential philosophy, 232, 259, 283

Faith *See* Belief

Falseness, 101–02

Family, in Hegelian phil., 150, 153, 163–65, 168–71; affected by society, 176

Father Taciturnus (Kierkegaardian pseudonym), 256–57

*Fear and Trembling* (Kierkegaard), 220, 224, 231, 244–45, 252, 255, 257, 260, 290; discussed, 245–48

Feuerbach, Ludwig, 300, 349–50

Fichte, Johann Gottlieb, 36, 45–46, 93

"Form of intercourse" *See* Production process

"Frankfurt Fragment of the System," (Hegel), 33

Frederick, William IV, 299

Freedom, Absolute *See* Absolutes, Freedom

Freedom, consciousness of, 161, 314; historical progress to, 136–38, 144–45

Freedom, idea of: Hegelian, 21, 75–76, 161–63; in human existence, 165; "negative", 165–66; Marx on, 382–83

French Revolution *See* Revolution, French

Freud, Sigmund, psychology of, 166

Fries, Jakob, 155

Future, idea of: Hegel on, 76–78, 178–79; Marx on, 339, 363–64, 381–82; various views, 191–201
*See also* Utopian societies

Gabler, 187

Gans, 298, 313

Garve, 7

"Geist," 9n., 59n.

*German Ideology* (Marx), 325, 343, 357–58, 364, 383; criticism of German socialism, 349–50; discussed, 349–56; quotes from, 365, 382

German Workers Alliance, 368

Germany, 299–300; Hegel on, 29, 138, 143–45; Burckhardt on, 195; Marx on, 326–28; revolution, 329–30
*See also* Prussia

God: Hegel, 9, 14–15, 55, 97, 106, 125, 132, 142, 171;

God: Hegel (*cont'd.*)
concept, 5; birth of 39–43; and dialectic, 120–21; as ever-changing, 124, 125; Kierkegaard, 227–28, 245–46, 248; existence of, 263, 272; as "nothingness," 279–80

*See also* Jena fragment on God (Hegel)

Goethe, Johann Wolfgang, 27, 32, 47, 54, 220

Haering, 20, 22, 25, 33

Hardenberg, Prince Friedrich Leopold von, 155

Hartmann, Nicolai, 35, 112

Haym, Rudolf, on Hegel, 18, 22, 29, 32, 61, 72, 73, 129, 142, 145, 151–52

Hegel, Georg Wilhelm Friedrich, 1770–1831, 3–184; Berlin period, 125–30, 151; childhood & youth, 18–20; death, 187; editor, 71–72; and French Revolution, 11–13, 21–25, 27, 37, 137, 145; Heidelberg period, 109–126; Jena period, 13, 32, 38–47, 109–10, 128; Nuremberg period, 72–82, 128; old age, 156–58; personality, 10, 11, 13, 39, 129, 171; and politics, 27–31, 150; reactionary period, 143–47, 164, 167; and revolution, 22–23, 29–30, 78; success, 126–30; teaching/ scholarship, 26–27, 30–34, 44–45, 72, 78–82, 109–110,

122–24, 125–30; and theology, 121, 142; Tübingen period, 20–25

*See also* Critique of Hegel

Hegel, Karl (son), 136–37

Hegelian Left, and Right, 187, 298, 314–15, 328

Hegelian System, 122; beginnings, 31, 33; components of, 42; decline of, 187; and dialectic, 34; in *Encyclopaedia*, 111–15; influence, 180–81; secret of, 43–44

*See also* Critique of Hegel, Dialectic, etc.

Heine, Heinrich, 296

Henning, 111

Hess, Moses, 300, 308, 353

Historical materialism, 5, 69, 345; description, 325, 364–67, 370, 371; outline of, 350-56

History: Hegelian, 6, 11, 13, 37–38, 392–93; dialectic interpretation, 66–67, 69, 99–100; future, 76–78; Marxian, man in, 337–38; economic determinant of, 339–40, 342, 345

*History of Philosophy* (Hegel), 37, 42, 123, 161, 163–64

*History of Reaction* (Stirner), 313

Hoffmeister, *Documents Contributing to Hegel's Development*, 38–39

Hölderlin, 11–12, 20–21, 26

*Holy Family* (Marx & Engels), 322; discussed, 325; dissolution of society, 331

Hotho, Henrich Gustav, on Hegel, 10, 126–27

Human personality, in Hegelian thought, 165–67

Humankind, theory of, in Kierkegaard, 254–55
See also Man, theory of

Humanism, 63, 121, 382; component of Hegelian thought, 42

Humboldt, Alexander von, 128

Humboldt, Wilhelm von, 32

Husserl, Edmund, 52

Hyndman, Henry Mayers, on Marx, 307–08

Idea, in Hegel. thought, 14; defined, 82; as pure knowing, 84; Marx's criticism, 378

Idea, Absolute See Absolutes, Idea

Ideas Regarding a Natural Philosophy (Schelling), 26

Ideological forms, 351–53, 366–67, 370

Ideology, concept of, in Marx, 350–53, 366–67

Impoverishment, 338
See also Pauperization, theory of

Impulses, theory of, 165–67

Indirect method, in Kierkegaard, 225–30, 247, 283–85

Individual: in civil society, 176; general and particular, 59; and history, 139

Industrialization, 177

Intelligence, 162, 165

Introduction to Nordic Mythology (Köppen), 313

Irony, concept of, 213–18; as negativity, 214–15; in Either/Or, 234–36

Jena fragment on God (Hegel), 38–44, 55, 64, 120, 171

Jena Logic, Metaphysics and Natural Philosophy (Hegel), 33

Jews, and money, 332–33

Job, 251

Johannes de Silentio (Kierkegaardian pseudonym), 244–45, 255

Journals (Kierkegaard), briefly cited, 204, 207, 210, 219, 220, 222, 226, 228, 243, 247–49, 251, 257–58, 276, 279; discussed, 206, 281–82

Jugendschriften (Youthful Writings) (Marx, 322)

Kant, Immanuel, 3, 36; and transcendental dialectic, 7–9, 284, 286; on logic, 86; and Hegel, 115; on nature, 119; on Enlightenment, 190–91

Kaufmann, Walter, quoted, 51

Kautsky, Karl, 322, 369

Kierkegaard, Sören Aabye, 1813–1855, 5, 9, 16, 34, 57, 195–97, 200–02, 308; autobiographical, 220–21, 240, 256; attack on Christianity, 208–10; childhood & youth, 203–06; death, 210; engagement, 219–20; cf. with Hegel, 286–91; literary production, 206–10, 220–225, 231–32, 281; cf. with Marx, 181–83; personal characteristics, 204–08, 210–11, as philosopher, 221–22,

Kierkegaard (cont'd.)
259–272, 274; as poetic writer, 221–22, 248, 260–61, 275–76; religious thought, 221–22, 232, 244–47, 249–50, 254, 257, 275–80; and dialectic, 181–82, 387; totality of thought, 107

Knowledge, in Kierkegaard, 253–54

Knowledge, Absolute See Absolutes, Knowledge

Köppen, Karl Friedrich, 299, 307, 313

Kuess, Nikolaus von, 42

Kühlmann, 349–50

Labor, theory of, 332, 336–45, 371, 374; Hegel on, 150–51

Landshut and I. P. Mayer, 323, 332

Lange, F. A., History of Materialism, 93

La Rochefoucauld, Francois, 285–86

Lassalle, Ferdinand, 368

Lasson, Adolf, 135

League of the Just, 358

Leibniz, Gottfried Wilhelm von, 87, 142n.

Lessing, Gotthold, 267

Leutewein, on Hegel, 10, 22, 23–24

Liberalism, 144–45

Logic, 101, 105–06; Hegel on, 86–90, 103, 104, 106

Logic, Science of (Hegel), 16, 34, 73, 96, 97, 108, 123, 148, 164; and dialectic, 83–84; discussed, 84–95, 98–107; and God, 42; criticized, 86–87

Logos, 92, 107; evolution of, 150

Love, 169–70, 179; for Don Juan, 237

Machiavelli, 329

Man, Kierkegaard on, 272, 277–78; Marxian theory of, 337–39, 341–43

Marriage, and children, Hegel on, 170–71; Kierk. on, 234, 235, 237–39, 256

Martensen, Hans Lassen, 209

Marx, Heinrich, 295–98, 304, 312

Marx, Karl, 1818–1883, 5, 34; on change, 195–202; childhood and youth, 295–297; and dialectic, 93, 181, 230, 379, 397; editor-journalist, 300–01, 304, 320–21; fame, 368; father, 295–98, 304, 312; and Hegel, 9, 16, 42, 67, 68–69, 73, 152–54, 158, 172, 189, 314–18, 323–25, 378; and Kierkegaard, 181–82, 183; London years, 302–03; personal characteristics, 304–311, 376; student, 304–05, 312, 313–16; claim to totality of thought, 107; as writer, 321–23

Marxism, 130–31; and political economy, 336–45; scientific, 93, 384; totality of, 35–36, 107

Material conditions of life, 173, 324, 352

Materialism *See* Dialectical materialism; Historical materialism

Mayer, *See* Landshut

Mehring, Franz, 350

Melancholy, 210, 255–56; as sin, 239

Metaphysics, 9, 13, 69, 106–07, 117–18

Mill, John Stuart, 336–37

"Moment," articles (Kierkegaard), 225, 232

Money, 332–35, 340

Morality, 62, 160, 163–64

Moral Spirit, 75–76

More, Sir Thomas, 179, 334, 381

Movement, 16, 388, 399–400
*See also* Self-movement of concepts

Mynster, Bishop, 208–09

Mysticism, as component of Hegelian thought, 42; Marx on Hegelian mysticism, 189


Napoleon, 12, 32, 37, 74–76, 78, 143, 351

Natural science, 119

Nature, 40, 119–21

Needs, theory of, 166, 167, 173–75; Marx on, 175, 354

Negation, principle of, 16–17, 56–57, 62, 66, 102; and positive, 104–06, 395; in freedom, 165–66; in later thought, 182–83; in dialectic, 192–93; expansion of, 199–200; radicalized by Kierkegaard, 290

Negativity (nothingness), 200, 214–15, 229–30; in *Either/Or*, 233, 247; in *Fear & Trembling*, 247; in Kierkegaard's dialectic, 270, 279

*Neue Rheinische Zeitung*, 301, 361, 383

Niethammer, brief citations of letters from Hegel to, 47, 70–72, 77–78, 83–84, 108, 122, 128, 156

Nietzsche, Friedrich Wilhelm, on systems, 35; nothingness, 57; *Will to Power* quote, 195–96; on existing culture, 197

"Night of the Unconditioned," *See* "Unconditioned, The Night of the"

Nohl, 26, 33

Nothing, concept of, 85, 183; in *Logic*, 88–89, 91; other views of, 199–200
*See also* Negation, Negativity

Novalis, pseudonymn of Hardenberg, Prince Friedrich Leopold von, 32


Objective Spirit, 62, 113, 149; as universal spirit, 160–61

Objective Will, 13, 163

Olsen, Regina, 219–20, 244–45, 249, 256

*On the Concept of Irony* (Kierkegaard), 204, 220; discussed, 212–218

*On the Difference between the Systems of Fichte and Schelling* (Hegel), discussed, 45–46, 115

*On My Work As an Author* (Kierkegaard), 223–26

Opposites, 37, 55, 89
   *See also* Contradiction, Theory of

Paradox, 107, 246, 263–64, 268–69; discussed, 286–89

Pascal, Blaise, 259–60

Passion, 139, 142; as content of paradox, 266

Pauperization, theory of, 176–177, 371; in *Capital*, 373–74

"perfectibility of man," 179

Personality *See* Human personality

Phenomena, law of, in Marx, 377; theory of, 51–52; in *Philosophy of Right*, 160–61

*Phenomenology* (Hegel), brief citations, 4, 13, 15, 16, 33, 35, 37, 149, 164, 171, 331–32; arrangement/structure, 48–50, 111, 112, 122–23; chapters in, 60–61; concepts, 48–50, 92; contents, 49–50; discussed, 47–69; cf. with *Divine Comedy*, 61; on French Revolution, 23, 137; influence of, 337, 342, 347; cf. with *Logic*, 97–98, 100–01, 103; preface to, 50–57; purpose of, 58; quote from, 90; Spirits, 62, 73, 76; writing of, 70–71; self-movement of concepts, 55–57

*Philosophical Fragments* (Kierkegaard), 220–21, 224; discussed, 259, 261–73, 289

*Philosophical Propaedeutics* (Hegel), 81–82

Philosophy, Hegel on: 11, 15, 46, 115, 156–57, 190; systematization of, 35; Marx on: 321–22, 329, 348; and philosophers, 351n.

*Philosophy of History* (Hegel), 135–36, 137, 138, 141, 142–43, 146

*Philosophy of Nature* (Hegel), 34, 97, 107; discussed, 113, 124

"Philosophy of Religion," (Hegel), 124

*Philosophy of Right and the State* (Hegel), 11, 13, 15, 17, 81, 130, 144, 317; ambiguity of, 167; description of society, 168–178, 329; discussed, 148–179; cf. with *Encyclopaedia*, 149–50; influence on Marx, 152–54; Marx on, 325–26, 364; Preface, 131, 152, 154–58, 165; structure, 159–167

"Philosophy of World History," (Hegel), 124, 132, 313–14; discussed, 135–47

Plato, 36, 138, 227, 381

*Point of View for My Work As an Author* (Kierkegaard), 222–23

Political economy, 153, 173, 336; discussed, 344–45, 364–67

Poverty, 374
   *See also* Pauperization, theory of

*Poverty of Philosophy* (Marx), 358, 360, 383

Practice and theory *See* Theory and Practice

Private property *See* Property, private

Production process, 350, 354–56, 365–67, 370–74, 391–93, 395–96

Progress, belief in, 128, 191, 192–93, 197

Proletariat, concept of, 330–31, 340, 359, 373–74

Property, 163, 165, 173

Property, private, in Marxian thought, 175–76, 331–32, 335, 336–41, 345, 384, 391–93

Protestantism, 19, 24, 125

Proudhon, Pierre Joseph, 335, 358–60

Prussia, 73, 131, 151–57, 164, 167, 188, 299–301; Hegel praise for, 143–44; reactionary, 313–14

Psychology: empirical, 166; Kierkegaard on, 253, 285


Reality *See* Actuality

Reason, 48, 50; and actuality, 155–56; Hegelian belief in, 190–92, 194; consciousness/unconsciousness in, 82; as state, 179

Religion, Hegel: as synthesis, 48, 115; Marx: as estrangement, 333, 389

Religious existence, 224, 246–47, 252–53, 271–72, 287, 289

*Repetition* (Kierkegaard), 220, 224, 244–45; discussed, 248–251, 252

Revolution, 196–97, 369, 383–84; dialectic thought, 69, 388, 394–96, 399; and economy, 339–40, 366–67; Kierkegaard on, 196–97; necessity of, 355–56, 359–60, 380; principle and technique of, 328–29; in 1848, 360–62; theory of, 317–18, 323–25, 327–29

Revolution, French, 11–13, 21–25, 37, 64, 74–76, 143, 145; Terror, 67, 137, 166

Revolutionaries, 328–29, 363–64

*Rheinische Zeitung*, 300, 320–22

Ricardo, David, 336–37

Right, concept of, 160–63, 164–65

Rjazanow, 323

Robespierre, 143

Rosenkranz, Johann Karl Friedrich, 38–39, 81

Rousseau, Jean Jacques, 13–14, 24, 63, 119, 191

Ruge, Arnold, 300–01, 306, 320–22

Rutenberg, 313


Saint-Simon, Count de, 353n.

Sand, George, quoted, 360

Savigny, Friedrich Karl von, 298, 313

Schelling, Friedrich Wilhelm von, 11–12, 20–21, 26, 30–31, 36, 45–56, 93, 187–89, 315; letters to from Hegel, 29, 47, 49, 71, 156

Schiller, Johann Christoph Friedrich, 32, 38

Schlegel, August Wilhelm von, 32, 47–48

Schmidt, Kasper See Stirner, Max

Schnurrer, 22

Schopenhauer, Arthur, 187–89

Schrempf, 244

Science, as basis of Marxian communism, 381; and dialectic, 100; and Hegelian thought, 5, 53–55, 94–95, 103–04, 114, 132–33; in formal logic, 87, 94, 101; and Marxism, 93, 384

Self-consciousness See Consciousness

Self-determination, as intelligence, 165

Self-estrangement, Spirit of, 15–16, 332, 341; discussed, 62–69
See also Estrangement

Self-movement of concepts, 55–57, 88, 94, 98, 103, 104–106, 116, 132, 289

Shakespeare, William, 334

Sickness Unto Death (Kierkegaard), 222, 224, 231–32, 255; discussed, 275–78

Sin, 272–277; melancholy is, 239; original, 253–55

Sittlichkeit See Ethics

Skepticism, Hegel's, 128–29; new, 198

Sketch of a Critique of Political Economy (Marx), 172

Smith, Adam, 336–37

Social Democratic Workers Party, 368

Social forms, theory of, 167–178

Socialism, scientific, 310–11, 384; three forms of, 359; German, 349–50, 357

Society, criticized, 343–44; communist, 381–82; self-estrangement of, 174
See also Utopian societies

Socrates, 213–18, 227–28, 277, 285, 286

Spirit, in Hegelian philosophy, 48, 332; conceived dialectically, 69, 192; as man, 137–138; negation of, 66, 74; progress of, 58–61, 116, 128; world-spirit and history, 12–13, 69, 76, 78
See also Absolutes, Spirit, God

Stages on Life's Way (Kierkegaard), 220, 224, 274, 282; discussed, 255–57

Stahl, Friedrich Julius, 69

State, as actualization of ethical life, 158, 163–64, 168–69, 171, 176–77; theories, 150, 155, 178–79
See also Prussia

Stewart, Dugald, 27, 173

Stirner, Max, pseudonym, 299, 313, 349–50

Subjective Spirit, 113, 165

Subjective Will, 163

Subjectivity theme, 261, 264–273, 283–85

Superstructure, in class theory *See* Ideological forms

Surplus-value, theory of, 369, 371–72

Synthesis, in Hegelian thought, 43, 48, 62, 132–33; in Kierkegaard, 289–91; result of dialectic, 386; classless society as, 399

System, in philosophy, 34–36, 46, 55, 58, 92, 98, 135; Kierkegaard on, 261–62

Theodicy, 142n.

*Theories of Surplus Value* (Marx), 322, 369–70

Theory and practice, relationship between: in Hegel, 30, 142, 156, 183, 317; in Marx, 317, 328–30, 357; in *Capital*, 371

*Theses on Feuerbach* (Marx), quoted, 325

Thing: in formal logic, 101; as idea, 102–03

Thought, 115; as freedom, 76; movement of, 56; perversion of, 64; Kierkegaard's projection of, 264

Thust, M., 227

*Three Discourses at the Communion on Fridays* (Kierkegaard), 226, 232

Tieck, 32

Totality, in Hegelian philosophy, 107, 118; aim of dialectic, 388; of social relations, 168

*Training in Christianity* (Kierkegaard), 278

Transcendental dialectic, 7–8, 286–88, 289–90

Trendelenburg, on Hegel, 188–89

Triadic structure, 44, 48–49, 55, 140, 149, 159, 168; of world, 118; of Hegelian system, 121

Truth, concept of; Hegelian, 5, 52–54; appearance in, 51; God as, 125; relativity of, 101–02; as whole, 44, 132; Kierkegaard, and indirect method, 228; and irony, 215–16

Tübingen Theological Institute, 20–21

Twentieth century, 201–02

Uncertainty, objective, 269–72

"Unconditioned, The Night of the," (Kierkegaard), 279

Universality, 113–14, 134; and civil society, 174; of *Capital*, 370–71

*Utopia* (More), 334

Utopian societies, 343–44, 381, 384, 399

Victor Eremita (Kierkegaardian pseudonym), 233, 255

Vigilius Haufniensis (Kierkegaardian pseudonym), 253

*Wage Labor and Capital*, lectures (Marx), 358

War, 179; declaration in *Communist Manifesto*, 359–60
Wealth, 150–51, 177–78, 331
Weitling, 309–10, 358
Westphalen, Jenny von (wife of Marx), 297, 304
Whole, concept of, in Hegelian thought, and truth, 4, 5, 55, 132–33; in dialectic, 93, 137; and falseness, 141–42; as Knowledge, 117
Will, 13, 165–66; development of, 160; objective/subjective, 163; process of becoming, 162
Windischmann, 128–29
Women, Hegel on, 170
*Works of Love* (Kierkegaard), 224
World; three-staged, 118; mood changed, 190–202; Kierk. on, 230; dominion, 359
Württemberg, Hegel on government of, 27–28